A Student's Dictionary of Psychology and Neuroscience

This is the essential reference work for any student studying psychology for the first time. Packed with easy-to-understand definitions and helpful diagrams, the new edition has been expanded to include the key concepts within the growing field of neuroscience, as well as greater coverage of positive psychology.

Key features include:

- over *2,500* entries
- *extensive cross-referencing* for easy navigation
- *mini biographies* of key psychologists
- *study notes* section
- list of *common abbreviations*

Also including a list of key references in the field and a guide to writing essays and referencing your work, this is the perfect accompaniment for any student newly encountering this fascinating subject, those taking related disciplines in the health or social sciences, or professionals wanting to familiarise themselves with key terms and ideas.

Nicky Hayes has been granted the British Psychological Society's Award for Distinguished Contributions to the Teaching of Psychology. She is a Chartered Psychologist, a Fellow of the British Psychological Society and an Honorary Life Member of the Association for the Teaching of Psychology.

Peter Stratton is Emeritus Professor at the University of Leeds. Following a distinguished career in developmental psychology, specialising in the learning abilities of neonates, he moved into systemic family therapy and became a founder and director of the Leeds Family Therapy and Research Centre.

A Student's Dictionary of Psychology and Neuroscience

Nicky Hayes and Peter Stratton

Routledge
Taylor & Francis Group

LONDON AND NEW YORK

First published 2017
by Routledge
2 Park Square, Milton Park, Abingdon, Oxon OX14 4RN

and by Routledge
711 Third Avenue, New York, NY 10017

Routledge is an imprint of the Taylor & Francis Group, an informa business

© 2018 Nicky Hayes and Peter Stratton

The right of Nicky Hayes and Peter Stratton to be identified as
authors of this work has been asserted by them in accordance with
sections 77 and 78 of the Copyright, Designs and Patents Act 1988.

British Library Cataloguing in Publication Data
A catalogue record for this book is available from the British Library

Library of Congress Cataloging in Publication Data
Names: Hayes, Nicky, author. | Stratton, Peter, author.
Title: A student's dictionary of psychology and neuroscience / Nicky
    Hayes, Peter Stratton.
Description: Abingdon, Oxon ; New York, NY : Routledge, 2017. |
    Includes bibliographical references.
Identifiers: LCCN 2017010620 (print) | LCCN 2017027055 (ebook) |
    ISBN 9781315208282 (Master eBook) | ISBN 9781138632400
    (hardback) | ISBN 9781138632417 (pbk.)
Subjects: LCSH: Psychology—Dictionaries. | Neurosciences—
    Dictionaries.
Classification: LCC BF31 (ebook) | LCC BF31 .S693 2017 (print) |
    DDC 150.3—dc23
LC record available at https://lccn.loc.gov/2017010620

ISBN: 978-1-138-63240-0 (hbk)
ISBN: 978-1-138-63241-7 (pbk)
ISBN: 978-1-315-20828-2 (ebk)

Typeset in Goudy
by Swales & Willis Ltd, Exeter, Devon, UK

Contents

Preface

In this new edition of A Student's Dictionary of Psychology, we have extended its remit to include the growing area of neuroscience. Recent developments, particularly resulting from the increased sophistication of scanning techniques, have resulted in a greatly extended awareness of the connections between psychology and neuroscience, and many students are involved in studying both. It seemed appropriate, therefore, to broaden our scope as an 'explaining dictionary' to include many of the common terms and processes involved in neuropsychological research, as well as those involved in psychology in general.

As before, our mission to explain rather than simply define means, we hope, that following up all of the relevant cross-references to a given topic should allow the reader to acquire a reasonably full overview of the area. In that sense, we have often referred to this dictionary as a kind of random-access textbook, rather than just a dictionary of major terms. Since our belief is that many of the people who use it in this way will be doing so in order to help them to write an essay, we have also included useful tips in how to go about this at the end of this book. Essays are one of the more common forms of assignment in psychology, but you will find that the tips are just as relevant if you are trying to put together an introduction or a discussion for a research project.

The main development in this new edition is the inclusion of neurological terms, but there is also increased coverage of cognitive psychology, social psychology and positive psychology. Some older definitions have also been updated: psychology has moved on in very many ways since the first edition of this dictionary was published back in 1988. At the end of this book, you will also find a list of classic references to which we have referred, as well as a list of common abbreviations. We hope you will find all these features useful.

Nicky Hayes and Peter Stratton

Acknowledgements

The existence of this dictionary owes much to the support and encouragement that Helga Hanks has offered the authors during the preparation of earlier editions of this book.

About the authors

Nicky Hayes is a Chartered Psychologist and Fellow of the British Psychological Society. She is now semi-retired, but during her academic career she conducted research into subjects as varied as organisational cultures, team management, the psychology of interactive science exhibits, and exam stress. She also had a wide-ranging teaching career, which involved teaching psychology in colleges and universities at levels ranging from GCE to postgraduate degree work. Her extensive knowledge of psychology and ability to draw connections between different specialisms mean that she is much in demand for her broad-ranging and informative guest lectures, both in the UK and abroad. In 1997, she was awarded the British Psychological Society's Award for Distinguished Contributions to the Teaching of Psychology, and she is a Fellow of the British Psychological Society and an Honorary Life Member of the Association for the Teaching of Psychology. She has published over 20 books, and her clear writing style has opened up an interest in psychology for many new readers and struggling students. Her university affiliation is with the University of the Highlands and Islands.

Peter Stratton is Emeritus Professor at the University of Leeds. Following a distinguished career in developmental psychology, specialising in the learning abilities of neonates, he moved into systemic family therapy and became a founder and director of the Leeds Family Therapy and Research Centre. He also established the Leeds Attributional Coding System, and for many years applied this system in various contexts through the work of the Psychology Business, alongside his academic and educational work in the Psychology Department of the University of Leeds and his work in family therapy at the Leeds Family Research Centre.

A

AA See *ambulatory assessment*.

ABBA design An example of *counterbalancing* of experimental conditions. The first condition (A) is followed by two trials of the second condition (B), then by one of the first. The effect is to average out *order effects*, although if all of the *practice effects* might take place during the first trial, it is better to run half of the participants with a BAAB sequence. An alternative use of the term is for experimental designs in which one group of participants experiences the experimental conditions in the order A then B, while the other group experiences them in the order B then A. The two uses can be distinguished by examining the number of trials that each participant is obliged to undergo.

aberrant Behaviour (or in biology, an organism) that deviates from what is normal, expected or desirable.

ability A capacity or *skill*.

ability tests *Psychometric* tests that are designed to measure what someone is already able to do, as opposed to what they might be able to learn in the future. See also *aptitude test*.

ablation The removal or destruction of part or parts of the brain by means of surgical techniques, usually involving the cutting or burning away of the tissue concerned.

abnormal A term applied to behaviour or people who have been classed as not normal. It is a potentially controversial label because of problems in defining *normality*. Abnormality can be defined in several different ways:

(i) as behaviour that is different from the *norm* (i.e. unusual);

(ii) as behaviour that does not conform to social demands;

(iii) as statistically uncommon behaviour, based on the assumptions of the *normal distribution*;

(iv) as behaviour that is maladaptive or painful for the individual; or

(v) as the failure to achieve *self-actualisation*, the humanistic view.

These criteria bring their own problems because, for example, they lead to the classification of highly regarded individuals such as artists and social reformers as 'abnormal'.

abnormal psychology The psychology of abnormal behaviour. This term has been largely replaced by *clinical psychology* when referring to the professional practice of abnormal psychology.

abreaction A process used in some forms of *psychotherapy*, especially psychoanalytically oriented ones, which involves the reliving of deep emotional experiences. During abreaction, repressed emotional disturbance is brought to consciousness, allowing a recognition of its existence and the opportunity for the client to develop new coping strategies.

abscissa The horizontal or *x-axis* of a graph. See also *ordinate*.

absolute refractory period The period of a few milliseconds immediately after the firing of a neurone. During the absolute refractory period, the neurone will not produce another electrical impulse, no matter how much stimulation it may receive. See also *relative refractory period*.

absolute threshold The minimum amount of stimulation required for an event to be detected. The absolute threshold of a particular form of *stimulus* is set at the point where 50 per cent of the signals with that physical value are detected.

abstract thought Thought that uses concepts which do not have an immediate material correspondence, such as justice or freedom. In Piaget's theory of cognitive development, the capacity for abstract thought is only acquired after the age of about 12 years. It is an essential aspect of Piaget's *formal operational stage*.

abuse

(i)   The use of substances inappropriately in a way that is damaging to the individual (e.g. excessive alcohol consumption, sniffing glue). See also *addiction*.

(ii) Inappropriate and harmful treatment of another person. See also *child abuse*.

acalculia See *dyscalculia*.

accent A distinctive pattern of pronouncing words and phrases that is shared by members of a social or regional group. In some circumstances, accent is taken as an important signifier of social status, and may thus determine the nature of *social interaction* between individuals. This is particularly noticeable in stratified societies such as that of the UK. See also *dialect, psycholinguistics, speech register*.

accommodation

(i)   In biological terms, the process of adjusting shape to fit incoming information (e.g. the process by which the lens of the eye adopts a different shape when the eye is focused on distant objects than when it is focused on nearby objects).

(ii) In Piagetian theory, the process by which a schema, or cognitive structure, adjusts to new information by extending or changing its form, or even by subdividing into a set of schemata with different applications. See also *assimilation, equilibration*.

account analysis A research method which involves analysing the accounts that people give of their experience. Developed in answer to the need for psychological research techniques that could deal with the subjective realities of human experience (as opposed to measures of behaviour), account analysis takes as its starting point the radical idea that what people say may have meaning. From there, it goes on to assert that a systematic approach to collecting people's own versions of an experience or event may be of value to psychologists seeking to understand human experience. Account analysis can take many forms, but generally involves two stages:

(i)   a systematic approach to the collection of accounts, generally through *interviews*; and

(ii) some reflective technique that allows the psychologist to extract ideas, themes or implications from the data, such as *discourse analysis, attributional analysis* or *thematic qualitative analysis.*

Account analysis forms an important part of the *ethogenic* approach to the study of social behaviour propounded by Rom Harré.

accounts The verbal descriptions that people give of their experiences. An *interpretivist* approach treats the account as the object of study in its own right. For example, if someone describes getting angry during an interaction, the account might be taken as indicating something about their private emotional state. Alternatively, researchers might study the description itself as an example of the form and features of accounts of emotional experiences.

acetylcholine A *neurotransmitter* that is found at the motor end plate and is therefore involved in muscle action. Some military nerve gases exert their effect by the destruction of the enzyme at the motor end plate, which breaks down acetylcholine, causing the latter to build up, producing uncontrollable muscle spasm. Other drugs prevent the uptake of acetylcholine at the motor end plate by themselves being picked up at the receptor sites, and so blocking the uptake of the neurotransmitter. The paralysing poison *curare* operates in this way, and *nicotine* has a partial effect of this kind.

achievement The successful reaching of a goal. Used particularly to refer to real-life successes and when evaluating a person's life.

achievement motivation The motivation to accomplish valued goals and to avoid failure. This concept became important in the 1960s as motivation theory became less dominated by physiological drives, and was generally studied as *need for achievement.*

achievement test A test designed to measure what a person has already achieved (e.g. a statistics examination). See also *aptitude test.*

achromatic colours A range of hues that is judged to be all of one colour (e.g. yellows or blues). Their wavelengths occur within a narrow band, although they may vary in intensity and saturation. 'Achromatic' usually means 'all of one colour'.

achromatopsia A type of specific brain damage that impairs the *perception* of colour without damaging other functions. See V4.

acoustic Regarding sound and sound quality.

acoustic store The part of the *working memory* system that acts as a short-term storage device for sounds and spoken words.

acquiescence bias The tendency to respond positively or affirmatively in surveys, no matter what the content of the question is. See also *questionnaire fallacy.*

acquired dyslexia *Dyslexia* that has come about as a result of an accident, stroke or illness.

acquisition

(i)   A term used to indicate that a particular skill or ability has been gained by an animal or human being. When applied to language, the term 'acquisition' is used to avoid drawing inferences about whether language has been learned or inherited. Stating that a skill has been acquired implies that the actual process by which the skill was obtained is not the issue being discussed at that particular time.

(ii)   The phase during a *conditioning* procedure in which the response is learned or strengthened.

acronym An abbreviation of a title consisting of the initials of each word, particularly common in discussions of psychological tests (e.g. BAS for British Ability Scale). Working groups sometimes develop acronyms that outsiders do not understand as a way of excluding non-members and producing a feeling of *cohesion*.

ACTH Adrenocorticotrophic hormone.

acting out The expressing of a wish, need or motivation, particularly when it is unrecognised or unconscious, in overt behaviour. Often the behaviour is aggressive and self-destructive and may be uncharacteristic of the person, who may have no idea why they behaved in that way.

action disorganisation syndrome See *frontal apraxia*.

action pattern See *fixed action pattern*.

action potential The electrical impulse produced by a neurone when its stimulation exceeds the threshold level, such that the neurone fires. See also *evoked potential*.

action research An approach to psychological enquiry that challenges the idealised view of the psychologist as an 'objective' scientist, standing apart from the subject matter and observing it dispassionately. Instead, action research takes as its starting point the idea that the presence of other people will always affect behaviour, so it is naive to assume that the activities of

the researcher will not influence the behaviour of the subject. Instead, an action researcher deliberately acts as a change agent within a given situation, and incorporates the effects of these actions as an integral part of the outcome of the research. Initially developed in an organisational context by Lewin (e.g. Lewin, 1946), action research has continued to be popular in organisational psychology. With the increased emphasis on *ecological validity* in psychological research, action research gradually gained acceptance in several other areas of psychological investigation. See also *new paradigm research, participant observation*.

action research cycle *Action research* is generally perceived as a cyclical activity, proceeding from an initial diagnostic or evaluation stage to the development of a change strategy, to an action and implementation stage, then back to another evaluative stage, and so on through the cycle.

action-specific energy The energy that is used to perform *fixed action patterns*, or innate behaviours. The idea is that the energy is generated purely as a result of an instinctive drive to perform the activity, and will overspill into *displacement* activities if it is not used in carrying out the particular action for which it has been generated.

activation An increase in neurological or physiological processing in one condition, relative to other conditions. See also *deactivation*.

actor–observer effect A finding in *attribution theory* that for unwanted events, people tend to make *dispositional attributions* about other people's behaviour (e.g. if you drop a vase, I conclude that you are clumsy) while attributing their own behaviour primarily to the effects of external circumstances (if I drop the vase, it must be because it was slippery): a *situational attribution*. Research has found that depressed people are more likely to make dispositional attributions about bad events that affect them, while people in a good or loving relationship extend the situational explanations to their partner's unwanted events.

actualising tendency A term coined by Rogers (1951) to describe the process by which people seek to develop their various potentials and to maximise their *personal growth*, once their need for *positive regard* from others has been satisfied. See also *self-actualisation*.

acuity The fineness of discrimination that a sense organ can achieve. Most commonly used with reference to vision, where visual acuity indicates the smallest objects that can be distinguished.

adaptation The process of adjusting to an environment in such a way that maximal benefit may be obtained from it, or at least in such a way that life may be continued in a reasonably productive manner. The term has highly specific meanings in the following fields:

(i) Physiology – the adjustment of bodily organs to particular environmental demands (e.g. the adaptation of the heart to living at a high altitude).

(ii) Evolutionary biology – how a species is matched to the environments in which it has developed.

(iii) Psychology – the process by which an individual achieves the best balance feasible between conflicting demands.

Piaget uses the term more specifically for the processes by which cognitive structures are made to correspond to reality. See *accommodation, assimilation*.

addiction A state of physiological or psychological dependence on some substance, usually a drug, resulting in tolerance of that substance such that progressively larger doses are required to obtain the same effect. Addictions are most clearly identified by a failure to function adequately when the substance is withdrawn (see *withdrawal symptoms*). The most common addictions are to socially accepted drugs such as nicotine and alcohol, although illegal drugs (e.g. *heroin*) and those initially taken as medical treatment (e.g. *tranquillisers*) often cause more public concern. Treatments have covered the full range of psychological and psychiatric techniques, but behavioural and group methods are most widely used. In everyday use, the term has been stretched to include needs which have become exaggerated to a degree that is damaging to the individual (e.g. 'addiction' to television, violent exercise or food). See also *dependency*.

additive factors method An approach to analysing *reaction time*, which divides responses to a stimulus into four stages: encoding, comparing, decision and response.

ADHD Attention deficit hyperactivity disorder. See *attention deficit disorder*.

adipose Fatty, or pertaining to fat. Adipose tissue in the body is tissue which stores fat, and adipocytes are cells specifically adapted for that purpose.

adipsia Cessation of drinking.

adjustment Originally, adjustment was regarded as little more than the avoidance of *maladjustment*, but it became a goal for therapy with the emergence of *humanistic* approaches to psychotherapy.

Modern therapists accept that many forms of adjustment are possible, avoiding value judgements about lifestyle. Broadly speaking, adjustment refers to the individual's achieving a harmonious balance with the demands of both environment and cognitions. The development of behavioural technologies to improve individual adjustment raised complex *ethical* considerations (e.g. whether *conditioning* techniques to solve problems of sexual adjustment could be adopted without consideration of values and morals).

adolescence The developmental period between childhood and adulthood. In some cultures, the transition is very brief and achieved through some form of *rite of passage*, but in Western cultures it extends from the onset of *puberty* around 12 years of age, to about 17 or 18 years of age. Research on adolescence has tended to emphasise the four developmental areas of *competence, individuation, identity* and *self-esteem*.

adoption studies Studies of heredity that look at children with a specific genotype (e.g. *identical twins*) who have been brought up in different adoptive families. The idea is that differences between the twins must be environmental in origin, while similarities are likely to be genetic. However, a common failing in these families is to omit control for the similarity of the environment (e.g. in some cases, the children have been brought up in the same district, and only a few streets away from one another).

adrenaline A hormone and *neurotransmitter* produced by the adrenal glands, which is particularly associated with emotional states. Adrenaline is involved in states of arousal, initiated by the action of the *sympathetic division* of the *autonomic nervous system*.

It is released as a *hormone* by the adrenal gland, and serves to maintain an activated state of the body such that a higher level of energy is produced by the autonomic functions. It also acts within the brain as a neurotransmitter, and again is involved in emotional states.

adrenergic pathway A 'pathway' or familiar route in the brain that involves *neurones* which release the *neurotransmitter* known as *adrenaline*.

aesthetics The study of the nature of beauty, or of pleasing perceptual experiences.

aetiology The study of causation. This term is particularly used to refer to the causes of illnesses and mental disorders.

affect

(i) A term used to mean emotion, but covering a much wider spectrum of feeling than the normal emotions. Affect includes pleasurable sensations, friendliness and warmth, pensiveness, and mild dislike, etc., as well as extreme emotions such as joy, exhilaration, fear and hatred. Broadly speaking, affect refers to any category of feeling, as distinct from cognition or behaviour.

(ii) As a verb: to influence, to have an effect. Note that the verb 'to *affect*' means 'to cause'. 'An *effect*' is a result. See also *effect*.

affect display Overt signs such as *posture*, breathing, *pupil dilation* and raising of fur, etc., which indicate the emotional state of the person or animal.

affect heuristic The use of emotional judgements to influence judgements or decisions. See *decision-making*.

affectionless psychopathy A term used by Bowlby to describe a syndrome in which an individual does not demonstrate any emotion, either positive or negative, towards any other human being. Affectionless psychopaths, according to Bowlby, are characterised by a lack of social conscience and a high level of delinquency. See also *psychopathic personality*.

affective blindsight The ability shown by some brain-damaged people who lack conscious *visual perception* to be able to detect and distinguish between different emotional stimuli. See also *blindsight*.

affective disorder A psychiatric term used to refer to syndromes in which the person appears to be producing inappropriate emotional responses. Alternatively, it may refer to a prolonged disturbance of mood or emotion, as in *mania* and *depression*.

affective domain The dimension or domain of the human psyche that is concerned with feelings, emotions and moods. See also *conative domain, cognitive domain, behavioural domain*.

afferent dysgraphia Additions or omissions of strokes or parts of writing that happen as a result of failing to utilise *visual* and/or *kinaesthetic* feedback effectively.

afferent neurone A nerve cell (*neurone*) that carries information in the form of electrical impulses from the sense organs to the *central nervous system*. Also known as a *sensory neurone*. See also *efferent neurone*.

affiliation The process of joining or the sense of belonging to a group. Nearly everybody feels a desire to belong, so affiliation has been treated as a need or motive. See also *affiliative needs*.

affiliative needs Needs that relate to a sense of belonging with, or friendship towards, other people. This rests on the idea that the wish for *affiliation* is a kind of *drive*, so that the strength of the need can be studied in the same kind of way that physiological needs are studied.

affordances In J.J. Gibson's ecological model of perception, affordances are the possibilities for action that are offered by a particular visual stimulus, or image in the visual field. The concept is becoming more widely used in other concepts, usually to indicate the possibilities for action offered by the subject being referred to.

afterimage An image that remains in the visual field after the original stimulation has ceased. Afterimages usually occur after particularly intense or prolonged stimulation of the retina (e.g. after staring at an illuminated light bulb). See also *negative aftereffects*.

age regression See *regression*.

agency The sense that we are in control of our own thoughts, actions and effectiveness.

agentic state The state proposed by Milgram in which the individual surrenders personal judgement and conscience to act as the agent of other people, and do what they instruct. See *autonomous state*.

aggression A term used in several ways, commonly to describe a deliberate attempt to harm another being. There is no agreed definition, partly because the term is applied sometimes to behaviour (hitting), sometimes to an emotional state (feeling aggressive), and sometimes to an intention (wanting to harm). There are several classifications of different kinds of aggression, the most useful distinction being between *instrumental aggression*, which is an aggressive act performed in order to achieve some other objective, and *hostile aggression*, which is motivated by antagonistic feelings and emotions.

agnosia A disorder of cognitive processing in which the person cannot create any meaning out of their sensory inputs. See also *integrative agnosia, Gerstmann's syndrome*.

agonist A drug that causes a *neurotransmitter* to have an increased effect. For example, it is suspected that cocaine is an agonist for the neurotransmitter *dopamine* and that is why it produces pleasurable sensations.

agoraphobia The most common form of *phobia*. Literally meaning a fear of open spaces, it is usually associated with a fear of interacting with other people. Agoraphobia results in a severe restriction of the sufferer's life, as he or she cannot enter any crowded area and may become unable to leave the house. Often, it is possible to recognise some way that this makes it unnecessary for the person to have to tackle some source of anxiety. Psychological treatments may attempt either to reduce the symptoms of the phobia by techniques such as *systematic desensitisation*, or to resolve the underlying anxiety.

agrammatism A condition in which the person can produce speech but it lacks grammatical forms, such as word endings or function words.

agraphia An impairment in writing ability that results from damage to the language areas of the brain.

agreeableness One of the main factors in the *five-factor theory* of personality, which reflects a tendency to be positive and conciliatory in interpersonal interactions and to seek positive affect from the company of other people.

aha! experience A sudden experience of enlightenment, in which the solution to a problem is perceived very rapidly, with little prior feeling that progress is being made towards the solution. An example of *insight learning*, the aha! experience was used by *Gestalt* theorists such as Kohler to argue against the *reductionist* approach to human learning put forward by the *behaviourist* school. See also *creativity*.

AI See *artificial intelligence*.

Ainsworth, Mary (1913–1999)

Mary Ainsworth was a Canadian developmental psychologist who was widely influential in the development of our understanding of infant *attachment*. In 1967, she published *Infancy in Uganda*, which was the outcome of a lengthy African field study that allowed her to identify some of the cultural variations in the care of human infants, and also some of the 'universals' of human attachment. Back in the UK, she went on to investigate detailed facets of attachment, and developed the *strange situation technique*, in which a child is exposed to an unfamiliar situation and its behaviour towards its caretaker is observed. This and other research resulted in the concepts of *secure* and *insecure attachment*, which have been extensively used in child therapy ever since.

AIP See *anterior intraparietal area*.

akinetopsia A type of specific brain damage that impairs the perception of movement without damaging other functions. See V5.

alarm reaction A term used to describe the series of physiological responses brought about by the activation of the *sympathetic division* of the *autonomic nervous system*. Investigated systematically by W. Cannon, the alarm reaction involves, among other changes, increased heart rate and blood pressure, producing an increased supply of oxygen to the muscles, changes to the digestive system, including rapid digestion of sugars for increased energy, and alterations in the composition of the blood such that clotting occurs more quickly. The effective result of these changes is that the body is prepared for extended and demanding effort.

alcoholic A person who has become dependent on the drug alcohol. Many problems dealt with by clinical psychologists are caused or aggravated by alcohol (e.g. some 30 per cent of cases of physical *child abuse*). Alcoholism is treated in a number of different ways by different practitioners, including clinical psychologists, with varying degrees of success. There is controversy over the question of whether total abstinence is essential for anyone who has been an alcoholic. Alcoholism is probably the most widespread and damaging *addiction*. See also *antabuse, Korsakoff's syndrome*.

alexia A condition in which written words cannot be recognised. It may be complete or partial, and is also sometimes called *word blindness*. It is not a result of poor vision, nor is it caused by failing to understand words, since they can still be understood when spoken. See also *pure alexia*.

alexythymia The inability to read one's own emotional state.

algorithm A routine procedure that will produce a correct answer with enough repetitions or applications. If an algorithm exists for a problem, you know it can eventually be solved simply by following the procedure.

alienation A state of feeling or perceiving oneself as separated from: (i) one's own feelings; or (ii) other people and society.

alienist An early title for psychiatrists, who treated 'aliens' (insane people).

all-or-none principle The principle that a neurone either fires or it does not, with no variation in the strength of the electrical impulse. It was originally thought that all nerve cells operate according to the all-or-none principle – implying a necessity for digital processing models of brain functioning, and fostering some *computer simulation* approaches to understanding cognition. However, more recent evidence suggests that all-or-none firing is uncommon within the brain itself, and that cortical neurones use variable coding.

allele One of a pair of genes. Most organisms have pairs of *chromosomes*, with matching genes situated on each chromosome. If the two alleles are different in form, one may be a *dominant gene* over the other (e.g. in eye colour, brown is dominant over blue), or both may contribute to the eventual phenotype (e.g. as in skin colour, where both alleles contribute to the final result). Partial dominance is also possible.

allocentrism A collectivistic characteristic of personality that involves people centring their attention and actions on other people rather than themselves. See also *collectivism*.

allocentric coding Visual coding that is independent of the observer's perspective (e.g. connecting the features of two different objects with respect to one another, as opposed to *egocentric coding*).

allocentric space A map of space in which the items have been coded relative to one another. See also *egocentric space*.

allograph A letter that has been specified for its shape (e.g. by its case, or as print rather than script).

allophone Different versions of the same phoneme, where the differences relate to individual variations in speech or acoustics.

Allport, Gordon (1897–1967)

G.W. Allport exerted a fundamental influence on the development of *trait theory* in the psychological understanding of personality. In an early study, he went through the dictionary and extracted some 4,500 words relating to personality, which he argued could be organised into three major types of personality trait: cardinal (ruling passions or obsessions), central (basic to shaping behaviour, although not as dominating as cardinal) and secondary (traits that we only show occasionally or just to intimates). His idea of personality traits has continued to this day, and is fundamental to many aspects of *psychometrics*. Allport also went on to study many other aspects of *social psychology*, including prejudice, rumour and religion.

alpha The first letter of the Greek alphabet, often used to indicate primacy or importance (e.g. the dominant males in a baboon troop are sometimes referred to as *alpha males*).

alpha level Also known as the 'alpha criterion', this is the maximum probability of making a *Type I error*, as a result of the statistical analysis of a set of data. In student research, the alpha level is usually set at $p < .05$, but it can be made more stringent by choosing a different level of *statistical significance*.

alpha male A term used in *ethology* to describe a top-ranking or dominant male

in a social group, and also used loosely about men who display an extreme level of stereotypical male characteristics. See also *dominance hierarchy*.

alpha waves Distinctive patterns of brain activity shown on *EEG* readings, consisting of a wave pattern of between 8 and 12 Hz, characteristic of a state of wakeful relaxation. See also *beta waves, delta waves*.

altered states of awareness Also known as altered states of *consciousness*, this term refers to the idea that there are qualitatively different mental states that will result in various psychological processes such as *attention* and *motivation* functioning differently. Sleep is an obvious example, but more subtle changes in the waking state have also been studied, including *hypnosis*.

alternate-forms method A system for judging the *reliability* of a psychometric test, which involves comparing the results produced by two different versions of the same test, given to the same subjects.

altruistic behaviour Acting for the benefit of other people without regard to personal cost or benefit. There is dispute about whether truly altruistic behaviour ever occurs. See also *reciprocal altruism*.

Alzheimer's syndrome A condition that resembles *senile dementia*, but which can occur much earlier in life, with some sufferers even being as young as 40 years of age.

amacrine cells Retinal cells that make cross-communications right across the retina, linking rod and cone cells and coordinating visual input.

ambiguous Having more than one possible meaning. An ambiguous stimulus is one that can be interpreted in more than one way (see Figure 1).

ambivalence The simultaneous existence of two opposed emotions, motivations or attitudes (e.g. love–hate; *approach–avoidance*, etc.). Each feeling has its own separate origin, so the two cannot be reconciled, and the person either alternates between the two attitudes or *represses* one of them.

ambivert A person who has achieved a balance between extreme *introversion* and extreme *extraversion*, as described by Eysenck.

ambulatory assessment (AA) A general term for a range of data-collection methods, including self-report, observation, and clinical or biological data collected in the course of the person's everyday life. It is mainly used in clinical contexts such as in the health services. See also *ambulatory self-report*, *Experience Sampling Method*, *Ecological Momentary Assessment*, *diary method*.

ambulatory self-report A form of *ambulatory assessment* in which the person keeps a record of how they are feeling or other clinical data at various points during the course of the day. See also *Ecological Momentary Assessment*, *diary method*.

Ames room A well-known *visual illusion* in which a room is constructed that, when viewed from a particular viewing point, appears to be normal, but actually has one corner much farther away from the viewer. An appearance of equal distance is achieved by carefully balancing the perspectives of the room and the levels of the floor and ceiling. The effect is that people or objects of the same size appear to be of different sizes (see Figure 2).

Figure 1 An ambiguous figure: is it B or 13?

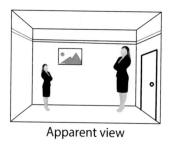

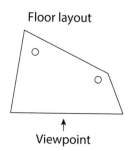

Floor layout

Apparent view   Viewpoint

Figure 2 The Ames room illusion

Ameslan A standardised sign language used by deaf and/or dumb people in America. A true language in its own right, several primate studies have involved the teaching of Ameslan to gorillas or chimpanzees, with a degree of success.

amnesia Loss of memory, normally from physical causes. *Retrograde amnesia* refers to loss of memory for events prior to the damaging event or disease; loss of memory of the few minutes leading up to severe concussion is the most common example. *Anterograde amnesia* refers to the loss of subsequent memory (e.g. impairment of the ability to code new memories after brain surgery or, as found in *Korsakoff's syndrome*, through long-term alcoholism).

amodal Not tied to any particular perceptual system.

amphetamine A drug that stimulates the *central nervous system*. It is usually prescribed in order to raise energy levels or to prevent sleep, and is abused (e.g. as 'speed') for the same purposes. Amphetamine is also used as an appetite suppressant to help dieters and to control *hyperactive* children.

amphetamine psychosis A state of acute paranoia that develops as a result

of taking large amounts of *amphetamine* over a period of time.

amusia An inability to process music – that is, to perceive the sounds received as making up a musical form. *Congenital amusia* occurs when the amusia is a result of brain injury or misfunction.

amygdala The part of the *limbic system* that appears to control emotion, aggression and the formation of emotional memory. An almond-shaped group of *neurones* located deep within the medial *temporal lobes*. See also *Kluver-Bucy syndrome*.

anaclitic depression A depression caused in infants aged between 6 and 18 months by prolonged separation from their mothers. The term was first used by Rene Spitz, and was an important concept in early studies of *maternal deprivation*.

anagram A puzzle or problem which consists of words with their constituent letters disarranged, such that all of the necessary letters are present but in the wrong order. The letters may be randomly listed (G AANMRA) or rearranged to resemble other words (A GRANMA). Anagrams are often used in laboratory problem-solving tasks.

anal stage The second of Freud's psychosexual stages, in which *libido* focuses on the anus. See also *oral, phallic stage*.

analogue An object or phenomenon that corresponds to or resembles another in at least some respects. The term is used:

(i)   in theories of memory referring to information stored in the brain from which a representation or image of an object can be generated;

(ii) in biology for different characteristics of different species that have the same functions; and

(iii) in electronics for information shown through a continuously variable quantity, such as analogue (circular) clock faces as opposed to *digital* watches.

analogy An image of speech that involves comparison of two objects, emphasising the similarity between them.

analysand That which is being, or has been, analysed. Used sometimes to refer to student analysts undergoing *psychoanalysis* as part of their training.

analysis

(i)   Identifying the constituent parts or links of a whole so that it can be better understood and interpreted (e.g. in statistical analysis).

(ii) A shorthand term for *psychoanalysis*.

analysis-by-synthesis A term used to describe a cognitive model in which the brain is seen as combining separate pieces of information about an event in order to make the best judgement about the nature of that event.

analysis of variance (ANOVA) A statistical procedure used to test whether groups of scores differ from each other. The principle is that if the scores are not being influenced in different ways, the variation (*variance*) of scores within each group will allow us to predict how much variation there will be between the means of the groups. If it turns out that the group means vary more than expected, we conclude that the groups differ (and have therefore been influenced in different ways). Several different sources of influence can be tested within a single ANOVA design, and the complex relationships or *interactions* between them can be analysed. See also *F ratio*.

analytical psychology The system of psychopathology and treatment devised by Carl Jung after his split from the Freudian school. It introduces concepts such as the *archetype* and the *collective unconscious*.

anaphor A pronoun or other word that takes its referent from a previous phrase or sentence.

anarchic hand syndrome Complex goal-directed movements of the hand that are not voluntarily directed by the hand's owner. See also *split-brain studies*.

anchoring In *social representation* theory, the process of making the social representation easier to grasp by setting it in a familiar context. In *decision-making* theory, anchoring refers to the process of establishing a set reference point or framework, from which an option is evaluated.

androcentrism The view that male behaviour is normal and that female behaviour compares unfavourably to this norm.

androgens Hormones produced mainly by the testes. They are responsible for the physical developments in the foetus that give rise to male characteristics, including the external genitalia. Later in life, they influence sexual activity and the expression of genetically controlled characteristics, such as the growth of a beard. See also *testosterone*.

androgyny The presence in one person (either male or female) of both male and female characteristics. In humans, there are no *sex differences* that are present in one gender and not the other – it is more a matter of the prevalence and strength of each tendency. Therefore, everybody mixes male and female characteristics to some extent, and the term androgyny is reserved for people who show both male and female characteristics to a significant degree. Research indicates that individuals who are psychologically androgynous tend to be mentally healthier than those who conform tightly to orthodox gender *stereotypes*.

anecdotal evidence Information quoted in support of an idea or theory that has been obtained purely from everyday experience or accounts, rather than from some form of systematic or controlled study.

anencephalic Without a *cerebrum*. Anencephalic infants usually survive for only a few days after birth, although some have been kept alive for up to six months. Anencephalic infants are of interest to students of *neonate* functioning, as observable differences between them and normal infants only seem to emerge after the first few weeks, implying that *cerebral cortex* activity may not play an important part in early infant behaviour.

aneurism A localised region of the artery in which its membranes have become over-elastic, and can easily become stretched and rupture. This produces an interference with blood flow to the brain, resulting in a *cerebrovascular accident*, or *stroke* – that is, loss of functioning for key abilities, usually movement and/or speech. See also *plasticity*.

anger An emotion based on a high state of *arousal*, often generated when someone else is judged to have violated a social norm of some kind.

angst A mental disquiet or anguish considered by supporters of *existentialism* to be the inevitable outcome of a full appreciation of the implications of personal responsibility and personal choice.

angular gyrus That part of the *cerebral cortex* which is involved in the decoding of visual symbols. The angular gyrus receives input from the *visual cortex*, and appears to process that information into a form equivalent to information which has been processed by the *auditory cortex*. The angular gyrus then passes messages on to the area known as *Wernicke's area*, where it is processed for comprehension. Accordingly, the angular gyrus plays an important role in the process of reading, and it is thought that damage to this area is the root cause of certain *dyslexias*.

animism The attribution of living qualities to inanimate objects or phenomena, and frequently the attribution of conscious awareness. Animism is a powerful trend in human thought processes, which has been studied mostly in the thinking of young children. It is commonplace in everyday speech (e.g. referring to the family car as a person, or the computer as a living thing), and occurs extensively in the belief systems of most cultures. See also *anthropomorphism*.

ANN See *artificial neural network*.

anodal tDCS A form of *transcranial direct current stimulation* that increases cortical *excitation* and results in increased levels of performance. See also *cathodal tDCS*.

anodyne A pain-relieving treatment or agent.

anomaly A noticeable deviation from what is expected or predicted.

anomia A type of *aphasia* where the person has consistent difficulties in producing the names of things they want to talk about.

anorexia nervosa A disorder in which the person becomes unable to eat and may starve to death. Anorexia is most common among teenage girls, and is often initiated by excessive dieting. Anorexia has been thought of variously as arising from a distorted body image, as a subconscious attempt to return to pre-pubertal physique and, by implication, social role, and as an expression of rebellion against domination by a mother figure. See also *bulimia, eating disorders*.

ANOVA See *analysis of variance*.

ANOVA interaction diagram A diagram that illustrates the way that two variables may interact with one another in the data (see Figure 3).

ANOVA model of attributions See *covariance*.

anoxia A reduced supply of oxygen to the brain or other tissues. It is particularly likely to happen to a baby around birth, and can result in brain damage.

ANS See *autonomic nervous system*.

antabuse The commercial name for the drug disulfiram, which produces an extreme reaction when taken in conjunction with alcohol. Usually administered by a skin implant that can last for a month or more, antabuse is used therapeutically in *aversion therapy* for *alcoholics*. The association between

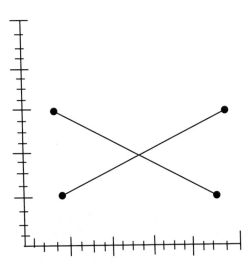

Figure 3 ANOVA interaction diagram

extreme nausea and vomiting and alcohol can sometimes produce a lasting aversion to alcohol, helping the alcoholic to deal with the problem.

antagonistic Having an opposite effect, working against or competing with something else. Antagonistic muscles work in opposite ways to one another (e.g. one set of muscles in the iris contracts to dilate the pupil of the eye, while a different set constricts it).

antecedent Taking place before the relevant event. An antecedent may be the cause of the event, but it cannot be assumed that it was. See also *causality*.

antecedent variables Factors in an experiment that precede (happen before) some other event. Because of the time relationship, the antecedent variable cannot have been caused by the subsequent event, and may even have been a cause of it. See *causality*.

antenatal To do with the period before birth.

anterior Towards the front, or the most forward area. See also *superior, posterior, inferior*.

anterior cingulate cortex An area of the brain in between the *frontal lobes* and the *limbic system*, which has been classified as belonging to either brain structure at various times. It is involved in detecting errors and monitoring complex responses, such as are required for the *Stroop* test. It is also involved in processing bodily signals which characterise *emotions*, and it has been proposed that its error-detecting and monitoring functions may be linked with an assessment of the value of proposed responses.

anterior intraparietal area (AIP) A part of the intraparietal *sulcus* that responds to 3D objects or manipulable shapes.

anterograde amnesia A form of amnesia (i.e. loss of memory) in which the person becomes unable to store new information, although memories that were laid down before the amnesia-producing event remain intact and accessible. See also *retrograde amnesia, amnesia*.

anterograde memory Memory for events that happened after brain damage which led to *amnesia*. See also *retrograde memory, retrograde amnesia, anterograde amnesia*.

anthropology The study of different human societies, involving a particular emphasis on social structures and belief systems. An anthropologist is one who undertakes such a study, often using non-participant observational techniques.

anthropometric To do with the measurement of parts of the human body, or of the human body as a whole.

anthropomorphism The process of attributing human characteristics to non-human objects or animals. Anthropomorphism, while accepted as a scientific fallacy, is common to all human societies: even in modern technological cultures, it is common for human beings to attribute intention (either benign or malevolent) to the actions of computers, spiders, etc. See also *attribution, animism, social representations, Lloyd Morgan's canon*.

anticipation A mental state of readiness for a specific event. See also *set*.

anticipatory schema A concept put forward by Neisser, whereby an anticipatory schema forms an essential *cognitive* component in the cyclic process of *perception*. An anticipatory schema consists of a set of cognitions derived from the individual's beliefs and experiences, based on observations of the situation, and concerning the most probable outcomes of action. This schema will be utilised in the selection of appropriate behaviour and actions. These in turn will change or modify the situation, producing a new sample of observations. These new observations then modify the anticipatory schema. Neisser considered this continuous cyclic process to be the key to an understanding of human cognition (see Figure 4).

antidepressants Drugs such as those known as 'tricyclics', which are used to treat severe *depression*.

antilocution Encouraging social *prejudice* by using verbal communication in a particularly negative way (e.g. by using emotively loaded words and *metaphors*).

anti-positivism An approach to research that emphasises the human interpretation of meanings and implications; introduced as a challenge to hardline *positivism*. See *qualitative research*, *hermeneutics*.

antisocial personality disorder A personality problem in which the individual shows a chronic disregard for social conventions or acceptable behaviour, typically acting in a disruptive or disturbing manner. See also *sociopathy*.

Anton's syndrome The mistaking of visual imagery as visual perception, which occurs in some blind people.

anxiety A stressful state resulting from the anticipation of danger. Anxiety has a physiological component (the *alarm reaction* or *fight or flight response*),

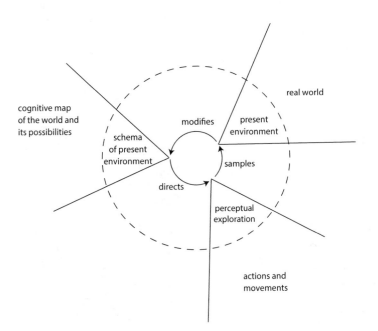

Figure 4 The perceptual cycle

a cognitive aspect, particularly in narrowing attention, and a subjective experience of discomfort. Each of these components may help the person to deal effectively with clearly recognised, real and immediate dangers, but can be damaging both psychologically and physically when the anxiety persists, as in occupational *stress* or unresolved *unconscious* conflicts.

anxiety disorder A general term for psychological disorders in which chronic anxiety, with debilitating consequences, is a prominent feature. Includes *panic attacks* and *phobias*.

anxiolytic drugs Drugs used to treat the symptoms of anxiety.

anxious attachment See *insecure attachment*.

apathy A mental state characterised by lack of interest in everyday or momentous events, and involving a disinclination to exertion or effort in order to effect or achieve results of any kind. The state is characteristic of *depression*.

aphagia A lack of eating, which can be induced experimentally by *lesions* in the *lateral hypothalamus*. Animals with aphagia show no interest in solid food, to the point of starvation. Aphagia is believed by some physiological psychologists (although not all) to be a mechanism in *anorexia nervosa*.

aphasia A disorder of speaking, sometimes brought about by *lesions* in *Broca's area* – the area of the cortex involved in speech production. The affected individual has serious problems in articulating words, although they have no difficulties in understanding language.

apnoea (apnea) Temporary stopping of breathing, common among premature babies. It is present in some adults during sleep, and is believed to result in the destruction of brain cells through *anoxia* in extreme cases. Apnoea is often associated with snoring.

apparent motion A term used to describe visual illusions that provide an appearance of movement even when no such movement is actually occurring. Examples of this are found in the *phi phenomenon*, the *waterfall effect* and *stroboscopic motion* stimuli.

appeasement behaviour Actions carried out by an animal that serve to stop or deflect aggressive behaviour from another. The term is particularly applied to antagonistic encounters deriving from territorial or sexual selection conflicts. See also *instinctive behaviour*, *sign stimulus*.

apperception The conscious awareness of an act of perception, with focused concentration on its full meaning.

apperceptive agnosia A failure to recognise objects, thought to be due to an impairment in perceptual processes. See also *associative agnosia*, *agnosia*.

appetitive behaviour Behaviour that is directed towards the satisfaction of some kind of desire, want or need.

applied psychology A general term used to classify areas of psychology in which theories are put to use in dealing with practical, non-laboratory situations. Applied psychology traditionally includes *clinical psychology*, *educational psychology*, *industrial psychology* and *occupational psychology*, but also includes other fields where psychological theories may be put to use, such as *environmental psychology* or *study skills*.

appreciative inquiry A model of social discussion and investigation that is based on the idea of the 'unconditional positive question', exploring possibilities, opportunities and strengths rather than focusing on problems or criticisms. Appreciative inquiry involves bringing in large numbers of people to the discussion, and exploring the positive insights they have to offer. It has achieved some popularity as a management tool, and is promoted as a solution to wider social problems. See also *positive psychology*.

apprehension

(i) In colloquial terms, a feeling of unease or dread concerning some future event.

(ii) In cognitive terms, the mental grasping or full comprehension of a concept or idea.

approach–avoidance conflict A pattern of behaviour often seen when an organism is inclined or required to approach something that has simultaneously attractive and aversive qualities (e.g. a parachute jump). The individual tends to oscillate between approach behaviour and avoidance behaviour, with approach behaviour typically dominant when the event or stimulus is more distant in time or space, and avoidance becoming more characteristic when the event or stimulus is closer. See also *conflict*.

apraxia A *motor* disorder caused by brain damage in the posterior parietal cortex, i.e. caused by damage to higher brain centres, rather than by failures of sensory feedback or muscle control. It results in the person having problems with motor planning. They may be willing to perform an action, but find it difficult to carry out the movements involved. See also *optic apraxia*.

aptitude The ease with which a person will acquire a new set of *skills* or abilities. An individual is said to have an aptitude for a particular skill if he or she learns that skill more rapidly and with more ease than other individuals with the same prior knowledge.

aptitude test A form of *psychometric* test designed to assess someone's potential or suitability for different types of occupation. See also *attainment test*.

archetypes Classic, powerful images which, according to Carl Jung, are held in the *collective unconscious* and recur frequently in folk art and mythology. Examples of Jungian archetypes are the earth mother, the sea as a symbol of rebirth, the omnipotent father, the inaccessible virgin, the knave, etc.

arcuate fasciculus A bundle of *white matter* (i.e. *myelinated* neurone fibres) that connects the *frontal lobes* with the temporoparietal region.

Argyle, Michael J. (1925–2002)

Michael Argyle was a major figure in British *social psychology*. His research concentrated on the positive applications of psychology and its use in helping people with social difficulties, and established the importance of *non-verbal communication*. He developed many techniques of social skills training to

(continued)

(continued)

help people improve their social interactions, and to provide ways of improving the social functioning of people with learning difficulties and those with *neurotic* and *psychotic* problems. Later in his career, his interest in shifting the emphasis of social psychology away from its concentration on problems led him to develop research into areas such as the psychology of happiness.

arousal A state in which the *sympathetic division* of the *autonomic nervous system* is activated, producing an *alarm reaction*, or a longer term response to *stress*. Arousal is characterised by very high levels of adrenaline in the bloodstream, and results in a general state of readiness to react in the organism. Depending on cognitive and environmental factors, this may result in anger, anxiety, exhilaration, excitement or, if the arousal is frequent and prolonged and the energy is not dissipated by regular demanding exercise, in long-term stress disorders.

arrhythmic Irregular, lacking in rhythm.

artefact (artifact) Anything that has been constructed. Used particularly about objects that have been made for everyday living by earlier civilisations. Within psychology, the word is most likely to be applied to aspects of data that result from the process of the research and so do not provide any information about the subject of the research, even though they seem to. For example, when patients are interviewed about their experience of hospital treatment, if they are still in hospital with the medical staff around, their reports will be much more positive than when they are at home. So the positivity of the accounts becomes an artefact of the situation.

articulation

(i)   Clear verbal expression.
(ii) Free movement through the action of a joint, sometimes extended to mean the assembly of joints and levers that make such movement possible (e.g. in *robotics*).

articulatory loop The part of Baddeley's model of *working memory* that performs rehearsal of information held for short periods of time. The articulatory loop is where incoming information is rehearsed in order to retain its immediacy, and therefore its availability for information processing.

articulatory suppression A term used in connection with the *working memory* model, and referring to the suppression or blocking of the activity of the *articulatory loop*. This is usually achieved by asking the participant to undertake some other cognitive task instead, such as counting backwards in threes.

artificial insemination The introduction of sperm into the uterus of a female by technical means rather than by sexual union. As the donor of the sperm may be unknown to mother and child, the technique has implications for family relationships and the possible selection of *genetic* characteristics.

artificial intelligence (AI) An area of research which aims to develop computer systems that will allow the computer to develop novel solutions to problems, or to produce other forms of 'intelligent' behaviour such as gathering relevant information to aid expert decisions. It is hoped by those involved that computer systems which can 'reason' will eventually be able to produce the same kinds of outcomes as those produced by human cognitive processes. Work on artificial intelligence has tended to concentrate on:

(i) knowledge-based systems, known as 'expert systems', which are capable of limited decision-making on the basis of prior input from a number of human experts;

(ii) human–machine interface research, such as the development of *voice recognition systems*; and

(iii) *robotics*, involving the development of sensing and manipulation devices such as might be suitable for manufacturing processes.

See also *computer simulation*, *parallel distributed processing*.

artificial neural network (ANN) See *neural network*.

Asch, Solomon (1907–1996)

Originally a Gestalt psychologist, Solomon Asch is most widely known for his research into *conformity*, in which he made the (then) remarkable discovery that people would be prepared to lie outright rather than disagree with the majority, even on a relatively simple task. The *Asch effect* generated a vast amount of research, and the basic observation remains fundamentally valid to this day – although of course it can be influenced by situation, motivation and even knowledge of previous Asch studies! One of Asch's most famous students was Stanley Milgram, who took Asch's work further to investigate just how far social *obedience* could extend. The work of these two psychologists, Asch and Milgram, has become seminal to any study of *social psychology*.

Asch effect A term used to describe *conformity* arising through awareness that, if the individual stated their own judgement openly, they would be responding differently to the rest of the group, and others would become aware of their dissent. Asch's studies of conformity involved a research participant placed in a situation in which the other group members had been primed to give obviously wrong answers to a relatively simple problem and the real participant had to answer openly, after the majority had answered (see Figure 5).

Asperger's syndrome A condition characterised by difficulties in non-verbal communication and social interaction,

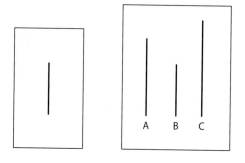

Figure 5 The type of test material used in Asch's study of conformity

which are generally accompanied by repetitive patterns of behaviour carried to the extent of actually interfering with, or restricting, the person's everyday living. Asperger's syndrome is considered to be a mild form of *autistic spectrum disorder*, but it is different from most of the others in that the person's use of language and intellectual abilities are unaffected.

assertion training A series of *therapeutic* techniques designed to enable the person to take an active or dominant role in social interaction.

assimilation One of two processes by which a *schema* in Piagetian theory is considered to develop. New information is said to have been assimilated when it is fitted into an existing schema and so can be understood in relation to earlier learning. Assimilation and *accommodation* are considered to be continuous cognitive processes, contributing to cognitive *adaptation*. See also *equilibration*.

association The linking of one thing with another in sequence. *Associative learning* is learning that has been acquired as a result of the connection of a *stimulus* with a response. During the period when psychology was attempting to account for all behaviours as

stimulus–response connections, association was seen as the central psychological process.

association cortex An older term given to those parts of the *cerebral cortex* that did not seem to have a specific, localised function. They have been thought of as the areas in which basic perceptual information is associated with more general knowledge. See also *equipotentiality*.

associative agnosia A failure to recognise objects, thought to be due to an impairment in *memory* for those objects.

associative learning Learning that involves making connections or associations between stimuli. *Classical conditioning* is the main example of associative learning, but see also *one-trial learning*.

associative priming The way that reactions to a stimulus are faster if that stimulus is associated with a stimulus that has been previously presented. See also *priming*.

assortative mating The tendency for organisms (including humans) to select those with characteristics similar to their own as sexual partners.

assumption An idea or set of ideas that is taken for granted in the formulation of an argument or theory. If made explicit, it is sometimes called an axiom.

astigmatism A disorder of vision in which lines at certain angles are not perceived with the same *acuity* as lines of different orientations. Recent research suggests that astigmatism may arise from the irregular development of *simple cells* or *complex cells* in the *lateral geniculate nuclei* of the *thalamus* – involved in the primary decoding of visual information.

asymmetrical Lacking in balance or evenness.

ataxia A neurological problem in which the coordination of muscle movements is impaired. It can arise from several causes, but is generally believed to result from some form of impairment of the *cerebellum*. See also *optic ataxia*.

attachment A close, emotionally meaningful relationship between two people in which each seeks closeness with the other and feels more secure in their presence. The attachment between mother and infant has been extensively studied, and some writers apply the term only to the relationship of the infant to the mother. Attachment has been the subject of much theorising by John Bowlby. There is substantial evidence that the quality of attachments in infancy affects *exploration* and *play* in the short term, and a wide range of cognitive and social functions throughout childhood. However, it is no longer believed that the infant always forms a major attachment exclusively to the mother. See also *bonding, contingency, imprinting, monotropy, strange situation technique*.

attainment test A test designed to assess the knowledge and skills that an individual has obtained, either through experience or through following a prescribed course of training. See also *aptitude test*.

attention A directed focus of awareness, such that the individual is maximally prepared to respond to a signal or other sensory input. See *selective attention*.

attention deficit disorder (ADD) A classification of children who are judged to have an inability to sustain attention. Such children are likely to be disruptive in school or at home, and if the condition is serious they are likely to have educational difficulties. The use of this diagnostic label means that the condition can be treated as a kind of illness. Previously, these children were labelled as *hyperactive* and as suffering from 'minimal brain damage'. ADD is often treated with drugs such as Ritalin, which are related to *amphetamines*. Although these drugs are usually used as stimulants, they also help to maintain attention, which seems to be the effect that is helpful to those concerned.

attention deficit hyperactivity disorder (ADHD) Those children in which ADD shows itself primarily in the form of a high level of activity.

attentional bias The tendency to focus attention on potentially threatening stimuli rather than neutral ones, when both are presented simultaneously. See also *selective attention*.

attentional blink The inability to report a target stimulus if it appears soon after another, reported stimulus. See also *selective attention*.

attenuation

(i) The shortening or limiting of an object or event.

(ii) A term used by Triesman to refer to the weakening of a signal being processed, as an essential part of a model of *selective attention*. See *filter models*.

attitude A 'mental set' held by an individual that affects how that person regards events and organises their cognitions. Attitudes are commonly held to have three essential components or dimensions:

(i)   a cognitive dimension, involving the beliefs and rationalisations that 'explain' the holding of the attitude;

(ii)   an affective dimension, involving the emotional aspects of the attitude, such as likes, dislikes, feelings of distaste or affection; and

(iii) a behavioural dimension that involves the extent to which the individual is prepared to act on the attitude that he or she holds.

However, recent approaches also include:

(iv)   a conative dimension, concerned with *intentionality*.

See also *prejudice, stereotype*.

attribution The process of ascribing reasons or causes to events. Causal attributions are often concerned with suggesting the possible motives or intentionality underlying people's actions, and a number of researchers have explored how variations in attributions can have wide-reaching effects. See also *attribution theory, covariance, animism*.

attribution theory An extensive area of *social psychology* dealing with the ways in which people attempt to account for their own and other people's behaviour. It is most concerned with the kinds of causes by which individuals account for their experiences – attributions about negative *life events* are considered to be particularly important. Attribution theory has been used to improve and extend *helplessness theory*, and is extensively used in *cognitive therapy*. Strictly, attribution theory deals with how people come to have their beliefs about the causes of events and behaviour, while attributional theory deals with the different forms (or *attributional styles*) that such beliefs may take. See also *covariance, social attribution*.

attributional analysis A research technique that involves analysing the attributions people make in conversations or written communication, to identify underlying meanings or patterns. See also *Leeds Attributional Coding System, discourse analysis, covariance*.

attributional error See *fundamental attributional error*.

attributional style The theory that individuals tend to believe in particular kinds of causes for a wide range of effects. Styles may vary in the extent to which they incline towards stable causes (ones that are unlikely to change in the future), global causes (affecting many things), and *internal–external* causes (such as character or situation). For example, of two people who have failed an examination, one may attribute the cause to the room being noisy (unstable, specific and external), while the other may believe it is due to their being stupid (stable, global and internal). Martin Seligman and others have produced evidence that individuals who incline towards using a stable, global and internal pattern of attributions may be particularly vulnerable to *depression*. See also *personal attributions, controllable attributions, Leeds Attributional Coding System*.

audience effects The effects produced by the presence of other people on an individual's behaviour. See also *social facilitation*.

audition The process of hearing. Auditory signals are processed by means of a complex auditory system. The outer ear collects the signals and focuses them inward, the middle ear amplifies the signals, the inner ear transduces the signals into *electrical impulses*, and the auditory nerve transmits the signals to the brain via a crossover junction with the auditory nerve from the other ear. Some primary decoding of the signals occurs in a region of the *thalamus*, and they are eventually interpreted in the *auditory cortex* of the *cerebrum*.

auditory agnosia A form of *agnosia* that is restricted to input through hearing.

auditory cortex That part of the *cerebral cortex* that is involved in the interpretation of sensory messages received by hearing. The auditory cortex is located on the *temporal lobe* of the *cerebrum*, immediately below the *lateral fissure*. See also *sensory projection areas, planum temporale*.

auditory leadership style See *autocratic leadership*.

authoritarian personality A specific, rigid pattern of personality characterised by punitive approaches to social sanctions and high levels of *prejudice* towards out-group members. Adorno showed that the cognitive styles of highly prejudiced right-wing conservatives had two distinctive traits:

(i) rigidity – maintaining a belief system even in the face of direct evidence showing that it is untrue or inefficient; and

(ii) intolerance of ambiguity – a tendency to take sides quickly and to be unable to cope with equivocal positions.

Adorno concluded that this was due to *defence mechanisms* – highly prejudiced individuals had to protect themselves against ambiguities which might challenge their ideas. Moreover, they had often been brought up by cold and highly authoritarian parents, producing a *reaction formation* whereby the child would displace his or her aggression towards authority figures on to minority groups in society. Adorno measured authoritarianism using the F scale (F for fascism). See also *prejudice, social identity theory*.

authoritative A term used by Baumrind to describe a style of parenting or a *child-rearing style* in which children are encouraged to participate in decision-making and to express their opinions, but the parent nonetheless has the final authority. This was in contrast with an *autocratic* approach, in which the child is not encouraged to express an opinion; or a *laissez-faire* approach, in which the parent has little involvement in the process of decision-making. See also *authoritarian personality*.

authority figure A person who represents power or established dominance in some way.

autism A serious disorder appearing towards the end of infancy, in which the child withdraws from all social contact, which seems to be aversive and distressing. Activity is directed towards inanimate objects and may give evidence of quite high intelligence, but speech is usually minimal. Although it is often called infantile autism, or childhood autism, the condition can persist throughout the person's life. There is little agreement about cause, although a majority of those who work in the area probably believe in an organic predisposition, and there is even less agreement about treatment. See also *theory of mind, broken-mirror theory*.

autistic Thought and fantasy determined entirely by the person's needs and wishes and not constrained by reality in any way. Daydreams are autistic, as is the isolation from immediate social contact through the absorbed use of iPhones and portable music, but the term is usually reserved for the more extreme and permanent removal from reality, such as is found in *schizophrenic* thought.

autistic spectrum disorders The concept of autistic spectrum disorders was introduced in the fifth edition of the *Diagnostic and Statistical Manual of Mental Disorders* (DSM-V), which groups together a range of developmental disorders, emerging during early childhood and characterised by four sets of symptoms: social and communication difficulties, stereotyped or repetitive behaviours, sensory issues, and cognitive difficulty or delay in cognitive processing. Autistic spectrum disorders may not include all of these, but generally include three out of the four. There are conditions identified as autistic spectrum disorders: *autism* itelf, *Asperger's syndrome*, childhood disintegrative disorders, and *PDD-NOS* (pervasive developmental disorders not otherwise specified). It is open to question, particularly with respect to the last of these syndromes, whether the classification represents a real problem or a trend to medicalise untypical or unusual

forms of childhood behaviour that in previous times were regarded as normal but distinctive.

autobiographical memory Personal memory of the development or experiences of our own selves throughout our lifetimes. See also *direct retrieval, generative retrieval, hyperthymestic syndrome*.

autochthonous A term used to describe a state arising primarily from events within the individual, such as thirst or hunger.

autocratic leadership A style of leadership characterised by lack of consultation or negotiation, and making frequent use of arbitrary commands. Also known as authoritarian leadership. See also *laissez-faire, democratic leadership, authoritative*.

autogenic Originating from the self; self-initiated (e.g. autogenic training in which the individual is trained to have internal control of their own relaxation).

autohypnosis *Hypnosis* that has been self-induced. Many forms of hypnotherapy concentrate on building up the individual's own skills in autohypnosis, so that they can develop strategies of *coping behaviour* for dealing with stressful events.

autokinetic effect A visual illusion involving the *apparent motion* of a stationary dot of light when it is perceived in a totally dark environment. The light appears to move in rapid jerks, because of the minute tremors made by the eyeball.

automatic processing The cognitive processing of information without conscious awareness or intention.

automatic routines Actions or sequences of actions which have become so habitual that we no longer need to pay attention to them. Much complex skill learning consists of developing automatic routines (such as changing gear while driving). One of the most powerful demonstrations of automatic routines in cognition is the *Stroop effect*, which shows how the automatic subroutine of reading conflicts with the visual identification of colours. See *automatisation*.

automatic writing Writing that is performed without conscious awareness by the writer. It is usually elicited under *hypnosis*, but it can be produced by sitting undisturbed for a long period and writing continuously with no attempt to control what is produced. After several hours, the product may give an uncensored glimpse into the unconscious. Or it may not.

automatisation The process of learning a skill or technique so well that it no longer requires conscious thought. See also *skill acquisition, automatic routines*.

autonomic nervous system (ANS) A network of unmyelinated nerve fibres running from the brainstem and spinal cord to the internal organs, which can activate the body rapidly, preparing it for action. The ANS has two main parts, the sympathetic and the parasympathetic divisions. Activation of the *sympathetic division* results in the body being rapidly prepared for action, producing the *alarm reaction*. It is strongly involved in active emotions such as excitement, fear or anger. Activation of the *parasympathetic division* involves more quiescent functioning such as digestion, tissue growth and repair, the storage of blood sugars and the building up of bodily reserves. The parasympathetic division is thought to be involved in the passive *emotions* such as depression, contentment or sadness.

There seem to be individual differences in the balance between sympathetic and parasympathetic arousal, and in the overall lability of the autonomic nervous system (see Figure 6).

autonomous morality The third of Kohlberg's three stages of *moral development*, in which the individual is considered to have reached a point where he or she arrives at moral judgements and decisions on the basis of his or her own reasoning, rather than simply by accepting the ideas laid down by society. In the first level of this stage, the person accepts social rules and moral codes because he or she considers them to have been democratically established for the common good. In the second level, a more individual judgement is achieved, and the person may eventually come to reject some commonly accepted social values that they feel to be unjust or immoral.

autonomous stage of skill acquisition When a skill has been developed so thoroughly that it doesn't need conscious attention, but can be performed more or less automatically. See also *cognitive stage of skill acquisition*.

autonomous state A reference to the theory of obedience outlined by Milgram, in which he proposed that human beings, as social animals, have two alternative and mutually exclusive 'states' of social being. One of these is known as the autonomous state, in which people act as autonomous individuals, and in which their personal conscience and morality inform and direct their choices of action. The other, known as the *agentic state*, occurs when people act simply as an agent for others higher up in the social order.

autonomy A state of independence and self-determination in the individual,

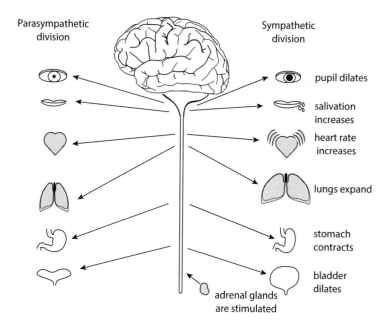

Figure 6 Connections of the autonomic nervous system

considered to be the ultimate goal of therapies based on *humanistic psychology* and *existentialism*.

autopagnosia An inability to localise body parts (e.g. pointing to the elbow instead of the knee) on oneself, other people or pictures, while still being able to use these parts effectively. This is one of the disorders that challenges the *sensory-functional distinction*.

autoshaping A procedure in *operant conditioning* in which a neutral stimulus is associated with a *reinforcer*, for example, by making a disc change colour whenever a food pellet is delivered, with the result that the pigeon's behaviour is *shaped* so that eventually it will peck the disc despite never having been directly reinforced for doing so. See also *behaviour shaping*.

autostereogram A complex two-dimensional image that appears to be three-dimensional if looked at for a prolonged period.

availability heuristic The 'shortcut' in human *decision-making* in which information that is readily available (e.g. as a result of having been recently discussed) is weighted more heavily than other, equally significant information. In other words, it is the idea that people make decisions using the information which comes most readily to mind.

avatar A fictional representation of a character, such as is used in computer *gaming* to represent the player.

average

(i) A colloquial term used to mean 'usual' or 'commonplace'.

(ii) An everyday term used to describe a statistical measure of *central tendency*, normally the arithmetic mean.

aversion therapy A technique of *behaviour therapy* that involves using *classical conditioning* to develop alternative behaviour patterns in the individual. It is done by the association of unpleasant stimuli or consequences with the maladaptive behaviour, such that the behaviour comes to be avoided. See also *antabuse*.

aversive Leading to avoidance behaviour. A stimulus or event that is unpleasant (such as an electrical shock) would be described as aversive.

avoidance learning The training of behaviour through a process of *negative reinforcement*, such that an *aversive* stimulus fails to take place if the behaviour is demonstrated. Avoidance learning is extremely resistant to *extinction*.

avoidant attachment See *insecure attachment*.

awareness A subjective state of being alert or conscious; cognisant of information received from the immediate environment. See also *altered states of awareness*.

axis A line along which objects can be arranged according to some measure, as when people are given a position along a line that indicates increasing height. A graph usually consists of more than one axis (the plural is 'axes'; see *x-axis*, *y-axis*, *z-axis*). Objects can also be placed at given distances from an axis, and rotate around it, as the earth rotates around the North–South axis.

axon The elongated 'stem' of a neurone, by means of which the electrical impulse is passed from one region of the nervous system to another. The axon is that part of the neurone found after the cell body, according to the direction of travel of the impulse. In *afferent* or *sensory neurones*, the elongated part of the neurone found before the cell body is known as the *dendron*.

B

babbling Vocalisation produced by infants, which includes the full range of human phonemes. In *Verbal Behaviour*, Skinner argued that language acquisition occurred as a result of *behaviour shaping*, with infant babbling as the *operants*, conditioned through the *Law of Effect*.

Babinski reflex A *reflex* shown by newborn babies in which scratching the sole of the foot produces extension of the toes. Absence of the reflex indicates a damaged motor system in a baby. Conversely, organic damage is indicated if the reflex is present in an adult.

baby talk The style of speech adopted by adults when talking to a baby, sometimes called *motherese*.

back-propagation A learning mechanism used in *connectionist modelling*, in which actual responses are compared to correct ones.

backward conditioning A variant of *classical conditioning* in which the *unconditioned stimulus* (UCS) precedes the *conditioned stimulus* (CS). There is some disagreement over whether backward conditioning is really possible. If it can occur, it is certainly difficult to achieve. See also *delayed conditioning, simultaneous conditioning, trace conditioning.*

balance theory A theory put forward by Heider, suggesting that we need to maintain a state of cognitive equilibrium between the different *attitudes* that we hold, and that our social cognitions will, if necessary, become modified in order to create or perpetuate such a balance. *Cognitive dissonance* is a later variant of the theory.

balanced design An experimental design in which sources of variation such as practice, fatigue or gender of subjects are balanced so that they will not be responsible for differences between groups. See *ABBA design.*

balanced scale A test or questionnaire in which sources of bias in the items are counterbalanced. For example, half of the items should be true and half false, so that any preference to answer 'yes' does not distort the outcome.

Bandura, Albert (1925–)

Bandura is, in an understated way, one of the most influential figures of twentieth-century psychology. He has been a major figure in the social cognitive aspects of psychology, in one form or another, for over 50 years. This includes a lengthy period in which social aspects of cognition were only accepted as a result of his experimental demonstrations of *modelling* and *imitation*, which ensured that, even during the *behaviourist* heyday, there was some recognition that not all learning consisted exclusively of *stimulus–response* connections and *conditioning*. In later years, Bandura developed an interest in personal agency and self-directedness, and contributed greatly to the psychological understanding of *self-efficacy beliefs*.

bandwagon effect The tendency, shown by all people, to believe a claim or hold an attitude if they believe that most other members of their group have that belief. See also *Asch effect*, *Barnum effect*.

bandwidth The amount of information that a communication channel can carry. For example, the amount of information that the copper wire of a phone line can carry is its bandwidth. The term is used about actual communication channels in the nervous system such as the optic nerve and also about hypothetical channels in models of *information processing*.

bar chart A statistical diagram in which the frequency, or amount, of two or more discrete variables is indicated by the length of a bar for each one. A *histogram* is a particularly accurate form of bar chart.

barbiturate A widely used drug, particularly given to promote sleep and to control epilepsy. Barbiturates are highly addictive and commonly abused, producing *amnesiac* disorders in long-term users.

Barnum effect An effect named after the circus entrepreneur T.P. Barnum, whose motto in dealing with the gullible public was 'there's a fool born every minute'. It is used to describe the widespread acceptance of certain common beliefs (e.g. astrological predictions, which are written in such general terms that they can be readily applied to anyone, but which are read by the credulous as being an exact description of their own individual character or circumstance). In cognitive terms, it refers to the tendency for people to engage in selective *perception*, noticing only what they wish to believe and ignoring that which does not accord with their expectations.

baroreceptors Receptors that detect blood pressure.

Bartlett, Frederic (1886–1969)

Frederic Bartlett is known as one of the pioneers of memory research. Rather than study memory in the abstract, like Ebbinghaus, Bartlett was interested in the human sense that people make of the information they are trying to remember. In a series of famous studies featuring the *serial reproduction* of a traditional Native American story called 'War of the Ghosts', he showed how we adjust and change information in order to make sense of it and to integrate it with what we already know. Bartlett is also one of the first psychologists to use the concept of the *schema* – often erroneously attributed to Piaget.

basal age On tests graded by age, the highest age level up to which all of the items are passed. It may be called 'basal mental age' in *intelligence testing*.

basal ganglia A group of brain cells associated with movement, cognition, emotions and learning. They link with nuclei in the *cerebral cortex*, *thalamus* and *cerebellum*. The basal ganglia are particular concerned with regulating action, and maintain a balance between stimulating movement and inhibiting it, to produce smooth action. They do this through two pathways: an *excitatory* pathway which stimulates movement, and an *inhibitory* pathway which reduces it. See also *Parkinson's disease*, *Huntingdon's disease*.

base rate or baseline The level or frequency at which a function is operating before any experimental or therapeutic procedures have been started. Measures taken before an intervention is started may be used as a prediction of what the level of functioning would have been without the intervention. For example, baseline heart rate may be measured for a few seconds before a stimulus and the recordings used to show whether the heart rate after the stimulus is consistently different; or the number of cigarettes smoked per day may be recorded for a month before a treatment starts, to see whether there is any change.

basic emotions Categories of emotion that are common to humans in all cultures, and generally considered to be innate. The six generally accepted basic emotions are *happiness*, sadness, *disgust*, *anger*, fear and surprise.

basic needs The most compelling human needs, such as those for food and the avoidance of pain. In Maslow's theory, these are at the base of a *hierarchy of needs*, and other requirements, even for physical safety, will be ignored until they are satisfied.

basic trust The development in an infant of total trust that the mother will provide for, protect and not harm the infant. It is the first of Erikson's eight stages of lifespan development, and is proposed as the most important task that the infant must complete. It is achieved as a result of the security provided by good mothering. Erikson also pointed out that a capacity for mistrust is sometimes useful, too.

basilar membrane A membrane that runs the length of the *cochlea*, in the inner ear, on which hair cells are located that effect the *transduction* of auditory vibrations into electrical impulses. The impulses are transmitted to the *auditory cortex* by the auditory nerve.

battered baby syndrome A term coined by C. Henry Kempe in 1962 in a paper that first alerted the medical profession to the widespread existence of infants who had been injured by their parents. See also *child abuse*.

Bayley Infant Development Scales Measures of infant development that assess infants on mental and motor tasks. First developed in the 1920s, and based on the work of Gesell, they are still the most widely used infant assessment. The *norms* are based on normal infants and rely heavily on the ability of the infant to perform motor tasks, but the scale is now used almost exclusively to assess the general development of children with motor impairments.

behaviour The movements or actions that a person or animal performs. If something is referred to as 'behavioural', it means that it is only concerned with actual behaviour, and not, for instance, with any cognitive aspects of an action or performance.

behaviour analysis A systematic method of observing behaviour that generally involves identifying discrete categories of activity, and taking regular time samples during an observational period. At these times, the number of occurrences in each category is recorded and noted. Although somewhat mechanical, the method can be useful in identifying recurrent patterns of problematic behaviour, which may then be addressed or challenged by professional therapists.

behaviour disorder A general term used to cover a wide range of psychological disorders in which the behaviour of the person is the major concern. More specifically, it applies to conditions such as *psychopathic personality*, *addictions* and *hyperactivity*. One feature of behaviour disorders is that they usually involve symptoms that are likely to bring the sufferer into conflict with society. See also *conduct disorders*.

behaviour genetics The study of the influence of *genes* on behaviour. Empirical work is particularly concerned with changes in inherited tendencies as a result of selection pressure, and with environmental influences on the expression of these tendencies. Practical considerations result in much of the work being carried out with organisms with very short breeding cycles, such as fruit flies (*drosophila*). Applied behaviour genetics has a history of a few thousand years in, for example, horse breeding. See also *eugenics*.

behaviour modification The therapeutic technique of treating psychological difficulties by dealing solely with the maladaptive behaviour that they produce. The process of behaviour modification operates from the assumptions that disturbed behaviour consists of inappropriate responses to stimuli arising from maladaptive learning, and that new responses may be acquired as a result of new learning. The therapy is based on *conditioning* techniques. Some researchers use the term behaviour modification to refer to those forms of treatment based on *operant conditioning* and imitative learning (e.g. *token economy*), and use the term *behaviour therapy* to refer to techniques based on classical conditioning (e.g. *aversion therapy*). In practice, behaviour modification is used for training to create or increase the desired behaviour, while behaviour therapy is used to treat psychological disturbance.

behaviour shaping The production of novel behaviours through the systematic adjustment of *reinforcement contingencies* – in other words, by rewarding simple behaviours until they are established in the organism's repertoire of actions and then rewarding only those variants of it which produce behaviour that is closer to the desired outcome. Once that in turn is established as a frequent behaviour pattern, only behaviour which is even closer to the desired outcome will be rewarded. Behaviour shaping can be used to produce behaviours that are completely unlike anything in the organism's previous repertoire, such as pigeons playing table tennis.

behaviour therapy The process of treating abnormal behaviour by using conditioning techniques to modify maladaptive symptoms. Behaviour therapy includes techniques such as *aversion therapy*, *systematic desensitisation* and *implosion therapy*. See also *behaviour modification*, *cognitive behaviour therapy*.

behavioural analysis Part of the procedure in *behaviour modification* in which the relevant behaviour is analysed in detail. The idea is that this analysis will reveal the *conditioning* processes that sustain it.

behavioural assessment A detailed analysis of the behaviours, including indicators of emotions and cognitive processes, that a person displays in a relevant context. Behavioural assessment is usually carried out to identify the objectives of a programme of *behaviour modification*. It generally depends on careful unobtrusive observation.

behavioural coding A research process in which categories of behaviour are defined and placed on a grid. Then the category is checked whenever that behaviour is observed.

behavioural correlates of attention The changes in behaviour or physiological state that people show when they are attending to something, such as turning one's head towards the source of a sound. See also *orienting reflex*.

behavioural domain One of the four domains of the psyche. The behavioural domain concerns what people actually do. See also *cognitive domain*, *conative domain*, *affective domain*.

behavioural genetics The study of the relationships between genetic inheritance and behaviour and/or cognition. See, for example, *imprinting*.

behavioural neuroscience The study of cognitive or social *neuroscience* in non-human animals.

behavioural pathogens Factors in a person's lifestyle that produce poor health and which can be addressed by psychological methods (e.g. smoking, excessive drinking).

behavioural psychotherapy *Psychotherapy* in which the emphasis is on getting the person to behave differently (e.g. by imitating successful models) so that they discover new ways of coping with their problems and stresses.

behavioural sciences A general term used for those sciences that are concerned with the understanding of behaviour, such as *psychology*, *ethology*, population genetics, etc.

behaviourism The school of thought first established by J.B. Watson in 1913, in which he argued that, to be truly scientific, it was necessary for psychology to concern itself only with that which could be directly observed, namely the behaviour of organisms. Watson considered that a complete understanding of human behaviour would eventually be developed through the analysis of psychological phenomena as complex chains of learned stimulus–response connections. The behaviourist approach, developed especially in America and Britain in the first half of the century, proposed that only the study of measurable behaviour was objective, and therefore scientific, and that therefore psychologists should study only behaviour and ignore 'mental' processes. Behaviourists also considered that all human behaviour ultimately consisted of links between a stimulus and a response, in much the same way as living matter consists of cells. This inherently reductionist argument led to much criticism of the approach, which eventually resulted in a considerable decline in its popularity. However, behaviourist assumptions left their mark on accepted methodology within psychology, and formed the dominant background against which the challenges posed by *new paradigm* research and *qualitative analysis* were evaluated. See also *association, reductionism, stimulus–response learning.*

belief bias The tendency to accept invalid but plausible explanations and to reject true but implausible ones, even when their validity has been demonstrated.

belladonna A drug, atropine, is derived from the plant belladonna, which dilates the pupils of the eye. Since *pupil dilation* is a significant *non-verbal cue* indicating interpersonal attraction, the drug was used as a cosmetic, especially in Italy – hence the name belladonna, meaning 'beautiful lady'.

belt region An area in the secondary *auditory cortex*, located in the *temporal lobes*, which receives information from the *primary auditory cortex* and also from the *medial geniculate nucleus.*

benign Used to describe conditions that do not pose any significant threat. Its opposite is 'malignant'.

benzodiazepines A group of commonly prescribed minor *tranquillisers* such as Valium. They are a form of barbiturate producing muscle relaxation, decreased anxiety and sedation, and are widely used to help people to cope with transient difficulties. Benzodiazepines are not *antidepressants*, and there is concern that their availability may cause people to put up with an unsatisfactory situation instead of taking positive action to deal with their problems.

bereavement The experience of losing a friend, relative or acquaintance as a result of their death.

beta waves A wave pattern observed in *EEG* recordings characteristic of an alert, wide-awake individual. See also *alpha waves, delta waves.*

between-group design A form of experimental design that compares the results obtained from two separate groups of participants. Because this makes results vulnerable to distortion arising from individual differences in the participants concerned, data of this kind need to be analysed using *independent-measures* statistics. See also *within-subjects design.*

between-group variance A measure of the variation found among the means of a number of samples. The measure is divided by the *within-group variance* to give an *F ratio*. These measures are usually computed within an *analysis of variance*. See also *variance.*

bias A systematic distortion. The term is used in two related ways in psychology, either as bias when making judgements (see *prejudice*), or as distortion of a statistical result because some factor was operating that had not been accounted for in the research design (see *artefact*).

biased sample An error in the way in which a particular *sample* has been selected, which results in that sample not being representative of the population as a whole. The classic example was a survey of American electors that was conducted by randomly selecting respondents from the telephone directory, thereby excluding all of the voters who could not afford telephones at that time.

Big Five personality factors See *five-factor theory.*

bilateral Occurring on both sides. In neuroscience, this usually means both sides of the *cerebrum*, but the word is also used in many other contexts.

bilateral transfer The demonstration of a skill learned by one side of the body (e.g. the right hand) by the other

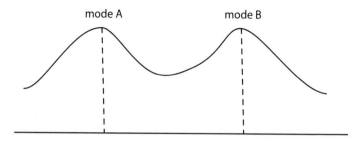

Figure 7 A bimodal distribution

half (demonstrated by the left hand). Bilateral transfer can be demonstrated with many motor skills – practice with one side will produce an improvement in performance by the other side.

bimodal distribution A set of scores that, when plotted as a frequency distribution, shows two separate peaks. Usually, this indicates that the scores do not all come from the same population, although it may mean that the source *population* itself is bimodal (see Figure 7).

binaural cue An indication of the direction of a source of sound arising from differences in the sounds reaching the two ears. For example, a sound which originates from one side will reach the ear on that side marginally sooner than it reaches the other ear. A crossover point for the auditory nerve means that the difference can be detected and the direction of sound analysed.

binding problem A problem encountered by those working in *cognitive psychology*, and particularly in knowledge *representation*, which has to do with linking together particular concepts or features, in order to perform mental operations. For example, if one wanted to exclude the rich and famous from a simulated model of personality and consumerism, it would be necessary to bind together the two features 'rich' and 'famous', so that the two features were treated together. In everyday language, we use conjunctions, such as 'and' or 'but' to do this, but *computer simulations* require specialist symbols or instructions to make the connections clear in the context; and the way these connections should be represented has become known as the binding problem.

Binet, Alfred (1857–1911)

Alfred Binet was a major figure in developmental psychology. Like Freud, he had studied mesmerism and *hysteria* under the neurologist Charcot, and he became Director of the Sorbonne Psychological Laboratory in 1894. His major contribution to modern psychology was the concept of age-related intelligence and the first *intelligence test*, developed with Theodore Simon in 1905, developed in order to identify children who required more educational assistance than standard French schools could provide. Binet insisted that the new tests should not be regarded as measuring fixed ability, but rather as an indicator of the current development of the individual. He was deeply concerned that they should not be used as any kind of social label, but as a guide for educational assistance. This was somewhat ironic in view of the *IQ test's* subsequent history.

binocular convergence See *binocular disparity.*

binocular depth cues Indicators of distance that depend on the use of both eyes. The main binocular depth cues are *binocular disparity* and the convergence of eye muscles (convergence is greater when looking at objects closer to the eyes than for objects further away). See also *depth perception.*

binocular disparity The difference in the retinal image received by the two eyes. The disparity between two images is greater for objects close to the eyes, and the difference is used to judge the distance of nearby objects.

binocular rivalry When two different stimuli are presented at the same time, one to each eye. For an auditory equivalent, see *cocktail party effect.* However, unlike the auditory version, in binocular rivalry the perceived stimulus will alternate between the two eyes, unless one eye is significantly dominant over the other.

binocular vision Vision obtained by comparing the images received by two eyes, such that *depth perception* can be achieved by comparing the disparity between the two images. See also *binocular disparity.*

binomial distribution This applies to data that have two mutually exclusive outcomes (heads/tails, adult/child), and it indicates the proportion of each ratio of scores which would be expected for each sample size. For example, if a coin is repeatedly tossed in sets of 20 times each, the distribution will indicate how often you would expect to get 20 heads, how often you would expect 19 heads and one tail, and so on. The actual proportions obtained can be compared with the expected proportions, to see whether it is reasonable to suppose that the scores came from the specified population (in this example, whether the coin is unbiased) (see Figure 8). With large samples, the binomial distribution becomes very similar to a normal distribution.

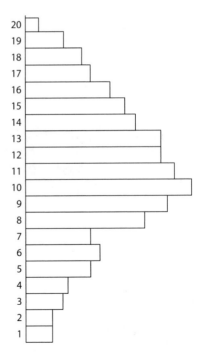

Figure 8 A typical binomial distribution

biodiversity A measure of the variety of animals, plants and microorganisms. Greater biodiversity in a given habitat is generally regarded as an indication of the health of that environment. There is concern that human activity is having significant effects in reducing biodiversity.

biofeedback A term used to describe a process by which control of *autonomic* functioning can be learned if the individual is provided with information about how the body is working (e.g. blood pressure or *galvanic skin response* readings). Typically, the person engages in relaxation exercises while being provided with such feedback, and it has been demonstrated that effective reduction of blood pressure and heart rate may be achieved in this way. Biofeedback is sometimes cited as an example of the practical application of *operant conditioning*, although this has been disputed on the grounds that the reward – knowledge of results – is a cognitive rather than a behavioural *reinforcement*.

biogenic A term applied to behaviours or characteristics with a biological origin.

biogenic amines The group of amines that are known to be particularly important in the functioning of the nervous system. They include *catecholamine* and histamine.

biological anthropology The study of the behavioural and anatomical *evolution* of human beings.

biological clock The idea that organisms contain a mechanism which maintains a fairly constant rate and which is responsible for controlling biological rhythms such as the sleep/wake cycle. See also *biorhythm, circadian rhythm*.

biological determinism The argument that human nature or human characteristics arise as an inevitable consequence of human biological characteristics. See also *reductionism*.

biological motion The ability to detect the presence of animal or human bodies from motion cues alone. Studies showing movements of limbs and joints through light-emitting diodes as points in an otherwise dark environment show that human beings are remarkably good at this. The perception of biological motion has been associated with activity in the *superior temporal sulcus*.

biological preparedness A state of readiness for a particular kind of *learning*, which comes about as a result of *genetic* factors. For example, a young gosling is biologically prepared to learn to identify and follow its mother soon after birth (see *imprinting*), or bees are biologically prepared to learn to identify flowerlike scents, or humans are biologically prepared to respond preferentially to other humans, as opposed to other animals, from birth. This form of learning is achieved much more easily than the learning of other information.

biological reductionism The idea that everything can be explained purely by reference to biological functions. See also *reductionism*.

biological therapy The treatment of psychological disturbance or mental illness by physical methods such as *drugs*, brain surgery or *electroconvulsive therapy*.

biomedical model A way of looking at health problems or psychological disorders that attributes them primarily to disturbances in biological functioning, which can be adjusted using medical techniques. See also *biopsychosocial model*.

biopsychology The study of the biological sources of individual functioning. The term usually has a slightly different emphasis to *psychobiology*, but there is no universally agreed meaning for either label.

biopsychosocial model The idea that health-related behaviours such as healthy lifestyles or addictions arise through a combination of biological, psychological and social factors, rather than being caused by any one of these alone. See also *biomedical model*.

biorhythm General swings or fluctuations of biological functioning, such as *circadian rhythms* or the menstrual cycle. Longer-term biological rhythms, such as annual variations, have been demonstrated in many animals, but evidence for their existence in human beings is not clearly established. The term has also been adopted by an industry that claims to calculate variations in functions such as creativity from the individual's date of birth. See also *Barnum effect, zeitgeber*.

bipolar Having two ends.

bipolar cells Cells that pick up information from one source and pass it on to another, such as are found in the second layer of the *retina*, or in some parts of the auditory system.

bipolar constructs or concepts The claim that, in human thought, concepts are defined in terms of opposite poles. For example, the concept of honesty entails the opposite pole of dishonesty. The most well-known theory constructed on this basis is George Kelly's *personal construct* theory.

bipolar depression A disorder of *affect* that involves swings between the two extremes of mania and depression. The condition is regarded as having a *biogenic* origin, and the swings can be halted by continuous treatment with *lithium*. The disorder is also called *manic depression* or manic-depressive psychosis.

birth cry A reflex cry that signals the start of breathing immediately after birth. It is possible for breathing to start without a birth cry.

birth rate The annual number of live births per 1,000 people in the population.

birth trauma An attempt to explain psychological disturbance as resulting from the trauma of being born. It was proposed by Otto Rank in the early days of *psychoanalysis*, but was largely abandoned. It has been revived more recently in relation to concern about the technological nature of some methods of managing birth.

bisexual A person whose sexual preference includes people of the same sex as well as those of the opposite sex.

bit A term used in *information theory* to define a unit of information. A bit of information is not a vague amount, but is precisely defined as the amount required to choose between two equal alternatives – it halves the uncertainty. For example, if you were searching for a randomly chosen word in this dictionary, one bit would tell you which half it was in, two bits would narrow it down to a quarter, and three bits to an eighth. Twelve bits would identify a specific word out of 4,096. The word 'bit' is a contraction of 'binary digit'.

black box A term used to describe an approach to psychological theory in which the internal workings of the organism are regarded as unknowable, as if they take place inside a 'black box'. One is left with the options of either:

(i)   guessing what is going on in the box by observing the relationships between inputs to the box and its consequent behaviour; or

(ii) claiming that it is not important to know what is going on in the box, and that only the relationships between input and behaviour should be studied.

The second approach was the one chosen by the supporters of *behaviourism*.

Blaint's syndrome Severe difficulty in spatial processing usually arising from bilateral lesions of the *parietal lobe*. It consists of a group of symptoms including *simultanagnosia*, *optic ataxia* and *optic apraxia*.

blank slate See *tabula rasa*.

blind scoring When the observer is unaware of the status of the event that is being scored (e.g. which condition of an *experiment* has produced the behaviour being observed).

blind spot A specific location on the *retina* of the eye where the neural fibres of the ganglion cells in the retina bunch together to form the optic nerve. The blind spot is so named because this part of the retina contains no photosensitive cells, but it is not normally noticed because the brain 'fills in' the area such that it appears to be continuous with the general background.

blindsight A condition of some people who are completely blind in the sense of having no visual awareness but who can still make some use of visual information. See also *affective blindsight*.

block design A method of designing the presentation of experimental material in which the same or similar stimuli or conditions are presented together, or in sequence. See also *event-related design*, *counterbalancing*.

blood pressure The force with which blood travels through the arteries and veins of the body. High blood pressure is a reliable indicator of long-term *stress*, and a precursor to many stress disorders.

blood–brain barrier A characteristic of the blood supply to the brain that prevents many substances from passing from the blood to the brain tissues. It protects the brain from many poisons, but also prevents some potentially useful drugs from being used in the brain.

bodily-kinaesthetic intelligence One of Gardner's seven forms of *intelligence*. This form deals with the ability to learn and execute complex physical skills.

body image The idea held by each individual of what their body is like. There is evidence of a physiological basis for a body image at birth, but each infant has to learn which parts of the universe are not part of its own body. Later, the body image extends beyond a *representation* of the body and comes to reflect an evaluation of bodily characteristics. The 'normal' pattern is to overestimate such characteristics as head size and attractiveness. The body image is an important part of the *self-image*.

body language A general term used to describe those aspects of *non-verbal communication* (NVC) that involve direct use of the body, such as *gesture*, *posture* and *proxemics*.

body-schema The body-schema is the internal representation that an individual has of his or her own body. According to Piaget, the very first *schema* formed by the infant develops from the first 'me – not me' distinction. For the older person, it includes ideas and memories of how the body is, has been and could be.

body-size effect An *illusion* in which inaccurate perception of one's own body size results in misjudgements of the size of perceived objects.

BOLD Acronym for blood oxygen level dependent information, used in *MRI scanning*.

bonding The formation of a strong relationship (*attachment*), usually applied to mothers and their infants, and usually during the period immediately following birth. Some claim that a strong bond may be formed at first contact between mother and baby, a view that has been called the 'Araldite theory' of bonding. Obstetric practices in many Western hospitals have been changed to facilitate bonding, but the significance of contact between mother and baby immediately following birth is still a matter of controversy. Some writers reserve the term 'bonding' for the mother's feelings for her baby, and 'attachment' for the infant's relationship to the mother. This usage assumes that there are two different, one-way processes, rather than a *transactional* shared relationship.

borderline disorder A disorder of personality. The term was originally applied to people judged to be on the borderline between *neurosis* and *psychosis*, particularly those believed to have an underlying psychotic disorder but who were coping reasonably well. It is now used much more broadly when describing people who show instability in their *emotions* and interpersonal relationships, but whose symptoms do not fit any diagnostic system.

boredom effects False research results obtained from a psychological study as a result of the participants becoming bored with carrying out tedious, predictable or repetitive tasks.

bottom-up approach An approach to research that sees theorising as a kind of jigsaw puzzle, in which the pieces are factual information about the subject under study, obtained through narrowly focused research. Bottom-up theories ignore higher-order levels of functioning, in contrast to *top-down approaches*, which take those as their starting point. Inevitably, each approach has its advantages and also its disadvantages. See, for example, *emergent properties*, *reductionism*.

bottom-up processing Perceptual processing that is initiated by the characteristics of the stimulus and leads on to higher forms of cognitive activity, as opposed to top-down processing, which begins from the higher levels. Marr's *computational theory of perception* is a classic example of bottom-up processing, and the term can also apply to Gibson's *ecological perception* theory.

bounded rationality The idea is that people are rational within their own environmental and cognitive bounds – in other words, that the decisions we make or the arguments we put forward are valid for our own personal worlds, even if not in an objective sense.

Bowlby, John (1907–1990)

John Bowlby originally trained as a psychiatrist, and became interested in the effects of separation on the development of the child. With James Robertson, he created some upsetting films of the effects on children of being separated from their parents for periods of over a week, which had a powerful effect on the ways in which children are treated in hospital and in temporary care. His theory of *maternal deprivation* was taken as saying that even brief separations from the mother during infancy can cause permanent damage, but there is still controversy as to whether Bowlby really made this strong claim. He did, however, include 'mother working full-time' on a list of situations that might damage children, producing a social debate which has not died down since the 1950s. He then turned to *ethology* as a source of understanding, and developed his theory of *attachment*, which has become one of the more important theories in *developmental psychology*.

box whisker diagram See *box-plot diagram*.

box-plot diagram A form of statistical diagram which indicates the *median* and *semi-interquartile ranges* of sets of scores, by using a square shape to indicate the median with lines (whiskers) coming out from top and bottom (or left and right) to indicate the range.

bracketing Systematically identifying and setting aside preconceptions, beliefs and opinions that might influence the interpretation of *qualitative data*.

brain A general term used to describe the complex of *neural* structures developed at the forward end of the spinal cord. In casual usage, however, many psychologists refer to the 'brain' when in fact they mean the *cerebrum* or the *cerebral cortex* (e.g. *split-brain studies*). Whether the whole brain or simply the cerebrum is meant must be deduced from the context.

brain scan A general term used to describe a non-invasive method of studying the living brain. There are many types of brain scan, but they tend to fall into three main categories: CAT or CT scans, PET scans, and fMRI scans. CAT scans map the brain by taking a number of X-ray photos that form 'slices' of the whole brain, and combining them to build up a full image. PET scans (*positron emission tomography*) work by monitoring a small amount of radioactive chemical that is put into the blood supply and indicates the increased uptake of blood by active brain cells. The third main approach is *functional magnetic resonance imaging* (fMRI), which is a rapid procedure that can be used to monitor cognitive processes as they happen. It is a popular method for researchers, partly because of its accuracy, but also because there are no X-rays or radioactive substances involved. See also *False Discovery Rate*, *magneto-encephalography*, *transcranial direct current stimulation*.

brainstem See *medulla*.

brainstorming A technique for developing new ideas, commonly used in advertising work and other *problem-solving* situations. A group engages in a period of intensive concentration in which any idea at all that comes to mind – regardless of how apparently inappropriate it might be – is noted. There is an agreement not to reject or ridicule any suggestion. At the end of that period of time, all of the ideas so generated are examined for their potential value as a solution to the problem in hand. Some recent research indicates that a group may produce more ideas if the individuals work on their own and then pool their suggestions. The term has become common in everyday usage for any type of idea-generating session, but the distinctive and most important aspect of brainstorming as a technique is that the idea-generating stage should be entirely separated from the evaluation stage.

brainwashing The technique of operating total control over a person's environment, with a consistent application of deprivation, debilitation and dread (the three Ds), so that the victim becomes amenable to adopting a completely new belief system or ideology. The process may depend on some form of *identification*.

brainwaves Overall electrical activity of the brain that can be detected outside the skull by an *electroencephalogram*. Or, in colloquial use, a good idea.

bridging inferences In reading, these are inferences made to link the current and preceding parts of a text, in such a way as to increase their plausibilty and coherence.

brightness The intensity of light stimulation.

brightness constancy The perceptual adjustment by which we perceive objects seen in widely varying light intensities as being of similar brightness. Brightness *constancy* arises because of the capacity of our perceptual system to work in context, and to deal with relative differences in intensity rather than with absolute ones. For example, we perceive a piece of paper in a dark cellar to be brighter than a piece of coal in daylight, even though the latter actually reflects more light.

Broadbent, Donald E. (1926–1993)

Donald Broadbent was a key figure in the development of cognitive psychology during and after the Second World War. His dual interest in engineering and the developing subject of psychology led him to study with Bartlett at Cambridge, where he became concerned with designing technological environments that were suitable for human use. His early research into *selective attention* was a major stimulus to *information-processing* models of human cognition. Although his subsequent research led him to reject this approach, and emphasise the importance of *probability* and *motivation* in cognition, it was never as influential as his early work had been.

Broca's aphasia The inability to formulate speech, resulting from damage to *Broca's area*.

Broca's area An area of the *cerebral cortex* at the base of the *frontal lobe*, usually on the *left hemisphere*, which is mainly concerned with the production of speech and the formulation of words. Damage to Broca's area can produce *aphasia*.

Brodmann's areas Brodmann developed a technique for dividing up the *cerebral cortex* for the purpose of mapping its different areas. Brodmann's areas consist of 52 regions of the cortex, labelled BA1–BA52, which are based on the relative distribution of cell types across the cortical layers.

broken-mirror theory A theory of *autism* which proposes that the social difficulties encountered by autistic people are the result of dysfunction of the *mirror system*.

Bruce, Vicki (1953–)

Vicki Bruce is a major contributor to the psychological understanding of perception in general, and face recognition in particular. Her perceptual research has contributed to a variety of different social applications, ranging from the design of new coins to raising awareness of the legal shortcomings of an eyewitness testimony. She is acknowledged as an international authority on the neuropsychology of face recognition.

Bruner, Jerome S. (1915–2016)

Bruner was a major figure in the cognitive revolution of the 1960s and 1970s, representing the 'human' side of cognitive psychology, as opposed to more mechanistic, *information-processing* approaches. His work emphasised the active nature of human cognition, and the role of meaning and intentionality. He regarded cognitive development as being closely linked to culture, and his research included studies of the role of cultural amplification in the child's cognitive development, as well as research into the development of representation. Bruner was also instrumental in introducing the Western psychological community to the work of Vygotsky, and in developing the concept of cultural input as scaffolding, supporting and structuring cognitive development.

bulimia or **bulaemia** A disorder of eating involving phases in which very large quantities of food are consumed, followed by vomiting, taking laxatives, or intense exercise. The victim therefore gains little nutritional value from the food, and may lose weight rapidly. Bulimia is considered to be closely related to *anorexia*.

burnout A condition that develops when a worker has been under continual stress. In this state, people suffer from fatigue, lack of motivation and depression. The most common outcome is to leave (or lose) the job in which burnout occurred. Burnout is seen as a particular risk in the helping professions.

bystander apathy A somewhat moralistic label applied by social psychologists to the phenomenon whereby onlookers fail to help in emergencies, even though they may be upset by what is happening. Concern about bystander apathy was aroused by the case of Kitty Genovese, who was stabbed to death in New York in 1964. About 40 people heard her screams for half an hour, but news reports stated that none of them called the police (although this may not be true). Much research has been conducted on the factors that determine whether onlookers will intervene or not, and the area has come to be known as *bystander intervention*.

bystander calculus model A way of interpreting the behaviour of bystanders that sees people as calculating the perceived costs and benefits of helping versus not helping, and responding accordingly. See also *bystander intervention*, *social impact theory*.

bystander intervention The involvement of onlookers in situations where, for example, help is required by another person. The likelihood of bystander intervention has been shown to depend on several factors, such as the onlooker's definition of the situation, the presence of other people who might be expected to provide the help needed and, to a lesser extent, the characteristics of the victim. The most powerful factor influencing the decision as to whether to intervene appears to be *diffusion of responsibility*.

C

CA See *conversation analysis*.

CAL See *computer-assisted learning*.

calibration Adjusting a scale to provide appropriate measures. Once a scale has been set up, for example, of non-verbal expressions of increasing anger, data can be gathered to give a measure of the strength of feeling at each point of the scale.

cancellation task A form of *visual search* task in which the person has to identify all the instances of a certain type of stimulus presented as part of an array, and cancel them out. It is often used to diagnose visual *neglect*.

cannabis See *marijuana*.

Cannon–Bard theory A theory of emotion put forward in the 1920s, in which it was stated that the psychological experience of emotion and the physiological reactions produced by the body (see *autonomic nervous system*) were completely independent of one another. Compare *interactionism*, *James–Lange theory*. See also *alarm reaction*.

Capgras syndrome A syndrome thought to result from a deficit in the emotional component of *face recognition*, in which the person reports that their partners, family members or friends have been replaced by imposters or 'body doubles'.

cardiac muscle Heart muscle. The term 'cardiac' refers to the heart.

caregiver/caretaker A general term used to refer to the person who looks after a child, thus avoiding the assumptions

inherent in the use of terms such as 'mother' or 'parent', and allowing for a wider range of possibilities. Despite being apparent opposites, the two terms are used with identical meaning.

carpentered environment An environment in which there are many straight lines and right angles (e.g. in modern buildings). Carpentered environments are highly characteristic of Western society, and this has been cited by some researchers (e.g. Gregory) as a possible explanation for some cultural differences in perception (e.g. that geometric illusions are perceived more or less strongly by people from different cultures) (see Figure 9).

Cartesian dualism The philosophical position proposed by Descartes, that the mind and the body are separate entities, each with its own way of operating. Cartesian dualism formed the fundamental assumption of Western medicine, which sees the body as a machine and the mind as being almost entirely separate, and it has also influenced (or distorted) many other areas of knowledge, including psychology. Gilbert Ryle described it as believing that the human mind is a 'ghost in a machine', and was influential in showing that dualism is an unhelpful assumption. Although the position is no longer widely supported when it is stated explicitly, it continues to be an assumption of much scientific research. Everyday language, too, makes it easy to slip into assuming a separation of mind and body. See also *dual-aspect theory*.

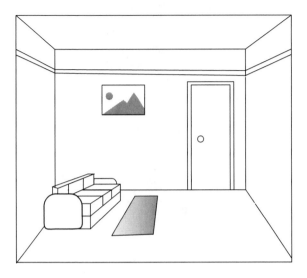

Figure 9 A carpentered environment

cascade model In cognitive psychology, this is a form of *information processing* in which information passes from one level to the next before it has been fully processed at the first level. In general research contexts, it is a way of obtaining a *sample* whereby each person asks several others to participate in a study, and they in turn ask several more – an approach also known as *snowball sampling*.

case history A detailed account of the background and previous experience of a single patient or client, which may be important in therapy or in the understanding of a particular psychological phenomenon, such as *anterograde amnesia*.

case-series study A form of research method that involves investigating several people with similar cognitive impairments. This allows the researcher to make meaningful comparisons, to identify symptoms in common and also to map out some of the variation between individuals.

case study A psychological study involving the detailed investigation of one particular case or individual. Case studies are extremely important in many areas of psychology, as they allow for an in-depth analysis of unusual circumstances and their outcomes, which may in turn throw light on more normal psychological events (e.g. the outcome of localised brain damage may serve to highlight the functions of a particular area of the brain). They are also used in situations where a detailed account rather than a limited set of standardised measures is required. However, the method has its own problems (e.g. subjective decisions about which aspects to describe) and difficulties of *replication*.

castration threat anxiety A Freudian concept, referring to the anxiety experienced by the young boy during the *Oedipus complex*. As the young boy's sexual interest is directed towards his mother, and his father is perceived as a rival for the mother's love, the child supposedly develops a fear that the father (being bigger and more powerful than he) may deal with the competition by castrating him.

CAT scan Computed axial tomography: a non-invasive technique for examining the structure of the brain, which consists of building up a three-dimensional X-ray picture of the brain. This is achieved by taking X-ray photographs of the brain in a series of sections. The sections are then combined using a computer. The resulting image shows up deformed or damaged tissue, and also blood clots or areas where the blood supply has been interrupted. See also *magnetic resonance imaging, positron emission tomography*.

catastrophe theory A mathematical theory that deals with changes of state which are sudden, substantial and not easily reversible (e.g. walking off a cliff). Many psychological phenomena look like this, with examples ranging from the spontaneous reversals of perception of a *Necker cube*, through experiences of insight (*aha! experience*), to the sudden onset of a *phobia*. It is always difficult to record significant psychological phenomena in a form that can be entered into a mathematical equation, and we do not yet know how useful catastrophe theory will be to psychology.

catatonia A state in which the muscles are extremely tense. The person may stay in a fixed posture for several hours, and in some cases if one moves a limb to a different position it will stay there. It is usually seen in people diagnosed as *schizophrenic*. If it is their major symptom, they are classified as suffering from 'catatonic schizophrenia'.

catecholamines A group of *biogenic amines*, including adrenaline and dopamine,

which play a role in neural transmission in the brain. It is suspected that an excess of catecholamines may be involved in *schizophrenia*.

categorical perception In cognitive psychology, this is the term used when a sound which is between two *phonemes* is perceived as being either one or the other of its neighbours, rather than being perceived as the intermediate sound that it really is.

categorical variable A variable that only varies by fitting into one category or another – in other words, nominal data. See also *levels of measurement, nominal scale*.

categorisation Grouping people into categories on the basis of chosen characteristics. When the category is one that the observer wants to see as indicating inferiority (e.g. a different class or race), social categorisation is the basis for *stereotyping*. Categorisation is also used for the process, which is fundamental in much *qualitative research*, of grouping basic codings into higher order concepts. So references in the data to playing sport, dancing and watching television might be grouped under the category of 'leisure activities'. See also *grounded theory*.

category specificity The idea that the brain represents different categories of information in different ways, or in different areas.

category-specific deficits Disorders resulting from certain types of brain damage, in which memory for particular semantic categories, but not others, is impaired.

catharsis The sudden release of tension or anxiety resulting from the process of uncovering repressed trauma or ideas during psychoanalysis. In a wider context, the process of catharsis is seen as the satisfying release of built-up emotional energy, often through *displacement* (e.g. enthusiastic support of team sports).

cathexis A term used in *psychoanalytic theory* to refer to the investment of intense energy, desire or meaning in a person, object or event. In many ways, cathexis can be thought of as being the opposite of catharsis.

cathodal tDCS A form of *transcranial direct current stimulation* that decreases cortical *excitation*, and results in decreased levels of performance. See also *anodal tDCS*.

caudal To do with the tail. See also *cephalo-caudal*.

causal attribution A reason given for why an event or characteristic occurred. See also *attribution*.

causality The process by which an event such as the action of a person or thing brings about some kind of effect. A fundamental cognitive process is to be alert to causal effects, or *contingencies*, and the recognition of contingencies is essential for *operant conditioning* to occur. *Attribution theory* is the study of how people decide which cause of an event to pay attention to.

CDS See *child-directed speech*.

ceiling effect An effect that occurs when a test is too easy, such that most people score near the top (or ceiling) of the scale. The result is that the test is unable to distinguish between individuals. The opposite situation is known as a 'floor effect'.

cell body The part of the *neurone* that contains the nucleus, the mitochondria

and other organelles specific to the cell's general functioning.

centile The point on a scale such that a given percentage of the relevant population would score at or below that point. For example, if the 60th centile for height in a given population is 1.75 metres, 60 per cent of those people will be that height or shorter.

central coherence The ability to use all of the information involved when interpreting a situation or spoken communication.

central dyslexia The disruption of reading that results from difficulty in accessing meaning or translating to speech, occurring after the visual word form has been processed. See also *deep dyslexia*, *pure alexia*.

central executive The core component in the theory of *working memory*. The central executive controls the interactions between the long-term memory and the currently active visual and phonological processors.

central fissure Also known as the *central sulcus* or the fissure of Rolando, this is a deep groove which runs from the top of the *cerebrum* downwards, separating the frontal and parietal lobes of the cerebrum. The *motor projection area* is located on the frontal edge of the central fissure, and the *somatosensory projection area* is located along the parietal edge.

central gray See *periaqueductal grey*.

central nervous system (CNS) The general name given to the network of nerve fibres and supporting cells that form the brain and the spinal cord. The central nervous system coordinates and regulates the major functions of the body, and operates with the other systems of the body, such as the *endocrine system* and the *autonomic nervous system*, to maintain integration and effective functioning of bodily and cerebral processes (see Figure 10).

central sulcus See *central fissure*.

central tendency See *measures of central tendency*.

centration A Piagetian term that refers to the preoperational child's tendency to focus on one central characteristic of a problem to the exclusion of other features (e.g. judging the volume of a jar of liquid purely by a single dimension such as height, rather than taking into account other dimensions such as width). Centration is considered by Piagetians to be a manifestation of *egocentricity*, which can lead to the inability to perform the process of *decentration*, and the inability to *conserve* number and volume.

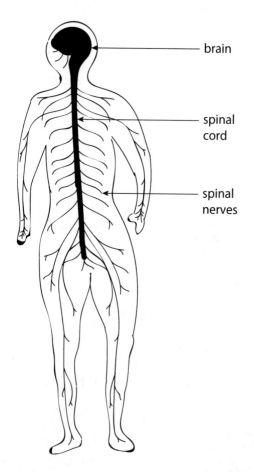

Figure 10 The central nervous system

cephalo-caudal Literally 'from head to tail'. A description applied to the development of motor coordination in infants by Gesell, who undertook some of the first systematic observations of infant development, and who proposed that infant development was largely *maturational*, and therefore always consistent in direction. See also *proximo-distal*.

cerebellum A large, cauliflower-like structure at the back of the brain, which is responsible for the mediation of voluntary movement and balance. The cerebellum is highly convoluted, and has two distinct lobes. It receives sensory input from the *kinaesthetic* nerve fibres and from the organs of balance in the inner ear, and coordinates actions into smooth sequences of behaviour.

cerebral cortex The outer part of the *cerebrum*, which has six or seven layers of neurones, and which covers the whole of the surface. The cerebral cortex consists of *grey matter*, and it is in the cortex itself that the information-processing functions of the cerebrum are considered to take place. The remainder of the cerebrum, below the cortex, consists of *white matter*, which is made up of *myelinated* nerve fibres that transmit information from one part of the brain to another. Parts of the cerebral cortex have highly localised functions, such as the *language areas* or the *sensory projection areas*, but some areas of it appear to have a generalised information-processing function, and are referred to by the term *association cortex*. Such areas were considered to conform to the principle of *equipotentiality* (i.e. they operate 'en masse', and the overall amount of cortex involved is more important than the specific location of that cortex). This model is currently under revision as a result of

information from brain scans. See also *cerebral hemispheres, cerebrum*.

cerebral hemispheres The two halves of the *cerebrum*, which are joined by a band of nerve fibres known as the *corpus callosum*. In general, the left hemisphere mediates the functioning of the right side of the body, while the right hemisphere is concerned with the left side. Various studies (e.g. Sperry, 1964) indicate that the two cerebral hemispheres, while similar in their general structure and in the projection areas, are concerned with different aspects of 'higher' mental functioning, the left hemisphere being more concerned with language, logic and mathematical functioning, while the right hemisphere is thought to be more concerned with spatial, artistic and musical abilities. See also *cerebral cortex*.

cerebral palsy A condition in which there is difficulty in motor control, resulting from brain damage, usually incurred around the time of birth. The most common form is spasticity, in which the muscles become stiff or paralysed. Intelligence may be unaffected, but people with cerebral palsy may have their cognitive ability underestimated because of their uncontrolled movements.

cerebrospinal fluid The fluid that fills the ventricles of the brain and the central canal running through the spinal cord. It carries nutrients to the *neurones* of the *central nervous system*.

cerebrovascular accident (CVA) See *aneurism*.

cerebrum A structure that in humans forms the largest part of the mass of the brain. The cerebrum is concerned with the processing of information and the coordination of voluntary responses, and as such it is also concerned with thinking and other cognitive functions. The cerebrum is divided into two major hemispheres, and each of these has specific areas that deal with localised functions, such as the *sensory projection areas*. Anatomically, each hemisphere of the cerebrum is divided into four lobes – the *frontal lobe*, the *parietal lobe*, the *temporal lobe* and the *occipital lobe* (see Figure 11). See also *cerebral cortex, cerebral hemispheres.*

chameleon effect The spontaneous mimicry of gestures or facial expressions during positive interpersonal exchanges. See also *mirror neurone, postural echo.*

change blindness A failure to notice the appearance or disappearance of objects in two alternating images. See also *attention.*

Charles Bonnet syndrome A condition resulting from an eye disease, in which people form extremely vivid and explicit visual *hallucinations*, which they may sometimes mistake for reality.

chartjunk Irrelevant and unnecessary data and/or information included in the presentation of statistical results.

chemotherapy The treatment of a disorder or clinical problem by means of drugs. Chemotherapy became a popular method of treatment for psychiatric disturbances during the 1950s, when psychoactive drugs such as *chlorpromazine* (Largactil) and diazepam (Valium) were introduced. The stronger drugs allowed the treatment of people with extreme behavioural disorders to proceed without physical restraint, and as such became widely used very quickly. Nowadays, the spectrum of psychoactive drugs available is extremely wide, including such groups as *antidepressants*, anti-anxiety drugs, *tranquillisers, amphetamines, barbiturates*

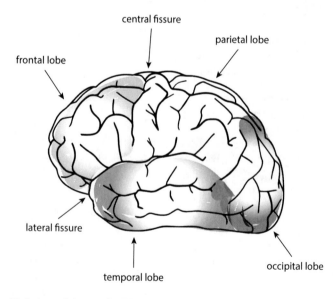

Figure 11 Lobes of the cerebral hemispheres

and several more. There is considerable debate as to the ethics and usefulness of many forms of chemotherapy for psychiatric or psychological disorder. See also *benzodiazepines*.

chi-square (χ^2) A *non-parametric statistic* that is applied to nominal data. The expected frequency of each event is compared with the frequency obtained in the research, and the chi-square indicates how likely it is that the differences could have resulted from chance variation.

child abuse The significant failure of a responsible person to care for a child appropriately. Physical injury, sometimes called non-accidental injury or NAI, was the first form to be widely recognised (see *battered baby syndrome*), and is still the most common form to be reported. However, it is now recognised that other forms of child abuse may be at least as common, though they are often more difficult to identify. The major forms of abuse can be grouped under the headings of physical, emotional and sexual, and in each case the abuse may be active or passive. See *failure to thrive, neglect, sexual abuse*.

child-directed speech (CDS) A special form of speaking that parents and other adults use with small children. While not the same as *baby talk*, it is characterised by simple sentence structures and an emphasis on relevant nouns.

child-rearing styles A generalised term used to refer to characteristic ways of handling or dealing with one's children. Between the 1940s and the 1960s, there was a considerable amount of research into the effects of child-rearing or parenting styles, much of which proved inconclusive. One problem seems to have been that no account had been taken of the effects of the child on the parents. See *transaction*.

childhood amnesia The way that early memories become lost as the child grows older. Five-year-olds often have quite clear memories of being 1 or 2 years old, but these fade with time, and have usually completely disappeared by the time the child is 11 or 12.

chlorpromazine A widely used antipsychotic drug, which is a derivative of phenothiazine. Chlorpromazine has a *sedative* effect, caused by raising the *threshold* for sensory information in the *brainstem*, reducing sensory input to the *reticular formation* of the brain, blocking the uptake of the *neurotransmitters adrenaline* and *noradrenaline* in the *sympathetic division* of the *autonomic nervous system*, and also blocking the uptake of *acetylcholine* by nerve fibres of the *parasympathetic division*. Chlorpromazine is sold under the trade names Largactil and Thorazine. See also *chemotherapy*.

choice reaction time The time someone takes to respond to a signal when experimental conditions require a choice to be made. In general, reaction time increases as the number of choices increases, in such a way that, if the reaction time is plotted against the square root of the number of choices, a straight line will be obtained.

chromatic adaptation Changes in the sensitivity to colour when the background lighting is altered. See also *colour constancy*.

chromatic colours Colours of varying wavelengths, which are perceived as having different hues (e.g. blue, red, yellow). See also *achromatic colours*.

chromosome Strings of DNA that appear in the nucleus of a cell shortly before division as thread-like structures, arranged in pairs. Chromosomes carry the genes that determine the physical characteristics of the individual, and as such are large-scale units of heredity.

chronic Continuing over a period of time. The term is usually applied to illnesses to distinguish persisting conditions (such as a depression that has been going on for years) from those that are expected not to last, or at least that have only just started and had a sudden onset. Those conditions are described as acute.

chronological age The age of an individual measured by standard units (e.g. in months or years). In the original formulation of the *intelligence quotient* by Binet, the measurement was obtained by comparing the chronological age of the child with the mental age. In this way, a comparison could be made as to how the child compared in learning skills with their contemporaries. Chronological age is measured from birth, and so may be misleading when applied to premature babies who are biologically younger than infants born at full term of the same chronological age. The age counted from the date of conception is called the 'gestational age'. See also *mental age*.

chunking The process by which, according to Miller, *short-term memory* can be extended. Miller's theory stated that short-term memory was of limited capacity, able to deal with only 7 plus or minus 2 items at a time. However, by grouping items of information into meaningful 'chunks', that capacity could be extended considerably (e.g. the figures 1, 0, 6, 6 would form four units treated separately, but just one 'chunk' if perceived as the date 1066).

cingulate gyrus Part of the *limbic system* that has been found to be involved in the detection of emotional and cognitive conflicts. See also *multiple-demand network*.

circadian rhythm A term used to describe bodily cycles that last for approximately 24 hours (e.g. cycles of temperature and of alertness). Many individuals show pronounced circadian rhythms, becoming 'attuned' to their daily cycle. Disruption of these cycles, such as occurs when travelling from one time zone to another, can produce an uncomfortable period of readjustment known as *jet lag*. Extensive research by Kleitman and others has investigated natural human periodicity in cue-free environments, such as caves in which lighting and temperature are kept constant. Physiological correlates of *diurnal rhythms* (e.g. fluctuations in body temperature) and the relationship between circadian rhythms and performance have been studied in this way. Circadian rhythms are also known as diurnal rhythms when referring to functions that occur during the day, and *nocturnal* rhythms for night-time activities. See *biological clock, zeitgeber*.

circular reactions These were considered by Piaget (e.g. Piaget, 1959) to be an essential mechanism of cognitive development during the sensorimotor stage. In circular reactions, the result of an action triggers a repetition of that action, or some variation of it. As a result, actions are repeated and become practised, and so competences are acquired and schemata are developed. At first, such reactions involve only the infant's own body and are called primary circular reactions. Later, the child progresses to *secondary* and *tertiary circular reactions*.

clairvoyance Seeing or perceiving without being physically present or receiving direct sensory input from the target. A considerable amount of research in *parapsychology* has been devoted to investigations of clairvoyance, particularly in the form of 'distance viewing' – identifying scenes from a distance of several hundred miles away. The military potential of the research meant that it attracted more funding than most parapsychology topics, but the outcomes were hotly disputed and remain equivocal. Other studies of clairvoyance include investigations of the actions of mediums and other 'psychic' practitioners.

classical concept A term referring to the classification of human concepts following work by J.S. Bruner and others on the development of thinking. Classical concepts are those in which the identifying properties of the concept are shown by every member of that class. For instance, all the cards of the 'diamonds' suit in a pack will show the diamond symbol, will be rectangular, etc. By contrast, although 'having four legs' would be an identifying property of the concept 'tables', not all members of the class would possess that identifying property. 'Tables' would therefore be a *probabilistic concept* rather than a classical concept.

classical conditioning The procedure of pairing an originally neutral stimulus with a stimulus that reliably produces a response, so that the neutral stimulus comes to produce a version of the response on its own. In Pavlov's original experiment, the neutral stimulus, called the *conditioned stimulus* or CS, was a bell which rang at the same time that the effective stimulus of food, called the *unconditioned stimulus* or UCS, was

presented. Eventually, the bell on its own came to produce some of the responses that food had elicited, such as salivation. These responses are called the *conditioned response* or CR. The original full response to food was called the *unconditioned response* or UCR. Pairing an arbitrary CS with a UCR may require over 100 trials before conditioning becomes established. However, when the UCR is a strong emotional response, such as fear, classical conditioning can be achieved in a single trial. Although it has been studied in the laboratory, there are many everyday situations in which stimuli are paired in such a way that classical conditioning will occur (see Figure 12). See also *eyeblink response*.

client-centred therapy A form of *psychotherapy* developed by Carl Rogers, based on a humanistic approach, in which the individual is considered to be the only person who can develop solutions or approaches to his or her problem, and the role of the therapist is to facilitate such development. Because the therapist is frequently dealing with highly approval-seeking individuals, the onus is on the therapist to use *non-directive therapy*, and to develop a genuine and warm relationship with the client, which will allow that individual to explore possibilities and options freely. See also *actualising tendency, positive regard, unconditional positive regard*.

clinical interview An approach to interviewing children that is less formal than a research interview, and is designed to allow them to display their modes of thinking. Clinical interviewing was a major component of Piaget's research.

clinical neuropsychology The study of how the brain and nervous system function, in psychological terms, using

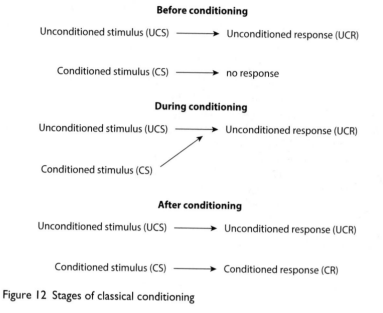

Before conditioning

Unconditioned stimulus (UCS) ⟶ Unconditioned response (UCR)

Conditioned stimulus (CS) ⟶ no response

During conditioning

Unconditioned stimulus (UCS) ⟶ Unconditioned response (UCR)

Conditioned stimulus (CS)

After conditioning

Unconditioned stimulus (UCS) ⟶ Unconditioned response (UCR)

Conditioned stimulus (CS) ⟶ Conditioned response (CR)

Figure 12 Stages of classical conditioning

information gained from investigating clinical cases. These include people with head injuries, brain tumours or disease, or people with specific mental deficits such as the inability to recognise faces or recall names. In recent years, advances in brain scanning technology have led to significant developments in clinical neuropsychology.

clinical psychology The branch of *applied psychology* that is concerned with the use of insights and methods obtained from theoretical psychology, research and clinical experience to assist people with problems in living, or with psychological difficulties. Over the last 40 years, the profession has shifted from providing assessments as requested by psychiatrists to functioning as independent therapists. Clinical psychologists may use a range of techniques, such as *cognitive therapy*, *behaviour therapy*, *psychotherapy*, *family therapy* and *biofeedback*. The major

specialisms are defined in terms of client groups (i.e. general adult, child, mental handicap, neurology and the elderly). However, clinical psychologists are increasingly to be found in community bases or working alongside general medical practitioners, and are also sometimes employed in industry.

cloning A technique which makes use of the fact that the genetic 'blueprint' for a whole animal is reproduced in the genes and chromosomes of each cell nucleus in its body. By culturing small groups of undifferentiated cells, it is possible to develop a complete individual of the same species, which is genetically identical to its parent animal. Successful cloning has been achieved in many different species of animal, ranging from frogs to sheep. The cloning of human beings to create a tightly stratified society forms a favourite theme of science fiction writers, but is unlikely to catch on in a big way, as the production of new human beings by traditional methods would appear to be both popular and effective.

closed questions Questions that may be asked during a research or a therapeutic interview that can be answered with a simple 'yes' or 'no'. An example would be: 'Have you gained insight into your own behaviour as a result of studying psychology?' See *open questions* for a more productive version of this question. Closed questions can be responded to in a way that closes down that part of the conversation, and so are regarded as bad practice in interviews. However, in practice, participants are well aware of the social requirements of an interview, and will usually only give closed answers (such as just saying 'no' in response to the question above) if they want to make some point.

closure A tendency to perceive incomplete objects as being complete. A triangle with a corner missing will, at a glance, be seen as the more familiar complete triangle (see Figure 13). The term is also used to refer more generally to the preference for completeness so that, for example, an unfinished emotional task like expressing dissatisfaction – not 'getting something off

the chest' – leaves us with a wish to complete the process.

cluster sampling A method of sampling that uses a 'natural' group (e.g. all the children in a class, or all of the PE teachers working for Highland Council).

CNS See *central nervous system.*

coaching A form of personal development in which the individual is supported by another person, or coach, whose role is to provide training, advice and guidance. It is most commonly used in work or organisational contexts, but a similar approach known as life coaching involves individuals providing the same roles to people to help them deal with their everyday lives and problems.

coaction A term used to describe the process of acting jointly with another person (e.g. working together on a task).

coarticulation The way that someone's production of a specific *phoneme* is affected by the phonemes immediately preceding and following it.

cocaine A drug obtained originally from the coca plant, and used as a local anaesthetic. Freud is credited with reporting the first medical use. The drug also produces a sense of euphoria if taken internally, and is often used as a *recreational drug*. It can produce *dependency*.

cochlea The coiled tube in the *inner ear* that transduces sound vibrations into electrical impulses (see Figure 14). See also *organ of Corti.*

cocktail party effect A term given to one of the well-established phenomena of *selective attention* – the way that individuals are able to monitor unattended information subconsciously, such that they pick up highly sensitive information (e.g. their own name) even when

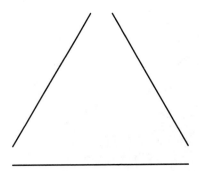

Figure 13 Closure

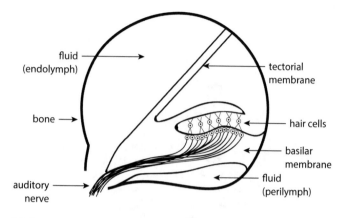

Figure 14 Section through the cochlea

attending to entirely different stimuli, and when they are unaware of the rest of the unattended message.

code of conduct A set of binding rules concerning appropriate behaviour and procedures, which must be observed by practising professionals. Agreement to conform to the relevant code of conduct is the basis for the issuing of licences to practise professionally.

codes of language A description of styles of language use that distinguishes two main 'codes' of language: *elaborated codes*, which involve a wide vocabulary and extensive use of nouns and explicit descriptions; and *restricted codes*, involving a more restricted vocabulary, a preference for pronouns, and the use of implicit in preference to explicit description. These codes were first described by Bernstein, who argued that:

(i)   elaborated codes were used far more by middle-class than by working-class families; and

(ii) the language code used would faci litate or inhibit cognitive development, owing to elaborated codes

being less dependent on context, and therefore more amenable to abstract conceptualisation.

Bernstein's work was heavily criticised, notably by Labov.

coding Also referred to as *encoding*, the term is generally taken to refer to ways in which information is represented cognitively (e.g. for storing in memory or for association with other information). Memories may be coded in a variety of ways, using many different modalities (e.g. *kinaesthetic* or *enactive* coding, visual coding or coding by *iconic representation*, auditory coding). See also *schema*, *representation*.

codon A sequence of three nucleotide bases which make up an amino acid. It is used to summarise a specific genetic instruction produced by the activity of DNA.

coefficient A numerical value that indicates the strength of a relationship, as in *correlation coefficient*. More generally, a coefficient indicates how much a variable is modified. For example, a ball with a coefficient of elasticity of 0.9 keeps 90 per cent of its momentum when it hits a hard surface, and so will bounce more than a ball with a coefficient of 0.4.

coefficient of determination A number that expresses how much of the variation in a data set can be accounted for by a particular correlation. It is normally calculated by multiplying the correlation coefficient by 10, then squaring it to obtain a percentage (e.g. a coefficient of 0.6 would account for roughly 36 per cent of the data).

coevolution A concept which acknowledges that natural selection is not a one-way process. While a species is adapting to its environment, the presence of that species will be having effects on the environment, including other plants and animals. In this way, *evolution* needs to be seen as a progressive mutual accommodation between species. The concept is similar to that of *transaction* in development.

cognition A general term used to refer to the 'higher' mental processes. Cognition would generally be taken to include such forms of mental activity as thinking and conceptualisation, *memory*, representation and mental *imagery*, *perception* and *attention*, reasoning and *decision-making*.

cognitive Referring to *cognition*.

cognitive architecture The overall framework being used to represent human cognition, or to model it in the case of computer systems.

cognitive behaviour therapy A method of psychological therapy derived from *behaviour therapy* but extended to take account of the patient's cognitions. The objective is to modify both maladaptive behaviours and maladaptive beliefs. See also *cognitive therapy*.

cognitive bias modification Cognitive training (e.g. of *memory* or *problem-solving*) that is typically designed to reduce bias, either from attention processes or from patterns of interpretation.

cognitive development The way in which *cognitions* develop during childhood. The major and most detailed theory of cognitive development is that produced by Piaget, although his theory is largely restricted to the ways in which thinking and understanding change through childhood. One of Piaget's most important contributions was to establish that the thought and logic of young children is not an inferior version of adult thinking, but has its own rules and is well adapted to the needs of the child. Cognitive development is not just a process of getting better at adult modes of cognition, but is a complex progression through different kinds of thinking and understanding. Other approaches to cognitive development include research into *metacognition*, *social cognition* and the child's *theory of mind*.

cognitive dissonance A concept put forward by Festinger, in which the main proposal is that people strive to maintain consistency between their differing cognitions. Should a noticeable inconsistency arise, this will produce a state of cognitive dissonance, which the individual experiences as uncomfortable and attempts to correct. Dissonance is reduced by adjusting one of the beliefs or *attitudes* involved in the inconsistency, so that the conflict disappears. See also *balance theory*.

cognitive domain One of the four domains of the psyche, concerned with reasoning, thinking and understanding. See also *behavioural domain, conative domain, affective domain*.

cognitive map An internal representation of a specific or general area that forms a plan or outline which can guide behaviour. The idea of cognitive maps was put forward by Tolman following work in which he demonstrated that rats which had been allowed to explore mazes freely would perform better when subsequently reinforced than rats which had not had such an experience. Tolman used the concept of cognitive maps to illustrate one of the ways in which cognition might be involved in learning, at a time when learning was largely conceptualised as a reflexive, *stimulus–response* process. Later research on cognitive maps in humans demonstrated, for instance, the way in which areas familiar to an individual would be perceived as larger and more complex than distant ones. Some cognitive theorists, including Tolman, have argued that cognitive mapping forms the basis of all internal representation.

cognitive miser Someone whose thinking patterns characteristically involve minimal levels of time and effort. See also *principle of parsimony*.

cognitive model An attempt to outline the theoretical mechanisms involved in a particular cognitive process, such as *problem-solving* or *selective attention*. A cognitive model is particularly likely to emphasise the role of information processing, as opposed to, say, habits or emotions.

cognitive neuropsychology An approach to *cognitive psychology* that focuses on combining neurological information with knowledge about cognitive processes. This includes the study of brain structure and functioning as it relates to psychological ability (e.g. the study of *acquired dyslexia* as a result of brain injury).

cognitive neuroscience An approach to research that aims to explain cognitive processes in terms of neurological mechanisms.

cognitive processes Mental activities such as thinking, reasoning, *memory*, the understanding and interpreting of *language, perception, decision-making*, and so on. The term is also used to describe specific activities within these areas, such as the way in which textual information is processed and interpreted during the act of reading.

cognitive processing The act of working on cognitive information by altering its structure, changing its form or exploring its meanings and implications.

cognitive psychology The branch of psychology that is concerned with the study of cognition. Cognitive psychology is generally taken to include the study of perceptual processes, *attention, memory, imagery, language, concept formation, problem-solving, creativity, reasoning, decision-making, cognitive development* and *cognitive styles*, but has often been assumed to exclude *learning*.

cognitive skill Competence in a defined cognitive task. The term is used in the study of skills to separate those skills such as verbal fluency and chess playing, in which the cognitive component is most important, from *motor skills*, in which the physical activity is what matters most.

cognitive stage of skill acquisition The first stage of skill acquisition, in which the individual is consciously aware of all of the procedures involved and how they should be connected. Behaviour or understanding at this stage tends to be slow and relatively clumsy, until the skill becomes more practised. See also *autonomous stage of skill acquisition.*

cognitive styles Distinctive patterns of cognition that characterise individuals. Work on cognitive styles has included investigations of *convergent* and *divergent thinking, field dependence* and forms of *intelligence.*

cognitive therapy In its narrow sense, an approach to the treatment of *depression* developed by Aaron Beck. Beck sees depression as resulting from a combination of a negative evaluation of the self, a negative view of present experiences and events, and negative expectations of the future. The sufferer then uses faulty logic to maintain this outlook. The therapist must be very active to modify the way in which the patient thinks, insisting on correct logic and challenging unrealistically pessimistic assumptions. Beck described specific techniques for use in cognitive therapy, but the term is now being used for a wider range of less well-defined approaches based on similar principles but applicable to a wider range of conditions.

cognitivism A way of looking at psychology that sees information processing as being the core and source of all behaviour. See also *computer metaphor.*

cohesion The tendency of members of a group to stick together rather than separate as individuals.

cohort Any grouping of people or animals. The term is most often used in psychology to refer to people of similar age, although the interest may be that they share some common experience. For example, European people who were born between 1935 and 1945 share the fact that their early childhood would have been affected by the Second World War.

cohort design A form of research design in which a group of participants is selected and then followed up at intervals (e.g. the children born in a particular year, or the members of a class of students graduating on one particular occasion).

cohort effect The effect of belonging to a particular cohort. The cohort effect is usually seen as a complication in developmental studies, because it may produce a difference between people of different ages that has nothing to do with ageing. For example, differences in IQ between 40-year-olds and 60-year-olds in the year 2000 may have been affected by the different ways in which children were fed in the 1940s and the 1960s.

cohort model The idea that word recognition begins by the initial sound triggering off a cohort of possibilities, which is then narrowed down as more sounds are produced, or by the context.

collective unconscious The concept, proposed by Carl Jung (e.g. Jung, 1964), that the human race has developed a shared unconscious mind which contains universal images called *archetypes.*

collectivism This is the moral or epistemological stance that emphasises the group and the imporance of its interests above those of the individual. See also *allocentrism, individualism.*

colour blindness The inability to detect certain wavelengths of light. Most colour-blind individuals are red/green colour-blind, that is, they are unable to distinguish between particular shades of red and their equivalent shade of green, but occasionally individuals are blue/yellow colour-blind. Colour blindness is found in about 1 in 10 males, and it is much rarer in females. It arises from a faulty gene carried on the X-*chromosome*, which in women is usually counteracted by the normal equivalent *allele* on the other X-chromosome. However, males have only one X-chromosome, and the Y-*chromosome* is shorter, so there is no chance of a 'healthy' gene to correct the fault.

colour constancy The process by which the perceptual system compensates for the appearance of objects seen under light of differing wavelengths. Colour is detected by the analysis of the wavelength of the light reflected from an object. In normal white light, the light reflected will show the true colour, but under coloured lights an object may reflect light of a very different hue, owing to the mixture of colours. However, the brain compensates for this by using its prior knowledge of the object and by *adaptation* to the viewing conditions, so the object is perceived as keeping its true colour.

colour vision The ability to detect the specific wavelengths of light reaching the eye, which facilitates fine discrimination of detail and the use of colour as a signalling medium. Colour is detected to some extent by the cone cells of the eye, but the full mechanisms by which human beings detect colour are complex and not yet fully understood. See *opponent processing*, *Young–Helmholtz theory*.

commisurectomy A surgical process of cutting the *corpus callosum* that connects the two *hemispheres* of the brain. After the operation, the two hemispheres can no longer communicate and so the functions that are localised within each can

be studied. The operation is only ever carried out for medical purposes, usually of reducing epileptic seizures, but studies of these patients have provided valuable information about the different specialisations of the hemispheres.

communication The process of transmitting information to another individual or group of individuals, and having it received and interpreted by them. Communication may be voluntary or involuntary – the individual who unwittingly signals that they are nervous by fidgeting, etc., is communicating this to the observer, although not voluntarily. Communication in human beings is complex and varied, and can be roughly classified into three general types:

(i)   *verbal communication* (using language or codes which stand for language);
(ii) personal *non-verbal communication* (such as the use of dress, posture, gesture or gaze to communicate); and
(iii) *ritual* (the use of highly structured events or familiar patterns of activity to communicate).

It is also possible to regard social networking and other forms of Internet activity as a fourth category, particularly given the extensive use of imagery in such communication.

communication channel The vehicle by which information is carried to its recipients. This could be television, a magazine, a mobile phone or other external device, but could also be a part of the nervous system. See also *bandwidth*.

community psychology The application of psychology to improving life for members of the community. The focus of community psychologists has been mainly on people whose capacity is reduced in some way (e.g. those who have lived in institutions for a long time). The term is used particularly for setting up environmental conditions such as sheltered housing, which will make it possible for such people to engage in some participation in the general community. See *social exclusion*.

co-morbidity The diagnosis of more than one psychological disorder in the same individual.

comparative psychology The branch of psychology that involves drawing comparisons between different species to gain insight into the mechanisms of behaviour. Some psychologists see the value of comparative psychology as being to shed light on human functioning, while others regard an understanding of animal behaviour as a legitimate goal in itself. Much of what has been called comparative psychology has in fact been the study of a single species of artificially bred laboratory rat. Comparative psychology includes many branches of learning theory (especially those in the behaviourist tradition), *ethology*, and any area of psychology that has been influenced by studies of animals (e.g. early theories of *attachment*).

compensation Using other resources to make up for a deficit (e.g. when a blind person makes exceptional use of sound stimuli). In psychoanalytic terms, it is a way of overcoming, or at least concealing, a defect in personality, particularly in Adler's theory of compensation for feelings of inferiority. Note that compensation does not necessarily mean *overcompensation*. In neurophysiology, compensation refers to the process in which an intact part of the brain may take over the functions of a damaged part.

competence The ability to perform tasks or carry out procedures in a way which means that they are likely to be completed successfully.

competitive drugs Drugs that compete for the same neurotransmitter *receptor site* as the 'natural' *neurotransmitter*.

complementary needs hypothesis The idea that people form relationships with one another because qualities in each person satisfy unmet needs in the other. This is the psychological version of the lay principle that 'opposites attract', and acts as a counterbalance to the *matching hypothesis*.

complex

(i) A description implying that the phenomenon in question is complicated, probably having many influencing factors.

(ii) A noun used to describe a complicated mass (e.g. 'a complex of reasons').

(iii) In terms of *psychoanalytic* theory, a noun used to describe a set of emotionally charged phenomena and feelings (e.g. the *Oedipus complex*).

complex cell A type of *neurone* found in the *visual cortex* of the brain. Discovered by Hubel and Wiesel in 1968, complex cells form part of a hierarchical arrangement of cells that serve the function of coding incoming visual information into simple shapes and patterns. For a full description, see *simple cell*.

compliance Conforming to accepted patterns of behaviour, or aquiescing in decisions. Kelman draws a distinction between *conformity* to others or to social norms arising from compliance, and conformity arising from the internalisation of the group norms or values. Compliance is perceived as an outward conformity, with the individual reserving opinion or inwardly disagreeing.

componential intelligence The part of Sternberg's *triarchic theory* of intelligence that deals with mental processes and aptitudes. Componential intelligence is considered to have three main elements:

(i) metacomponents, which are the higher-order processes involved in, for instance, planning and decision-making;
(ii) performance components, which are involved in actually carrying out a task, such as the ability to count or calculate, or reason logically; and
(iii) knowledge-acquisition components, which are concerned with how we go about acquiring or learning new information.

See also *intelligence test*.

compulsion A repetitive, stereotyped behaviour that is both unnecessary and unwanted, but which the individual still feels they have to carry out. It is usually associated with obsessions. See also *obsessive–compulsive disorder*.

compulsive personality disorder See also *obsessive–compulsive disorder*.

computational modelling The construction of computer programs designed to replicate a function or process observed in animals, humans or society in general.

computational theory of perception A theory developed by Marr, who proposed that we are able to identify objects because of various computations or calculations applied by the brain to the visual image received by the retina. Computational theory emphasises the characteristics of edges and boundaries in the visual image, and suggests that the brain uses these to build up an increasingly complex series of representations of the object, until eventually a three-dimensional picture can be produced.

computed axial tomography See *CAT scan*.

computer-assisted learning (CAL) The use of computer programs written to enable students to learn at their own pace. The user works through factual material and exercises, with corrective feedback from the computer. Also known as 'computer-assisted instruction' (CAI).

computer metaphor Thinking of the brain as if it were a computer. Using what we know about computers as a *metaphor* in this way was especially useful in the early days of information theory, because it provided a whole language in which to talk about the brain as an *information processor*. However, it also distorted some areas of cognitive psychology by de-emphasising the human side of cognition.

computer simulation The use of computers to replicate human thought strategies and patterns of behaviours. Research on computer simulation has involved the study of the use of *heuristics* in reasoning, and of probabilistic judgements in decision-making. It is hoped by those involved that such research will eventually shed light on human *cognitive processes*. In *industrial psychology*, computer simulation often provides a safer, cheaper or more ethical way of examining what will happen to the process being simulated, under a variety of conditions. See also *artificial intelligence*.

conative To do with intentionality. The *conative domain* was one of the three domains of the human psyche outlined by Galen in the second century BC, the other two being the *affective domain* and the *cognitive domain*. This distinction was maintained in *attitude* theory, where a given attitude was considered to have three components:

(i) an affective or emotional component;

(ii) a cognitive or rationalised component; and

(iii) a conative or behavioural component, which is concerned with the individual's tendency to act on the attitude in question.

However, in more recent years, it has been recognised that conation is not the same as behaviour. Conative means 'to do with will and intention', and as such is a fourth domain. In many ways, this represents a seriously neglected area of human psychology.

conative domain The domain of human personality or human nature that is concerned with intentionality, will, decisions and planning. In early models, the conative dimension was seen as acting in conjunction with the *affective* and *cognitive domains* of personality. With the advent of behaviourism, and its determinist view of human nature, the conative domain disappeared and a behavioural domain was substituted. More recently, psychologists have begun to investigate conative aspects of human nature again, and the term is beginning to reappear.

concept A set of ideas and properties that can be used to group things together. It is a generalised idea that may be abstract (e.g. 'justice') or concrete (e.g. 'furniture'). Human cognitive processes are often considered to progress by the formation and elaboration of concepts, resulting from increased experience. See also *classical concept, construct, probabilistic concept, schema, mental model*.

concept formation The name given to the process by which an individual comes to develop mental categories that will allow objects and events to be classified and grouped together. A considerable amount of research on cognitive development has emphasised concept formation.

conceptual priming A form of *priming* that is based on the meaning of the stimulus.

conceptualisation The process of organising information into specific concepts or categories. Also used to describe the first stage in speech production, when ideas are first formed.

concordance interval A way of expressing where the mean is likely to fall in 95 per cent of a set of samples. See also *variance*.

concordance studies Family studies which aim to assess genetic similarity within families and so calculate the probability that a member of the family will develop an inherited psychological or physiological disorder.

concrete operational stage This is the third of Piaget's four stages of *cognitive development*, characterised by the child's fascination with the material world and strong inclination to collect facts and statistics. Children in the concrete operational stage were considered unable to deal fully with abstract concepts, and able to deal only with those aspects of experience that had a material equivalent or which could be represented in a concrete fashion, although recent research suggests that this may have been overemphasised. The stage was considered to last from approximately 7 to 11 years of age. See also *formal operational stage, preoperational stage, sensorimotor stage.*

concurrent validity The degree to which a test or measurement agrees with another measure of the same thing, taken at the same time. See also *validity.*

conditional positive regard A concept introduced by Carl Rogers, which refers to the satisfaction of the basic need for positive regard in human beings. The term 'conditional positive regard' refers to approval, love or respect given only as a result of the individual behaving in 'appropriate' or socially acceptable ways. A person who has encountered nothing but conditional positive regard throughout their life will, according to Rogers, become unable to satisfy the need for *self-actualisation.* Autonomous action, or exploration of their own potential, necessitates taking a certain amount of risk, in that it could conceivably result in social disapproval. The formation of a relationship that provides *unconditional positive regard* for the individual provides the security for such self-actualisation to take place, and this is the goal of Rogerian *client-centred therapy.*

conditioned reflex A physiological *reflex,* or autonomic response, produced in response to a stimulus that would not normally produce such a reaction, but has come to do so as a result of the process of *classical conditioning.*

conditioned reinforcer An event or stimulus which has acquired the property of strengthening a learned (conditioned) response, such that the learning is less likely to become extinguished. See also *secondary reinforcement.*

conditioned response (CR) A response that is produced under specific conditions, as a result of being associated through a training process with a particular stimulus, known as a *conditioned stimulus.* The training process consists of repeatedly pairing a novel stimulus with one that will elicit the desired response automatically. After a while, the new stimulus will come to elicit the response independently, at which point the response is said to have become a conditioned response. See *classical conditioning.*

conditioned stimulus A stimulus that brings about a response as a result of repeated association with an *unconditioned stimulus.* See also *classical conditioning, conditioned response.*

conditioning A term used to describe the process of learning. Learning is considered by behaviourist psychologists to be the process of acquiring and reproducing specific behavioural responses under specific conditions – hence the term 'conditioning'. There are normally considered to be two major forms of conditioning, usually referred to as *classical conditioning* and *operant conditioning.*

conditions of worth A concept proposed by Carl Rogers concerning the way in which the individual's self-concept is affected by the *conditional positive regard* that they have experienced throughout life. Conditions of worth are an internalised set of values by which individuals assess their own behaviour. In people who have experienced only conditional positive regard throughout life, such conditions of worth may come to represent unrealistically high standards of conduct, giving the individual a negative self-concept, and inhibiting the expression of their need for *self-actualisation*.

conduct disorders A group of *behaviour disorders* in children in which aggression or the breaking of rules is involved.

cone cells Cone-shaped cells found in the retina of the eye that effect the *transduction* of light waves into electrical impulses which are subsequently transmitted to the brain for interpretation. Cone cells are particularly concentrated in the *fovea*, and consequently colour perception is better in the centre of the visual field. They contain a photosensitive pigment known as iodopsin, which breaks down on exposure to light. Different cone cells are maximally sensitive to light of different wavelengths. The two major theories of colour vision, the theory of *trichromatism* and the *opponent processing* theory, are both based on the fact that there are three types of cone, which are sensitive to different wavelengths of light, and therefore responsive to three different colours, but the theories disagree as to how colours are combined.

confabulation The process of constructing memories so that they fit with an opinion or view of what the memory should be about. Through confabulation, a memory becomes adjusted or changed, often as a result of discussions that have reshaped the meaning of the event.

confidence level See *statistical significance*.

confidentiality The ethical principle that details concerning individuals who have participated in research projects should be kept private and not made available to those outside the project. See also *ethical issues*.

confirmation bias A tendency in decision-making to accept only information that confirms what the person already believes or wishes to believe.

conflict The result of opposed motives applying simultaneously. Most conflicts (e.g. between the desire to stay and finish an essay versus the duty to go out with friends) are easy to resolve. Some are much more difficult, and result in an inability to act and the abandoning of both objectives. (If you really could not decide whether to write or go out, you might solve the problem by sitting in front of a piece of paper and daydreaming about going out.) Difficult conflicts of various kinds have been studied experimentally, often with rats. *Approach–avoidance conflicts* in which a goal is both desired and feared are the most common, and readily result in inaction. Avoidance–avoidance conflicts (choosing between the frying pan and the fire) can easily occur and are very stressful if a choice has to be made. Usually of less concern are approach–approach conflicts, when going towards one desired goal means leaving another (the mythical donkey that starved to death halfway between two piles of food).

conformity The social process by which people in a group or in a social situation engage in behaviour that appears to be socially acceptable, that is, they go along with the social expectations apparent at the time. Conformity is often divided into *compliance* (conforming while inwardly disagreeing) and *internalisation* (conforming as a result of internal agreement with the behaviour). Normative conformity refers to the process of conforming as a result of the existence of strong social norms directing the accepted behaviour. Informational conformity is the process by which an individual may conform with others on the grounds that they are better informed about the situation, while ingratiational conformity refers to conformity with the specific purpose of achieving social approval, or a feeling of 'belonging'. The classic experiment in the field was conducted by Solomon Asch, who instructed groups of people to pretend to misjudge the length of a line, and found that members of the group who had not received this instruction felt under strong pressure to conform. Conforming to group pressure is sometimes called the *Asch effect*.

confounding variable A factor or *variable* in a study that causes a change in the *dependent variable* (the measures being obtained), but which is not the *independent variable* or main condition of the study. Many of the techniques of experimental methodology are ways of dealing with confounding variables. If, for example, the sex of the research participants is likely to influence a result, this may be dealt with:

(i)   by eliminating the factor (use only female research participants);

(ii) by controlling for sex (equal numbers in each group so that the effect cancels out); or

(iii) incorporating it as a variable in the design (record male and female participants separately and examine the effect of sex on the dependent variable).

congenital A characteristic that is built into the person. Congenital characteristics may be genetically specified (e.g. eye colour) or caused during *gestation* (e.g. hearing impairment due to rubella during fetal development).

congenital amusia See *amusia*.

congruence A general term used to refer to behaviour, attitudes or ideas that are in accord and not in conflict with other behaviour, attitudes or ideas. See also *balance theory*.

conjunction fallacy The mistaken belief that a combination of two events is more likely to happen than those events happening singly.

connectionism The theory that *learning* is achieved by processes in which the connections between *neurones* are reinforced by use. As a result, *neural networks* are set up that in some way represent the experience of the organism. Connectionism is the fundamental principle of many approaches to *computer simulation* inherent in the use of *parallel distributed processing* systems to simulate human reasoning. The ability of such systems to produce novelty, in the form of unexpected or unanticipated outcomes (*emergent properties*), has been hailed as a major breakthrough in the development of *artificial intelligence*. See also *Hebb*.

connectionist models See *connectionism*.

connector neurone Neurones found in the *grey matter* of the brain and spinal cord that link and pass impulses on to other neurones. Connector neurones are also known as *relay neurones* or *multipolar neurones*. They are spidery in form, having several *dendrites* that enable the transmission or receipt of information to or from many other neurones (see Figure 15).

connotative meaning The meaning that is implicit in a particular term or

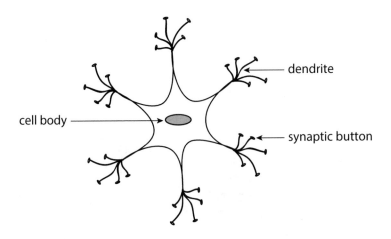

Figure 15 A connector neurone

phrase, although possibly not made explicit. See also *denotative meaning*.

consanguinity Literally, 'being of the same blood', but also meaning that two people have genes in common, being descended from the same parent or member of a previous generation. The word usually appears in the context of marriage. Most societies forbid marriage between close relatives, as such individuals are more likely to produce genetic defects in any offspring.

conscience An acquired mental framework for making judgements about the moral 'rightness' or 'wrongness' of actions. The idea of conscience contains strong overtones of duty and obligation. Doing things that conflict with the conscience causes internal anxiety or distress. See also *moral development, superego*.

conscientiousness One of the main factors in the *five-factor theory* of personality, which reflects a tendency to undertake tasks in a systematic and responsible manner, to respect social obligations and to value moral and ethical principles highly.

conscious That part of the mind that is readily available to awareness. Mental activities or contents that are not available are called *unconscious* when it is thought that they are being actively suppressed in ways originally described by Freud, and non-conscious when they are simply processes which are carried out without awareness. Processes that can be brought into consciousness, but only with difficulty, are said to be *preconscious* or *subconscious*.

conscious process A mental process of which the individual is aware as it is happening.

consciousness The awareness of one's own mental processes, or the state of having this awareness. The state of being aware of one's perceptions, thoughts and feelings is vivid and undeniable, but extremely difficult to study. The major issue is whether consciousness has any function or whether, as the behaviourists claim, it is just a by-product of behaviour. As developments such as *information theory* have provided a language for describing private mental events, psychologists are returning to the study of phenomena such as consciousness. See also *unconscious*.

consensus A common or generalised agreement, usually concerning *social norms* or acceptable behaviour; also used to refer to agreement between theories or ideas. In the *covariance* model of *attribution theory*, consensus is one of three factors believed by Kelley to influence the kind of *attribution* made for a specific situation or event. If a person is observed shouting, a relevant question is whether everybody else is shouting. If so, and the condition is one of high consensus, it is assumed that there is something about the situation that is responsible for the behaviour. If nobody else is shouting (low consensus), then the behaviour will tend to be attributed to some characteristic of the individual. See also *consistency*, *distinctiveness*.

conservation The ability to recognise that volume, number or mass do not change when the physical appearance of the way in which they are presented changes. In Piagetian theory, the ability to conserve is developed towards the end of the *preoperational stage*. Prior to that time, if the child is presented with, for example, two identical balls of clay and one of them is rolled into a sausage shape, the child will say that the longer one contains more clay. Piaget considered this to arise from the process of *centration* – the child's tendency to focus on a single, central attribute of objects rather than taking several different aspects of its appearance into account. However, more recent studies (e.g. by Donaldson) have demonstrated that the language used in relation to the child and the social situation of the experiments may have produced the result, and that children may be able

to conserve at a much earlier age than Piaget suspected. See also *social cognition*.

consistency One of three factors in Kelley's *covariance* model of attributions. The more consistently a person produces the observed behaviour, the more likely we are to see it as arising from their disposition, and not the situation. See also *consensus*, *distinctiveness*.

consolidation The process by which momentary or ephemeral changes in brain activity are altered into permanent structural changes in either the brain or in cognitive processes such as *memory* or *learning*. See also *reconsolidation*.

conspecific Applying to or including other members of the same species.

constancy See *perceptual constancy*.

constancy scaling The process by which the perceptual system adjusts to distance, by mentally 'scaling up' objects that are far away, such that they are not perceived as being smaller. It is considered that constancy scaling may provide an explanation for certain *visual illusions* (e.g. the *Ponzo illusion*).

constitution The inherited physiological structure of an individual. There have been attempts to relate psychological tendencies to the physical type of the individual, notably in Sheldon's theory of *personality*, but relationships are weak and inconsistent.

construct A term used in *personal construct* theory to define concepts in a precise way. It is proposed that our cognitive system is made up of *bipolar constructs* (e.g. illness–health and honest–dishonest). A large part of the theory is concerned with the relationships between constructs (e.g. a particular individual may have the idea that honest people tend also to be healthy). See also *core construct*.

construct validity A test of the validity of a psychometric test or measurement that involves seeing whether it makes sense in terms of accepted theory. See also *validity*.

constructionism See *social constructionism*.

constructive memory The general term given to memory for meaningful material that has been affected by the individual's own pre-existing *schemata*, values or *attitudes*. Since Bartlett, it has been observed that people rarely remember events or information accurately, but instead tend to adapt their memories to make more sense and accord with their own cognitions and cognitive styles. This is known as constructive memory.

constructive perception A theory of perception spearheaded by Richard Gregory that emphasises how perceptions are organised, structured or developed as a result of cognitive processes such as expectation, *emotion* or memory. Such perceptions are not simple 'snapshots' of reality, but expressions of cognitive processing, even though they may feel perfectly 'real' and a reflection of the external world. Gregory proposed this theory as an explanation for *visual illusions*, and it is often contrasted with the theory of *direct perception* spearheaded by J.J. Gibson.

constructivism The view that *cognition* is about constructing a coherent system of meaning within the person, rather than about understanding reality. Constructivists are likely to regard reality as unknowable, and also of less significance for the social sciences than the meaning systems that people create. However, they do not claim that reality does not exist, but just that it is a more effective strategy to study how we construct our meanings. The theories of Kelly and Piaget are major examples of constructivist theories in psychology. See also *positivism, social constructionism*.

consumer psychology The application of psychological principles to understanding consumers or customers. The marketing industry was an early user of behavioural principles, but psychoanalytic concepts dominated by the middle of the twentieth century. Today, there is a much broader range of psychology to draw on, and consumerism has become a more important component of Western society. Psychology is used extensively in market research both for research techniques and for interpretation of findings about consumer behaviour. In advertising, the areas of perception, memory, habituation, humour and aesthetic judgement are crucial. *Decision-making* is relevant to how people decide to allocate their incomes, while consumer activities in areas such as choice of organic foods, fashion and health are not yet well understood. Other areas could benefit from much more attention to psychological knowledge. For example, 'relationship marketing' pays little attention to psychological research into human relationships. Consumer psychology seems likely to continue to grow as a user of psychology and a source of employment for psychology graduates.

contact hypothesis The idea that *prejudice* can be significantly reduced if two groups have sufficient everyday contact with one another. Unfortunately, while the contact hypothesis has some validity, history shows that it is not proof against the manipulation of *social identification* by others (e.g. politicians).

contagion The communication of a disease by direct or indirect contact. In psychology, the term is also used to describe the involuntary repetition of *innate* behaviours such as yawning.

content analysis The *quantitative analysis* of verbal material, such as information obtained during interviews, from open-ended questions in questionnaires, or from reference material (e.g. children's reading books). Content analysis initially involves the identification of a number of defined categories – usually predefined by the researcher, but sometimes developed as a result of an initial inspection of the data. Once the categories have been defined, the number of times that each category of information occurs throughout the material is counted. In the case of more active data, such as the content analysis of video recordings, simple counting may be replaced by timing the duration of the activity of interest. See also *qualitative analysis*.

contention scheduling The idea that when several schemata are activated at one time, the most appropriate one will be selected. Damage to the contention scheduling mechanism has been proposed as an explanation for action errors made by patients with prefrontal lesions. See also *prefrontal cortex*, *lesion*.

context The general setting or environment in which an event or a phenomenon occurs. There is evidence to suggest that *memory* is highly context-dependent, and that re-establishing a context will provide cues which facilitate the retrieval of memories. Similarly, the context of a communication or an utterance may be an important influence on how it is understood. See also *state-dependent learning*.

context-bound Limited to one particular setting and not applicable to others. The phrase 'context-bound' is particularly used to refer to Bernstein's descriptions of *restricted codes* of language. He argued that the restricted code preferred by working-class language users is closely tied to the specific situation in which the utterance is made, owing to its reliance on pronouns rather than nouns, and on nuances of tone of voice. This, Bernstein argued, serves to inhibit *abstract thought* and conceptualisation in the restricted language code user.

context-specific Relating only to that particular situation or environment, and not applying in other circumstances.

contextual intelligence The part of Sternberg's *triarchic theory of intelligence*, which emphasises that intelligent acts always take place within a context. Something that is an intelligent thing to do in one context may be stupid in another. Contexts range from being very specific, such as the demands of the immediate circumstance or situation, to very broad, such as the assumptions made by an entire culture or society.

contiguity How close two stimuli are together in time. For example, in *classical conditioning*, this would mean the closeness in time of the *conditioned stimulus* (CS) and the *unconditioned stimulus* (UCS).

contingency Any case in which one event has a raised probability of following another. In such circumstances, an observer is likely to assume that the first event caused the second. *Reinforcement schedules* are examples of contingencies that have been experimentally manipulated. Research with infants has shown a high degree of alertness to events that are contingent on an action of the infant. For babies, contingent events are only likely to be provided by *caregivers*, and so this alertness is believed to play an important part in orienting babies towards members of their own species. More generally, providing infants with contingent events has been suggested as a basic process of attachment and of the development of *self-efficacy beliefs*.

continuity The expected consistency of various characteristics as the individual develops. Most developmental psychologists expected the *intelligence quotient* to stay reasonably constant as the child grew older, but it is now recognised that its continuity has been overestimated. In fact, there is remarkably little continuity in any kind of measurable characteristic over anything more than short time periods. Most psychologists, like most other people, seem to believe in continuity, and some are producing more sophisticated models of development to account for the lack of continuity in their data. See also *transaction*.

continuity hypothesis The belief that later functioning can be predicted from a knowledge of that individual earlier in their life. There are two forms of continuity hypothesis:

(i)   Characteristics such as personality and intelligence are relatively stable, so that if they are measured at one age, they will predict the strength of equivalent characteristics later in life.

(ii) Significant events early in life will have permanent consequences (e.g. Freud's belief that early trauma is responsible for later psychopathology). This is known as the 'main effects' model. It can be contrasted

with *transaction* as an alternative explanation for lasting effects.

Continuity is a major issue in *developmental psychology* because the evidence for either form of continuity has been very weak, despite good theoretical reasons and common-sense assumptions which suggest that it should be true.

continuous variable A variable, such as height, that can take any value within a range, as distinct from a *discrete variable* such as being pregnant, which can only be one of a set number of values. A continuous variable can take any value, including fractions, so with enough data it is always possible to find a score between any other two.

contralateral On the other side. This term is of interest to psychology because most of the brain's relationship with the rest of the body is contralateral (e.g. the left *cerebral hemisphere* controls the right side of the body).

control condition One of the conditions in a research study in which the *independent variable* does not operate. Participants in the control condition give a basis for comparison with the experimental condition. For example, in a study of the effects of inducing stress, the control condition would be the one in which participants were not subjected to stress. See also *experimental group*.

control group A group in an experiment that is used for comparison with an experimental group. The control group experiences all of the conditions of the study in the same way as the experimental group, with the sole exception of the *independent variable*. In this way, by comparison of the results produced by the control group and the experimental group, the effects of the independent variable may be observed without contamination from the experimental situation itself.

control processes Processes that use *feedback* in order to keep the functioning of a system within defined limits. The term has its clearest use in engineering and physiology, and has been extended to psychological functions by analogy. See also *homeostasis*.

controllable attributions *Attributions* of a kind which imply that the person believes they have control or at least influence over the process (e.g. believing that you passed an exam because of your hard work is a controllable attribution). In *attributional analysis*, it is not always clear whether the controllability is intended to apply just to the cause, just to the outcome, or to both.

conventional morality This is the second of the three stages of *moral development* proposed by Kohlberg. Individuals at this stage consider that society's rules are by definition moral. In the early part of the stage, the individual adopts moral codes in order to avoid social sanctions. In the second part of the stage, such moral codes or rules are seen as intrinsically right because they facilitate the smooth operation of society, and therefore should not be challenged. See also *autonomous morality*, *pre-moral stage*.

conventional norms Accepted rules of conduct that are approved by society in general. See also *social norms*.

convergent evolution A process whereby the same or similar evolutionary pressures produce an outcome that is extremely similar to an outcome produced in an entirely unrelated species. The classic example here is the octopus

eye, which bears a number of structural similarities to the human eye despite having evolved independently in a species (almost) unrelated to human beings. See also *evolution*.

convergent thinking Problem-solving that works consistently towards a defined solution; a way of thinking that assumes there is a single right answer and that the way to reach that answer is to work directly towards it. It has been pointed out that within the educational system, students are trained in convergent thinking, and that *intelligence tests* depend entirely on convergent thinking ability. Rather less justifiably, it is then assumed that convergent thinking is opposed to *creativity* and is inferior to creative or *divergent thinking*. It could be argued that the reason why most people use convergent thinking most of the time is because it works for most problems.

converging operations An approach in which several methods with differing strengths and weaknesses are used to tackle a given research problem or issue. See also *triangulation*.

conversation analysis (CA) An aspect of the study of *discourse* in which attention is paid to the ways that people operate their conversations. The research process is to collect naturally occurring conversations and produce a very detailed *transcript* in which pauses, intonation and stresses are indicated along with the words. CA then investigates how people manage aspects of the conversation such as coordinating taking turns, and the 'repair processes' by which people correct misleading impressions.

conversion effect When a change in public or private attitudes occurs as a result of *minority influence*.

coordinates The number on each *axis* that indicates how an event scores on that *variable*. On a graph, the coordinates of the event on the *x*- and *y-axes* together show exactly where it is positioned.

coping behaviour A general term given to behavioural strategies or techniques that allow an animal or human to reduce the amount of stress experienced in a given situation.

core analysis The main analytical process involved in *grounded theory*, which involves exploring concepts that have emerged from the data and using these to reinterpret the data, in an *iterative* cycle.

core constructs A term used in *personal construct* theory to describe those *constructs* that are most closely associated with a person's *self-concept*. Core constructs are ones with which the individual identifies strongly and that tend to be utilised in a wide variety of situations.

core principles The principles of respect, integrity, competence and responsibility that form the core of the *ethical guidelines* operated by researchers and practitioners in psychology. See also *ethical issues*.

corpus callosum The band of neural fibres that connects the two hemispheres of the cerebrum. *Split-brain studies* involve the study of behavioural and learning changes produced when the corpus callosum is cut, such that the two hemispheres operate independently and cannot pass information to each other.

correlated-measures t-test See *dependent t-test*.

correlated-subjects design See *repeated-measures design*.

correlation A statement of a relationship between two *variables*, such that changes in one tend to be accompanied by changes in the other. In a positive correlation, when one variable increases, the other increases (e.g. tall people tend to be heavier, while shorter people tend to be lighter, so there is therefore a positive correlation between height and weight). If two variables show a negative correlation, then as one increases, the other decreases (e.g. reaction times get longer as the visibility of the stimulus diminishes). A perfect positive or negative correlation will show changes in the two variables that are exactly proportional to one another, whereas a weaker correlation will show more variability in the extent to which the two measurements match up. See also *correlation coefficient, scattergram, coefficient of determination*.

correlation coefficient This is a numerical statement of the extent to which two variables vary together. A correlation coefficient is expressed as a number between +1 and 1, with +1 representing a perfect positive correlation (i.e. when one variable increases, the other shows an increase which is precisely proportional to it) and 1 representing a perfect negative correlation (i.e. one where a decrease in one variable shows a precisely proportional increase in the second). In situations where there is little or no relationship between the two measurements, the correlation coefficient will be close to zero. See also *Pearson's product–moment correlation, Spearman's rank–order correlation coefficient*.

correlation matrix A way of presenting a number of *correlations* between a set of variables. The variables are listed at the head of the columns and the start of the rows, with the correlation between the two variables being

	Practice	Motivation	Achievement	Sociability	Personality
Practice	1	0.45	0.32	0.23	0.15
Motivation	0.45	1	0.51	0.002	0.41
Achievement	0.3	0.51	1	0.37	0.24
Sociability	0.23	0.002	0.37	1	0.62
Personality	0.15	0.41	0.24	0.62	1

Figure 16 A correlation matrix

recorded at the intersection. The matrix has the same form as the mileage grid in a road atlas. Statistical packages allow users to display significant correlations so that it is easy to see how the variables relate to each other (see Figure 16).

correspondence bias Another name for the *fundamental attributional error*.

correspondent inference theory A form of *attribution theory* that uses the three characteristics of consistency, consensus and distinctiveness to attribute blame or responsibility. See also *covariance, fundamental attributional error*.

cortex A general term used to refer to the *cerebral cortex*.

cortical blindness A form of blindness that results from damage to the *visual cortex* rather than to the eye or optic nerve. See also *hemianopia, blindsight*.

cost–benefit analysis A process in which an attempt is made to quantify the costs and the benefits of a given course of action. If it is possible to compare the estimates of cost and benefit, a decision can be made about which action will produce the best ratio of benefit to cost.

cot death See *sudden infant death syndrome*.

counselling The term has two rather opposed meanings:

(i) A form of therapy derived from the *non-directive therapy* of Carl Rogers in which the client is supported while they gain insight into their problem and work on finding their own solution.

(ii) Guidance on practical personal problems such as vocational choices, problems in studying, etc. These counsellors are much more active in providing information, offering advice, etc.

counterbalancing A strategy used in the design of those experiments in which it is possible that the order of presentation of the conditions of the study could produce an unwanted effect, such as a *practice effect* or a *fatigue effect*. Counterbalancing involves systematically varying the order of presentation of the conditions such that, for example, half of the participants would have condition A followed by condition B, while the other half would have condition B first, followed by condition A. See also *order effect, ABBA design*.

counter-conditioning In *behaviour therapy*, the *conditioning* of a response that is incompatible with an existing undesirable behaviour. Someone who is afraid of spiders might be trained to relax whenever they think of a spider, so that their first reaction prevents them from feeling fear.

counterfactual reasoning The ability to argue or reason about non-existent relationships.

counter-transference In psychoanalytic therapy, but presumably occurring in many other contexts as well, the feelings produced in the therapist by the patient. These are regarded as a valuable clue to aid understanding of what is happening to the patient and the effect that they have on people in their outside relationships. If the therapist notices feelings of irritation or a wish to protect the patient, this can be used to help the patient to understand what is going on in the session and to clarify the effects that they have on other people. It will also help the therapist to identify the nature of the patient's *transference*.

covariance An approach to *attribution theory* that identifies blame and responsibility in terms of *consistency* (whether the person always acts in that way), *consensus* (whether other people act in that way) and *distinctiveness* (whether the person only acts that way towards that particular target).

covert Hidden or disguised; non-apparent.

covert attention Internal shifts of attention that do not involve external physical signs such as changes in eye movement or breathing.

covert orienting The change of attention from one location to another without involving movement of the eyes or the body. See also *orienting*.

covert research Research in which the person who is carrying it out remains hidden from the participants, or at least their role as researcher is concealed. As a result, the participants are unaware that any research is taking place.

CR See *conditioned response*.

creative intelligence A form of intelligence that is concerned with novelty and developing creative or new forms of output rather than simply solving pre-existing problems.

creativity The ability to produce novel products or solutions to problems. Creativity has been studied as a counterpart to intelligence, represented by *divergent* and *convergent thinking* abilities, respectively. However, it is difficult to devise tests, as a creative response is by definition unpredictable, so correct answers cannot be specified in advance. In fact, there is no agreed way of measuring how creative any particular achievement may be. Moreover, it is probably even less appropriate than with intelligence to think of creativity as a quality of which an individual has a certain measurable amount. Despite these difficulties, E. Paul Torrance has produced a test of creativity which includes classic items such as 'How many uses can you think of for a brick?' and claims that results obtained from the test show that school education reduces the child's creativity. The classic theory of creativity is that it requires preparation (doing the groundwork), an *incubation period* (a period of unconscious processing), inspiration (a sudden insight) and verification (checking that the solution works). More recent theories, for example those of Edward de Bono, usually involve claiming that creativity results from a random element in thinking. It seems unlikely that Leonardo da Vinci's output could be accounted for in this way. The present state of the field is that we have no plausible theory of how creativity happens, no reliable way of measuring the creativity of a person, and no real idea of whether creativity happens because of characteristics of the individual, or because of particular kinds of circumstances. We clearly need a creative solution to these problems, but we do not have much idea of how to achieve this.

cretinism A severe *congenital* condition caused by a lack of thyroxine, sometimes because of a lack of iodine in the pregnant mother's diet. The result is severely stunted physique and brain development.

crib death See *sudden infant death syndrome*.

criterion A standard or yardstick by which a judgement or evaluation is made. One use of the term is for the level of probability required for a statistical result to be regarded as significant. The usual criterion is a probability level of less than 0.05.

criterion validity A way of assessing the *validity* of a test by comparing the results of the test with an existing criterion. Often a test is easier to apply than a real-life criterion. So if the test gives results that are close to the criterion measure, then the test can be used in its place. For example, a pen-and-paper test of aggression might give results that are close enough to a criterion of violent behaviour to be used in place of observing the person in situations where such behaviour is likely. Unfortunately, there are not many cases in psychology in which there is a measurable absolute criterion. For example, we cannot say what the 'real' IQ of a person is, and so

we cannot check the validity of a new test in this way. The best we can do is see whether the new test gives results that are similar to well established tests such as the *WAIS*.

critical period A time period during the development of the individual in which a particular function can readily be acquired. Outside that specific age range, it will be difficult or impossible to acquire the function. The function may result from physical development (*maturation*) or from *prepared learning*. *Imprinting* in ducklings is a well-known example, and in human infants if three-dimensional vision is not achieved by the age of about 2 years, then it may never be acquired. According to a strict definition, a critical period is a well-defined time during development, and the function should be impossible to achieve either before or after this period. However, outside of physical growth processes, examples of strict critical periods are rather rare. It is now known that even imprinting can be achieved well after the end of the normal critical period. In human development, it is now more common to speak of *sensitive periods*, but even this looser term has often been applied too enthusiastically. For example, it is not very helpful to refer to a critical or sensitive period for language acquisition when language can be acquired at any time during a period of at least 12 years, and possibly longer.

critical value The value of a *test statistic* which must be obtained in order to state that the results have achieved *statistical significance*. For some significance tests, the value obtained has to be higher than the critical value, while for others it has to be less – it depends on which test is being used.

Cronbach's alpha A *correlation* measure of a scale's *reliability*. To be considered acceptable, a *psychometric* scale should usually have a reliability measure somewhere between 0.7 and 0.8.

cross-cueing The process observed in patients in *split-brain studies*, by which one hemisphere of the brain transmits information to the other. In a typical experiment, an object may be shown to one side of the person's brain only. Later, the object is shown to the other side of the brain, and the person is asked questions about it. Although in such patients the *corpus callosum* has been cut so no direct transmission of information between the cerebral hemispheres is possible, people may produce feedback on the correctness of the answer offered by an imperceptible nod, frown or other physical signal. This is recognised by the other side of the brain, so that the question can be answered correctly. Cross-cueing of this nature can often be extremely rapid and subtle.

cross-cultural study A study that involves the comparison of people from different cultures.

cross-modal transfer The transfer of information from one sensory mode to another. For instance, *figure-ground perception* learned as a result of experience with touch may also be applied when the subject is using vision. This kind of transfer is frequently found with those who have acquired a new sensory function (e.g. people blind from birth who have obtained their sight through an operation performed in adulthood).

cross-sectional study A method of research in developmental psychology that involves comparing individuals of different age groups (e.g. measuring the moral judgements of 6-year-olds, 10-year-olds and 14-year-olds). Such an approach is cheaper and easier to carry out than a *longitudinal study*, in which the same children would be repeatedly measured at different ages, but it may present other problems. One example is post-war studies of psychological decline with ageing. Older people were found to have lower *intelligence quotients* than a younger sample. However, this was probably due to a *cohort effect*, because their diet and education as children in 1920 were inferior to the diet and education available to the younger sample who were children in 1970. Thus, age differences found through cross-sectional samples may not be a direct result of the ageing process.

crystallised intelligence A form of *intelligence* that reflects how good the person is at dealing with clearly structured, predictable types of problem. It draws on existing knowledge such as vocabulary, arithmetic or general information. See also *fluid intelligence*, *multiple intelligences*.

CS See *conditioned stimulus*.

cue Something that gives an idea or a hint about something. More specifically, a cue is information that activates a *schema*. A cue in *memory* theory, for instance, is a remembered item that connects with further information, allowing the individual to retrieve more. In *perception*, a cue is the item of information that is used by the brain to direct the interpretation of specific stimuli. A *depth cue* is that part of the information which is used to calcuate how far away something probably is.

cultural neuroscience An interdisciplinary approach to knowledge that links *cultural psychology*, *neurogenetics* and *neuroscience*.

cultural psychology The branch of psychology that is concerned with explaining how societies and cultures influence, shape or even determine psychological processes. Cultural psychology has been particularly concerned with challenging the *ethnocentricity* apparent in much psychological research, wherein the white North American culture has been used as the norm or standard for all of humanity. The idea that the rest of the world does not automatically share the same values or principles, while a revelation to some, is producing a much-needed balance in modern psychological research.

culture A general term used to describe the set of accepted ideas, practices, values and characteristics that develop within a particular society or people. Although most modern societies are *multicultural* to some degree, the word 'culture' is often, although not accurately, used interchangeably with 'society'.

culture-free and culture-fair tests During the 1960s and early 1970s, considerable efforts were made to develop *psychometric* tests (e.g. IQ and personality tests) that would avoid cultural bias by being free from reference to culture altogether. In practice, the diversity of cultures was so great that such tests proved impossible to develop. Researchers had to content themselves with an attempt to establish tests that, instead of being completely free of cultural influences, allowed a fair assessment of those from other cultures. Such culture-fair tests are psychometric tests that do not provide an advantage to members of one culture over another. In practice, however, culture-fair tests are also extremely difficult to achieve, owing to cultural diversity that produces differences not only in background knowledge and skills, but also in motivation and attitudes to tests. It is also very difficult for those compiling the tests to be fully aware of their own cultural assumptions. It could also be argued that, since the culture itself is not fair, a biased test will give more accurate predictions (e.g. a test that gives an advantage to middle-class academic values will more accurately predict which children will do best in school).

culture-specific Occurring in, or belonging to, a particular culture.

cumulative record or cumulative curve A graph in which each successive point shows the total number of responses up to that time. It can be used to show the progress of *operant conditioning*, and has the advantage that the steepness of the curve gives a direct indication of the rate of responding.

curare A paralysing poison used in blowpipes by some South American Indians for hunting. Curare achieves its effect by being picked up at *receptor sites* in muscle fibres, thus blocking the uptake of acetylcholine such that messages from the central nervous system are not received. Curare therefore prevents voluntary muscle action, but does not affect the actions of involuntary muscles. Animals that have been killed with curare die from suffocation but, if respirated artificially until the curare has worn off, will stay alive. Consequently, curare has proved useful in several psychological studies investigating, for example, the effects of muscle actions on cognitions.

cutaneous To do with the skin.

D

dark adaptation The process by which light-sensitive cells in the *retina* adjust their sensitivity to light, such that they will fire even in response to very faint stimuli. Full dark adaptation in the human being takes approximately 20 minutes, beginning with a rapid period of adaptation while the *cone cells* adjust, followed by a longer period for the *rod cells* to achieve maximal sensitivity.

Dark Triad A group of three *personality traits* that represent unpleasant or malevolent personal qualities. The three traits are *narcissism*, *Machiavellianism* and *psychopathy*, each of which incorporates minor undesirable traits such as *egotism*, selfishness and the tendency to manipulate others. Some researchers have argued that the Dark Triad traits can be mapped onto the *five-factory theory* of personality traits, but as polar opposites. For example, psychopathy might be regarded as a polar opposite of *agreeableness*, while Machiavellianism would be an opposite of *conscientiousness*, and narcissism an opposite of *extraversion*. Other researchers have found a less clear one-to-one relationship between the five factors and the Dark Triad, although there is general consensus that some kind of negative *correlation* between them does exist.

data A general term for all forms of recorded information. Usually, the term is used for the scores obtained in a *survey* or an *experiment*. Note that 'data' is a plural word, the term for a single score being 'datum', so it is wrong to write

'the data is . . .'. Unfortunately, there is no standard singular word for a collection of data, but 'result' or 'information' will often suffice.

data-driven technique Any approach to analysing data in which the form of the analysis is shaped by the data rather than by fitting the data into an existing structure. For a major example, see *grounded theory*.

data set The set of scores or other data obtained from one group of participants in a study.

datum A single score or other item of data. Datum is the singular of the word *data*.

daydreaming The activity of engaging in fantasies or imaginative speculations during quiescent waking periods. Some research suggests that daydreaming may be instrumental in promoting positive mental health for the individual, perhaps through the clarification of goals and ambitions.

db See *decibel*.

deactivation A decrease in neurological or physiological processing in one condition, relative to other conditions. See also *activation*.

debriefing A verbal summary of the nature and purpose of a study or activity, given to participants once the study has ended. See also *ethical issues*.

decay Reduction in the size or strength of something over time. Using the word decay implies that there is no specific cause of the reduction. The output of a sensory *nerve* that has been briefly stimulated will decay rapidly. *Habituation* is a process in which response strength decays over repeated exposure to the *stimulus*.

decentration The process by which an individual is able to step out of their own mental perspective, and to take another person's point of view. According to Piaget, the ability to 'decentre' only emerges during the *preoperational stage*, and forms a part of the gradual reduction of *egocentricity* which Piaget saw as central to *cognitive development*.

deception Deliberately misleading people or causing them to believe what is known to be untrue. In psychological research, this refers to misleading experimental participants as to the purpose of a particular study. Deception used to be the norm in psychological research, and was even considered to be absolutely necessary in order to avoid *volunteer effects*. However, the growth of ethical concerns in psychology means that deception can only be used where it is absolutely unavoidable: alternative strategies must be adopted wherever possible. See also *double-blind control*, *ethical issues*.

decibel (db) A measure of sound levels. The decibel scale involves a progression which is nearly logarithmic, such that a doubling in perceived intensity is represented by an increase of approximately three units on the decibel scale.

decision-making The study of how people go about making decisions, and the factors which may mislead them into making decisions that are not optimal. Research into decision-making includes the study of the *knowledge frame* of the decision, and

the *heuristics* that lead to sources of bias such as *anchoring*, *entrapment*, *hindsight bias* and *groupthink*. See also *satisficing, own-age bias, affect heuristic, availability heuristic*.

decision support system A computerised system constructed in order to help people make decisions in situations where the problem cannot be clearly specified.

decision theory Any theory that attempts to explain how decisions are made. In practice, the term is most often applied to theories that apply mathematical models to human decision processes. See also *receiver-operating characteristic curve*.

declarative knowledge Factual knowledge about the world. See also *procedural knowledge*.

declarative memory A form of *long-term memory* that involves memory for both facts (*semantic memory*) and events (*episodic memory*), and is essentially about knowing. It is also sometimes described as *explicit memory*.

deconstruction The process of identifying how scientific theories, literature and social science generally come to reflect the social assumptions and conventions of their time, or of those propounding the theories. For example, in deconstructionist terms, the association of Konrad Lorenz with the German Nazi party would not be seen as unconnected with the theory of *aggression* that he propounded.

deduction Drawing conclusions about specifics from general principles. As one of the major forms of reasoning, deduction has been studied by psychologists interested in cognitive areas such as *problem-solving*. See also *induction*.

deductive methodology The approach to research that has been dominant in psychology, and which uses research to test predictions from theory. See also *hypothetico-deductive method, induction*.

deductive reasoning Reasoning that is based on the principle of establishing a set of premises, or statements which will automatically produce a particular conclusion. See also *induction*.

deep dyslexia *Dyslexia* in which the person's comprehension of words is affected. See also *surface dyslexia*.

deep dysphasia A condition that produces significant difficulty in repeating spoken words, or non-words. The difficulty may involve both *lexical* and *semantic* errors.

deep structure A term coined by the linguist Noam Chomsky to describe the universal properties of basic grammar, supposedly common to all languages. It was the similarities of deep structure which allowed for Chomsky's proposed innate *language acquisition device*, a theoretical construction by which he explained the infant's readiness to acquire human language.

default mode network A group of *neural networks* in the brain that are more active when the brain is at rest than when the person is engaged in an active task. See also *resting state paradigm, functional integration*.

defence mechanism A strategy that protects the *ego* or *self-concept* from real or imaginary threat. First proposed by Freud, defence mechanisms may take many forms, of which a few of the most common are: *repression, reaction formation, projection, rationalisation, identification* with the aggressor, *intellectualism* and *denial*. Although Freud classified defence mechanisms as neurotic or psychotic, the fact is that everybody uses them sometimes as a way of avoiding unwanted information about themselves or the outside world. However, they all have the disadvantage of distorting one's understanding of reality.

defensible space An approach to housing design that emphasises perceived ownership of open areas and has been shown to reduce crime and vandalism. See also *environmental psychology*.

deficiency motive A motivation that arises because of a perceived deficiency of some kind. The deficiency can range from *physiological needs* (e.g. food) to higher needs, such as the desire for recognition. Deficiency motives are distinguished from 'abundancy motives', in which it is judged that the organism is trying to acquire more of the material than is needed for comfortable survival.

degeneration In *neurophysiology*, the deterioration of neural tissue that occurs through lack of stimulation, injury or lack of nutrients. In stimulus deprivation studies, some damaged perceptual functioning that was originally thought to result from cognitive deficits was later found to be caused by neural degeneration.

degrees of freedom (df) The number of possible options for variation that exist in a *data set*. For example, if a set of two scores have a given total, then the first score can vary, but the other one must be fixed in order to reach the desired total. This gives one degree of freedom. A set of three scores producing a fixed total would have two degrees of freedom, and so on. The size of the score on a statistical test needed for a given level of *significance* will depend on the number of degrees of freedom, so tables of significance are generally arranged in terms of degrees of freedom.

degrees of freedom problem A term used in *neuroscience* to describe the way that there are potentially an infinite number of motor solutions which can come into play to produce a single action on an object.

deindividuation The process by which individuals come to feel that they are simply part of a corporate entity, such as group or crowd members. Deindividuation involves the individual surrendering the immediate perception of independence and *autonomy*, and feeling as though they have merged anonymously with the other people involved. It is commonly found in military units in action, and is often believed to be common in mobs. See also *diffusion of responsibility*.

delayed conditioning A form of *classical conditioning* in which the *conditioned stimulus* is presented several seconds before the *unconditioned stimulus*, but with both coming to an end at the same time. By comparison with *simultaneous conditioning* or *trace conditioning*, delayed conditioning is considered to be the most effective.

delta waves Long slow wave patterns that can be observed in the *electroencephalograms* of people in deep sleep. Delta waves begin to appear during the third level of sleep, and are most common during level 4 sleep. See also *sleep cycles*.

delusion A belief that is mistaken yet firmly held, despite contradiction by evidence and logic. Delusions of grandeur may occur in *schizophrenia*, and delusions of persecution are common in *paranoia*.

delusions of control The sense or belief that one's thoughts and actions are under external control, and not subject to personal volition. The opposite of *agency* beliefs.

demand characteristics Those features of an experimental or similar setting that elicit unusual or situation-dependent forms of behaviour from subjects participating in the study. These would include factors such as *experimenter effects* producing bias, expectations held by the participant as to the 'correct' way to behave in a psychological study, the effects of trivialised or meaningless tasks that necessitate uncommon strategies to deal with them, and the wish to give the experimenter the result they want. See also *implacable experimenter*.

dementia A state in which the cognitive abilities of a person are so damaged that they are no longer able to function independently. The term is now used almost exclusively for permanent physical deterioration of the brain. The most common form is senile dementia, which can occur in old age but has a variety of causes. See also *Alzheimer's syndrome*.

democratic leadership An approach to *leadership* in which the leader consults with team members, and decisions are generally taken on the basis of consensus. See also *laissez-faire*.

dendrites The branched structures at the end of the *axon* of a *neurone* that are used for the transmission or reception of *neurotransmitters*, and so contribute to either the *excitation* or the *inhibition* of the electrical impulses through *synaptic transmission*. A dendrite characteristically ends in a swelling, or *synaptic knob*, which carries vesicles containing a neurotransmitter. *Receptor sites* on the dendrites of the adjoining neurone pick up the neurotransmitter.

dendron That part of the elongated stem of a *neurone* that is found before the cell body, taking the same direction as that in which the impulse travels. See also *axon*.

denial A defence mechanism or aspect of one's own psychological functioning in not acknowledging the existence of a threatening event or utterance. Denial is most commonly found in children, although it is not uncommon as an adult defence mechanism.

denotative meaning The specific or symbolic meaning of an utterance or term. The denotative meaning of something is that which is simply and necessarily contained in the use of that term, without any of the additional associations or implications which a listener may understand. See also *connotative meaning*.

deoxyribonucleic acid (DNA) The compound that forms the basic units of *chromosomes* and is therefore fundamental to reproduction.

dependency

(i) A term used to express an unbalanced relationship in which one individual relies consistently on the support or aid of another. In this sense, the term was formerly used to describe the relationship of an infant to its mother, but has now largely been replaced by *attachment*.

(ii) A term used to describe reliance on a particular drug or therapy, which falls short of physiological *addiction* but is characterised by a psychological reliance such that the individual feels unhappy or uneasy in its absence.

dependent t-test A two-sample *statistical test* for *interval scale* and *ratio scale* data, where the two samples consist of paired data sets taken from the same individuals under differing conditions. It is also known as related-measures t-test, repeated-measures t-test or correlated-measures t-test. See also *t-test, independent t-test*.

dependent variable The variable that is measured as an indicator of the outcome of an *experiment*. If an experiment is set up to assess the effect of coffee on speed of essay writing, the dependent variable would be the measure of writing speed. The dependent variable is so named because, if the experimental *hypothesis* is valid, its value will depend on the condition of the *independent variable* that has been set up.

depictive representations Cognitive *representations* which are similar to images or pictures, in that they organise information spatially and graphically.

depolarising Reducing two conditions or positions from their extremes to something more moderate or similar. For example, depolarising an argument involves getting both participants to modify their positions slightly so that they can find room for agreement, or can agree to differ.

depressant A drug that reduces or depresses physiological functioning, particularly *central nervous system* activity. Alcohol is the most widely available depressant, although its effects may be concealed temporarily by its capacity to induce euphoria. The term may also be applied to psychological influences that have the effect of lowering mood. See also *stimulant*.

depression A reduced state of both physiological and mental functioning, usually associated with feelings of unhappiness. The most common symptoms are a loss of interest and inability to enjoy any experiences, sadness, loss of appetite, sleep disturbances (especially early in the morning), passivity, and suicidal thoughts or intentions. However, even very severe depressions may only involve a few of these symptoms. The term is used for a very wide range of conditions, extending from 'ordinary unhappiness' through to *psychotic* disorders. Psychologists will therefore indicate when they are using the term to refer to a serious clinical condition either by the context or by attaching further labels – either 'clinical depression' or a specific term for a particular form of depression. The more common of these are *bipolar depression*, *endogenous depression* (thought to be caused internally), *exogenous* or *reactive depression*, and psychotic depression. Other forms of depression are 'agitated depression', in which the individual is agitated, restless and irritable, and 'retarded depression', when they are slow, apathetic and difficult to get moving.

depressive attributional style An *attributional style* in which people are likely to explain bad events in terms of causes that are stable, global and internal. Some would add personal and uncontrollable to this list. There is evidence that habitually explaining things in this way is associated with *depression*, especially for people who encounter a significant number of negative life events. The work on depressive attributional style grew from Seligman's theory of *learned helplessness*.

deprivation Having some important resource or positive environmental condition removed, usually producing distress or at least discomfort. See also *privation*, *maternal deprivation*.

depth cue A perceptual factor that gives an indication of how far away an object or image is. See also *depth perception*, *monocular depth cue*.

depth interview A technique of generating data for *qualitative research*. Participants are interviewed individually in a way that is designed to get them talking in detail about significant issues in their lives. Depth interviews are used extensively in qualitative research. See also *focus group*, *interview*.

depth perception The interpretation of distance from *sensory* information. Depth perception relies on two main sets of *depth cues*, namely *binocular depth cues* and *monocular depth cues*. Binocular cues include *retinal disparity*, *binocular convergence* of the eye muscles and *accommodation* of the lens, while monocular cues include height in plane, *superposition*, shadow, *gradient of texture* and colour, relative size, and *motion parallax*. Auditory depth perception involves the interpretation of attenuated signals, such that sounds which are further away are fainter, and also of phase shifts in the wavelengths of sound, such that sounds which come from further away appear to be muffled compared to nearer ones.

descriptive statistics Statistics that summarise or illustrate *data sets* (e.g. as summary tables, *measures of central tendency* or diagrams). See also *inferential statistics*.

desensitisation A procedure that will reduce the responsiveness of the person concerned. It is used mainly for behavioural techniques that reduce or eliminate inappropriate emotional responses, usually anxiety. The basic procedure is to present weak forms of the feared stimulus while using stronger forms of a stimulus that produces a response incompatible with anxiety. The strength of the feared stimulus is then gradually increased without triggering the fear response. This is called *systematic desensitisation* and is an example of *counter-conditioning*.

determinism The belief that everything that happens is the result of an identifiable cause. This assumption leads to a definition of science as being about finding causes. Within psychology, determinism is strongest among *behaviourists* and *Freudians*. Both approaches were attempts to account for all of human behaviour in terms of fundamental causes. The assumption has been undermined by physicists deciding that at the basis of all matter, the principle in operation is indeterminism. More broadly, the shift against determinism has taken the form of *postmodernism*. In practice, most psychologists seem to regard themselves as freely choosing (non-deterministically) to study the (deterministic) causes of behaviour. This is yet another example of the *actor–observer effect*. See also *existentialism*.

development The processes of change and growth over the lifespan. One aspect is physical development, which is strongly influenced by *genetic* tendencies. The other is psychological development, which is much more directly influenced by environmental factors. See also *lifespan*.

developmental disorders Disorders that appear to result from a failure of developmental processes, and which can be expected to distort future development.

developmental dyslexia The basic form of *dyslexia*, shown by children who have difficulty with reading and make mistakes in a characteristic form

(e.g. getting words and letters in the wrong order). The term 'developmental' is added primarily to distinguish it from *acquired dyslexia*, in which the difficulty starts later in development.

developmental norms The expected level of performance of children at a specific age. For example, in a given *population*, the *norms* for the number of words spoken might be 50 at age 18 months, 400 at age 3 years, etc. Developmental norms can be used to give a precise indication of how uncommon any unusual performance by a child may be. Identifying a level of performance as being exceptionally poor is only the first step in deciding whether any further action is desirable. See also *intelligence*.

developmental psychology The psychological study of development. Some distinction is made between developmental psychology, which is the study of the laws and processes of development, and child psychology, which is more focused on empirical techniques for studying children at specific ages. However, the terms are often used fairly interchangeably, and the phrase 'experimental child psychology' has come into use to preserve the distinction. Major theories of development have been propounded by Freud, Gesell and Piaget, among others. All of the large-scale theories were established in the first half of the twentieth century, and most are restricted to childhood. However, there is reason to believe (or at least hope) that development continues throughout adulthood. The field of *lifespan developmental psychology* has therefore become active in recent years, but as yet has no major theory as a basis. In fact, developmental psychology in general seems to be proceeding quite adequately at present without much reliance on overall theories of development. Instead, there are theories to deal with restricted areas such as *attachment* and *language*, and a focus on a number of more or less practical issues. The areas of greatest interest include the growth of cognitive and social *competence*, the *nature–nurture* or genetic–environment debate, the question of continuity, the way in which a child develops a *theory of mind*, applications to education and to parenting, the importance of *play* and *creativity*, and, more recently, the family.

deviation In everyday terms, an expression of how different a particular behaviour is from accepted *social norms* or assumptions. In *statistics*, it refers to how much a particular score differs from the *mean* for that group. See also *standard deviation*.

Diagnostic and Statistical Manual of Mental Disorders (DSM-V) This is produced by the American Psychiatric Association, and subject to periodic reviews. It is generally referred to as DSM, followed by the version number: the version at the time of writing is DSM-V. The manual was produced as an attempt to standardise diagnosis, and it can be a useful way of finding out what is currently regarded as good practice in diagnosis in the United States. However, the empirical evidence for its *reliability* and *validity* have been disappointing, although perhaps not less so than for any other psychiatric technique. See also *International Statistical Classification of Diseases and Related Health Problems*.

dialect A distinctive pattern of grammatical forms and vocabulary that originates from a particular region.

The point at which a dialect becomes distinctive enough to be seen as a language in its own right is largely a matter of social judgement, rather than of any linguistic criteria. Some linguists, for instance, regard the West Indian Creole dialect or Hong Kong English as distinctive languages in their own right, since, although they may have originated as forms of English, they contain their own distinctive grammatical forms and vocabularies. The same situation pertains to a number of European languages, such as Flemish, where considerable social action was required in order for it to be regarded as a separate language rather than a regional dialect. It may be observed, therefore, that the social recognition of an extremely distinctive shared form of speech as a language rather than a dialect has everything to do with the acknowledged social status of the group which uses that form of language, and relatively little to do with the linguistic structure of the form of speech itself. See also *accent*, *psycholinguistics*, *speech register*.

dialectics A form of argument or theorising in which one argument (referred to as the thesis) is combined with another, apparently opposing argument (referred to as the antithesis), to produce an entirely new outcome (referred to as the synthesis). The synthesis combines elements of both arguments, and so avoids seeing the issue as an 'either/or' conflict. The clearest example of dialectics in psychology is the modern perception of the classic *nature–nurture debate*. While the two were seen to be opposing influences for many years (development as produced by either genetics or environment), they are now viewed as working together in a dialectical relationship in which each contributes to the other's functioning, and also to the final outcome. The end result is a synthesis of both genetics and environmental experience that amounts to more than just the sum of the two processes operating independently. For example, some aspects of environmental experience might not occur if the individual did not have the genetic attributes that attracted them, while some aspects of genetic potential may never become fully realised without the environmental circumstances that bring them out and encourage them to develop.

dialogical self This is a theoretical approach that is concerned with how the internal sense of self and the external dialogue with society interconnect. The idea is that the internal self actually comprises a number of different 'selves', each of which have different social connotations and connections. It also includes our awareness of significant others, and our ideas about their own minds and how they work. These internal personas provide the basis for a continual dialogue concerning the self and the external world, and they shape our communications and interactions with the external world. What it all boils down to is the idea that the inner self is not simply individual and separated from society, but extended into its society and inextricably linked to it, and the 'other' is not external or separate, but also part of ourselves.

dialogism In literature, this means the representation of the author's thoughts through a dialogue between two or more characters. In psychology, it has to do with the way that we incorporate different 'selves' or the viewpoints of different people, in dialogue with each other, as part of our own sense of *self*.

diary method A research method, often used in *developmental psychology* and increasingly in clinical contexts, in which a detailed written record of chosen aspects of behaviour is kept over time. In child research, the diary is often written by parents, which not only makes life easier for the researcher, but also means that information can be recorded about times and events that are not available to the researcher. See also *qualitative research*, Ecological Momentary Assessment, Experience Sampling Method.

diaschesis When a brain *lesion* in one location disrupts the functioning of other areas of the brain that are structurally intact.

diathesis-stress model Also known as the *vulnerability model*, this is a way of looking at mental illness which emphasises that although the person's vulnerability to the problem may come from *genetic* factors, it is their lifetime experience and social stresses which result in the mental illness actually developing. So the origins of the problem lie in the interaction between genetic vulnerability and environmental factors.

dichotic listening task A method for investigating *selective attention* by presenting two different messages through the two sides of a set of headphones, and asking the research participant to attend to one message only. Dichotic listening tasks are usually monitored by asking the person to engage in *shadowing* (i.e. speaking the attended message out loud as they listen to it) (see Figure 17).

dichotomous variable A discrete *variable*, such as being pregnant, that can only take one of two values.

attended ear

non-attended ear

Figure 17 A dichotic listening task

dichromatism A term used to describe forms of *colour vision* in which the individual is lacking in sensitivity to specific wavelengths of light. Normal colour vision is trichromatic in that three major wavelengths make up any given colour, but some colour-blind individuals use dichromatic vision to interpret specific hues (i.e. using two major wavelengths only). See also *colour blindness*.

DID See *dissociative identity disorder*.

diencephalon Also sometimes referred to as the *forebrain*, this consists of subcortical *grey matter*, and includes the *thalamus*, *hypothalamus* and the *mamillary bodies*.

difference threshold See *relative threshold*.

diffusion of responsibility The process by which individuals may fail to act in a situation requiring *bystander intervention* as a direct result of the presence of several other onlookers. The perception is that this implies that the responsibility is shared, which reduces the pressure on each separate individual to act.

diffusion tensor imaging (DTI) A technique that measures the differences in concentration of *white matter* and *grey matter* using *MRI imaging*.

digit span The number of unrelated digits (numbers or letters) that a person is able to recall accurately after just one hearing. In most people, it is usually within the range of 7 ± 2, and shows a (relatively weak) correlation with measured *intelligence*. See also *short-term memory*.

digital Coded in simple on–off (binary) units, as in computerised information. This is also the traditional view of the firing of *neurones*. See also *all-or-none principle*.

diglossia The ability to speak more than one version of one's own language (e.g. being able to converse freely in a regional *dialect* and also in formal 'received pronunciation' English).

diploid Having a full complement of *chromosomes* (i.e. a pair of each kind). Different species have different numbers of pairs of chromosomes. See also *haploid*, *gene*, *meiosis*.

dipole A pair of positive and negative electrical charges, separated by a short distance.

dipole modelling A method of dealing with the *inverse problem* by making assumptions about how many regions of the brain are actually critical in producing observed scalp potentials. However, these are probabilistic judgements, and if accuracy is required it is preferable to use *fMRI* or another scanning technique.

direct perception A model of perception developed by J.J. Gibson which emphasised that in the real world, most if not all of the information required for accurate perception is actually present in the visual field (e.g. *gradient of texture* or *superposition*). Even if it is not apparent from a static viewpoint, this information becomes evident through movement and interacting directly with the world. Consequently, there is no need for inference or *hypothesis testing* in real-world perception. See also *top-down approach*, *bottom-up processing*, *ecological perception*.

direct reciprocity The idea that we provide help to others in order to receive help from them at some future date. See also *altruistic behaviour*.

direct retrieval A form of *autobiographical memory* in which information is recalled involuntarily, as the result of some environmental or social cue. See also *generative retrieval*.

directed forgetting Forgetting that happens because of a deliberate intention to forget – either by the person or, for example, through a hypnotic instruction. See also *denial*.

directed retrospection A research technique in which people are asked to categorise, pretty well immediately, the thoughts they have just had. See also *protocol analysis*.

directed thinking Thinking that is directed towards a particular goal (e.g. *problem-solving*).

discontinuity A break in a sequence or set of actions. In most psychological contexts, this implies that earlier and later characteristics (i.e. those separated by the break) are entirely independent and will have nothing to do with one another.

discounting principle The idea that the existence of other possible causes reduces the role or importance of another specific cause.

discourse Deliberate or conscious forms of *communication*. Discourse is usually taken to mean words, but some examples of *discourse analysis* have included analyses of photographs, murals or even toothpaste packaging.

discourse analysis A general term covering various ways of analysing spoken or written communication. The term 'discourse' avoids the assumptions built into terms such as 'conversation'. There are a number of techniques of discourse analysis, such as identifying the recurrent *semantic* themes of a discourse, or its use of *metaphor*. Linguists apply a more specific meaning to the term, relating to natural breaks in the discourse. See also *content analysis*, *social representations*, *conversation analysis*.

discourse markers Spoken words or phrases that do not contribute directly to the literal content of what is being said, but enhance the communication in other ways (e.g. by indicating the speaker's *attitude* towards it). See also *discourse analysis*.

discovery learning A form of educational practice studied particularly by J.S. Bruner, in which students operate mainly by *deduction* and *inference*, with guidance and resources being provided by the teacher. Discovery learning emphasises the student's own activity and enquiry, rather than the teacher's transmission of information. See also *schema*.

discrete variable A variable, such as the total of scores on a *questionnaire*, that can only have one of a set number of values, as distinct from a continuous variable such as height. If it can only take one of two values, it is called a *dichotomous variable*.

discrimination

(i)   The skill of distinguishing one stimulus from another, possibly learned through selective *instrumental learning* or *classical conditioning*.

(ii) The practice of drawing arbitrary distinctions between one set of people and another, such as is found in a group of highly prejudiced individuals taking steps to limit or restrict access to privileges or resources by a minority group. See also *prejudice, social identification*.

discriminatory stimulus A stimulus in *operant conditioning* that provides a cue to indicate when a particular response is appropriate or not.

discursive To do with *discourse*.

disembedded thought Thinking that is not applied in a relevant context, but is required to take place independent of context. Many of the criticisms of Piagetian approaches to the understanding of the child's cognition centre around the idea that the child was required to engage in disembedded tasks. When these tasks were put in an appropriate social context, children were noticeably more successful at them. See also *naughty teddy*.

disengagement A theory of ageing proposed by Cumming and Henry, according to which the elderly undergo a process of systematic disengagement or withdrawal from society, reducing their amount of participation in and integration with society. The process was thought of as a way of coping with the deaths and illnesses of partners and friends, and as a possible preparation for approaching death. Cumming and Henry proposed that this behaviour had a possible biological origin. The theory has been heavily criticised, mainly on the grounds that the social pressure on old people to withdraw from society is high, and that, for many, society offers few alternatives.

disgust A negative emotion containing strong elements of rejection and repulsion. It is thought that disgust might have its *evolutionary* origins in avoiding the ingestion of contaminated foodstuffs.

displaced aggression Aggressive behaviour directed towards a target that is not the original source of frustration. Typically, *aggression* becomes displaced because the original target is unreachable, or because it would be inexpedient for the individual to direct aggression towards the original source. For instance, it may be risky for someone to express directly the aggressive feelings generated by an unpleasant boss, and such feelings may become displaced on to family members instead.

displacement The process of channelling undesired or inexpedient impulses to alternative outlets. An example would be the application of aggressive tendencies to becoming the best chess player in the college. When the outcome of displacement is regarded as socially desirable, the process is also called *sublimation*.

display rules The amount of self-control or regulation of emotional expression that is expected in the presence of other people. See also *face*.

disposition A tendency to behave in a particular way. When used by developmental or clinical psychologists, the term implies an inherited tendency, and is used interchangeably with predisposition. When used in the context of *motivation* and *personality*, it is a general term for any relatively stable behavioural tendency, and no genetic basis is implied.

dispositional attribution Believing that a person's behaviour is caused by their character or *personality*, rather than the situation that they are in. People are usually more likely to make dispositional attributions about the behaviour of other people, and to account for their own behaviour in terms of the situation they were in – the *actor–observer effect*. See also *covariance, fundamental attributional error, situational attribution*.

dissociation A separation of two parts of an individual's mental life so that each can function separately or even in contradiction to the other. Extreme forms are *amnesia* and *dissociative identity disorder*, but milder forms are more common (e.g. when someone is competitive at work but not at home).

dissociation of function The idea that *cognitive* functions are separate and

distinct, such that when one cognitive function is damaged or impaired, others continue to work appropriately and are unaffected.

dissociations In *neurology*, the term is used to refer to impaired cognitive functions that have arisen as the result of localised brain damage, while other similar or related cognitive functions have been left intact. *Double-dissociations* occur when two apparently independent cognitive functions have been impaired by the same localised injury (in more than one individual). While dissociations are useful for indicating possible localisation of function, it needs to be borne in mind that the cortex has multiple connections, and that simple *reverse inference* is not always an appropriate explanation.

dissociative disorders A group of disorders in which the usual connections between *memory, identity* and *consciousness* have been broken.

dissociative identity disorder (DID) A rare condition in which a person functions with two or more distinct personalities. The personalities may alternate and each have their own memories and social life, while seemingly quite unaware of each others' existence. DID is not a form of schizophrenia, but a development of a phenomenon that is quite common and normal in childhood. It was previously called *multiple personality* disorder. See *dissociation*.

dissonance A state in which a cognitive discrepancy is produced between two events, such that one cognition is in direct contradiction to another. Typically, *cognitive dissonance* results in an attitude change, such that the dissonance is reduced.

distal stimulus A stimulus that is out there in the real world. Contrast with *proximal stimulus*.

distance cues See *depth cue*.

distance effect The observation that people find it easier to determine which of two numbers is the larger if there is a significant distance between them, and take more time to process a judgement about two adjacent or similar numbers.

distinctiveness A concept in *attribution theory* that concerns how unique an event or behaviour is. Distinctiveness is one of three major criteria used to formulate attributions for any given situation based on their *covariance*. The other criteria are *consistency* and *consensus*. If a person is shouting on a particular occasion, we might ask whether they usually shout in other contexts as well. If not, the condition is one of high distinctiveness, and we would tend to assume that there is something about the situation that is producing the behaviour. If other occasions produce shouting (low distinctiveness), then we would attribute the behaviour as a characteristic of the person.

distraction A strategy for *emotion regulation* that involves diverting attention away from the emotive stimulus or situation, and focusing on information which is neutral or positive.

distributed practice A procedure during *learning* in which time gaps are interspersed during the practice. For example, if you were trying to learn the contents of a chapter, you might take a short break at the end of each section. This approach has been found to lead to more effective learning than *massed practice*, in which no breaks are taken.

distribution The pattern made by a set of scores when grouped according to frequency. Theoretical distributions are the pattern that would be produced by scores that conformed precisely to a mathematically defined function. The most important of these in psychology is the *normal distribution*, but each statistic has its own distribution.

distribution-free tests See *non-parametric statistics*.

diurnal rhythm A *biorhythm* in which activity and alertness peak during the daytime. It is a form of *circadian rhythm*.

divergent thinking Thought that ranges far more widely than is conventional. Tests of divergent thinking are often included in *creativity* tests, as it is assumed that highly creative individuals will be able to utilise novel frameworks more readily than those with a more conventional style of cognition. See also *convergent thinking*.

divided attention A situation in which two tasks are performed at the same time. See also *selective attention*, *dichotic listening task*, *multitasking*.

dizygotic twins Twins that have developed as a result of the simultaneous production of two ova by the mother, both of which have subsequently been fertilised and developed fully. Unlike *monozygotic twins*, they resemble each other genetically only to the extent that ordinary brothers and sisters do. Dizygotic twins are also known as fraternal twins.

DLPFC See *dorsolateral prefrontal cortex*.

DNA See *deoxyribonucleic acid*.

document analysis Research that is carried out by examining written records or other forms of documentation.

dogmatism A *personality trait* involving rigid adherence to a chosen point of view, and intolerance of people who hold alternative positions. See also *authoritarian personality*.

domain specificity The idea that a given neural node or cognitive module will respond specifically to one type of input (e.g. colours or faces) but not to others.

dominance A term used loosely by *ethologists* to refer to privileged access to resources, rights of way, or generation of appeasing treatment by other members of a social group.

dominance hierarchy A concept first proposed in 1922 by Schjelderuppe-Ebbe after observation of a consistent order of precedence (the pecking order) among hens when the latter had been given restricted access to food supplies. Dominance hierarchies became popular as *ethological* concepts throughout the 1950s and 1960s, and were considered to present a basic model of social organisation for most animals, but the existence of linear dominance hierarchies has been increasingly called into question by ethologists in recent years.

dominant gene A gene that is more likely to be expressed in the individual's development than a matching gene (*allele*) with a different physical implication. For example, if an individual inherits a gene for red hair and a gene for dark hair from their parents, the dark-haired gene, being dominant, will be the one that is expressed. Red-hair genes are *recessive* and will only be expressed in the *phenotype* if both alleles code for red hair.

dominant hemisphere The half of the brain that controls language function and usually other aspects of dominance such as handedness. For most people, the left hemisphere is dominant, and they are right-handed.

dopamine A *neurotransmitter* involved in reward and motivational pathways in the brain, and possibly implicated in some psychiatric disturbances. The tranquilliser chlorpromazine (Largactil) seems to work by blocking dopamine *receptor sites*, while *amphetamines* effect an increase in the levels of dopamine and *noradrenaline*. The symptoms of *Parkinson's disease* can be alleviated by the drug L-dopa, which increases dopamine levels in the brain. The implication here is that a dopamine deficiency may be causing the problem.

dopamine hypothesis The hypothesis that *schizophrenia* is caused by an excess of dopamine in the *limbic system*.

dopaminergic Involving the actions of the *neurotransmitter dopamine*.

dorsal Towards the top. See also *ventral, lateral, medial*.

dorsal stream Sometimes called the dorsal visual stream, this is a term used to describe the visual pathway that goes from the *occipital lobes* to the *parietal lobes*, and has been shown to be involved in *attention* and visually guided action. See also *ventral stream, fusiform face area*.

dorsal visual stream See *dorsal stream*.

dorsolateral prefrontal cortex (DLPFC) An area of the *cortex* that is involved in manipulating information in *working memory*. For example, it becomes more active if someone is presented with a recognisable sequence of numbers rather than a random set.

double bind A situation in which the individual appears to be confronted with alternatives, but in fact whatever they do will be wrong. For example, a father might forbid his son to climb a tree. If the boy climbs the tree, he is punished for disobedience, but if he does not, his father indicates that he is disappointed at the boy being so 'soft'. Double binds seem to be particularly common in families, and Gregory Bateson, who invented the term, initially proposed that *schizophrenia* was caused by growing up in a family in which double binds were used frequently. This theory has now been abandoned, but systemic family therapists recognise that double binds are a common and destructive feature of many disturbed families.

double-blind control An experimental *control* in which neither the person conducting the experiment nor the research participants in the study are aware of the experimental *hypothesis* or conditions. Double-blind controls are precautions against *experimenter effects*, and are considered essential in tests of new drugs or assessments of *therapeutic* procedures. But see also *deception*.

double-dissociation The observation that some people with brain damage may show normal ability on one task but impaired ability on another, while someone else with apparently the same problem shows the reverse effect.

double obligation dilemma The ethical issue involved when the use of *deception* would make a very significant contribution to our social knowledge or awareness, but might involve distress or anxiety on the part of individual research participants. See also *ethical issues*.

Down's syndrome A *congenital* disorder in which the individual possesses an extra *chromosome*, giving rise to a series of distinctive physiological characteristics, often accompanied by mental retardation and language difficulty. It was once called 'mongolism', a term that originated because of a slight resemblance of children with Down's syndrome to Mongolians, but which is now no longer used in psychological literature.

dream analysis Finding hidden meanings in disguised symbolic form by interpreting the content of dreams. Dream analysis is an important tool of the *psychoanalytic* schools of thought proposed by Freud and Jung. It is considered to form an important set of clues to the *unconscious* mind, because dreaming is thought to express unconscious wish fulfilment expressive of the individual's deepest conflicts and desires.

dreaming Mental activity that occurs during sleep. Dreams typically have vivid imagery, an emotional content, and occur during a particular phase of sleep (*REM sleep*). They also have the characteristic of being rapidly forgotten on waking. It seems that all humans dream, but most dreams are not remembered. Freud proposed that the function of dreams was to preserve sleep by seeming to fulfil wishes that would otherwise disturb the sleeper. More recent theories propose that dreams are the by-product of the processing of information that has come in during the day and needs to be incorporated into the cognitive system.

dreamwork A term used by Freud to refer to the complex process by which unconscious wishes and fantasies are disguised in dreams, appearing in symbolic form. See also *latent content*, *manifest content*.

drive An energised state in which the person or animal is motivated by the need to satisfy some lack or want (usually physiological in nature).

drive-reduction theory The theory that *motivation* occurs, and behaviour is energised, mainly or entirely as a result of the need to alleviate or reduce drives. It is a rather negative theory in that it assumes that all drives produce tension or *arousal*, so that the organism is always motivated to minimise drive states. The failure to encompass enjoyment and activities that deliberately increase arousal (such as exploration and sky-diving) was one reason for the decline of the theory. See also *secondary drives*.

drug A chemical substance, usually non-nutritive, which exerts an effect on the body. See also *recreational drugs*.

DSM-V See *Diagnostic and Statistical Manual of Mental Disorders*.

DTI See *diffusion tensor imaging*.

dual-aspect theory The idea that mind and brain are two aspects of the same thing, but described at different *levels of analysis*.

dualism See *Cartesian dualism*.

dual-memory theory A model of *memory* first proposed by William James in 1890, and later developed by (among others) Miller, and Atkinson and Shiffrin. Dual-memory theory postulates two independent memory systems, namely a limited-capacity, immediate or *short-term memory* (STM), and a large-capacity, *long-term memory* (LTM). The Atkinson and Shiffrin model proposes that STM forms a first stage to LTM storage, and that material is transferred from STM to LTM by means of *rehearsal* (see Figure 18). See also *levels of processing*.

dual-process dependency model A way of analysing social influence by separating normative social influence coming from knowledge that has been directly learned from others about norms and socially accepted standards, from informational social influence, which has been learned more indirectly from the media, etc. The dual process dependency model assumes that these two forms of influence are entirely separate, and exert different pressures on the individual.

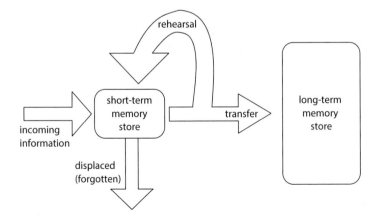

Figure 18 A dual-memory theory

Dunning-Kruger effect The finding that people who are less skilled are more likely to overestimate their abilities than people who are more skilled. See also *self-efficacy*.

dyad A pair, usually of people, who are engaged in some kind of interaction. Dyadic interaction means interaction just between two people, with no one else involved.

dyadic interactions Interactions between two people, usualy face to face.

dynamic equilibrium A state of a system which is unchanging, not because all of its components are locked into fixed positions (static equilibrium), but because the components are continually changing in relation to each other in such a way that the system as a whole is stable. It can be a useful metaphor for human systems that are much more likely to become stable (or stuck) in this way.

dynamometer A machine for measuring muscular strength, particularly of hand grip.

dysarthria Impaired ability to contract the muscles, resulting in difficulty in movement. It is associated with *lesions* to the *cerebellum* and the left *basal ganglia*.

dyscalculia A difficulty with performing arithmetical calculations, similar to *dyslexia* and generating many of the same debates.

dysexecutive syndrome A cognitive impairment that affects the ability to plan and organise deliberate behaviour. It is thought to arise from damage to the *prefrontal cortex*.

dysfunctional Working or operating in such a manner as to be a positive handicap to the individual or originating body. In general, the prefix 'dys' is used to mean faulty or presenting a problem.

dysgraphia A type of *learning difficulty* that involves difficulty in writing (i.e. with performing the physical actions involved in writing). It often overlaps with other disorders such as difficulties in writing at speed, but does not seem to be related to difficulties of comprehension. Dygraphia has been associated with misfunctioning of a specific writing area, known as Exner's area, in the *frontal lobe*. See also *phonological dysgraphia, dyslexia*.

dyslexia A general term for disorders involving a failure to learn to read, or specific difficulties in the interpretations of words or letters, despite adequate general *intelligence*. Dyslexic problems may take many forms, and there are a number of theories as to origins, and various therapies. See also *developmental dyslexia, phonological dyslexia, phonological mediation*.

dyspraxia An impairment in the ability to perform deliberate actions. See also *orofacial dyspraxia*.

E

eardrum The part of the ear that forms a barrier between the outer ear and the middle ear. The ear drum, or tympanic membrane, is a taut membrane that vibrates in response to sound. These vibrations are transmitted to the middle ear, where they are amplified, and then passed on to the *cochlea* for transduction into electrical impulses.

eating disorders A general term for disturbed behaviour involving food. Such disorders include *anorexia nervosa* and *bulimia*.

EBA See *extrastriate body area*.

Ebbinghaus, Hermann (1850–1909)

Hermann Ebbinghaus is famous for pioneering the systematic study of *memory*, and for establishing rigorous laboratory methods to ensure *standardisation* of both subject matter and research procedures. He did this by using lists of nonsense syllables (consonant-vowel-consonant groups with minimal prior meaning) and carefully *standardised procedures*, and identified a number of consistent memory processes, such as the four Rs (recall, recognition, redintegration and relearning savings), which described different degrees of remembering. Although not the first, he is often credited with being one of the most influential of the early experimental psychologists, partly because of his vigorous defence of the experimental approach.

---

echoic memory A very brief form of immediate or *short-term memory* for sound information, which fades quickly. We may, for instance, be reading or concentrating on something else, and only become aware that the doorbell has rung because of the brief echoic memory it has left behind.

echolalia The repetition of the last heard item of speech, sometimes exactly and sometimes with what appears to the listener to be a mocking intonation. It is sometimes, though not always, a symptom of an underlying psychiatric disorder such as *schizophrenia*. See also *echopraxia, mirroring*.

echopraxia The automatic and often uncontrollable copying of other people's actions or movements, sometimes, though not always, a symptom of an underlying psychiatric disorder such as *schizophrenia*. See also *postural echo, mirroring*.

Ecological Momentary Assessment (EMA) A form of *diary method* that involves sampling what the person is doing in their everyday lives at random moments throughout the day. It has four distinct characteristics: (i) events or phenomena are recorded as they occur; (ii) the recordings depend on careful, usually randomised timing; (iii) the recordings will often involve repeated events, which can be usefully compared; and (iv) they are made in the person's own environment. See also *Experience Sampling Method, ambulatory assessment.*

ecological perception The approach to perception proposed by J.J. Gibson, who argued that it is not possible to understand perceptual processes outside the context of the individual's active engagement with the physical world. When that context is taken into account, many of the problematic aspects of visual perception disappear. For example, many visual illusions are based on 'snapshots' of a scene or image, and result in hypothesising about the likely implications of the visual stimulus. In the real world, however, perceivers move around, and so other aspects of perception such as *gradient of texture, superposition* and *motion parallax* become relevant, and the apparent illusion disappears. Gibson argued that perception does not involve hypothesising when it is studied in its ecological context rather than as a decontextualised phenomenon. See also *direct perception.*

ecological validity *Validity* is concerned with the question of whether a given psychological technique really assesses that which it purports to measure. Ecological validity is, as its name suggests, concerned with whether a given technique truly corresponds to its equivalent in an everyday, 'natural' setting. The issue centres around whether artificially controlled laboratory simulations of human situations can really be considered to be equivalent to the behaviour that human beings display during the course of their everyday lives, given what we know about *demand characteristics* and *self-fulfilling prophecies.* For example, it is questionable whether minimal group studies of *social identification* are really examples of the same psychological processes as are produced by belonging to a given ethnic or occupational group, since these are highly confined and restricted laboratory studies that deliberately exclude all the complexities of social life. The term is particularly associated with J.J. Gibson's approach to studying perception in realistic settings. See *ecological perception.*

ecology The study of the interaction of organisms and environments.

ECT See *electroconvulsive therapy.*

edema See *oedema.*

educable mentally retarded An American term corresponding to the obsolete British category of *educationally subnormal,* and implying a delayed mental development such that the child cannot cope with normal schooling, but is still educable if special help is provided. Specifically, the category is applied to children with an IQ between 50 and 69. Below 50, the American term is 'trainable mentally retarded'. See also *mental handicap.*

educational psychology One of the major professions of psychologists. In the UK, practitioners are employed within the educational system to deal with psychological issues concerning children in school, and to assess and monitor the progress of children with special needs. They are usually based in School Psychological Services or Child Guidance Clinics. In some areas, the work is largely taken up with assessing children who are having difficulties in school, and making recommendations about which kind of educational setting they need. Other areas have been able to develop much more varied work, ranging from therapy with individual children and their families, through curriculum development and teacher training, to consulting with the school on more effective management structures. Training courses usually last for three years and award a doctorate, but require the applicant to have a good psychology degree, training as a teacher and two years of teaching experience before starting the course.

educationally subnormal (ESN) A classification for children who are unable to cope with normal schooling. A Government Act in 1981 ruled out the use of all of the terms which had been set up to label children with mental or physical handicaps, so these terms are now obsolete. When a child has 'special needs' a report is prepared by an *educational psychologist* which defines the strengths of the child and the areas in which special help will be required. It is hoped that this will prevent children experiencing *labelling* which inevitably becomes derogatory and difficult to remove.

EEG The *electroencephalogram*, which is a recording of changes in the overall electrical activity of the brain. EEGs are taken by attaching several electrodes to different parts of the scalp, and using these to detect neural activity in the different regions of the brain. A *polygraph* converts these fluctuations into a written record and/or sends them for computer analysis, so that particular patterns of activity or responses to specific stimuli can be identified. Specific frequencies (*alpha*, *beta* and *delta waves*) are reliably associated with different mental states, and patterns of EEG response can be used to identify a disposition to fits (seizures) and other forms of brain dysfunction or *levels of sleep* (see Figure 19). See also *error-related negativity*.

effect

(i)   When used as a noun, an effect is a result or outcome (e.g. 'the effect of his or her action').

(ii) When used as a verb, it means to bring about a consequence (e.g. 'I may effect a change in your understanding'). This is an entirely different meaning from 'affect', and students need to be careful not to confuse the two, as the entire meaning of a sentence may be changed by such a mistake.

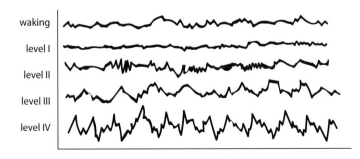

Figure 19 EEG patterns in sleep

For more detail, see *affect*.

effect size The extent to which a particular variable being investigated has produced a result. In studies with human beings, because of the complex range of factors that are always involved, effect sizes are rarely large, but even small ones can be *statistically significant*.

efference copy A representation or copy of a motor signal that is used to predict the sensory consequences of an action. For example, the reason why we are unable to tickle ourselves is that the efference copy of the action is sent to the *sensory projection area*, so we know what to expect and therefore the unpredictability in the stimulation is lost.

efferent neurone See *motor neurone*.

effort after meaning A term used by Bartlett to describe the ways in which individuals attempt to organise their memories, and to make sense of them, if necessary altering the content of the specific information in order to do so.

efMRI See *event-related functional magnetic resonance imaging*.

ego In Freudian theory, the part of the personality structure that deals with external reality and balances pressures of the *id* and *superego*. Literally, the word means 'I', and its more general use is to refer to the sense of *identity* or self.

ego-defence mechanisms See *defence mechanism*.

ego-ideal The image an individual holds of the person they would like to be. Also known as the *ideal self-image*.

ego-state A term from *transactional analysis* that describes the basic structures of feelings which lead to a person adopting particular ways of relating to someone during an interaction. At any one time, a person may be relating as a parent, an adult or a child.

egocentric coding Visual coding that is entirely dependent on the person's individual perspective, by comparison with *allocentric coding*.

egocentric heuristic A strategy commonly used when listening to others, in which what is said is interpreted entirely with respect to *idiosyncratic*, personal knowledge rather than with respect to knowledge that is held in common with the speaker.

egocentric space The map of the immediate (or distal) environment that is coded entirely in respect to the person's awareness of the position of their body.

egocentric speech Speech that is simply involved in monitoring and directing the child's internal thought processes and has no communicative function. According to Piaget, this is a significant part of the child's acquisition of speech. It forms a valuable tool of thought, with which the child performs mental *operations* on the external world.

egocentricity or egocentrism A central concept in Piagetian theory, egocentricity refers to the idea that children take their own perspective as central, assuming that other people have the same understandings, motives and needs as themselves. It is not a moralistic concept, and has nothing in common with selfishness or *egotism*, but instead is concerned with the child's perception of *association* and *causality*. The process by which the child gradually comes to differentiate itself from the external world, through the development of the *body-schema*, to recognise that objects have permanent existence, and to be able to achieve *decentration* and see things from another's viewpoint are, for Piaget, significant milestones in the reduction of egocentricity. When used of adults, the term has implications of selfishness, although perhaps it should just imply a delayed cognitive development.

egoism A tendency to give an excessively high priority to one's own needs and wishes, and a correspondingly low priority to those of other people. For a comparison, see *egotism*.

egotism A consistent tendency to overvalue oneself, and therefore to undervalue other people. It differs from egoism in that egotists tend not to be interested in other people, whereas egoists need a good understanding of others in order to exploit them. Egotistical attitudes tend to be clearly displayed, whereas egoism may need to be concealed to be effective. See also *Dark Triad*.

eidetic imagery Commonly referred to as photographic memory, eidetic imagery is memory that has been encoded by means of a particularly detailed visual image, such that the individual is sometimes able to identify details from the image which are unlikely to have been noticed on first exposure. Eidetic imagery is relatively common in children, occurring in about 10 per cent of cases, but tends to disappear around late adolescence, and is rare in adults. See also *iconic representation*.

eigenvalue A quantity calculated in multivariate statistics, which indicates the contribution of one factor, or independent variable, to the variance of the dependent variable.

Einstellung A term coined by the Gestalt school of psychology to refer to *mental sets* that influence problem-solving

by inducing a rigidity of thought. This then precludes the perception of alternative strategies or solutions.

elaborated code A term used by Bernstein to refer to the form of language commonly used by middle-class families, characterised by an extensive use of nouns, explanations and synonyms. Bernstein's use of the term 'code' is contentious, as are many other parts of his theory. This is mainly due to the theory having been associated with the *verbal deprivation hypothesis* of class differences in language use, which argues that restricted language use implies restricted cognitive possibilities. See also *codes of language, restricted code*.

elaboration In cognition, the addition of information to a representation or *schema* that already exists in the cognitive system. This may involve incorporating new information (through *assimilation* or *accommodation*) or relating the representation to other stored information. See also *elaborative inference*.

elaboration mnemonics Ways of storing information by deliberately expanding each item of information to be stored. This is done by exploring relevant related information and adding details, or working to transform the information in some other way. Elaboration is thought to work because it encourages cognitive processing of the information. See also *mnemonic, levels of processing*.

elaborative inference This is the adding of detail to an existing memory or cognition by drawing on prior knowledge or theories. See also *elaboration mnemonics*.

Electra complex A term introduced by Jung as a female counterpart of the *Oedipus complex*. Most theorists, including Freud, rejected use of the term. See also *penis envy*.

electrical impulse A short burst of electricity. In most psychological contexts, this refers to the electrical impulse produced by a *neurone* when it is stimulated. See also *all-or-none principle*, *synaptic transmission*.

electrical potential A term often used to refer to the *electrical impulse*, or spike of electrical energy, that is generated by a *neurone* when it fires.

electrical stimulation of the brain (ESB) See *ESB*.

electrocardiogram (ECG) A recording of the electrical discharges that appear on the surface of the body as a result of the activity of the heart. In psychology, the ECG is used mainly as a way of recording the rate at which the heart is beating, as changes in heart rate may indicate the presence and strength of a number of processes such as *stress* and the *orienting reflex*.

electroconvulsive therapy (ECT) A treatment for *endogenous depression* that involves passing an electrical current through the brain, thus simulating a severe epileptic fit. This controversial treatment induces temporary amnesia and often results in the alleviation of some forms of depression. However, there is considerable concern both as to how appropriately it is actually used in the psychiatric context, and with regard to the possibility of long-term damage to memory and concentration.

electrode A device that will pick up or transmit electrical activity wherever it is placed. Normally, it takes the form of a small metal disc, coated with a jelly to improve electrical contact, and fitted to a larger adhesive disc so that it can be securely attached to the skin.

electroencephalogram See *EEG*.

electromyography (EMG) A method for measuring the amount of electrical activity associated with muscle movement.

electroshock therapy (EST) American term for *electroconvulsive therapy*.

EMA See *Ecological Momentary Assessment*.

emblems A category of non-verbal signals identified by Ekman and Friesen, which involves those non-verbal cues which have a direct and culturally understood meaning, and which stand for something. *Gestures* with specific meanings, or uniforms denoting specific *role* functions, are examples of emblems.

embodied cognition The idea that the movement or internal state of the body can be used in cognition. See also *enactive representation*.

embodiment The sense that the self is located within the body.

embryo An organism in the earliest stages of development following conception. In lower species, the animal is called an embryo until hatching or birth. In humans, the period of the embryo extends to two months from conception, by which time different organs are becoming visible, and the term *foetus* is then used until birth.

emergency reaction See *alarm reaction*.

emergent properties Properties or characteristics that appear in groups or complex combinations, and which could not have been predicted from the characteristics of the individual elements which make up that group. One of the chief arguments against *reductionism* as a form of argument concerns its assumption that complex behaviour, whether it be social or individual, can be explained simply by reference to its component parts. This does not take into account the emergent properties that become apparent when elements are combined into a higher-order whole. For instance, it would not have been possible to predict that group decision-making can result in highly polarised decisions simply from looking at the decision-making patterns of individual group members (see *group polarisation*), or to have identified the phenomenon of *groupthink* from research into individual cognitive processes.

EMG See *electromyography*.

emic approaches Approaches to knowledge that address indigenous local phenomena or experiences which are culture-specific rather than universal. See also *etic approaches*.

emotion Subjective feelings that have positive or negative value for the individual. Beyond this statement, the definition must depend on the particular theory of emotion being held. Most current theories regard emotions as a combination of physiological response with a cognitive evaluation of the situation. The idea that emotions are the source of action has become less popular, and in fact the term has only a remote link with any idea of motion, having come into English from the French word *emouvoir*, meaning 'to excite'. Some definitions would reserve the term emotion for fairly intense and fairly brief experiences. It is certainly useful to distinguish emotions from *states* (such as hunger, sexual desire and frustration), which may give rise to emotions, and also from behaviours such as *aggression*, which may indicate the presence of an emotion, but which are not themselves emotions. See also *basic emotions, mood*.

emotion generation A term used to describe a spontaneous emotional reaction to a situation or event.

emotion regulation The use of deliberate strategies to change or adjust emotional or *mood* states, most commonly used to minimise negative emotions. See also *mindfulness*.

emotional disorder A set of disorders in which children show high levels of shyness, *anxiety* and *dependency*. The term is also used more broadly to refer to a wide range of psychological disturbances that involve inappropriate emotional experiences, such as *mania* and *depression*. For this sense, an alternative term is *affective disorder*. See also *conduct disorders, affect*.

emotional intelligence A term used to describe social and emotional sensitivity, which is a combination of complex skills essential for smooth social interaction and maintaining social harmony. Although previously overlooked, they are now considered to be a basic form of *intelligence* in their own right.

emotional stability A more neutral term used to describe the trait of *neuroticism* in the *five-factor theory* of personality.

emotive A description of behaviour as expressing an emotion. Usually, use of the term implies a strong emotion, though the actual emotion may not be identified.

empathy A feeling of emotional understanding and unity with another, such that an emotion felt by one person is experienced to some degree by another who is empathic to them. The term is sometimes used when indicating how much capacity an individual has to be empathic towards others. It is thought to be important for psychotherapists to be empathic. See WEG.

empathy-altruism model The idea that *altruistic behaviour* is motivated by empathic concern for other people.

empirical Such as can be measured. Empirical observations are those that can provide a level of objective data which can be assessed in one form or another. Using the term 'measure' loosely, almost all psychological forms of investigation may be considered to be empirical.

empiricism A philosophical school of thought, highly influential in psychology, which argued that only that which can be directly observed or measured can be meaningfully studied. See *behaviourism*.

enactive representation According to Bruner, this is the first *mode of representation* developed by the young child. Enactive representation involves the storing of information in the form of *kinaesthetic* sensations, such as the way that most adults would recall the sensation of a fairground waltzer or helter-skelter. In the world of the infant, 'muscle memories' would be adequate to cope with most of the information encountered by the child. As the child develops and its world widens, further forms of representation are added to its repertoire, such as *iconic representation* and *symbolic representation*. See also *embodied cognition*.

encoding The processing of information in such a way that it can be represented internally, for memory storage. The term is also used when data are transferred into a standard form such as a computer file. See also *encoding specificity*.

encoding specificity The idea that retrieval from *memory* will depend on the overlap between the information available at the time of *retrieval* and the information stored in the *memory trace*. For example, if someone is trying to remember a sentence such as 'the girl was dancing', then 'music' might form an effective *cue*, which stimulates retrieval, whereas 'coat' probably will not.

encounter group A therapeutic technique devised by Carl Rogers, in which clients are placed in a situation which facilitates openness and honesty about their self-concept and their feelings concerning the others in the group. Once the initial barriers were down, Rogers considered that such a group would provide the emotional support and *unconditional positive regard* needed for each member to deal with their problems and to explore their options for personal growth. See also *client-centred therapy*.

endocrine system This is the general term for a system of glands, distributed throughout the body, which release *hormones* into the bloodstream. The endocrine system is generally involved in the maintenance of specific conditions of the body, such as pregnancy or aroused states, rather than in particular acts or behaviours. The main gland of the endocrine system would appear to be the *pituitary gland*, which is located in the brain and directly connected to the *hypothalamus*. The pituitary sends messages to many of the other glands of the system, and is closely linked to the homeostatic mechanisms of the body. Some of the other glands of the endocrine system are the *pineal gland*, the thyroid and thymus glands, which are involved in growth regulation and immune mechanisms, the *testes*, and the adrenal glands.

endogenous Within the body. Compare *exogenous*.

endogenous depression *Depression* that has come about without any apparent cause, and which persists over an extended period of time. The term implies that the depression originates within the individual, rather than being a response to external circumstances. See also *reactive depression*.

endogenous orienting Attention that has been directed by the aims or goals of the person doing the perceiving. See also *selective attention, exogenous spatial attention*.

endogenous spatial attention Attention directed towards a particular location, which has been directed by personal goals or intentions. See also *exogenous orienting*.

endorphins A group of neurotransmitters, mainly found in the *limbic system*, which were originally termed 'endogenous morphine'. This later became contracted to endorphin, and the group includes the similar *enkephalins*. They are substances with chemical structures closely resembling morphines, produced in the brain in response to demanding exercise, pain, anxiety or fear. It is considered that the feelings of euphoria that often accompany strenuous exercise are produced by the actions of endorphins, and that the similar experience produced by the opiates *heroin* and morphine occurs as a result of their being picked up in *receptor sites* specific to endorphins.

engineering psychology The application of psychology to human–machine interaction. It includes the selection and training of people to operate machines, and advice on the design of machines so that they can be efficiently used by human operators. See also *applied psychology*.

engram An outdated expression, the physical form in which an experience is recorded in memory. See *memory trace*.

enkephalins A specific set of neurotransmitters belonging to the general group of *endorphins* that are produced in response to pain or demanding exercise.

entrapment The process in *decision-making* whereby it becomes difficult to make the decision to get out of a bad situation because too much has already been invested in trying to make it work. The American war in Vietnam was a classic example of entrapment, and carried on for many years even after it was apparent that America could not win. A more mundane example would be that of feeling unable to scrap an old car because of the money that has already been paid out to keep it on the road – the owner feels obliged to try to keep the car on the road, even at additional cost, because otherwise the money that has already been spent is seen as wasted.

environment The total external context in which an individual operates. The concept of environment is usually used to include both physical surroundings, and their characteristics and social contexts and interactions. However, it may be used more specifically to include all the different facets of the physical, but to exclude the social aspects. See also *ecology*.

environmental determinism The view that behaviour, personality or psychological characteristics originate as a direct consequence of individual learning and environmental influences, and are not significantly influenced by *innate* factors.

environmental psychology The study of how the environment influences and channels individual behaviour. Environmental psychology includes the study of such factors as *territoriality* and *personal space*, *ergonomic* design, and the physical attributes of surroundings.

environmentalism The doctrine that all significant determinants of behaviour are to be found in the environment. Strict behaviourism is one version of environmentalism.

EPI The *Eysenck Personality Inventory*, a questionnaire designed to assess people on the two *personality traits* of *extraversion* and neuroticism (see *neurosis*). These were proposed as the two main traits underlying *individual differences* in *personality*, each representing several second-order traits.

epidemiology A research technique in which the distribution of the events or other features under study is plotted in order to identify patterns or regularities. Distributions are usually plotted geographically (e.g. studying whether identified cases of incest are more prevalent in some areas of a city than others). Alternatively, other forms of distribution may be applied (e.g. as in epidemiological studies of the incidence of AIDS in subgroups within the *population*).

epigenetics Changes to the way that a *gene* is expressed which have been driven by the environment. For example, it has been shown that early *abuse* or *neglect* can influence glucocorticoid receptors, such that they respond differently from those in animals or humans who have not experienced early stressors of this type.

epilepsy The most common serious neurological condition, usually symptomatic of an underlying brain disorder. Everyone has a seizure 'threshold' (i.e. a potential to have epileptic seizures, which are unpredictable but transient abnormal electrical discharges in the brain). Seizures can manifest themselves in different ways, depending on which area of the brain is involved. Generalised seizures involve both hemispheres of the brain simultaneously, producing a temporary loss of consciousness, whereas partial seizures begin in a localised area of the brain and may produce few visible symptoms. Epilepsy can be managed by medication, with reasonably high success rates, and in some cases it can be treated by surgery, most commonly the removal of the *temporal lobe* of the brain.

epinephrine The American name for *adrenaline*.

epiphenomenalism The kind of account or theory in which a phenomenon is seen as an *emergent property* of some more fundamental process, and therefore to be studied in terms of the more basic process. An epiphenomenal approach would see mind as being just a direct outcome of brain activity.

episode analysis According to Harré, it is episodes, rather than acts or actions, that should form the basic unit of social analysis, since that is the more meaningful unit in human experience. Harré proposed that episodes could be viewed using a dramaturgical metaphor, which would encourage the researcher to consider social roles, social scripts, non-verbal signals, discourse and social meaning, and many other facets of *social psychology*, providing a more rounded view of what is happening than conventional approaches. See also *ethogenics*.

episodic buffer A passive and rapidly decaying component of *working memory*, which acts as a brief store of integrated information about an event or situation.

episodic memory Memory for specific events, episodes or phenomena. See also *semantic memory*.

epistemology The study of knowledge, and the ways in which what counts as knowledge may vary from one discipline or field to another. For example, a similarly worded question about the family might occur in both sociology and psychology examinations, but different epistemological demands would be applied in the evaluation of the answer. In the sociology examination, the student would be required to consider the relationship of the family to society, while in the psychology examination a consideration of interpersonal processes and roles would be more appropriate. What counts as knowledge in each subject is different, and it is the consideration of such differences that is the subject matter of epistemology. See also *postmodernism*.

EPQ Eysenck Personality Questionnaire. See *Eysenck Personality Inventory (EPI)*.

equal-interval scale A system of measurement in which the difference in value between consecutive units is consistent throughout. For example, in an equal-interval numbering scale, the difference between 30 and 31 is of exactly the same magnitude as the difference between 36,005 and 36,006. Equal-interval scales with a fixed zero are known as ratio scales. Children are introduced to ratio scales from a very early age, as they first learn to count, and adults continue to use them (e.g. in dealing with money). See *levels of measurement*.

equilibration In Piagetian theory, the process by which *schemata* are developed to take account of new information. If new information that is encountered fails to fit into an existing schema, the individual is thrown into a state of cognitive discomfort known as disequilibrium. Through the two processes of *assimilation* and *accommodation*, the schemata are adapted or adjusted such that the new information can be handled and the cognitive balance is restored. This is the process of equilibration.

equilibratory senses The *kinaesthetic* senses based on receptors in the *semicircular canals* of the inner ear, such as the senses of balance and *proprioception*.

equipotentiality The now outdated principle outlined by Lashley after his investigations of the *cerebral cortex*, that those areas termed *association cortex*, concerned with learning and memory, seemed to be equal in their potential to carry out these functions – in other words, that such functions were not localised, but were organised across the whole of the association cortex. See also *Law of Mass Action*.

equity theory The idea, from social exchange theory, that people choose relationships in which they will benefit to about the same extent as they contribute. There is some evidence that if people feel either disadvantaged or over-advantaged in a relationship, they will be dissatisfied.

ergonomics The study of the relationship between energy expenditure and work. As such, ergonomics includes the study of design and physiological limitations, and of other factors influencing efficiency in both mechanical and human–machine systems.

Erikson, Erik (1902–1994)

Erik Erikson was a developmental psychoanalyst most widely known for coining the term 'identity crisis', and for his lifelong development theory. Developed at a time when much psychoanalytical theory focused only on childhood, Erikson's assertion that psychological development continued throughout adulthood and even into old age was radical, and resulted in his influence extending into mainstream psychology, as well as within the psychoanalytic world. His idea was that each stage of life required the resolution of certain psychological conflicts, and the way that these were resolved formed the foundation of how that person went about resolving later ones. See also *psychosocial stages*.

ERP See *event-related potential*.

error bars Ways of indicating how much variation is associated with any given point on a graph. Error bars form the 'whiskers' on a *box whisker* or *box-plot diagram*.

error-related negativity A distinctive pattern in *EEG* recordings that shows up when an error is made.

error variation The amount of variation that occurs within the groups in an *analysis of variance* (ANOVA) calculation.

ESB The usual abbreviation for a form of direct electrical stimulation of the brain that appears to function as a powerful reinforcer of behaviour, and to give highly pleasurable sensations. Experiments conducted in the 1960s seemed to imply that there was a direct *pleasure centre* in a particular region of the *hypothalamus*. Stimulation of this area in rats, given as a reward for lever-pressing, produced an extremely high response rate, and in terminally ill cancer patients produced reports of feeling 'wonderful' or 'happy' (Campbell, 1973). It was thought that this might be the root of all motivational states.

However, the 'pleasure centre' concept presents some difficulties. For instance, unlike other forms of learning, it extinguishes very quickly. The effect is also not linked to one particular location in the brain: animal studies show that self-stimulation can occur from electrodes implanted in the *amygdala*, the *lateral hypothalamus* and the *orbitofrontal cortex*, and appears to tap into a wider *reward pathway* in the brain.

ESM See *Experience Sampling Method*.

ESN See *educationally subnormal*.

ESP See *extrasensory perception*.

EST See *electroshock therapy*.

esteem needs One level of the *hierarchy of human needs* proposed by Maslow. Esteem needs include the need for achievement and social recognition, and are considered to achieve importance once *physiological*, *safety* and *social needs* have been met. See also *self-esteem*.

esthetic See *aesthetics*.

ethical Concerned with rights and wrongs. Owing to the scope of psychological interests and the potential for psychological damage, ethical issues have become of great importance in modern psychology. They include such aspects of psychological practice as the use of *deception* in experimental work, the investigation of characteristics that are potentially threatening to the *self-concept* (cf. Milgram's work on obedience), the use of animals in research, and questions of confidentiality in professional practice. Professional psychological associations usually have special committees that evaluate and provide guidance on ethical issues.

ethical guidelines A set of rules drawn up by a professional body that set out the principles which should be observed in conducting research. Ethical guidelines are used to inform the work of *ethics committees*, which give permission for research to be carried out. See also *ethical issues*.

ethical issues The set of concerns about the conduct of research and the treatment of research participants that resulted from an increased awareness of the *social responsibility of science* in the later part of the twentieth century. Ethical issues became particularly influential as a reaction to the manipulative and often damaging research conducted from the 1930s to the 1970s, in which participants' rights were often disregarded, and many suffered distress, pain or even lasting damage. See also *ethical guidelines, ethics committee, informed consent, deception, debriefing, confidentiality, double obligation dilemma*.

ethics committee A group of knowledgeable people brought together to evaluate proposed research, in order to ensure that it will conform to the appropriate *ethical guidelines*. Ethics committees became necessary as a reaction to many research projects carried out in the first two-thirds of the twentieth century, which disregarded the rights of, or consequences to, research 'subjects' in the name of 'science'. The growth of the *social responsibility of science* movement from the 1970s onward eventually saw the demise of this attitude, and the acceptance of *ethical issues* in research. However, the complexity of ethical issues and problems such as the *double obligation dilemma* made committee judgements necessary.

ethnocentricity A condition in which the perceptual framework and social assumptions of an individual are entirely bounded by, and defined in terms of, the experience of their own social, ethnic or national group. Ethnocentricity is therefore a form of cognitive (or rather sociocognitive) *set*, which leads to assumptions about one's own group's practices, beliefs or assumptions as setting the standard of 'rightness' or objectivity, and thus leads to undervaluing, or even failing to recognise, alternatives. Probably deriving from mechanisms of *social comparison*, ethnocentricity appears to be a fundamental and extremely common aspect of human thinking. It is clearly recognisable when we are looking at the arguments of those belonging to different social groups, although difficult to recognise when we are looking at our own. Arguably the most powerful benefit of education, travel, contact with others of different backgrounds, etc., is that it can sometimes have the effect of reducing the extent of the individual's ethnocentricity. Regrettably, however, this is not an inevitable consequence of any of these experiences.

ethnography A set of research techniques first developed by anthropologists for the study of other cultures.

It was then taken up by sociologists in studying subcultures within their own societies (e.g. the study by Whyte, 1934) of urban gang culture reported in his book *Street Corner Society*. Because it is difficult to recognise the rules and processes of a culture when you are living in it, the techniques of ethnography are essential for social psychologists who want to analyse how a culture works. The first step is to gather data, usually by observation and interview, but the researcher may join the people being studied in *participant observation*, and may also use other material such as letters and diaries, and cultural products such as magazines and television. A rich description is then created and checked back with well-informed members of the cultural group. Finally, the insider's form of description is converted to a psychological or 'expert' account.

ethnomethodology The study of the common-sense knowledge by which social actors know how to behave. We are usually not fully aware of the knowledge we draw on to operate socially, in which case it is called 'tacit knowledge'. The main research technique used to uncover this tacit knowledge is *conversation analysis*.

ethogenics An approach to social enquiry outlined by Rom Harré in an attempt to identify some of the more meaningful aspects of social interaction. Properly speaking, ethogenics is a philosophy rather than a methodology, but there are two outstanding methodological implications of the ethogenic approach. The first of these is that it is the episode, rather than the act or action, which should constitute the basic unit of social enquiry, since social life is experienced in real life as a succession of meaningful episodes. Harré

suggests that a dramaturgical metaphor may be helpful in *episode analysis*. If an episode is thought of as being similar to an act in a play, then a number of features of the situation become significant in interpreting it – characters, setting, scripts, *non-verbal communication*, prior episodes, plot and so on. Analysis of these different aspects of the episode would therefore link diverse areas of psychological knowledge to provide an insight into what is going on. The second methodological implication of the ethogenic approach is that the accounts which people give of their experiences should be taken to have equal validity to an external 'objective' analysis, since the way in which we perceive and experience social life is just as important in determining social interaction. *Account analysis*, in Harré's model, has two stages, the first being the process of collecting the accounts themselves, and the second consisting of a critical reflection of the meanings contained in those accounts. See also *emergent properties*, *new paradigm research*, *qualitative analysis*.

ethological observation Observing behaviour in the natural environment.

ethology The study of behaviour in the natural environment. Ethological studies of animal behaviour have been conducted throughout the twentieth century, and were systematised by the work of Konrad Lorenz and Niko Tinbergen. More recently, the ethological approach has been applied to the study of human behaviour, most notably in the fields of *mother–infant interaction* and *non-verbal communication*.

etic approaches Approaches or forms of knowledge which are considered to be valid across cultures, aiming to address the universality of traits or characteristics. See also *emic approaches*.

eugenics A set of political beliefs based on the idea that intelligence and personality are fixed inherited characteristics determining role and position in society. Eugenicists believe that breeding should be restricted among those of the 'lower' classes of society, and that those of subnormal intellect or undesirable personality should be sterilised to prevent the spread of such genetic characteristics. Eugenic ideas were widespread in Western Europe and America before the Second World War, mainly as a result of the work of Francis Galton, and formed the basis of the Nazi policy of 'exterminating' those considered to be of inferior racial characteristics. Eugenic laws were also enacted (and in some cases are still current) in several states of the USA, and there are many cases on record of individuals classified as mentally subnormal having been involuntarily sterilised as a result of these laws. In the UK, they were more likely to have been kept in institutions, and so prevented from engaging in procreative sexual activity.

euphoria Extreme happiness; a feeling of being elated or 'high'.

European social psychology A school of thought in social psychology that derived from theories developed by European psychologists, particularly through the 1970s and 1980s. One of the central theories in this approach is that of *social identity theory*, particularly associated with the work of Henri Tajfel (e.g. Tajfel, 1982). Social identity theory is concerned with how people internalise social group membership and interact as representatives of their social group, rather than as individuals. Another core theory in European

social psychology is that of *social representations*, developed by the French psychologist Serge Moscovici (e.g. Moscovici, 1984). This is concerned with the shared beliefs that emerge in society and which serve to legitimise and rationalise social action. A third area of interest is research into social and collective *attributions*, for example in the work of Miles Hewstone (e.g. Hewstone, 1989). European social psychology can therefore be perceived as a body of theory spanning several different levels of explanation in social life. It emerged particularly with the foundation of the *European Journal of Social Psychology* in 1971, and has been proposed as a marked contrast to the largely problem-centred and, some say, reductionist approach represented by much of American social psychology. See also *social attribution*.

evaluation apprehension Also known as 'test anxiety', this is the fear of being assessed or appraised by others, which can distort research results by causing people to act in ways that are different from their usual manner.

event sampling An observational technique in which the occurrence and form of specified events is noted each time they occur. The technique is used for *observational studies* of relatively rare events such as quarrels between children in a playground. See also *time sampling*.

event-based prospective memory A form of *prospective memory* that involves remembering to do something or perform an action when the situation becomes appropriate (e.g. to buy a needed item of stationery when shopping).

event-related design A method of designing the presentation of experimental material in which different stimuli or conditions are intermixed together. See also *block design, order effect.*

event-related functional magnetic resonance imaging (efMRI) A form of *functional magnetic resonance imaging* that compares the patterns of electrical activity resulting from two or more different events (e.g. giving correct or incorrect responses on a memory test).

event-related potential (ERP) The amount of change in the electrical activity of an area of the brain, measured at the scalp, which is linked to the timing of a particular cognitive event or the response to a stimulus. See also *inverse problem.*

evoked potential A measure of brain activity obtained by taking an *EEG* reading at the same time as exposing the individual to some form of stimulation – usually visual. The resulting changes in the EEG record are known as the evoked potential. In practice, the stimulus is usually applied repeatedly and the responses averaged so that the signal can be distinguished from the background noise.

evolution A gradual process of genetic change in which the genetic characteristics of a whole species are altered over many generations, effecting a physical change that serves to adapt the individuals of that species more fully to their environment. Individuals in a species do not change, but owing to the genetic reshuffling that occurs as a result of *sexual reproduction*, or to mutation, each individual varies genetically from its parents. If the variation is one that confers an advantage in terms of the adaptation of the animal to its environment, then that individual is likely to become stronger and healthier, or in

some other way more likely to breed and to pass on its favourable genetic characteristic to its offspring. Gradually, over time, weaker members of the species become less efficient at surviving, and so the 'new' genetic characteristic becomes more widespread in the population. This process is known as natural selection. Over millions of years, this results in the development of whole species that are specialised to their environment.

Although evolutionary arguments are frequently voiced in terms of modern humankind, these are unlikely to have much substance, owing to:

(i)   the relatively few generations involved in 'modern' life styles; and

(ii) the tendency of humankind to modify its environment to suit itself, thus obviating the need to alter the species to suit the environment.

See also *coevolution, sociobiology.*

exchange errors Errors of speech in which words or parts of words swap places.

excitation The process by which a *neurone* is rendered likely to fire. Excitation of neural impulses occurs either through direct stimulation of sensory neurones from sense receptors receiving information from the environment, or through the stimulation of a number of *excitatory synapses* making connections with that particular neurone.

excitation transfer When the arousal caused by one set of stimuli becomes transferred to another (e.g. when the arousal caused by economic anxiety becomes transferred into aggressive behaviour towards out-group members, as in *scapegoat theory*).

excitatory synapse A *synapse* that, when stimulated, renders the neurone receiving the neurotransmitter more liable to generate an *electrical impulse*. Although stimulation from a number of excitatory synapses is usually required to set off the nerve impulse, reception of the appropriate *neurotransmitter* serves to lower the *threshold of response* of the neurone, thus contributing to the eventual production of the impulse.

executive functions Functions that are concerned with bringing together and coordinating information from a range of other sources, usually for the purposes of *decision-making*. A 'central executive' with this type of role is a feature of current models of *working memory*. In *neuropsychology*, the term refers to the control processes needed to coordinate the operation of more specialised areas or components of the brain.

existentialism A philosophical approach which argues that individuals can only be understood in terms of their existence in the world and the choices with which they are faced. Existentialists stress self-determinism rather than environmental or developmental *determinism*, and emphasise the responsibility that each individual has for his or her actions within society, on the grounds that the individual is always free to act differently, to say 'no', and to accept the consequences. Existentialism was extensively propounded by Jean-Paul Sartre, and has been taken up by many psychological theorists. Probably most notable of these was R.D. Laing, who, in *The Divided Self*, proposed an existentialist theory of *schizophrenia*

that directly challenged orthodox psychiatric approaches and stimulated investigation of several alternative forms of therapy in cases of psychological disturbance, such as *family therapy*.

exogenous Outside the person. Compare *endogenous*.

exogenous depression A depression that is believed to have been caused by external events, usually called a *reactive depression*.

exogenous orienting Attention that is externally guided by a stimulus. See also *endogenous orienting*, *selective attention*.

exogenous spatial attention Attention directed towards a particular location, which has been directed by an external stimulus, such as a sudden sound or flash of light. See also *exogenous orienting*.

expectancy effect An improvement appearing to result from therapeutic techniques, but really caused by the fact that the client expected to feel better as a result of the treatment. See also *self-fulfilling prophecy*, YAVIS.

Experience Sampling Method (ESM) A type of *diary method* in which participants are asked to stop and make a note of what they are doing at specific intervals during the course of the day, week or relevant research period.

experiential intelligence The part of Sternberg's *triarchic theory* of intelligence that is concerned with what the individual has learned from their own personal experience.

experiment A form of empirical investigation or study in which variables are manipulated in order to discover cause and effect. An experiment will involve at least one *independent variable*, which will be set up in such a way as to pro-duce changes in a *dependent variable*.

experimental design The process by which an experimental study is organ-ised so as to allow for investigation of the possible effects of the *independent variable* upon the *dependent variable*, with as little contamination as pos-sible by *confounding variables*. See also *counterbalancing*, *experimenter effects*, *matching*.

experimental group A subgroup of the research participants in an experiment who all receive the same version of the experimental condition. When there is only one experimental condition, the experimental group is compared with the *control group*. In more complex designs, there will be several experi-mental groups, each experiencing a different condition.

experimental hypothesis Also known as the alternate or alternative hypoth-esis, this is the prediction that the outcome of an experimental procedure will occur as a result of the variables under investigation. In reality, the experimental hypothesis can never be fully proven; instead, the *null hypothesis* can be refuted with varying degrees of certainty. See also *statistical significance*.

experimental method The use of con-trolled experimental situations to test *hypotheses*. The term is rather vague, largely because there is no agreed defi-nition of what constitutes an *experiment*.

experimental neurosis It is possible to induce apparently neurotic behaviour in laboratory animals by training them to perform a task and then gradually making it impossible. Experimental neurosis was first studied by Pavlov and presented as a basis for controlled study

of *neuroses* in humans. Subsequently, doubts were raised about whether the mental states of the animals were really similar to those of neurotic humans, and the research was abandoned. A similar process occurred more recently with the study of *learned helplessness*.

experimental philosophy The branch of philosophy that, during the eight-eenth and nineteenth centuries, became increasingly concerned with the study of the human mind, and which drew on *empirical* observations for its conclusions. Experimental philosophy became transmuted into psychology towards the end of the nineteenth century. The 'founding fathers' of psychology, Wilhelm Wundt, Herman Ebbinghaus and William James, were simultaneously the last of the experi-mental philosophers.

experimental psychology Those bran-ches of psychology that are firmly based in laboratory experimentation. The term was used to cover such areas as learning, memory and perception, but it has now been largely replaced by the wider area of *cognitive psychology*.

experimenter effects Experimental problems producing a biased result brought about by the influence of an experimenter (e.g. through research par-ticipants responding to the person who conducts the experiment). Experimenter effects may occur indirectly, because of the personal characteristics of the exper-imenter (e.g. their age, sex or other such feature), or directly, as a result of the beliefs or unconscious bias being trans-mitted to the research participants, and producing a *self-fulfilling prophecy*. The latter is usually controlled by using the *double-blind control* technique. See also *demand characteristics*.

expert systems *Artificial intelligence* systems which are designed to carry out tasks of organising information in ways that support human decision-making.

expertise A high level of competence produced by a considerable amount of practice, and resulting in extremely skilled knowledge and/or behaviour.

explicit memory Memory that involves the conscious *retrieval* of information. See also *explicit memory bias*, *declarative memory*.

explicit memory bias The tendency of explicit memory to retrieve more negative information than positive or neutral information. See also *impact bias*, *implicit memory bias*.

exploration Activity undertaken in order to gain information. Vigorous exploratory behaviour is characteristic of the young of many species, and is often studied in conjunction with play. Daniel Berlyne proposed a major distinction between diversive exploration, in which the environment is investigated to identify sources of possible interest, and specific exploration, in which attention is focused on a specific object or phenomenon. Specific exploration is usually more systematic in investigating the properties of the object. Some research has investigated which properties of objects are most likely to elicit exploration, but a major reason for being interested in exploration is that it appears to originate largely within the child or animal. It is therefore a potential source of self-motivated *learning*.

exposure therapy A general term for treatments of *phobias* or *anxiety disorders* that deal with the problem by exposing the person to the relevant stimulus, either gradually as in *systematic desensitisation*, or in a concentrated episode as in *implosion therapy*.

expressed emotion Emotion that is apparent to an observer by being shown in facial expression, posture, gesture or other *non-verbal cues*. Expressed emotion is often genuine, but can be simulated such that it does not reflect an underlying emotional state.

extended cognition The use of technology of various kinds to amplify cognitive capacity (e.g. the use of print for storing knowledge, or computing to increase the capacity for calculation).

external attributions See *internal attributions*.

external locus of control An aspect of *locus of control* which refers to a belief that control of events, or more specifically of *reinforcements*, is outside the person. See also *internal locus of control*.

extinction

(i) A term used in both *classical* and *operant conditioning* to refer to the dying out of a response as a result of lack of reinforcement. In *behaviour therapy*, learned associations, such as phobias, are treated by procedures designed to effect extinction of the stimulus–response connection, by organising circumstances in such a way that it will not be reinforced (see Figure 20). See also *spontaneous recovery*.

(ii) In neurological contexts, this term is sometimes used to describe an outcome of damage to the parietal lobe that produces lack of awareness of a stimulus in the presence of competing stimuli.

For example, if a stimulus is presented to either the right or the left side of the area being fixated on, the person will perceive its presence. But if two stimuli are presented simultaneously, one to the left and one to the right of fixation, someone with a parietal lesion may only perceive one and be completely unaware of the presence of the other. See also *neglect*.

extraneous variables Additional influences or factors that can affect research results, and which cannot be or have not been completely controlled by the research design (e.g. the state of the weather, or the participant's family interactions prior to the study).

extrapyramidal system A linking pathway between the *cerebellum* and the *basal ganglia* that connects a set of brain structures involved in the control of movement.

extrasensory perception (ESP) Perception that does not depend on the usual sensory processes. ESP is one of the class of paranormal phenomena and, in common with other forms, evidence that it actually happens is contentious. There is also the rather odd scientific status that if it could be explained in terms of known laws, it would cease to qualify for the title. See also *parapsychology*, *telepathy*.

extrastriate body area (EBA) An area of the *visual cortex* that responds more to whole bodies and body parts than to faces or objects.

extraversion A term originally coined by C.G. Jung to describe individuals who are outward-directed and sociable in their behaviour. Extraversion as a personality trait was adopted as one of the main personality dimensions by Eysenck in his two-factor model of *personality*, in which he included such second-order factors as risk-taking, impulsiveness and *sociability*. See also *EPI*.

extrinsic External, or deriving from sources outside the individual or situation. Contrast with *intrinsic*.

extrinsic motivation *Motivation* that comes from outside the person, such as working to receive gifts or payments. Extrinsic motivation is generally regarded as less desirable than *intrinsic motivation* because the performance is

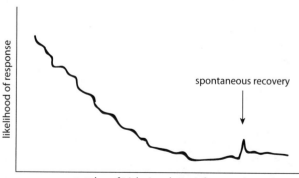

Figure 20 The extinction of a learned response

likely to stop rather quickly as soon as the motivator is withdrawn. However, Allport believed that a process he called the 'functional autonomy of motives' operated, so that eventually an extrinsically motivated behaviour becomes valued for its own sake.

eye contact Mutual gaze, or the amount of time that two people spend looking at each other simultaneously. Eye contact is sometimes taken as an indicator of intimacy; eye contact with unknown individuals tends to be avoided. Prolonged eye contact with neutral or hostile facial expression is taken as a threat gesture, and tends to be responded to by either aggressive or avoidance behaviour. It is a powerful signal in all primates, including human beings.

eyeball test The process of visually examining a data set, usually when the raw data have been reduced to a manageable form by some kind of processing. While the process is open to bias, and cannot lead to statistical conclusions, it does make use of human capacities to identify patterns, including those that are unexpected. Such patterns might be missed by more formal techniques of analysis that specify in advance what comparisons should be made. An eyeball test may also detect artefacts and gross errors in the data. It is therefore useful in checking that the data are not badly corrupted (see GIGO), and in choosing which *statistical tests* will be most appropriate.

eyeblink response This term is commonly used in two contexts:

(i) To describe the tendency to blink more rapidly when under stress or in conditions of anxiety, which means that it has been used as an indicator of lying. See also *polygraph*.

(ii) To describe a *reflex* reaction to a puff of air at the corner of the eye. This reflex is easy to condition, and has been used in many *classical conditioning* experiments. Research using this form of conditioning has indicated the involvement of both the *cerebellum* and the *hippocampus* in the formation of *memory*.

eyeblink startle response A blink that has been elicited by a sudden and unexpected simulus such as a loud bang. See also *eyeblink response*.

eyebrow flash A recognition signal that consists of rapidly raising the eyebrows as a greeting to the individual who is recognised. The eyebrow flash seems to be common to all human cultures, and to some other species. It is therefore considered to be *innate*.

eyewitness testimony Evidence given in court by witnesses to an event or crime. This is a major area of research in psychology, largely owing to research led by Elizabeth Loftus, who showed how vulnerable such testimony is to external influences such as the phrasing of questions or other forms of suggestion. Research into eyewitness testimony draws on theories and research into *perception*, *memory* and *thinking*. See also *own-age bias*, *misinformation effect*, *false memory*.

Eysenck Personality Inventory (EPI) A *personality assessment* created by Hans Eysenck. The EPI presents a rating scale from which the dimensions of introversion–extraversion and neuroticism–stability can be measured. A later version, called the Eysenck Personality Questionnaire (EPQ), also aims to measure *psychoticism*. See also *five-factor theory*, *Dark Triad*.

Eysenck, Hans Jurgen (1916–1997)

One of the most controversial figures in psychology, Eysenck studied psychology under Cyril Burt, whose belief in inherited *intelligence* was absolute. Eysenck adopted a similar position, from which he vigorously joined in the *nature–nurture* debates of post-war psychology. His work at the Maudsley hospital in London generated an interest in *personality*, which he also saw in terms of fixed, inherited traits, and in conditioning processes. Despite obtaining his data mainly through self-report questionnaires such as the *Eysenck Personality Inventory* (EPI), and despite his nativist stance, Eysenck identified himself as a *behaviourist*. Perhaps the most valuable manifestations of this identification were his many challenges to *psychoanalysis*, which began in the 1950s and continued through to the 1980s.

F

5-hydroxytryptamine See *serotonin*.

F ratio The statistic obtained when one measure of the *variance* of a set of scores is divided by a second measure of variance. When the *degrees of freedom* of the two sources of variance are known, tables can be used to judge the probability that the ratio could have arisen by chance. The main use of F ratios is in *analysis of variance*. Another use you may encounter is because the *t-test* relies on the two groups being compared having been drawn from populations with the same variance. You can test this assumption by dividing the smaller variance by the larger and checking the tables to see whether the ratio is *significantly* greater than 1 (which is what it will be if the two variances are identical). Note that whether or not your two groups have different means, finding that one has a significantly higher variance than the other may be important in its own right. For example, imagine two teaching techniques that produce the same average result for a group of students but the first has much lower variance than the second. You would use the first method for training in which it is essential to minimise mistakes, but the second if you were hoping to produce a few students with exceptional abilities.

F scale A measure of authoritarianism developed by Adorno as part of his *authoritarian personality* theory. It measured authoritarianism through nine sub-traits: (i) conventionalism; (ii) authoritarian submissiveness; (iii) authoritarian aggression (hostility towards those who challenge authority); (iv) anti-intraception (a tough-minded punitive approach); (v) superstition and stereotype (a belief that events are externally controlled rather than controllable by the individual); (vi) power and 'toughness' (a tendency to behave in a dominating manner); (vii) destructiveness and cynicism; (viii) projectivity (a tendency to project unconscious impulses onto others); and (ix) sex (an exaggerated concern with sexual misbehaviour). See also *prejudice*.

face

(i) The front part of the head, important in *non-verbal communication*.

(ii) A concept of self-esteem and respect, particularly important in Asian interaction, in which competition is seen as less imortant than a resolution to a deal or agreement that allows both parties to gain esteem and maintain 'face' during and as a result of the transaction. See also *unconditional respect for persons*.

face inversion effect The finding that faces are much harder to recognise when seen upside-down, whereas other objects are relatively easy to identify.

face recognition The way that we identify familiar faces as belonging to people that we know. A major model in this area was proposed by Bruce and Young (1986), who proposed that face recognition is a distinct cognitive skill, and that the brain has specific *face recognition units*, which come into play when we encounter people that we have met before. Lesions to or deficits in these units can produce prospagnosia. See also *other-race effect*, *Capgras syndrome*.

face recognition unit (FRU) Neural units proposed by Bruce and Young (1986) in their model of face recognition, which contain stored knowledge of familiar faces, including their three-dimensional structure. An alternative model based on neurological research (Haxby *et al.*, 2000) suggests that these neural units might not exist as independent entities, but that the *superior temporal sulcus* processes the dynamic aspects of faces while the *fusiform face area* is involved in recognising familiar faces. Other parts of the brain may also contribute input to face perception. See also *person identity node*.

face validity An assessment of the *validity* of a test obtained by inspecting the items and judging whether they are likely to generate a measure of the phenomenon that you want the test score to measure. It is entirely possible for a test with good face validity to be a poor measure, and for one with low face validity to be effective. But it can still be a useful preliminary indication.

facial affect programme A strategy for inducing behavioural change by making the individual aware of the sensations arising from facial expressions that are different from those which they use habitually. It is thought that encouraging the continued use of positive facial expressions will provide positive *feedback* both through social interaction and through muscular interpretation. See also *facial feedback hypothesis*.

facial electromyography A technique for measuring the degree of tension in facial muscles by recording the electrical discharges of the muscles. The aim is to obtain a systematic and objective measure of facial expression by mapping the muscle tensions occurring in different expressions.

facial expression Characteristic patterns of arrangements of the muscles in the face, which provide important *non-verbal cues* in social interaction. Facial expression may be used either to express understanding, attitudes and emotions, or as specific cultural signals with clearly defined meanings. Some researchers have found that basic emotional expressions seem to be common to all human cultures, and are also found in blind babies, which would seem to imply that they are innate. However, other facial expressions show cultural variability, and seem to be acquired through social interaction.

facial feedback hypothesis The idea that our experience of *emotion* arises at least in part from our interpretations of the arrangement of our facial muscles. The effect is used in studies of mood when people are asked to make, say, a depressed face as part of a procedure for changing their mood, through muscular feedback.

facilitator A person whose role in a therapy or research group is to help the process go in the right direction. It is used to describe the person running a group, in order to avoid using a label such as 'leader' or 'trainer', which would imply that they are controlling the process – even if they are, really.

factor analysis A statistical technique much loved by psychometricians, which involves the analysis of large and complicated sets of data in such a way as to draw out the underlying pattern of correlations. Groups of measures that all intercorrelate are identified as a 'factor', and the researcher can then examine the measures to see what they all have in common, and then speculate about the cause of or reason for the grouping. The technique requires a large amount of calculation, usually undertaken by computer. It also requires an ability to interpret the results provided.

factors Variables that can affect the item being researched. In a *factor analysis*, each grouping of variables is called a factor. See also *independent variable, confounding variable*.

failure to thrive (FTT) A condition of poor growth in infants, usually defined as being in the bottom 3 per cent for that age, sex and population. In some cases, there is a physiological problem that accounts for the poor growth, but in the majority of cases there is no organic cause and the condition is called 'non-organic failure to thrive'. FTT was once believed to be a direct result of emotional deprivation, and in its extreme form was called 'deprivational dwarfism'. It is now widely recognised that the basic problem is that the child does not receive enough food to sustain appropriate growth, although this in turn is likely to result from emotional or other difficulties of the parent, the child, or both. See also *child abuse*.

fallacy A false assertion used as the basis for a sequence of logical argument, or for a belief.

false belief task A research procedure used in order to identify the presence or otherwise of a *theory of mind* (TOM). In a typical false belief task, Child A watches while Child B hides an object.

Child B then goes out of the room, and Child A continues to watch while the researcher moves the object to a different hiding place. Child A is then asked where Child B will look for the object when they return. Children who have developed a theory of mind will recognise that Child B is unaware of the researcher's activities, and will therefore look in the original hiding place. Those without a theory of mind, such as very young or *autistic* children, will predict that Child B will look in the place where the object really is. See also *mindblindness*.

false consensus effect The tendency to assume that one's own attitudes or actions are typical of most people (i.e. to overestimate their frequency in the general population).

False Discovery Rate (FDR) A technique for correcting *statistical* comparisons that is based on a threshold developed from a number of random data sets. It has the effect of producing a more conservative estimate than might be observed without this correction. It is commonly used to allow for the random activity of neurones in research based on *brain scanning*.

false memory A memory that feels real to the individual experiencing it, but has arisen as a result of suggestion or other factors distorting the information which was originally stored. See also *eyewitness testimony*.

falsifiability The idea that a scientific prediction can be shown to be untrue by empirical investigation. Karl Popper argued that falsifiability lies at the heart of scientific research, and conventional experimental design is based on this principle. See also *hypothetico-deductive method*.

family therapy An approach to psychological treatment in which the whole family is the focus, rather than an individual patient. Early approaches were derived from *psychoanalysis* and treated the family as if it had psychological processes similar to those of individuals. Recently, methods have been developed from *systems theory* which recognise that, while the behaviour of a component may seem strange when it is seen in isolation, it will make much more sense in the context of the complete system. Applied to individuals, and recognising that families are one of the most significant systems within which most people function, this approach has led to a new way of looking at psychological disturbance. It assumes that in many cases, the 'symptoms' shown by an individual are a meaningful response to their circumstances. More specifically, disturbed behaviour is likely to be an attempt to regulate relationships, or solve problems, within the family. The literature contains many examples of spectacular success using 'systemic family therapy', but there has been little systematic evaluation of the techniques. See also *Leeds Attributional Coding System*.

Family Wise Error (FWE) A statistical technique used to correct for errors in statistical comparisons. It is based on the number of tests which have been conducted, and assumes that sufficient tests will show a smoothness in their collated outcomes, as a result of the summation of random processes.

fantasy The conscious mental construction of images of events or objects. It is generally a pleasurable activity that may indicate psychological health, and may be useful in creatively exploring possible courses of action. The content of fantasy, like that of dreams, may reflect major unresolved conflicts, and an excessive investment in fantasy indicates the existence of psychological problems. See also *daydreaming*.

FAS test A test of verbal fluency in which people are asked to generate as many words beginning with F as they can, in a limited period of time. It is sometimes used to detect people with lesions in the left lateral area of the *prefrontal cortex*, who often show particular impairment in this task.

fatigue effect An experimental effect brought about by the subject's being tired, bored or otherwise affected by the duration of the experimental procedure. It can contaminate experimental results because it may appear that people are less good at later tasks when in fact they are just getting tired. See also *counterbalancing, order effect*.

FBA See *fusiform body area*.

FDR See *False Discovery Rate*.

feature detection theory The idea that we recognise objects by comparing them with a stored 'list' of distinctive features. See also *pandemonium model*.

Fechner's law A principle in *psychophysics* which states that the sensation experienced by an individual increases as a logarithmic function of the stimulus intensity. In other words, the physical increase in stimulation required for a perceived increase in intensity is not constant, but is systematically greater for higher intensities. For example, switching a light on may be perceived as a substantial increase in brightness when the room was previously dark, but may be hardly noticeable during bright sunlight. See also *absolute threshold, just noticeable difference, relative threshold, Weber's law*.

feedback Information that enlightens the individual about the effect or outcome of a course of behaviour which has been enacted by that person, thus allowing a sequence of actions or behaviour to be modified if necessary or desirable. See also *biofeedback*, *negative feedback*.

FEF See *frontal eye field*.

feminist research A term used for research that aims to be compatible with, and to advance, feminist concerns. Some feminists insist that the term also implies a specific kind of methodology, which rejects rigid, *positivistic* assumptions and is more reflexive and respectful of its sources. Others do not see this as a necessary characteristic of feminist research as such, but see its focus as providing a counter to implicit patriarchal assumptions in traditional research. See also *deconstruction*.   .

Festinger, Leon (1919–1989)

Leon Festinger is perhaps most famous for his theory of *cognitive dissonance*, which showed how people will reduce the tension arising from incompatible beliefs and actions by changing beliefs that contradict behaviour, rather than changing behaviour to fit in with beliefs. Festinger also developed *social comparison* theory, which formed an important backdrop to Tajfel's later development of *social identity theory*, and also identified the importance of propinquity (i.e. physical closeness) in the formation of relationships. His emphasis on real-world research was developed as an outcome of studying under the social psychologist Kurt Lewin.

field dependence/independence An aspect of cognitive style concerned with whether a person is dominated by context when making judgements (field dependence), or whether they can ignore distracting contextual information (field independence). It may be tested by the accuracy with which a person can judge the orientation of a line when it is surrounded by a frame at a different angle, or when the person is in a chair that can be tilted away from the vertical. Large *individual differences* have been found that seem to relate to other areas of cognitive functioning.

field experiment Experiments conducted in the *real-world* environment but involving some experimental manipulation of the natural setting.

field study Research carried out in the natural setting in order to achieve *ecological validity*. A field study may involve simple observation, *participant observation*, or may be a *field experiment*.

fight or flight response See *alarm reaction*.

figuration A form of *objectification* in which the idea becomes attached to a specific image or concrete item (e.g. the way in which the concept of 'green' has become used to represent ecological activities of various types). See also *social representations*.

figurative language Language that involves imagery, *metaphor* or idiom, and is not expected to be taken literally.

figure-ground organisation The tendency of our *visual perception* to organise incoming information (which arrives in the form of light waves of varying intensities and wavelengths) into meaningful units or figures set against a background (see Figure 21). Figure-ground organisation was intensively studied by the Gestalt psychologists, who identified several principles of perceptual organisation that served to make up figure-ground discrimination. These were collectively known as the *Law of Prägnanz*, and included the *principle of closure*, and the principle of 'good Gestalt'.

figure-ground perception This is a general term used to refer to those aspects of perception that derive from *figure-ground organisation*. For instance, it would include areas such as *pattern perception*, which is dependent on the organisation of visual information into figures against backgrounds.

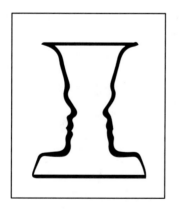

Figure 21 Figure-ground organisation

file-drawer problem The recognition that the criteria used by journals, and the profession of research psychology generally, might result in bias in reporting research findings. Specifically, dozens of researchers could have attempted *replication* of an important finding, each one discovering that their research failed to produce the same results. Knowing that journals do not generally publish negative findings, most of the researchers will not write the research up, and the others may find their paper rejected by the journal. So all the negative findings end up in filing cabinet drawers while the original report remains unchallenged. Newer techniques of *meta-analysis* attempt to judge whether a file-drawer bias might be significant.

filial imprinting See *imprinting*.

filter models Theoretical models of plausible cognitive mechanisms. The best-known filter models were put forward to explain the process of *selective attention* by psychologists such as Broadbent, Triesman and Deutsch. Each of these represented a more or less complex attempt to explain how incoming information is channelled such that only a selected part of it is received, rather than the overwhelming whole (see Figure 22).

first-order intentionality A degree of *intentional stance* which makes the inference that the individual acting has beliefs and desires, and is acting accordingly. See also *second-order intentionality*.

fissure A deep groove or channel. In psychology, this generally refers to the grooves on the surface of the brain. See also *cerebral cortex*.

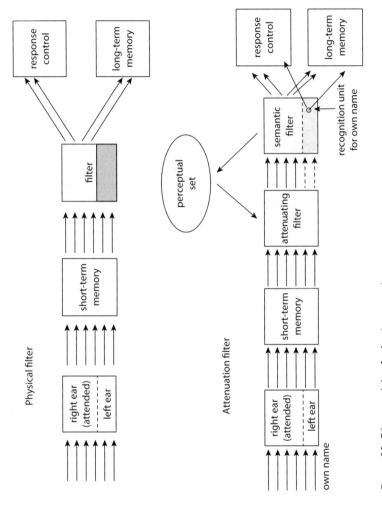

Figure 22 Filter models of selective attention

fit

(i) Statistically, how specific data match up to general sets, or to *measures of central tendency*.

(ii) In evolutionary terms, fitness refers to how well an organism is adapted to its environment.

(iii) In everyday use, the term has two meanings: whether a person or animal is generally healthy and able to engage in demanding physical activity, or how well something conforms to another.

five-factor theory The five-factor model of personality, also known as the Big Five, reflects the major personality traits measured by psychometric tests. It was first developed in response to the proliferation of personality traits being measured by numerous tests. Factor analysis showed that responses to these traits clustered around five major groups, reflecting higher-order factors which were named *extraversion, neuroticism, conscientiousness, agreeableness,* and *openness to experience.* The first three traits to be identified were neuroticism, extraversion and openness to experience, often summarised as NEO. Conscientiousness and agreeableness were added to make the Big Five, as those traits reflected sets of factors that didn't seem to be covered by the first three. See also *personality trait, EPI, Dark Triad.*

fixation In *psychoanalytic theory*, the failure to progress from an earlier stage of development (e.g. oral fixation) or an earlier relationship (e.g. mother fixation). The term is also used more broadly with reference to any relationship that is seen as inappropriately intense and dependent.

fixed action pattern A complex sequence of behaviour that is genetically pre-programmed so that all members of the species show the behaviour when it is needed. Neither learning nor practice are needed for the behaviour to be performed perfectly. Fixed action patterns have been intensively studied by ethologists, and involve sequences of behaviour that have been inherited as a complete unit. See also *sign stimulus.*

fixed-interval reinforcement A *reinforcement schedule* in which reinforcements, or rewards, are given only after a set period of time since the last reinforcement became available. After a suitable *acquisition* period, this method of administering reinforcement tends to produce a high level of responding around the time of the reinforcement, and a low rate of responding at other times. It has a low *resistance to extinction.*

fixed-ratio reinforcement A *reinforcement schedule* in which reinforcements, or rewards, are given only after a set number of responses has been made since the last reinforcement. Fixed-ratio reinforcement schedules produce a very rapid *response rate*, but have a low *resistance to extinction.*

fixed-role therapy A method of treatment derived from *personal construct* theory in which the client agrees to adopt particular ways of behaving that are clearly different from (although not opposite to) their usual style. The method seems to be particularly effective in undermining a belief that only one kind of behaviour is possible.

flashbacks Intense emotional memories of specific events or situations, often traumatic, that come back to the person suddenly and involuntarily. They are often associated with *post-traumatic* *stress disorder*, but may also result from the inappropriate use of *hallucinogens*.

flashbulb memory A form of memory that is associated with powerful experiences, and in which the memory contains a high level of contextual information as well as the specific information. Researchers have investigated flashbulb memory using questions such as 'Where were you when you heard that President Kennedy was shot/ Princess Diana died/Space Shuttle Challenger exploded?', and these studies show that people retain extremely clear memories of exactly where they were and what they were doing at the particular moment of time when they heard the news. However, there is reason to doubt the accuracy of flashbulb memories, vivid though they may be.

flooding See *implosion therapy*.

flow The apparent movement of the visual field that occurs as a result of the perceiver moving around and being active in their environment. Flow is a central construct in Gibson's theory of *direct perception* – also known as *ecological perception* – which argues that the visual field itself contains enough information for the perceiver to navigate around its world, without the need of additional cognitive inference, by contrast with Gregory's theory of *constructive perception*.

fluid intelligence A form of intelligence that is creative and adaptable, and can deal with unusual or unpredictable circumstances. See also *crystallised intelligence, triarchic intelligence, intelligence*.

fMRI A type of *MRI scan* that provides a dynamic image of blood oxygenation in particular areas of the brain, often as the person undertakes particular activities. It is particularly useful because it shows which areas of the brain are being used at any given time. For more detailed information, see *functional magnetic resonance imaging*. See also *PET scans*.

focal therapy An approach to psychotherapy in which a specific focus (problem) is identified early in the therapy and efforts are concentrated on this focus for the remainder of treatment. The method was developed as part of the attempt to make *psychotherapy* shorter and more cost-effective.

focus group A form of group *interview* that was developed in market research (see *consumer psychology*) as a cost-effective way of gathering the views of consumers. They were originally called focus groups because the job of the interviewer (moderator) was to bring the group to a focus on the issue. The conclusion about the general wishes of the group would then be apparent. As techniques for analysing group qualitative data have developed, there is less stress on working the group towards a consensus, but the name is still used for the increasing variety of group discussions. Much of what social psychologists and psychotherapists have learned about how people function in groups can be applied to research using focus groups. Factors such as *conformity* and *social desirability* may produce an unproductive consensus, especially if the interviewer allows their motivations to be visible. Oppositional behaviour or simple showing off by individuals can also reduce the usefulness of a focus group. Focus groups can be used to research what people want, but are often used by marketeers and politicians to find out how to make what they have already decided to offer acceptable to the public. See also *Leeds Attributional Coding System*.

focus of expansion The point in the visual field towards which the viewer is moving. This point does not seem to move, but the rest of the visual field appears to expand around it as the viewer gets closer. See also *motion parallax, ecological perception*.

focused attention See *selective attention*.

foetus An organism in the later stages of gestation, up to the time of birth; in humans, from the ninth week after conception. Before this time, it is called an *embryo*.

forebrain See *diencephalon*.

forensic psychology The application of psychology to legal matters, including work on the reliability of witnesses, evidence given by children, the consequences for children of possible court actions, and the causes of criminal behaviour.

forgetting The failure to retrieve information when it is wanted. Broadly speaking, theories of forgetting can be sorted into seven major approaches: decay theory (the idea that memory traces gradually decay over time, unless they are strengthened by being retrieved); *interference* theory; *amnesia* brought about through physical causes; *motivated forgetting*; lack of appropriate *cues* for retrieval; lack of the relevant context for retrieval; and inadequate processing during storage (see *levels of processing* theory).

formal operational stage The last of Piaget's four stages of *cognitive development*. In the formal operational stage, the individual has become capable of abstract thought and can conceptualise possibilities that are outside direct experience. Piaget considered this to be the highest form of cognitive activity, and one that is shown only in human beings, and from the age of about 12 years at the earliest. The preceding stages he viewed as steps towards this point, which, on the (outdated) theory that '*ontogeny recapitulates phylogeny*', illustrated the stages by which abstract logic had evolved. See also *concrete operational stage, genetic epistemology, preoperational stage, sensorimotor stage*.

forward model In neuropsychology, this is the idea that we use the brain's awareness of motor programs to predict what an action will feel like, and what its effect on a proposed target will be.

fovea That part of the retina that receives the clearest and most sharply focused image. The fovea is roughly central to the retina, and is composed entirely of *cone cells* that, through their discrimination of colour, allow for the distinguishing of fine details, at the cost of some loss of sensitivity to faint signals. See also *retina, rod cells*.

fractional anisotropy A form of *diffusion tensor imaging* that measures the concentration of water molecules in *white matter*, indicating its concentration in particular areas or *neural pathways*.

framing effect The source of errors in *problem-solving* that arises from the influence of irrelevant situational factors (e.g. the place someone is in at the time, or the social context).

fraternal twins Twins which have developed from two separate ova, such that they bear the same resemblance and relationship to each other as normal *siblings*. Twins of this kind are also known as *dizygotic twins*. See also *identical twins, monozygotic twins*.

free association A technique much utilised by Freud and subsequent psychoanalysts, as they considered that it provides important clues to the workings of the *unconscious* mind. Free association consists of the individual producing an uncensored, non-calculated account of what they are thinking and feeling during the session. Because the spontaneous expression avoids intervention and possible censorship by the *ego* (the conscious mind), the nature of the responses made during a free association session indicates the concerns and preoccupations of a person's unconscious. The agreement to engage in free association is called the 'basic rule' of *psychoanalysis*, and is regarded as essential for its success.

free recall The act of producing memories without the use of specific cues, or other forms of memory assistance or structuring.

freeloaders People who receive the benefits of collective action, without contributing to it themselves. See also *social loafing*.

frequency A count of the number of times an event, or the score in a given category, occurs. Frequency data are tested by *non-parametric statistics* such as a *sign test* or *chi-square*.

frequency theory A theory concerning how information contained in sound waves is transmitted to the brain. Frequency theory states that the wavelength, or frequency, of the sound affects the rapidity of transmission of electrical impulses along the auditory nerve, with sounds at higher frequencies producing more rapid transmissions. When the frequency rises to a point that would require firing at a more rapid rate than the neurones concerned can manage, the *volley principle* comes into effect, with neurones taking it in turns to fire, producing bursts or volleys.

Freud, Sigmund (1856–1939)

Freud was the founder of *psychoanalysis*, an attempt to provide a complete account of human psychology, and then to base a method of treatment on it. Freud proposed that the child develops through a progression of *oral, anal, phallic, latency* and *genital stages*, incorporating the *Oedipus complex* and the development of the *id, ego* and *superego*. This developmental frame, showing how the *unconscious* is formed, provides a basis for Freud's account of adult psychopathology. He saw coping with *anxiety* as a major drive, and argued that we build *defence mechanisms* to protect the ego against threat from the id and the superego. Within therapy, he recognised *transference* of feelings for familiar people on to others, such as the psychoanalyst. Psychoanalysis had a profound impact, not only on psychology, but within sociology, literature and Western society in general. Many of the strongest ideas, such as *repression* or the *continuity hypothesis*, have become so widely accepted that they are no longer seen as particularly Freudian.

Freudian slip A mistake that can be interpreted as revealing unconscious wishes, fears, etc. Freud argued that all apparently accidental happenings reveal something of the unconscious.

Friedman's ANOVA A statistical technique allowing researchers to identify and locate significant differences between several different samples. See also *analysis of variance*.

frontal apraxia Also known as *action disorganisation syndrome*, this is a disorder that results from damage to the *frontal lobes*, in which people have no difficulty with object recognition or using isolated objects, but are unable to undertake routine tasks that involve several steps or subgoals – such as making a cup of tea.

frontal eye field (FEF) The part of the *frontal lobes* that is responsible for voluntary movement of the eyes.

frontal lobe The general term given to the front part of the brain, located above the *lateral fissure* and in front of the *central sulcus*. In the early part of the twentieth century, the frontal lobe was thought of as the seat of aggression, from the discovery made by Monitz in 1930 that chimpanzees which had experienced lobotomy (the surgical removal of the frontal lobe) showed a decrease in aggressive behaviour. This led to considerable popularity for lobotomy as an operation to treat those with *psychosis*. The discovery that similar results could be achieved by the severing of connections between the frontal lobe and the rest of the cortex just above the lateral fissure (*leucotomy*) led to equal popularity for the latter operation. However, it transpired that many other functions were also impaired, including generally the capacity for

autonomous functioning and decision-making. Although the frontal lobe has few localised functions, it seems to be involved in much generalised cortical activity. See also *occipital lobe, parietal lobe, temporal lobe, frontal apraxia*.

FRU See *face recognition unit*.

frustration Both the act of preventing an organism from reaching a goal, and the emotion aroused in the organism by this experience.

frustration–aggression hypothesis The proposal, particularly associated with Leon Berkowitz, that aggression is caused by some kind of frustration. It also tends to assume that frustration always leads to aggression. This theoretical model has achieved widespread popularity, and is supported by comparative studies of overcrowding in animals, as well as by studies of human behaviour.

FTT See *failure to thrive*.

functional autonomy of motives See *extrinsic motivation*.

functional fixedness A form of *Einstellung*, or *mental set*, in which the individual is unable to deviate from using objects in a manner consistent with their normal functioning. For instance, in a problem-solving exercise, functional fixedness may prevent someone from realising that something such as a jug, usually used to contain liquids, could also be turned upside down and used as a support. See *problem-solving*.

functional integration The way that different areas or networks in the brain communicate with one another. See also *resting state paradigm, default mode network*.

functional magnetic resonance imaging (fMRI) A method of brain scanning that images the oxygen uptake of brain cells, and thereby indicates which brain cells are in use at any particular time. It works by identifying the magnetic fields of water molecules in brain cells, which are influenced by the strong magnetic field of the scanner, and slightly different when the cell is using blood than when it is quiescent. A whole fMRI brain scan only takes about two seconds, so researchers can use this method to explore brain activity and cognition (e.g. by asking the person to read a word, or think of a special event). The scan then indicates changes in the activity of different areas of the brain as they do it. It is a popular method for researchers, partly because of its accuracy, but also because there are no X-rays or radioactive substances involved. See also *multiple-demand network, multi-voxel pattern analysis, event-related functional magnetic resonance imaging.*

functional neuroanatomy The analysis of physical areas and structures of the brain in terms of the phsyiological or cognitive functions that they are known to be involved in, or to determine.

functional specialisation The way that different regions of the brain are specialised to deal with different functions.

functionalism The claim that psychological phenomena are best understood in terms of their functions rather than their structure (the claim of *structuralism*). Concepts such as *adaptation* and *role*, and therapeutic methods such as systemic *family therapy*, represent a functionalist approach.

fundamental attributional error The general tendency to attribute people's behaviour to internal causes, character or *dispositions. Attribution theory* has shown

that we consistently overestimate such causes and underestimate the influence of circumstances. The effect is so strong that we even attribute the behaviour of inanimate objects to motivations and dispositions (see *animism*). However, an exception may be made when a person explains their own behaviour (see *actor–observer effect*).

fundamental frequency The lowest frequency component of a particular sound. This normally determines the perceived pitch of the sound, but see also *missing fundamental phenomenon.*

funnelling Organising the questions in a questionnaire in such a way that the first ones are very broad in scope, but later ones become more and more focused.

fusiform body area (FBA) A region of the inferior *temporal cortex* that responds preferentially to whole bodies, rather than to body parts. See also *fusiform face area.*

fusiform face area An area in the fusiform gyrus in the *temporal cortex*, which forms part of the face recognition system, but is also involved in recognising other objects. See also *face recognition unit.*

future shock One of several theories about the stress imposed by transitions and *life events*. The idea was introduced in a book with the same title by Alvin Toffler to describe what he claimed were the traumatic effects of our present rapid progress into the future. Toffler proposed that people could be protected against the effects of change by maintaining some areas of stability in their lives.

FWE See *Family Wise Error.*

g See *general intelligence factor*.

GAF See *Global Assessment of Functioning scale*.

Galton, Francis (1822–1911)

Francis Galton was a pioneer of systematic measurement, and developed several statistical techniques, including the concepts of *correlation* and *regression*. He set up a Psychometric Laboratory in London, which members of the public could visit and, for a penny, obtain a range of personal measurements, such as lengths and widths of parts of the body, strength of grip or kicks, etc. Using these data, Galton found that human capacities tended to fall along a normal distribution curve. Reasoning that psychological abilities were presumably dependent on physical ones, he then concluded that capacities such as *intelligence*, too, must be normally distributed. Unfortunately, this, together with studies of high-achieving families, led him to develop the idea of *eugenics*, or selective breeding of human beings to promote higher intelligence or other desirable characteristics, which ultimately became the rationale for the Nazi concentration camps, as well as US immigration and other social policies.

galvanic skin response (GSR) Also known as galvanic skin resistance, this is a highly sensitive measure of *arousal*, registering even such slight increases in arousal as are produced by a disturbing thought or a slight pain. It refers to the electrical resistance of the skin, which changes as a result of increases in the rate of sweating. GSR detectors form an important component in *polygraphs*, which record a range of physiological indicators of psychological events, and may be used as *lie detectors*.

gambler's fallacy A belief that if a chance event occurs, then it is less likely to occur on the next trial. If red comes up several times running on a roulette wheel, there is a (mistaken) tendency to believe that black is more likely on the next throw. This universal tendency has been of interest to cognitive theorists, as it is a failure to follow probabilistic logic, and so may shed light on how humans assess probability. It may best be seen to reflect the fact that genuine instances of random sampling without replacement are uncommon in real life, and not as a failure to judge probabilities accurately. The gambler's fallacy is therefore a normally effective strategy that becomes inappropriate in certain rather artificial circumstances.

game The psychological uses of this term are similar to the ordinary meaning except that the idea of playfulness is usually absent, so a game is an activity within defined limits in which all of the participants operate according to agreed rules. Much social interaction can be regarded as a game, with plenty of scope for problems when the rules and the limits of the game are not made explicit. Eric Berne was one of the first to explore this concept in his book *Games People Play*. *Game theory* is a specific approach which expresses the rules of the game in mathematical terms so that the possible strategies can be precisely identified and their consequences predicted. See also *zero-sum game*.

game theory An approach to the mathematical modelling of social interactions that is largely concerned with how an individual's success in making choices is influenced by the decisions of others. Although still popular in some areas of *cognitive psychology*, game theory tended to fall out of favour as psychologists increasingly recognised its inability to take account of more complex social factors. See also *payoff matrix*, *individualism*, *prisoner's dilemma*.

gaming Engaging in digital games. These may be platform-based, Internet-based, or stand-alone, and include many types of game, such as sporting replications, action-adventure games or problem-solving games. The term is most commonly used for prolonged engagement with computer games, often through an Internet-based network. See also *avatar*.

Ganong effect The observation that an ambiguous phoneme is more likely to be perceived as a sound which produces a word rather than as a non-word.

GAS See *general adaptation syndrome*.

gate control theory A theory of pain control which holds that pain awareness is mediated by 'gates', or neural pathways which permit the passage of information about *nociception*. Control of these gates either chemically or psychologically may be useful in mediating or reducing chronic pain.

Gaussian distribution See *normal distribution*.

gaze cueing A term describing how the direction of one person's eye gaze can automatically cue another person or people to look in that direction. See also *joint attention*.

gender identity The awareness individuals have of themselves as a member of their sex. It emerges from the relationships between the beliefs they have about appropriate *sex roles*, *behaviour*, and their perception of themselves. For example, a small man who regarded size and muscularity as indicators of masculinity would modify his gender identity accordingly.

gene A unit of heredity that consists of a small segment of a *chromosome* made up of DNA (*deoxyribonucleic acid*). Each gene exerts its influence on the body by triggering protein synthesis – usually the production of an enzyme, but sometimes a protein that contributes to the production of a particular type of cell in the body. The word gene is also used loosely and erroneously in *sociobiology* to mean 'a unit of natural selection'.

gene-culture coevolution The idea that while culture can influence *gene* frequencies in a *population*, genes may simultaneously influence culture (e.g. through physiological predispositions).

gene-environment correlations See *gene-environment interplay*.

gene-environment interplay The interaction between genes and their environment. This is generally considered to involve four types of mechanism:

(i)   Direct environmental influences affecting the timing and degree of functioning of the genes (e.g. an enriched diet in childhood producing a larger individual).

(ii) *Heritability*, which varies according to environmental circumstances.

(iii) *Gene-environment correlations*, which are genetic influences on people's exposure to different environments (e.g. genotypes may influence whether people seek out risk-taking experiences or highly stimulating environments).

(iv) *Gene X-environment interactions* that happen when a person's susceptibility to a trait or problem results from a particular combination of genes and environmemt, such as the development of lung cancer as a result of smoking.

gene X-environment interactions See *gene-environment interplay*.

general adaptation syndrome (GAS) A long-term response to stressful stimulation identified by Selye in 1949. It is characterised by extremely high levels of *adrenaline* in the bloodstream, but without the rapid heart and pulse rates and changes to internal organs normally associated with adrenaline release. Selye's research indicated that the effects are always the same, regardless of the source of the *stress*. GAS has been shown to result in increased susceptibility to illness, possibly through a decline in the number of white blood cells and antibodies produced by the body.

general intelligence factor (g) The idea of one overall capacity of *intelligence* suggested by Galton and Spearman. Many psychologists consider this to be a contentious view, arguing that intelligence is a combination of many differing skills and attributes. Most intelligence tests are based on the assumption that a generalised intelligence factor, or 'g', can be calculated as a result of administering a set of specialised subtests, and it is as a consequence of this belief that the *intelligence quotient*, or IQ, has been so widely applied. See also *triarchic intelligence*.

general mental ability tests Another term for intelligence tests, and one that is preferred in occupational testing circles, since its use circumvents the controversial issues and criticisms associated with the terms *intelligence test* and *IQ*.

general problem-solver (GPS) A computer program, devised in the early 1970s, that emphasised the use of *heuristics* in tackling specific problems, and which formed the prototype for many subsequent attempts at *computer simulation* within the general field of *artificial intelligence*.

generalisation The process by which a learned response will occur in more situations than those in which it was first learned – it will also be applied to similar situations. See also *conditioning*.

generalisation gradient The relationship between the strength of a given response and the similarity of the triggering stimulus to the original stimulus. When eliciting a generalised response, a stimulus that is very similar to the original stimulus will produce a strong response, while one that is less similar will evoke a weaker response (see Figure 23).

generalised anxiety disorder A nonspecific psychological problem that consists of high levels of anxiety or panic attacks which can be generated in many different contexts and don't appear to be related to a single stimulus or set of stimuli.

generation gap The differences in attitudes and expectations that become apparent between widely differing age groups, as a result of changes in society and culture over the decades.

generative retrieval The deliberate or voluntary retrieval of details about autobiographical memory. See also *direct retrieval.*

genetic(s)

(i) In the singular, concerning the origin of something. Used particularly to refer to the development of abilities and characteristics of children (see *genetic epistemology*), but also applied to the development of characteristics in a species or the development of the species itself. See also *ontogeny, phylogeny.*

(ii) In the plural, genetics refers to the study of *genes* and their actions. See also *behaviour genetics, Lamarckian genetics, Mendelian genetics.*

genetic determinism The idea that human psychological characteristics are determined primarily by genetic mechanisms, established at conception. For example, H.J. Eysenck argued that the personality traits of *extraversion* and *neuroticism* were genetic in origin, and unlikely to be significantly affected by environmental experience. Its converse – *environmental determinism* – asserts that human characteristics have been produced primarily by environmental influences. In fact, both forms of *determinism* are exaggerating the case. See also *dialectics.*

genetic engineering The process of altering genetic characteristics through microscopic surgical or chemical intervention, usually by inserting a new section of *chromosome* into an existing one, such that when the chromosome

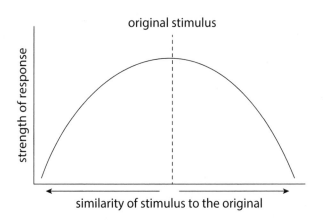

Figure 23 The generalisation gradient

is replicated, the new portion is also replicated and becomes part of the organism's overall *genotype*.

genetic epistemology The title for a theory of the growth of knowledge and understanding. It is usually reserved for Jean Piaget's theory charting the development of the child's cognitive functioning through a series of stages. See also *Lamarckian genetics*.

genetic psychology The psychology of development (not of *genetics*). It covers the psychological development of both individuals and species, but the term is no longer widely used.

genetic reductionism The idea that an understanding of genetic influences is all that is needed to understand human behaviour or human social phenomena. While this links with *genetic determinism*, and can be seen as another facet of that particular belief structure, the difference is that determinism refers to causality – what has caused this to occur – while reductionism is concerned with what we need to study in order to understand something fully. See also *reductionism*.

genetic transmission Passing information from one generation to the next by means of *DNA*, the genetic material that carries information about the nature of individual development, and which is found in each cell nucleus. Genetic transmission may be asexual, in which case the information is transmitted in very much the same form as it was in the parent organism, or it may be sexual, in which case each individual in the next generation receives a new set of genetic information, formed as a combination of genes from each parent. See also *allele*.

genital stage In *psychoanalytic theory*, the final stage of *psychosexual* development, beginning at puberty, in which the adult forms of sexual desire and activity are acquired.

genome The complete set of genetic information in an *organism*.

genome-wide association study (GWAS) A phenotype-led study involving thousands of participants, which uses small variations of the *genome* to identify 'hot spots' (i.e. areas where individuals of the same *phenotype* have distinctive genetic similarities).

genotype The term used to describe the full set of genes possessed by an individual, which have been replicated throughout the cells of the body. Because many genes will not encounter the circumstances in which they would become active, and others are recessive, so that their action is suppressed by a *dominant gene*, less than 50 per cent of the characteristics coded in the genes actively contribute to the structure or characteristics of the individual (the *phenotype*). However, all of the components of the genotype are available for passing on to offspring.

genotype-first An approach to genetic analysis in which different *alleles* or *genotypes* are used to identify variations in the *phenotype*. See also *phenotype-first*.

geometric illusions Forms of *visual illusion* that have their effect through the way the perceptual process deals with static visual forms such as line drawings.

Gerstmann's syndrome A set of four cognitive deficits (acalculia, finger agnosia, agraphia and left-right disorientation) occurring together, which are believed to result from damage to the left *parietal lobe*.

Gesell, Arnold L. (1880–1961)

Gesell developed a theory based on the *maturation* of the nervous system, claiming that its development is fully controlled biologically. He observed that foetal and *neonate* development is *cephalo-caudal* and *proximo-distal*, and he argued that behaviour arises from the fixed order in which the physiology of the child unfolds, and the set of stages through which it proceeds. Most existing assessments of infant development are based on the *Bayley Infant Development Scales*, which were created using Gesell's theory and observations. Apart from his theory, Gesell was a gifted observer of child behaviour and an early user of film and photography. He provided a good example, rare in psychology, of descriptions (at six-month intervals from birth to 10 years) of what real children were like. However, just as Skinner pushed conditioning beyond its limits as an explanation for all behaviour, so did Gesell with biological explanations. In both cases, psychologists have learned from the process, but have not accepted the more extreme claims.

Gestalt principles of perception An attempt to describe the important features of perceptual functioning through a set of principles that are consistent with the Gestalt emphasis on wholes. See also *Law of Prägnanz*.

Gestalt psychology A form of psychology, popular in Europe in the first half of the twentieth century, which gathered support in opposition to the mechanistic approach of the *behaviourism* school in America. Gestalt psychology emphasises the holistic nature of the human being, and opposes stimulus–response reductionism, on the grounds that the whole is more than the sum of its parts, and that there are many aspects of perception, memory and learning processes which cannot be understood in terms of collections of smaller units, but which are complete and unitary in themselves. The Gestalt emphasis on *cognitive psychology* provided an important background to the cognitive revolution of the 1960s and 1970s.

Gestalt therapy A method of *psychotherapy* developed by Fritz Perls that works in the 'here and now' rather than the past, and aims to increase the person's awareness of how all of their psychological processes are integrated. The emphasis on understanding the person as a whole is derived from *Gestalt principles of perception*. Gestalt therapy was one of the influential concepts in the later development of *mindfulness*.

gestation The period before birth when the *embryo* or *foetus* is growing, or 'gestating', in the womb.

gesture A mode of *non-verbal communication* in which information is conveyed by movement, usually (but not always) of the hands and arms. Gestures tend to vary considerably from one culture to another, and the same sign may have a very different meaning even in neighbouring countries.

Gibson, Eleanor J. (1910–2002)

Eleanor J. Gibson became known as the 'grand dame' of American developmental psychology. In the UK, she was best known for her research into infant depth perception, particularly studies involving the *visual cliff*. Eleanor Gibson was concerned that cognition should be understood in terms of the way that it relates to environmental demands and the survival requirements of the organism. Her later research into child cognitive development reflected that concern.

Gibson, James J. (1904–1979)

The husband of Eleanor Gibson, James J. Gibson is recognised as one of the most influential theorists in the field of perception. His theory of *ecological perception* argued that it was important to understand perception from the point of view of the ecological function which it served for the organism. As a result, he directly challenged the *top-down theories* of perception put forward by Gregory and others, arguing that there was no need for inference in perception because the visual field – or more specifically the *optic array* – contained enough information to make sense of incoming information, particularly when the movements of the observer and their interactions with their environment were taken into account. He therefore emphasised aspects of perception such as the *flow* of the optic array, and the *affordances* for interaction offered by objects within the visual field. See also *ecological perception*.

GIGO An acronym for 'garbage in, garbage out' – produced by computer users to point out that if one's *data* are rubbish, then running them through a sophisticated statistical program on a computer will just turn them into different rubbish.

glia An alternative term for *glial cells*.

glial cells Small cells that are found among the *neurones* of the nervous system. Their main function seems to be to provide nutrients and to absorb excreted waste from the neurones.

Global Assessment of Functioning (GAF) scale A scale used to measure 'psychological health' that focuses on how well adapted the individual is to their circumstances.

global attributions *Attributions* in which the chosen cause is of a kind that is likely to affect many outcomes (e.g. attributing your unusually intensive revision to the fact that the result of the exams that you are taking will influence your whole future career). When the cause has only minor consequences, it is described as a specific attribution.

go/no-go test A test of response inhibition in which the person is required to respond accurately to a series of trials in which they are presented with a rapid sequence involving stimuli which mean that they should respond and other stimuli which mean that they should not respond. It reflects activity in the medial *prefrontal cortex*, as does the *Stroop* test.

goal setting theory The idea that working towards and achieving goals is a fundamental part of human motivation.

gonads General term used to describe the sex glands – either the *testes* or the ovaries.

GPS See *general problem-solver*.

gradient of colour One of the *monocular depth cues* that indicates the distance of objects from the observer. Gradient of colour refers to the way in which the colours of distant objects appear to be greyer and less vivid than those of nearer objects. The brain utilises the relative intensity of the colour to deduce probable distances.

gradient of texture One of the *monocular depth cues* that indicates the distance of objects from the observer by utilising the extent to which fine details of texture can be discriminated. Nearer objects present a finely detailed appearance, whereas those that are further away appear to be smoothed out, and detail is lost (see Figure 24).

grammar A set of rules set up to specify how a language is constructed. Grammar is more concerned with *syntax* than with *semantics*, but particularly within *psycholinguistics* it is likely to be concerned with both. The objective of grammar is to have a set of rules that will generate all acceptable sentences within a language, but no others. As with *logic*, there may be a problem in that a particular set of rules that does the job may not correspond to the rules that humans use to achieve the same objective. The most widely accepted form of grammar in psycholinguistics is that produced by Noam Chomsky, known as *transformational grammar*.

grandmother cell The hypothetical idea that there are specific neurones in

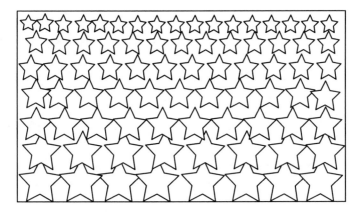

Figure 24 Gradient of texture

the brain that only respond to one specific stimulus, such as the sight of one's grandmother.

grapheme A basic unit for describing writing, in much the same way as a *phoneme* is a basic unit for describing spoken sound. The idea is that writing is made up of combinations of graphemes.

However, this does not mean that a grapheme simply corresponds to a letter, since a single letter may contain more than one grapheme 'element'.

graphemic buffer A form of *short-term memory* store that holds information about individual letters immediately prior to spelling a word.

Gregory, Richard (1923–2010)

Richard Gregory specialised in the study of visual perception, and in particular optical illusions. He became well known in psychology partly as the author of one of the first truly accessible textbooks (*Eye and Brain*), but also because of his work on optical illusions, and the experience of a blind person who had sight restored in later life. Gregory proposed a top-down model of perception, suggesting that the brain makes inferences from limited information based on its past experience and knowledge, which was challenged by Gibson for real-world perception, but remains a likely explanation of many less real-world experiences. He was also the founder of the Bristol Exploratory, one of the first hands-on science centres that illustrated in practice many of his theoretical observations. See also *visual illusions*.

grey matter or **gray matter** The term given to the densely packed mass of neuronal cell bodies and unmyelinated fibres found on the inside of the spinal cord and on the outside of the *cerebrum*. See also *white matter*.

grid cells Neurones within the medial *temporal lobes* that respond when an animal is in a particular location in a part of their environment. These cells operate in such a way that they produce a repeating grid-like structure, so cells may fire in multiple locations, but always in respect to the same position within that cell of that grid. See also *hippocampus*.

grounded theory An approach to research that specifies that data be acquired in ways which ensure that the information collected has not been influenced by theoretical assumptions. The data are then explored in detail, until some organisation of the material, such as recurrent themes or principles, emerges. Using this information, theoretical claims can then be made through a process of *induction*. See also *qualitative analysis, core analysis*.

group norm The generally accepted standards of a particular social group. These may be standards of behaviour, achievement, attitude or other characteristics, but they are generally considered to be what counts as acceptable, and used as the criteria to which group members should conform.

group polarisation The *emergent property* of groups in which people can be shown to make more extreme decisions when acting as a group than when they are acting as individuals. This was first identified with the *risky shift* phenomenon, in which groups were shown to make riskier decisions than would be made by the individuals that comprise them. However, more recent research shows that, under certain conditions, groups may also make more cautious decisions, so the term group polarisation was adopted as one which described the phenomenon without making assumptions as to the direction in which the group would shift.

group selection theories Models of evolutionary processes which are based on the idea that a trait may evolve because it helps the species as a whole to survive. Although popular in the 1960s, through the work of Wynne-Edwards and others, this approach to understanding evolution was largely discredited in favour of individual survival mechanisms, and in particular by the dominance of *sociobiology* in the 1980s. In more recent times, with the increased awareness of *coevolution* and similar mechanisms, some variants of group selection theories are beginning to be regarded as academically acceptable once again.

group test A psychometric test that is administered to several people at once, by a single tester, such as some of the school-type *intelligence tests*.

group therapy *Psychotherapy* carried out with a number of people who come together at agreed intervals for the purposes of the therapy. There are many different forms of group therapy, corresponding to most of the varieties of individual therapy, but all could be claimed to have three major advantages over individual therapy:

(i) cost-effectiveness, as a single therapist sees several patients simultaneously;

(ii) group processes that aim to ensure that the participants will have genuine interactions with each other and real emotional experiences, which will relate meaningfully to their experiences in daily life, and which can be used effectively by the group therapist; and

(iii) the support offered by group members to one another.

groupthink One of the *emergent properties* that can occur in tightly knit groups with a high level of consensus and group loyalty. Groupthink is the phenomenon whereby a consensual view of reality emerges within the group, so that unpleasant (and more realistic) alternatives to the way in which the group sees the world are not taken into consideration. Indeed, attempts to bring more realistic perspectives to bear on the situation are often perceived as being disloyal. The process therefore results in the group making silly or at times tragic decisions. The classic example of groupthink was the American military decision to invade Cuba at the Bay of Pigs – a decision that turned out to be a military disaster, and one which could have been easily foreseen if those making the decision had been able to make a realistic appraisal of the situation. Groupthink can occur in any tightly knit group with strong leadership, and was therefore also apparent in many of the governmental decisions made during the Thatcher and Blair years in the UK. Investigations of groupthink suggest that conscious and deliberate efforts to promote debate and to admit unwelcome possibilities are required to overcome it.

growth motive A term used in *humanistic psychology* models of *personality* to describe the tendency of human beings towards personal growth and development, not only through the acquisition of new skills and experience, but also through cognitive re-evaluation and an increased sense of personal control and autonomy. Humanistic psychologists consider this to be a very basic motive in the human being, and fundamental to an understanding of mentally healthy behaviour.

GSR See *galvanic skin response*.

gustatory perception The *perception* of taste, which uses sense receptors in the tongue and in the nasal epithelium.

GWAS See *genome-wide association study*.

gyri The plural of *gyrus*.

gyrus A ridge on the *cerebral cortex*. See also *sulcus*.

H

habit In behaviourist terms, a habit is described simply as a *stimulus–response learning* sequence. In cognitive psychology, it is seen as a set of automatic routines and subroutines in which the individual engages, and which, owing to frequent exercise, requires little conscious cognitive input. The learning process involved in acquiring a habit may involve *classical conditioning*, but will not be *habituation*.

habituation A very basic form of learning that involves gradually ceasing to respond to a non-significant stimulus that is repeatedly experienced. Ceasing to notice the ticking of a clock is a typical example. Habituation can be distinguished from fatigue by the fact that a small change in the stimulus will result in the response reappearing, a process called 'dishabituation'. Habituation is essential in that it allows organisms to concentrate on those properties of stimuli which have significance for them, and to avoid having the cognitive system overloaded with irrelevant information. For example, car drivers do not habituate to the sight of red at the top of a traffic light, but they are likely to have difficulty in remembering the colour of the stripes painted on the poles.

haemophilia A genetic disorder that results in excessive bleeding when the body is even slightly wounded, owing to an inability of the blood to clot. As a classic example of a *sex-linked trait*, haemophilia is found in many psychology textbooks, although the psychological implications of the disorder are obscure.

hallucination A vivid and convincing mental image that may appear in any sensory modality. The person experiencing it may be unable to believe that no sensory stimulation was involved. Hallucinations are regarded as one of the most reliable signs of *schizophrenia*, although they may also be caused as a side effect of *psychoactive drugs*. See also *Charles Bonnet syndrome*.

hallucinogen A drug that induces *hallucinations* or other unusual forms of perception. The most commonly used hallucinogens are psilocybin and LSD (*lysergic acid diethylamide*), but there are many others, including mescaline and the hallucinogen contained in the fly agaric mushroom. Traditionally, hallucinogens have formed an integral part of religious and social ceremonies in many parts of the world. In the West, they are normally used as *recreational drugs*, although there have been several instances of artists and creative writers utilising their effects to obtain special insights for their work, and one or two investigations of their usefulness in certain kinds of *therapy*.

halo effect An effect in which people or objects who are judged positively on one characteristic are also judged positively on others. For instance, a person who is judged to be physically attractive is more likely also to be perceived as being more amusing or intelligent than a physically less attractive individual of similar personality. See also *impression formation*.

handedness The term for specialisation in the use of one hand that develops in humans during the first years of life. Often the preferred foot or the preferred eye are not on the same side as the preferred hand. Handedness is thought by some to be related to *hemisphere dominance*. Since the right cerebral hemisphere controls the left side of the body, and vice versa, people who are right-handed are thought to be left-hemisphere dominant, while left-handed people are right-hemisphere dominant. However, the evidence relating handedness to cerebral dominance is at times contradictory, despite the plausibility of the idea.

haploid Having half the usual number of chromosomes – just one from each pair. Some social insects such as bees and ants are mostly haploid, as are reproductive cells (ova and sperm). See also *diploid, gene, meiosis.*

happiness A central focus in *positive psychology*, happiness is a positive state of being, in which the person is aware that they are in a positive *mood* and content with being so. Happiness can be an ephemeral state for some and a common one for others, but although it has been traditionally seen as a *personality trait*, modern researchers have shown that it is possible to learn to become more generally happy, through appreciation of the positive aspects of living and the challenging of negative *attributions.*

haptic To do with the sense of touch.

Harré, Rom (1927–)

Rom Harré is a distinguished social philosopher and psychologist. He developed the social psychological approach known as *ethogenics*, which identified two important methodological approaches: *episode analysis* and *account analysis*. Episode analysis takes the view that real everyday living is experienced as a series of episodes, and that the episode is therefore the most meaningful unit to adopt in any study of social experience. Account analysis emphasises the importance of discourse and memory in making sense of experience, and contributed greatly to the development of *discourse analysis.*

Hawthorne effect The phenomenon whereby when changes are introduced into a work environment in order to bring about an increase in productivity, there may be a temporary increase in productivity just because those changes have been tried. An entirely useless change may therefore appear to work unless the effects are tested over a reasonable period of time. Hawthorne effects illustrate the importance of social factors and expectations in the working environment. See also *organisational psychology.*

HCI See *human–computer interaction.*

head-related transfer function (HRTF) The way that sounds become distorted by the unique shape of one's own ears and head.

health belief model A theory which argues that the health beliefs people have are directly linked to their actions, and in particular to their adopting behaviours that are known predictors of health, or otherwise.

health psychology Originally health psychology was concerned with the psychological factors in medical conditions. It has now become a broad term to group together the areas of psychology that are concerned with different aspects of both physical and mental health and illness.

Hebb, Donald (1904–1985)

Donald Hebb was an influential Canadian neuropsychologist, who was concerned with exploring how learning and experience impacted on the brain. He argued that it was the repetition of connections between neurones which stimulated the development of synapse development, making familiar or more practised connections more likely to direct the neural impulse than novel or unfamiliar ones. Hebb challenged the mechanistic stimulus–response models of the behaviourists, arguing that the connection was also mediated by the organism, making it S–O–R (stimulus–organism–response) rather than S–R (stimulus–response). Although disregarded for a while, more recently his theoretical work has become widely accepted as the basis for *neural network* theory.

Hebb's theory of synaptic learning Hebb argued that it was the repetition of connections between neurones which stimulated the development of *synapses*, forming cell assemblies so that familiar or more practised connections are more likely to direct the neural impulse than novel or unfamiliar ones.

hedonic relevance The issue of whether a cause leads to effects that have direct positive or negative consequences for the person concerned. A cause has hedonic relevance for someone if it produces something pleasant or unpleasant. For instance, a government ruling that student income was to be halved would have direct hedonic relevance for students. It would not, however, be personalised. See also *personalism, attribution*.

hedonism In philosophy, hedonism is the idea that pleasure or happiness is the highest good. In psychology, it is the idea that it is fundamental to human beings to seek pleasure and to avoid pain, and that this in itself is a valid explanation of much behaviour.

helping Giving aid or assistance to someone. Psychologists have studied helping behaviour as a contrast to *bystander apathy*, and find that our 'natural' response seems to be to help others who appear to need it, but that this can be impeded by social and/or cognitive anxieties.

helplessness theory See *learned helplessness*.

hemianopia Cortical blindness that results from damage to the primary *visual cortex* in one hemisphere, and is therefore restricted to one half of the visual field.

hemiplegia Damage to one side of the *primary motor cortex*, which results in an inability to move the other side of the body.

hemispatial neglect A failure to attend to stimuli on one side of the perceptual field, opposite to the side of the brain *lesion* producing the neglect.

hemisphere bias The idea in popular culture that there is a distinction between right-brain activities and left-brain activities, that engaging in these different activities generates different approaches to life in general, and that people can be divided into 'right-brain' and 'left-brain' types. This belief involves an extensive mythology that has built up from a few valid neurological observations. While there is some evidence that logic and calculation, for example, tends to involve the left hemisphere more than the right, there is (a) some activity on both, and (b) no justification for the idea that the right *cerebral hemisphere* is therefore more emotional because *emotions* are the opposite of logic. Similarly, the observation that activities such as art appreciation or listening to music (for non-musicians) tend to involve more activity in the right brain has been exaggerated to the idea that (a) only the right hemisphere is involved, and (b) artists and musicians are therefore right-brain people, as opposed to writers and accountants who are left-brainers. (Incidentally, it has also been shown that trained musicians tend to generate left-hemisphere activity when listening to music.) There are some neurological tendencies towards hemisphere bias – for example, the location of most (but not all) language functioning on the left hemisphere, and evidence that the left side of the face (controlled by the right hemisphere) is more expressive of emotion.

But these tendencies do not justify the widespread popular beliefs that have grow up about this area. See also *hemispherectomy*.

hemisphere dominance The observation that, in most individuals, one *cerebral hemisphere* of the brain is more influential or has greater control over the body than the other side, thus possibly producing right or left *handedness*, etc.

hemispherectomy An operation that involves the removal of one entire *cerebral hemisphere*. Studies of left hemispherectomy in severely brain-damaged patients have shown interesting, often puzzling recovery of language functioning and linguistic memory that was not evident when the damaged hemisphere was *in situ*. These cases call into question the accepted idea that language is firmly localised on the left hemisphere, and rather suggest a hologram-like storage mechanism whereby each hemisphere is capable of taking over the functions of the other, but does not do so in everyday functioning. See also *hemisphere dominance*.

hemodynamic methods Ways of analysing brain activity by recording blood flow (e.g. *PET scans*).

hemodynamic response function (HRF) Changes in the *BOLD* response that occur over time.

hereditarian A term used to describe a theory or approach that emphasises inherited mechanisms and genetic influence, and excludes, or minimises, other factors. See also *genetic determinism, genetic reductionism*.

heredity The processes by which part of the biological potential of the parent is transmitted to the offspring. In sexual reproduction, this involves half of the genetic material of each parent combining to form the complete genetic structure of the offspring. See also *chromosome, gene*.

heritability A statistical concept designed to indicate how much of a given trait can be deemed to have come about as a result of *genetic* influences. The concept of heritability, while widely accepted in behavioural genetics and regarded as largely unproblematic when applied to physical characteristics, is often challenged when it is applied to behavioural or psychological characteristics because of its assumption that transmission through families is evidence that the trait concerned has been inherited. This leads into the twin study debates, and a political history in which the concept was seriously misused to inform racist and divisive social policies. See also *heritability estimate*.

heritability estimate A figure which purports to state the proportion of influence exerted by *genes* on the individual's development, despite the fact that many developmental geneticists and psychologists (e.g. Hebb) have demonstrated unequivocally how inseparable genetics and the environment are. The most well-known 'heritability estimate' is that of 80 per cent genetic influence on the variation in intelligence, put forward by Jensen in 1969 on the basis of Cyril Burt's fraudulent data on twin studies. Controversy concerns not so much the estimate of 80 per cent as the conclusions to be drawn from any estimate of heritability.

hermaphrodite An individual who possesses the primary sexual characteristics of both sexes at the same time. True hermaphrodites have gonads, one of which has developed as an ovary and the other as a testis. They could therefore produce an ovum and fertilise it themselves, and so potentially produce offspring without assistance from any other individual. The condition is extremely rare, and is not likely to be the true explanation of unexpected pregnancies.

hermeneutics The study of meanings in social behaviour and experience. It is concerned with meanings on a number of levels, ranging from the conscious and unconscious, personal and social to the cultural and sociopolitical levels. Rather than simply looking at the generalities of behaviour, or at statistical information, hermeneutics is concerned with the interpretation of experience, and the ways in which various forms of symbolism are used to convey meaning in human life.

heroin Heroin is a powerful analgesic of the opiate group, originally developed as a non-addictive painkiller. However, it was soon found that as a substance it is extremely addictive, producing *tolerance* very rapidly, and leading to increased doses of the drug being necessary for the same effect. It is probably the most abused of all the narcotic drugs. In addition to its analgesic properties, heroin induces profound mood changes, leading to relief from tension and producing a state of drowsy contentment. Accordingly, its use and abuse as an illegal drug is most widespread in the poorer sector, but occurs throughout society. In addition to the problem of tolerance, addiction to heroin produces a high level of susceptibility to infection and disease. In chemical terms, heroin has a structure very similar to the *endorphins* and *enkephalins* that are produced naturally in the brain in response to prolonged exercise, and it is picked up at the same receptor sites.

hertz (Hz) A measure of frequency, one hertz being one cycle per second.

In the audible range, the frequency determines the pitch of a sound or tone. Tones of higher pitch produce more frequent cycles, and hence are said to be of a higher frequency. See also *frequency theory*.

Hertzberg, Frederick (1923–2000)

Frederick Hertzberg was an influential organisational psychologist, whose main contribution to *applied psychology* was concerned with developing an understanding of employee motivation. His dual factor theory of motivation argued that there were two types of influencing factors: *hygiene factors*, which were concerned with the basics of working life such as pay, relationships with others, company policy, and the like; and *motivator* factors such as achievement, recognition, the work itself, and so on. Hygiene factors do not produce positive motivation, but are often the cause of dissatisfaction at work, while positive motivation depends on motivator factors.

---

heteroceptors Presynaptic areas that are able to receive messages from *neurones*. See *synapse*.

heterogeneity A set which is varied, or showing a large number of differences. A heterogeneous sample is one in which the research participants are of many different kinds. 'Hetero-' as a prefix means 'different' or 'other'. See also *homogeneity*.

heteronomous morality The second of Piaget's stages of *moral development*, this is also known as the 'moral realism' stage. At this point, morality is considered to be subject to the laws of others. In other words, the child accepts as right and proper the rules given by authority. See also *autonomous morality*.

heterosexism A judgemental approach which assumes that only conventional male/female relationships are acceptable, and that homosexuality is abnormal, inferior, to be despised or at best pitied. See also *homophobia*, *prejudice*.

heterosexual Having sexual inclinations towards members of the other sex. See also *homosexual*.

heuristics Problem-solving strategies that involve taking the most probable or likely options from a possible set, rather than working systematically through all possible alternatives. Heuristics provide a way of reducing a complex problem to a manageable set of tasks with only a slight risk that the solution lies among the alternatives excluded at the start. Heuristics differ from *algorithms* in that they do not guarantee a solution. See also *problem-solving, decision-making*.

hidden observer The term given to the experience of a dispassionate 'inner self' that observes the individual in stressful situations, or during day-to-day living. Such an experience is particularly common during *hypnosis*, in which the hidden observer is felt to have experiences that are parallel to, but not the same as, the hypnotised self. In *psychotherapy*, the objective part of the therapist that comments on their feelings and involvement with the patient is called the 'observing ego'.

hierarchy A structured form of organisation constructed in levels, with each level overshadowing or dominating the lower ones. The idea of hierarchy is used in many different ways. For instance, a hierarchy of concepts refers to the ways in which concepts may be stored in the brain, such that general concepts contain within themselves smaller constituent units. The analysis of organisations is almost always formulated in terms of hierarchies.

hierarchy of human needs Maslow's hierarchy of human needs refers to the idea that needs become important in a systematic progression. Lower, more 'basic' needs such as those for food and security are important first, and 'higher' needs such as those for beauty and *self-actualisation* only become important once the lower levels have been satisfied. The theory applies both developmentally and to the mature person. According to Maslow, children must be adequately satisfied at one level before they start to develop motivations at the next level, so the higher stages are not reached for several years, and self-actualisation may take at least 30 years to achieve. Adults may be stuck at a low level if they have never experienced sufficient satisfaction at that level, but even those who have progressed higher may cease to be motivated at the upper levels if they are seriously threatened in a more basic way. For example, the need for dignity ceases to matter if you look up and find you are in danger of being run down by a bus (see Figure 25). See also *social needs*.

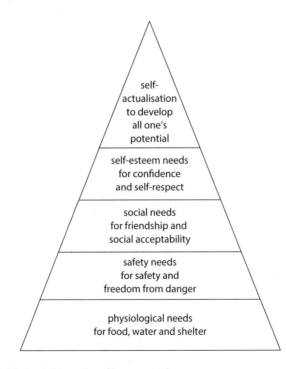

Figure 25 Maslow's hierarchy of human needs

higher-order conditioning See *secondary reinforcement*.

hill climbing heuristic A basic *heuristic* used in *problem-solving*, in which the person focuses on 'one step at a time' – in other words, on making moves that appear to bring them closer to the overall goal.

hindsight bias The tendency to regard decisions or choices that have already been made as having been the only practical or realistic option. Hindsight bias describes the way that we are strongly predisposed to justify or rationalise the benefits of our previous decisions. As a result, we often make these appear to have been clearly thought out, or simply a matter of logical choice, when in reality those decisions were taken in a much more impulsive manner, or according to much less rational criteria. See also *decision-making, cognitive dissonance*.

hippocampus A part of the *limbic system* that seems to be particularly concerned with memory processing. People with surgical damage to both sides of the hippocampus have subsequently experienced an inability to store or recall new information, although earlier memories remain intact and can be retrieved at will. A famous study of London taxi drivers (Woolett and Maguire, 2011) showed that the amount of time they spend in the job correlates positively with the volume of the right hippocampus. See also *grid cells*.

histogram An accurate type of *bar chart* in which the length and area of the bars represents precisely the relative proportions of the variables being illustrated. See also *descriptive statistics*.

holistic Complete, treating its subject matter as a coherent and indivisible unit. For example, a holistic approach to medicine would involve dealing with the whole person, including their own experiences, stresses and understanding of the situation, rather than simply treating the symptoms.

holistic processing Cognitive processing that involves integrating information from different sources to produce a meaningful whole (e.g. in *face recognition* or everyday *depth perception*).

hologram A portrayal of a three-dimensional image as a projection from a small unit or a two-dimensional surface, in such a way that the image can be examined from different angles and shows the appropriate parallax. A complete holographic image may be reconstructed from a proportion of an original, although some clarity of detail is lost. Understanding the perception of holograms poses a unique problem to psychology, which as yet seems far from resolution. Holograms are also of interest to psychologists because in some ways the *cerebral cortex* appears to function similarly. It seems possible that information is not stored in a specific location, but is available in any large enough area of the cortex. See also *hemispherectomy*.

holophrase A single-word utterance that conveys the meaning of a whole sentence in itself (e.g. 'Lost!').

home range The area within which an animal habitually forages for its food. This is not necessarily the same as the area that an animal will defend against other members of its species – many species have overlapping home ranges, but distinctive territories. See also *territoriality*.

homeostasis The process of maintaining a stable condition or state by detecting and reducing differences from a goal state. The classic simple example is a central heating system where the thermostat turns the boiler on when the temperature drops and turns it off when the temperature is high enough. The basic process involved is called *negative feedback*. The concept has been widely used to describe the maintenance of physiological balance in the body, with metabolic functions kept at an optimal level through the operation of mechanisms that correct imbalances. Homeostasis in the human body is maintained through a variety of mechanisms, tightly mediated by the *hypothalamus*. *Drives* are considered to arise directly from such homeostatic mechanisms. For instance, the hunger drive is purportedly initiated when blood-sugar levels in the body fall below a certain level. This produces food-seeking behaviour, until food is ingested and satiation is reached. The concept of homeostasis plays an important part in *systems theory*, and can therefore be applied to how psychological stability is maintained in people and their families.

homogeneity Similarity or likeness. Something that is homogeneous is the same overall, showing little variability. A homogeneous group of research participants will have been selected so that all of them score similarly on essential measures. For example, one might recruit a sample of 25-year-old middle-class mothers, each with one preschool child. This would be a homogeneous sample for research on child-rearing (although not necessarily for research in other fields, e.g. religious attitudes). A mixed sample is described as heterogeneous. The prefix 'homo-' means 'the same'. It is not related to the Latin 'homo', meaning 'man'. See also *heterogeneity*.

homogeneity of variance One of the criteria used for the selection of a *parametric statistics* test. Homogeneity of variance refers to the *variance* or 'spread' shown by the populations from which the data samples have been taken. The purpose of parametric analytical techniques such as the *t-test* is to compare the *means* of two samples, in order to determine whether they are different enough to have come from different populations. However, the formula for estimating the variance of the parent population relies on the two sample variances being similar, so if they are not, a t-value would be misleading. For this reason, homogeneity of variance is an important criterion for using a t-test, and variance is usually checked using an F-test (See *F ratio*). Note that finding a *significant difference* in the variances of the two samples might be just as important as finding a difference in their means (see Figure 26).

homograph A word that has a single spelling but two or more different meanings, such as 'set' or 'hamper'.

homophobia Hostility to homosexuals as a group. See also *reaction formation*.

homophone A word that sounds similar to another word, but which is spelt differently and has a different meaning (e.g. 'stair' and 'stare').

homosexual Having sexual inclinations towards others of the same sex. The prefix 'homo-' is derived from the Greek, meaning 'the same', and not from the Latin, meaning 'man'. The term therefore applies equally to men and women. See also *heterosexual*.

homunculus In *physiological psychology*, this refers to the two areas on the *cerebral cortex* on which areas of the body are mapped in relation to motor

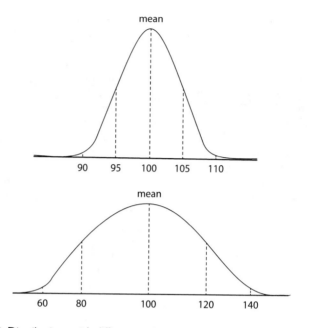

Figure 26 Distributions with different variances

and sensory functioning. The area is a representation of the body in which size is proportional to sensitivity, so a fingertip gets relatively much more space than an area on the back, because it is so much more sensitive. The term is also sometimes used to express the ancient idea that there is a miniature human operating within the body (e.g. a miniature perceiver looking at the image received by the eyes). See also *homunculus problem*.

homunculus problem The problem of the 'inner observer' found in some models of *thinking* or *perception*, which implies that the brain is acting as if it were another observer, or small person, observing the individual's mental processes. It is a problem because we would then need to propose another 'inner observer' to explain how the first observer makes sense of what it sees, and so on, ad infinitem.

hope A feeling of positive expectation – the desire that a positive event or situation will come to pass. See also *positive psychology*.

hormones Chemicals released into the bloodstream that produce changes in the functioning of the body. Hormones are produced by the glands of the *endocrine system*, which operate in close conjunction with the *hypothalamus*.

hostile aggression Aggression in which the objective is to inflict harm on the other, as opposed to *instrumental aggression*, which is undertaken for some other purpose. See also *aggression*.

HPA See *hypothalmic-pituitary-adrenal axis*.

HRF See *hemodynamic response function*.

HRTF See *head-related transfer function*.

hub-and-spoke model A model of memory which proposes a central 'hub' of *semantic memory* that is not dependent on any particular mode, but which feeds into a range of *modes of representation* based on sensory and motor systems such as vision, hearing, sensation, etc.

hue The term used to describe a particular wavelength, or tint, of a colour. It is a subdivision of the broader categories of colours. For instance, there are different hues of green.

human–computer interaction (HCI) The study of how human beings interact with and use computers, including ergonomic design, human-friendly displays such as the WYSIWYG (what you see is what you get) system for documents, or the desktop interface popularised by Mac and replicated in Windows, and studies of just what people actually use computers for.

humanistic psychology An approach within psychology that emphasises the whole person and their scope for change. Humanistic psychologists reject the *reductionist* approach of many researchers, which sees human action simply as collections of separate mechanisms, and they also argue against the dehumanisation and 'objectifying' of human behaviour produced by trivial laboratory investigations and behaviouristic attitudes within psychology. Instead, they argue that psychologists should take more account of the whole person, including *attitudes*, values and responses to social situations (including experiments). To attempt to study people in a fragmented way is, they consider, to ignore the essence of what it is to be human. There are many humanistic psychologists, of whom *Carl Rogers* is perhaps the most famous.

humour Communication that is amusing. Humour has primarily been studied in terms of its use in social processes, and in the hidden meanings of jokes. There is no satisfactory theory of the psychological processes involved when something is experienced as funny. There is a widespread belief and growing evidence that frequent use of humour and laughter is associated with positive physical and psychological health.

humours of the body The dominant theories of personality and of physical and mental health over some 2,000 years, until the nineteenth century, were in terms of the balance between four types of bodily fluids or humours. Everyday expressions such as being in 'a bad humour' combine the two concepts.

Huntingdon's disease Also known as Huntingdon's chorea, this is a genetic disease that involves contorted postures and flailing limbs (chorea). It occurs through the degeneration or death of inhibitory neurones in the indirect pathway between the *basal ganglia* and the *thalamus*. The indirect pathway acts to reduce unwanted muscular movement, while the direct pathway acts to increase or accelerate it. Overactivity of the indirect pathway produces movement inhibition as in *Parkinson's disease*, while overactivity of the direct pathway produces chorea, as in Huntingdon's disease. See also *hyperkinetic, hypokinetic*.

hygiene factors Factors in the working environment, identified by *Hertzberg*, which are concerned with the working conditions of the individual, such as shift organisation, staff facilities and organisational structure. In investigations of job satisfaction, Hertzberg found that bad hygiene factors contributed considerably to job dissatisfaction, but that incentives known as 'motivators' (e.g. promotion prospects, a sense of goals, etc.) were necessary to produce job satisfaction itself. See also *organisational psychology*.

hyper- A prefix indicating a high or excessive level of some function.

hyperactivity A condition of excessive and apparently uncontrollable activity in children, sometimes referred to as hyperkinesis. There is controversy over the reality of the condition, but there are some children whose activity is maintained at such an extreme level that the label seems to be unavoidable. It is also clear that many children who are labelled as hyperactive are just rather more active than their parents or teachers find convenient. The condition is strongly associated with difficulties in maintaining attention, leading to boredom, and it may be this aspect, rather than the activity level itself, which is fundamental. Hyperactivity can be effectively treated with drugs related to *amphetamines*. Although these drugs are usually used as stimulants, they also help to maintain attention, and it seems to be this effect that is useful to hyperactive children. The term hyperactivity has been replaced with *attention deficit hyperactivity disorder* (ADHD).

hypercomplex cell A type of cell, discovered by Hubel and Wiesel, that is located in the *thalamus* and the *visual cortex*, and which receives information from *complex cells* concerning basic images occurring in the visual field. Hypercomplex cells collate this information, so as to respond to simple patterns and shapes, and are thought to represent the basis of *figure-ground perception* (see Figure 27).

hyperkinetic An increase in movement, often involuntary. See *Huntingdon's disease, basal ganglia*.

hyperlexic Hyperlexic children are those who learn to read extremely quickly, with little apparent difficulty. See also *dyslexia*.

hyperphagia Excessive eating that may be induced by lesions to the hypothalamus. See also *set weight*.

hyperscanning Recording the activity of two or more different brains at the same time. Hyperscanning has been shown to be a useful technique in investigating the neural correlates of experiences such as trust or *empathy*.

hyperthymestic syndrome A distinctive example of *autobiographical memory*, concerning an exceptional ability to remember the events of one's own life.

hypnagogic imagery Vivid visual imagery that is experienced during the transition from waking to sleep. It often takes the form of an unusually clear image of an object that has been the subject of intense concentration during the day, but the most common image is of falling. Hypnopompic imagery, which is rarer, is a similar kind of imagery that occurs during waking.

hypnosis An *altered state of awareness* (or consciousness) usually induced by voluntarily allowing one's actions to be directed by another person (the hypnotist). The major characteristics of the state are heightened suggestibility and concentration of attention on the hypnotist. Some research participants appear to achieve a very high level of this state, called a hypnotic *trance*, in which they feel totally controlled by the hypnotist. Researchers have argued that hypnosis is just a matter of suggestible

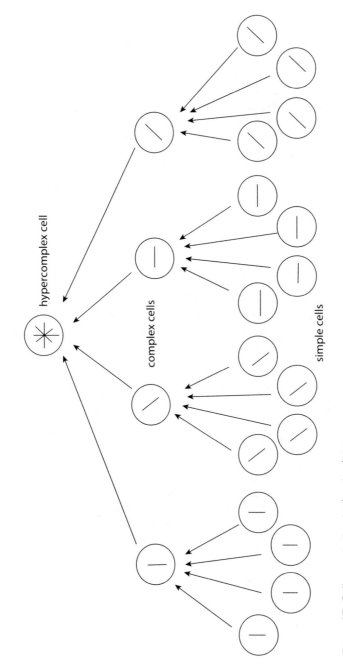

hypercomplex cell

complex cells

simple cells

Figure 27 Cell organisation in the visual cortex

people role-playing a trance state, although others have found evidence of EEG records of a changed pattern of brain activity during hypnotised states. See also *hypnotherapist, autohypnosis*.

hypnotherapist A practitioner who uses *hypnosis* for therapeutic purposes. It can be argued that hypnosis itself has no direct therapeutic effects, but that it can be used effectively within a cognitive-behavioural approach for purposes such as reducing anxiety.

hypokinetic Lacking in spontaneous movement, as in *Parkinson's disease*. See also *hyperkinetic*.

hypothalamus A small but important part of the brain, located immediately below the thalamus (hence the name). The hypothalamus is generally concerned with maintaining *homeostasis* in the body, and its functions seem to be partly localised. For instance, lesions to specific nuclei within the hypothalamus in rats have been shown to produce excessive eating, resulting in obesity.

hypothalmic-pituitary-adrenal axis (HPA) A *neural pathway* that is activated during *stress*, producing changes in stress-related hormones.

hypothesis An idea that is not proven, or which is advanced as a tentative suggestion or possible explanation. In terms of formal experimental method, a hypothesis is an idea, derived logically and consistently from a specific psychological theory, that contains an explicit prediction which can be verified or refuted by some kind of empirical investigation, usually an experiment. See also *null hypothesis*.

hypothesis testing See *hypothetico-deductive method*.

hypothetical construct An idea or factor that is not empirically evident, or demonstrable in reality, but is proposed as a theoretical explanation for some phenomenon or experience.

hypothetico-deductive method The technique of investigation outlined by Popper as being central to the scientific method. It consists of investigating by means of the formulation of an explicit *hypothesis* containing an explicit prediction as to what would happen in a given situation. An empirical investigation is then set up to test the hypothesis (i.e. to see if the prediction was true). If the hypothesis is to be retained because the prediction worked, that would be taken as support for the theory from which the hypothesis was derived. On the other hand, if the hypothesis is refuted, that would be taken (in an idealised world) as evidence against the original theory, and an alternative explanation would have to be found. See also *Type I error, Type II error*.

hypovolemic thirst Also known as osmotic thirst, this is the thirst that arises when the body's internal fluids have been depleted, as opposed to thirst brought on by advertising or other social pressures.

hysteria A physical symptom, with no apparent physical cause, but which appears to have some psychological function. An example would be temporary blindness or a paralysed arm that prevented someone from performing a job which they hated but dared not leave. Such symptoms are not under voluntary control. See also *psychoanalysis*.

Hz See *hertz*.

I

IAT See *implicit association test.*

ICD See *International Statistical Classification of Diseases and Related Health Problems.*

iconic representation The coding or representing of memories by utilising sensory images (from the Greek 'icon', meaning 'image'). Iconic representation is usually used to refer to visual imagery, and was considered to be the second *mode of representation* to develop, according to Bruner. See also *enactive representation, symbolic representation, eidetic imagery.*

ICSS See *intercranial self-stimulation.*

id The primitive part of the unconscious personality, according to Freud, characterised by extreme emotional reactions and demands for immediate gratification. The function of the id is to fulfil the instinctual needs, but it operates according to the *pleasure principle* and may be satisfied by fantasising the desired object. Therefore, the infant has to begin to develop the *ego* in order to deal with reality.

ideal self-image The internalised concept of the perfect version of ourselves that, according to Rogers, is held by every individual. The ideal self-concept is used as a yardstick by which the actual self's behaviour is judged. Accordingly, it expresses the individual's internalised *conditions of worth.* Highly neurotic clients are often distinguished by an unrealistically high ideal *self-concept*, resulting in continual anxiety and a recurrent sense of failure.

idealism A tendency to believe that events will occur, and people will behave, in the best possible way. An idealist will wish and hope that other people, as well as themselves, will behave for the best.

identical twins See *monozygotic twins.*

identification A process seen as essential by both social learning and psychoanalytic theorists because it is an efficient way of acquiring new characteristics. It is the second stage of the *social learning* process outlined by Bandura, the first of which is *imitation.* Identification refers to the internalisation of imitative learning, such that it becomes incorporated into the individual's *self-concept.* For instance, a person starting a new job may spend the first couple of days consciously imitating others in that role. After a while, they come to internalise the new role, and are able to generalise their learning to novel situations. Freud proposed that models would be chosen when they were seen as successful in solving those problems which the person found most urgent, or had power over. During the Oedipal phase, the strongest identification is with the parent of the same sex as the child, and so an appropriate gender identity is formed. A person may identify with a particular individual, or with a particular social *role.*

identity The sense an individual has of the kind of person that they are. According to Eric Erikson, the major task of adolescence is to establish a stable sense of identity that will remain relatively constant as the person moves between different situations. A failure to achieve a secure identity results in identity diffusion, which leaves the young adult unable to enter into commitments or close relationships for fear of being taken over by the other person.

identity formation The process of forming an identity. The identifications made throughout development play an important role, and adolescents in particular will try out different kinds of identity and use feedback from others to decide which to retain and which to abandon.

ideology A comprehensive belief system with an implication for acting in prescribed ways, such as Marxism. When the term is used to refer to psychological theories, it usually has a critical overtone. For example, calling behaviourism an ideology implies that its adherents have an irrational commitment to the theory.

ideomotor apraxia A condition resulting from damage to the left *parietal lobe*, in which people have difficulty in planning and carrying out an action, for example in response to a request, even though they are able to copy such an action.

idiographic Attempting to understand the functioning of individuals, as opposed to the search for general laws of behaviour. Idiographic approaches to human *personality* examine characteristics that are considered to be common to all individuals but which, in their operation, make each person unique. For instance, *personal construct* theory represents an idiographic approach, whereas most other *psychometric* approaches, which are concerned with comparing people with one another, do not. See also *nomothetic*.

idiolect An individualised form of language use, specific to a particular individual or small group. See also *dialect*.

idiosyncratic Special to that particular individual; characteristic of that person but not of most people.

idiot savants People of very low general intelligence who have an exceptional ability in one specific area, such as being able to perform very elaborate mental arithmetic extremely quickly.

illusion Something that tricks the senses into a false interpretation of what is there. Illusions may operate in any sensory mode (e.g. the *McGurk illusion* is an example of an auditory illusion). However, the best-understood ones are *visual illusions*. These have been extensively studied because they offer a chance to see how the visual system works. See also *constancy scaling*.

illusory conjunction When the features of two different stimuli are mistakenly combined to produce a *perception* of a single object.

illusory correlation The impression that two events or facts are connected because they happen at the same time, when really there is no such connection between them. This is another source of bias in *decision-making*.

illustrators Non-verbal signals that serve to amplify or demonstrate what someone is saying. See also *affect display*, *emblems*.

imagery Mental representations that recreate sensory impressions. Visual imagery refers to an impression of something as it would be directly seen; auditory imagery is a representation of something being heard. An image is usually of a fairly specific object, but may sometimes be more diffuse (e.g. an image of autumnal colours). The study of imagery has been a major area in memory research, as it forms one of the main systems for *encoding* and representation of memories. See also *hallucination, iconic representation*.

imitation The understanding and reproduction of the actions of other people. This is distinct from simply copying a specific action or sequence of behaviour, which is generally described as *mimicry*. Imitation is a social learning process that is common in young mammals but particularly important in humans of all ages. It provides an extremely rapid form of learning and a mechanism of early *socialisation*. See also *identification*.

immediacy of reinforcement The concept in *operant conditioning* that, in order for a particular behaviour to be learned, it must be reinforced immediately (i.e. as soon as it has taken place). Delayed reinforcements could mean that alternative behaviours occur in the mean time, and become accidentally strengthened through becoming associated with the reinforcement. See also *Law of Effect*.

immediacy principle The idea in language theory that the person is analysing for meaning as soon as they hear the first syllable of a spoken word.

immediate memory A term occasionally used instead of *short-term memory*.

impact bias An over-estimation of reactions to loss, exaggerating intensity and/or duration. See also *memory bias*.

implacable experimenter The situation in classic experimental research in which the experimenter appears entirely unaffected by the participant's behaviour. This was a significantly influential factor in Milgram's studies of *obedience*. See also *demand characteristics*.

implementation intentions Plans for action that are consciously aimed at achieving a specific goal (e.g. weight loss), based on specific information about how that goal could be achieved.

implicit Unspoken and/or assumed. The term is also used to refer to cognitive processes that are not available to the conscious mind.

implicit association test (IAT) A test that provides an implicit measure of *racism* by recording response times to the categorisation of words and names.

implicit attitudes Attitudes that are not overtly expressed, but which form the cognitive underpinnings of general statements and beliefs. For example, the idea that individualism is the dominant feature of human psychology is a commonly held but implicit attitude among North American researchers. See also *social representations, cultural psychology, prejudice*.

implicit learning The learning of complex information without any awareness that it has been learned.

implicit memory Memory that does not rely on conscious recollection. See also *explicit memory, non-declarative memory*.

implicit memory bias The way that tests of implicit memory show a tendency to better memory of negative information than to neutral or positive information. See also *memory bias, interpretive bias, impact bias*.

implicit personality theory The ideas about how personality traits are grouped together, often taken for granted in everyday living. For example, traits such as 'ambitious' may automatically be grouped with 'aggressive' and 'energetic', or 'kind' could be grouped with 'gentle' and 'peacable'. This means that individuals who are known to have one particular characteristic are often reacted towards as if they also possessed the full range of associated traits. They are treated in accordance with the unspoken and assumed theory of personality held by the people whom they encounter. See also *personal construct*, *halo effect*.

implosion therapy Otherwise known as *flooding*, this refers to a technique of *behaviour therapy* in which the phobic individual receives direct and extended exposure to the feared stimulus, until they become relaxed with it. For instance, someone who has had a car accident and is frightened of going out may be repeatedly shown film of cars approaching them. As they become used to this, the fear dies away and, through *classical conditioning*, a more relaxed attitude becomes associated with the stimulus. See also *systematic desensitisation*.

impression formation The process of creating favourable or unfavourable impressions on other people. The study of impression formation has included research into *primacy effects*, *non-verbal communication* and *stereotyping*, since all of these contribute to the judgements people make about one another.

impression management The presentation of the self to others in as favourable a way as possible. See also *self-presentation*, *social self*, *social desirability scale*.

imprinting The process involving following of the mother that occurs during a *critical period* shortly after birth in some species, most notably in ducks and geese. The 'following' behaviour can be elicited by any moving object during the hours, or perhaps days, after birth, and the animal seems to have a strong *innate* tendency to learn about and in some way identify with the object. The learning is very resistant to change, and later in life social and sexual behaviour may be directed at animals or objects that resemble the imprinted stimulus. Attempts have been made to explain the *attachment* of human infants to their mothers as a form of imprinting, but the two processes are quite different, and it seems that the main features which they had in common at the time when the theory was proposed was that neither could be satisfactorily explained.

impulsivity A behavioural tendency to make immediate responses without reflection, or to seek immediate rewards.

in vitro By laboratory methods. The term is usually used to refer to 'test-tube' conception, in contrast to *in vivo* methods.

in vivo By natural methods, or in real life. Usually used to refer to conception that has occurred through sexual intercourse, as opposed to the creation of embryos using *in vitro* methods.

inattentional blindness A failure to detect something appearing in the visual field because *attention* is directed away from it.

incentive A stimulus that has value, either positive or negative, for an *organism*.

incentive theory A theory of motivation which distinguishes between the expectation that a goal can be achieved (*incentive* motivation) and the strength of the need for the goal (*drive* motivation). The amount of effort made to achieve a goal is a function of both kinds of motivation, so high drive alone may be ineffective if paired with low incentive. For example, I would very much like a million pounds, but do not expect success, so I am not doing anything about it. Equally, high incentive (I am sure I could get spam for dinner if I tried) will not generate goal (or spam) seeking if my drive is low because I do not like the stuff. Practically, the theory indicates that if an organism is not working towards a goal, it is necessary to know whether to increase need (life will be really wonderful if I can pass my psychology exam) or incentive (there is still enough time to look up all the terms I do not understand).

incidental learning Learning that takes place without conscious awareness or intention, simply as a result of what the animal or person is doing. See also *latent learning*.

inclusive fitness An evaluation of an animal's likelihood of survival by comparison with others of the same species. This particular form of evaluation takes 'survival' as referring to the perpetuation of the animal's genes, rather than the survival of the individual. See also *sociobiology*.

incubation period The period during the creative process in which ideas seem to develop and become formulated at a totally subconscious level. Typically, this has been preceded by an acquisition period, in which ideas are experimented with and tested out, and is followed by a period of insight, and then intense creative activity, in which the artist-writer-creator produces the final work. Although not all creative individuals appear to operate within this four-stage model, it seems to be a common sequence for many, and the incubation period – in which work on the idea seems, on the surface, to have ceased – is its distinctive feature. See also *creativity*.

independent-measures design The kind of study that involves comparing the scores or responses from two or more separate groups of people, such that one group experiences one of the experimental conditions and the other group experiences a different condition. See also *repeated-measures design*.

independent self A form of social *identification* in which the person's goals and beliefs are seen as entirely separate from those around them. See also *allocentrism, collectivism*.

independent t-test A two-sample statistical test for interval or ratio data in which the two samples consist of separate and independent individuals, which means that the test has to be able to account for variations in the scores arising purely from individual differences. See also *dependent t-test*.

independent variable The variable that an experimenter sets up to cause an effect in an experiment. An independent variable may have two or more conditions, and research participants' responses to each of them are studied. Independent variables may be existing features (e.g. males versus females) or be created by the experiment (e.g. dark versus light conditions). The variable is described as independent because it is not affected by the experimental procedures. See also *dependent variable*.

indirect reciprocity A name given to a form of *altruism* that involves helping other people who may never be in a position to reciprocate (e.g. who one may never meet again). The assumption is that there is still some kind of benefit or exchange involved, such as reputation enhancement. See also *reciprocal altruism*.

individual differences The study and measurement of the significant ways in which individuals differ from each other. Some studies of individual differences deal only with intelligence test scores, but the area is usually taken to include any reasonably stable characteristics or abilities. It therefore includes *personality traits* and psychological dysfunctions.

individualism A *reductionist* approach to knowledge or social understanding which holds that what human beings do originates entirely within the individual, and that although social contexts may exert influences, these are only contributing factors to behaviour rather than determining it. The opposite of *social determinism*, or in other contexts of *collectivism*.

individuation The process of becoming separate. It is used particularly about people during the transition from adolescence to adulthood, when they separate from and become independent of their families. Jung felt that individuation could not be fully achieved before middle age.

induction Deducing general principles from a collection of specific instances. Theories such as *psychodynamics* and *learned helplessness* have been arrived at by a process of induction. It can be a creative process leading to a theoretical statement that efficiently combines a large number of individual facts. Induction contrasts with *deduction*, which works in the opposite direction. The term can also be used to refer to something being created in another person or thing. For example, if we say that page 75 is really exciting, this may induce in you a wish to turn to that page – or it may induce a feeling of disbelief.

inductive methodology An approach to research that starts with observation and data collection guided as much as possible by the phenomena being investigated. Theory comes later by a process of induction. *Grounded theory* is a particularly clear form of this approach.

industrial psychology The application of psychology to industrial situations. Industrial psychologists study the effects of environmental influences on people at work, of organisational influences, such as the effects of different management structures or styles, of social relationships within an industrial setting, or of sources of *stress* and industrial accidents. See also *applied psychology*.

infancy The period of human development before the child is able to speak, usually taken as the first year or two of life.

infant-directed speech See *motherese*.

infantile autism See *autism*.

infantile sexuality A supposition, originating with Freud, that the sensual pleasures and motivations of infants have a sexual basis. The issue became one of great controversy, and in some respects rests on the definition of sexuality. However, it is also the case that Freud was indicating a previously unrecognised aspect of infant functioning when he pointed out the pleasure that all infants obtain from activities such as oral stimulation and masturbation.

inferential statistics Statistics in which assessments about probability are made. Inferential statistics usually take the form of statistical tests, which examine the characteristics of the data sets and estimate the likelihood that these have arisen purely through chance. See also *hypothetico-deductive method, descriptive statistics, null hypothesis*.

inferior Towards the bottom. See also *anterior, posterior, superior*.

inferior colliculus A set, or nucleus, of cells in the midbrain that carry out an important stage in auditory information processing, much as the nucleus known as the *superior colliculus* does in the *visual system*.

information processing An approach which analyses cognitive processes in terms of the manipulations of information that are involved. As computers have become capable of progressively more sophisticated operations, information processing has become accepted as a plausible approach to understanding *perception, decision-making*, etc. The approach is more directly involved with computers when they are used to run models of particular cognitive processes (known as a *simulation*) to see how the model would work in practice. See also *mental chronometry*.

information theory An approach to understanding the functioning of the brain in terms of processing of information. Information theory uses concepts and techniques developed by engineers studying the flow of information, and has played an important role in the study of *selective attention*.

informed consent An agreement to participate in a research project or other event that is based on full knowledge and awareness of what is involved, including any foreseeable physical, psychological or social consequences. See also *presumptive consent, prior general consent, ethical issues*.

infrasound Sound that is too low in pitch to be detected by the human ear. Some animals, notably pigeons and whales, are able to detect infrasound of extremely low frequencies, and it has been suggested that they may use geological sources of infrasound to help them to navigate. See also *ultrasound*.

in-group A name given to the main group being referred to when describing *intergroup behaviour*. If *social identification* is seen as being all about 'them' and 'us', then the in-group is 'us' while the *out-group* is 'them'.

inhibition

(i) The process by which a *neurone* becomes less likely to fire. Inhibitory synapses raise the *threshold of response* for the next neurone, thus rendering it likely to fire only in response to extreme stimuli.

(ii) A process in learning whereby a response becomes increasingly less likely to occur with repeated presentations of the stimulus. The term inhibition is generally used to refer to a damping down or restraining of a behaviour, as a result of overuse or some other kind of direct stimulation.

(iii) The idea of a specific memory becoming lost or distorted as a result of further information. See *interference*.

(iv) Suppression of a social response or emotional reaction.

inhibition of return The reduced probability of returning one's *attention* to a stimulus or object that has just recently been attended to.

inhibitory synapse A synapse which operates in such a way that the nerve cell which receives its message becomes less rather than more likely to fire, so the passage of the neural message is inhibited, rather than passed on. Compare *excitatory synapse*.

innate Literally meaning inborn. It also means unlearned, or present at birth, and is used synonymously with inherited or *genetic*. Compare *congenital*.

innate releasing mechanism (IRM) A term used by Tinbergen to refer to the stimulus that triggers off an *instinctive behaviour*. Examples are the moving shape that stimulates pecking in a young herring-gull chick, and that which provokes 'freezing' in turkey chicks. The behaviour released by an IRM has direct survival value, either in avoidance of predators or in obtaining food. Currently, the term *sign stimulus* is preferred for referring to these signals, as it avoids the implicit assumptions about internal mechanisms contained within the term IRM.

inner ear The third main division of the ear. It is that part of the ear with direct connections to the brain via the auditory nerve. The inner ear contains the *cochlea* – a long, fluid-filled tube containing hair cells that transduce the vibrations of sound information into electrical impulses. It also contains the semicircular canals, which detect orientation of the body and motion in a similar fashion (i.e. by means of hair cells that fire when stimulated by motion or vibration). See also *middle ear*.

inner scribe The part of the *visuo-spatial scratch pad* that deals with spatial and movement information.

insecure attachment A type of *attachment* in which the infant lacks certainty and confidence in its relationship with its primary *caregiver*. Insecure

attachments are generally classified into two types: insecure/anxious attachment, and insecure/avoidant attachment. Infants (or older persons) with insecure/anxious attachment show high levels of *stress* on separation, and are difficult to console when reunited with the caregiver. Those with insecure/avoidant attachments are less demonstrative although still distressed on separation, and tend to avoid contact when reunited with the caregiver. See also *secure attachment*.

insight

(i)   In learning or creativity, a sudden and complete realisation of the solution to a problem, usually involving a restructuring of the person's perceptions. The process was regarded as particularly important by the *Gestalt* psychologists.

(ii)   An awareness of one's own psychological processes, *unconscious* fears and wishes, etc. Forms of *psychotherapy* that work specifically to increase insight, such as *psychoanalysis* and *humanistic* therapy, are often known as 'insight therapies'.

insight learning Learning that occurs as a result of a sudden flash of inspiration, in which the solution to a particular problem or task is perceived in an instant. See also *learning set, aha! experience*.

insomnia A general name given to the inability to achieve regular sleep. There are many different kinds of insomnia, and also many causes of it, but one of the most common is stress or tension. However, sleep research shows that many insomniacs do actually sleep for far more hours than they realise: they dream that they are lying awake. See also *sleep cycles*.

instinct A term now avoided as much as possible, but once used to refer to those aspects of human experience that were deemed to have been inherited and to be immutable. The concept of an instinct is always directed towards function (e.g. 'an instinct for' security, motherhood, etc.), and is therefore of very little value in describing or explaining behaviour itself. An instinct for security might manifest itself in a variety of ways. To one person, it might mean having money safely invested; to another, it might mean having a comfortable home; while to yet another, it might mean becoming increasingly self-reliant and able to survive with as little money as possible. Such potential diversity of behaviour means that the concept itself is of dubious value, and has largely been replaced by the term *instinctive behaviour*.

instinctive behaviour Behaviour that occurs as a result of the direct action of genes. Such behaviour typically shows certain distinctive characteristics:

(i) *stereotype* (the behaviour is stereotyped, being fixed and not modifiable by the individual);
(ii) there is a complex sequence of behaviour, not just a reflex response;
(iii) it arises in individuals even if reared apart from their own species;
(iv) it does not require prior learning or practice; and
(v) it is *species-specific behaviour*.

Such behaviour appears to be relatively common in fish and birds, but rather less so among the higher animals, which tend to rely more on adapting their behaviour through *learning*.

institutionalisation The effect on a person of living in an institution for a long time. Institutions such as psychiatric hospitals are likely to develop procedures that are very different to those in the outside world. As the inmates adapt to the regime, they develop patterns of motivation and behaviour that could prevent them from functioning successfully in the outside world. Ironically, the phenomenon operates most clearly in just those institutions (e.g. mental hospitals and prisons) that are supposed to improve the client's ability to function within society. It has been suggested that the reason why staff in institutions fail to take the process of institutionalisation into account is that they themselves are subject to it.

instrumental aggression *Aggression* that occurs because it will result, directly or indirectly, in a desired outcome for the individual showing the aggression (i.e. it serves a purpose).

instrumental learning Learning that occurs as a direct result of the beneficial or pleasant consequences which it has for that individual. The term is often used synonymously with *operant conditioning*.

insula A region of the *cerebral cortex* that is buried beneath the *temporal lobes*. The insula is involved in *pain* and *gustatory perception*, and has also been shown to respond to the experience of disgust.

integrative agnosia A form of *agnosia* in which people have difficulty combining parts into wholes. It is usually diagnosed using *Gestalt*-based perception tasks.

intellectualisation A way of coping with anxieties by denying the emotional component of a situation, and concentrating on an abstract logical account of the details of the situation and one's own response to it. It is one of the *defence mechanisms*.

intelligence In general, the ability of an individual to understand the world and work out appropriate courses of action. Within psychology, there is no more precise definition that is generally accepted, although the old claim that 'intelligence is what *intelligence tests* measure' is uncomfortably accurate in terms of how it is often viewed in psychological research. See also *Intelligence A, B, C, intelligence quotient, intelligence test, triarchic intelligence.*

Intelligence A, B, C Classifications developed by Hebb and Vernon in an attempt to express the relative contributions of experience and inheritance to an individual's intelligence. The term Intelligence A was used to describe the total potential intelligence of an individual, given that particular genotype and an ideal environment from conception. Intelligence B was conceived as an unknown proportion of Intelligence A – that amount of their potential which the individual had been able to realise throughout their life. Intelligence C referred to the unknown proportion of Intelligence B that can be measured using an *intelligence test*. In formulating this model, Hebb was applying the genetic distinction between *genotype* and *phenotype*, and arguing that to talk of the relative contributions of genetics and environment as if they were alternatives or could be quantified was inherently misleading (see Figure 28).

intelligence quotient (IQ) A score devised by Binet in an attempt to express the relationship between a child's *mental age* and its actual or *chronological age*. The quotient was obtained by dividing the child's mental age (obtained by using a variety of age-related tests) by its chronological age, and then multiplying the result by 100. This meant that 100 became the normative figure – a child who had a mental age appropriate for its chronological age would score 100, children who were advanced for their years would score above 100, and those who were behind would score below 100. Although Binet repeatedly expressed his concern that this should not be taken as indicative of a child's potential to learn, but simply of its achievements so far, IQ scores have been systematically

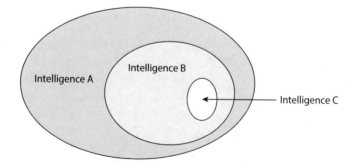

Figure 28 A possible model of Intelligence A, B, C

misused to represent a static measure of the individual's intellectual capacity. In addition, despite the normative nature of IQ scores, in many cases they have been erroneously treated as *equal-interval* data, and used as the basis of elaborate statistical calculations such as those underpinning the concept of *heritability*. Such research has formed the basis for such outcomes as compulsory sterilisation laws in the USA (see *eugenics*) and differential schooling systems in many countries, and has contributed to the concepts of racial inferiority that resulted in the attempted genocide of the Jews and Gypsies in the Second World War. Although the original formulation of IQ had some diagnostic value, its widespread misuse and abuse in society have resulted in its use being regarded with considerable suspicion.

intelligence test A standardised set of tasks from which intelligence can be estimated. All tests should have been fully assessed for *reliability* and *validity*, but a great variety is now available, to some extent reflecting problems that have been identified during the history of mental testing. Of the most widely used tests, the *Stanford–Binet test* is a direct descendant of the original test devised by Binet to give a single measure of IQ. The *WAIS* provides 12 sub-scales that measure different aspects of intelligence. *Raven's progressive matrices* attempt to eliminate cultural bias by having items and administration that do not depend on the use of language. The subsequent British Ability Scale is an attempt to incorporate later psychological work on intelligent performance, such as Piaget's ideas.

intentional stance This can be defined as the tendency to explain or predict the behaviour of others in terms of their *intentions* or intentional states. It has been articulated into four different orders of intentionality, depending on the sophistication of the assumptions made about the actor. See also *zero-order intentionality*, *first-order intentionality*, *second-order intentionality*, *third-order intentionality*.

intentions Plans for action or goals towards which actions are directed. See also *conative domain*.

interaction A situation in which one thing reciprocally affects another, such that an exchange takes place. The term is used particularly with reference to *social interaction*.

interactionist The interactionist perspective within *physiological psychology* is a direct contrast to the traditional approaches of *reductionism*. Rather than seeing physiology as the direct cause of behaviour, an interactionist perspective emphasises how environment, cognition and physiology may all have a reciprocal effect on one another, such that each may influence the other in achieving a given effect. Within this approach, physiological variables that are usually regarded as causes may equally well be seen as results.

intercranial self-stimulation (ICSS) Electrical self-stimulation of the brain, in which electrodes are placed in one of the *pleasure centres* of the brain, and the individual is able to stimulate it voluntarily.

interdependent self A form of social identification in which the individual's beliefs and goals are strongly linked with those of other members of their family or social group. See also *collectivism*, *allocentrism*, *individualism*.

interference The concept in *memory* theory that information may become lost or distorted because of the storage of additional information. The interference theory of *forgetting* was a popular approach in memory research throughout the 1950s and 1960s, and it centred around the idea that memories could become displaced because of the storage of similar information. Interference was considered to be of two kinds:

(i)   *proactive interference*, in which material that had been learned first interfered with the acquisition of later information; and

(ii) *retroactive interference*, in which information that had been acquired at a later stage interfered with the retrieval of previously learned material.

intergroup behaviour The behaviour of two distinct groups towards one another. See also *social identity theory*.

intergroup conflict Aggression or hostility between different social groups. See also *social identity theory*, *prejudice*.

intergroup rivalry Rivalry between groups, which in certain circumstances can be created simply by dividing some people into two groups, giving the groups different names, and putting them in competition for resources. See also *minimal group paradigm*.

intermittent reinforcement Reinforcement which is given only in some instances of the desired behaviour, and not every time that behaviour occurs. See also *schedule of reinforcement*.

internal attributions *Attributions* in which the chosen cause is internal to the person concerned, rather than arising from circumstances, in which case they would be described as external (e.g. perceiving your examination

success as having been caused by your own hard work and/or ability, rather than by luck). Internal causes are often equated to *dispositional attributions*, although this can sometimes produce conceptual difficulties (e.g. 'is hard work a disposition?').

internal consistency A measure of *reliability* that looks at the similarity of results produced by different parts of a *psychometric* test which are deemed to measure the same characteristic or trait.

internal–external scale A scale originally devised by Rotter in the 1950s to measure whether a person believes the causes of events to originate within themselves (*emotions*, abilities, effort) or outside (powerful other people, luck). See *locus of control* for one use of such a scale, and *attribution theory* for another.

internal locus of control One extreme of *locus of control* which refers to a belief that control of events, or more specifically of *reinforcements*, comes from inside the person. See also *external locus of control*.

internal validity The extent to which an individual item in a test measures the same thing as the other items. See also *validity*.

internalisation Making something part of oneself. Freud was concerned with the child internalising the moral values of its parents, as expressed in their system of rewards and punishments. The term is now used more broadly, particularly in areas such as *conformity*, where its use distinguishes research participants who have fully adopted and internalised certain ideas from those who express them for expediency.

International Statistical Classification of Diseases and Related Health

Problems (ICD) This is the main alternative to the *Diagnostic and Statistical Manual of Mental Disorders*. It is produced by the World Health Organization and differs from the DSM in that it covers health as a whole, including mental disorders but not primarily focusing on them. Its classification of mental disorders differs significantly from that of DSM-V (e.g. it classifies schizotypal disorder as a mild or arrested form of schizophrenia, whereas DSM-V classifies it as a personality disorder). The two systems also disagree on the classification of other kinds of personality disorder, and even how many there are. It is the more common system used for diagnosis outside of the United States.

interneurones Neurones within the *central nervous system* that connect sensory input (brought by *sensory neurones*) with motor output (carried by *motor neurones*). Also called *connector neurones*.

inter-observer reliability The extent to which two observers observing the same events agree about what they have observed. Also known as *inter-rater reliability*.

interoception Sensitivity to bodily stimuli. Interoception may be conscious or unconscious. See also *kinaesthesia*, *proprioception*.

interpersonal Occurring between people. The term may apply to an interaction between two or more people, to feelings between people, or to other psychological processes by which two or more people influence one another.

interpersonal attraction The study of what determines whether a person will find another individual attractive. After decades of research investigating a great range of subtle variables, it has emerged that people are attracted most to those whom they find physically attractive and who are geographically close to them.

interpersonal intelligence A form of intelligence that is concerned with how effectively the person is able to interact with other people. It includes communicative and empathic skills as well as the ability to relate well to others. See also *multiple intelligences*, *emotional intelligence*.

interposition See *superposition*.

interpretation

(i)   The sense made of events or stimuli by people in their everyday lives.

(ii) A trained skill used by therapists, which aims to identify significant unconscious conflicts in order to clarify and deal with them.

In *psychotherapy*, it refers to the activity of the therapist in pointing out underlying meanings in the patient's activities or cognitions. In *psychodynamic* therapy, interpretations are made to uncover the *defence mechanisms* of the patient and to describe the patient's *transference* reactions, with the aim of making the patient's *unconscious* processes explicit.

interpretive bias The tendency for people to interpret ambiguous stimuli or situations as being potentially threatening.

interpretive repertoire The range of images and metaphors used in conversation to interpret or illustrate a particular perspective or set of ideas.

interpretivism An approach to social research which starts from the position that it is the meanings of the experience which are important. Interpretivism developed within psychology in opposition to the idea that it is meaningful to study objective reality. *Personal construct theory* is a good example of interpretivism. See also *hermeneutics*.

interquartile range The spread of a set of scores between the end of the first quartile and the start of the fourth quartile (i.e. between the 25th and 75th percentage points) of a distribution. See also *semi-interquartile range*.

inter-rater reliability The extent to which two independent raters of the same object, behaviour or event (e.g. of the attractiveness of photographs) agree in their ratings. See also *reliability*.

interstitial fluid The fluid that surrounds cells in the body.

interval scale See *equal-interval scale*.

intervening variable An unobservable process that is proposed to account for the relationship between input and output. The characteristics of intervening variables can be studied by manipulating the *independent variable* and observing the effects on the *dependent variable*.

interview A conversation between a professional and a respondent designed to provide the professional with a certain kind of information. The nature of the interview will be influenced by its function, which may be evaluation of the respondent (for a job, therapeutic, or research). The form of the interview may be fully specified in advance (structured interview), and resemble a verbally administered questionnaire. Research interviews usually have a list of *open questions*, which indicate to the participant the areas for discussion, but allow new areas of interest to be explored. These are called semi-structured interviews.

A selection interview may also be planned in more or less detail, or be conducted without any prior consideration of what information is wanted and how it is to be obtained. Research has shown interviews to be an inaccurate method of selecting, but this may be because the interviews studied had not been carefully constructed with clear objectives. See also *depth interview, focus group, rapport interview* and *transcription*.

interviewer effects The usually unwanted effects that an interviewer can have on respondents when they are influenced by their values, motivation to obtain a particular result, or personal qualities of the interviewer. Sometimes these effects can operate through the structuring of interview questions, which lead the participants to talk about particular topics in a particular way. At other times it may be that non-verbal signals by the interviewer affect the process without either participant being aware of the fact. Researchers working within a *positivist* paradigm would regard interviewer effects as a contamination of the objective reality that the research is investigating, and therefore to be eliminated if possible. *Constructionist* researchers see the interview itself as defined by the interaction between the interviewer and respondent, in which case it would make no sense to talk about eliminating the effect of the interviewer, but it should be reflexively reported as accurately as possible. See also *depth interview, focus group*.

intrapersonal Within the person – a term used to refer to internal processes that do not involve interaction with others.

intrinsic Internal, or deriving from internal, pre-existing factors. See also *intrinsic motivation, extrinsic*.

intrinsic motivation Motivation that comes from the nature of an activity rather than from an external reward (*extrinsic motivation*). Examples are being motivated by pride in achievement or pleasure derived from the activity.

introspection The process of self-examination, or looking within one's own experience in order to gain insight into psychological phenomena. Although notoriously unreliable in many respects, introspection can sometimes provide valuable insights that could otherwise be missed.

introspectionism A school of thought, prevalent in the early years of psychology as an independent discipline from philosophy, in which investigations were conducted through systematic and often detailed introspection by one or two highly trained psychologists. Although often castigated as 'armchair psychology' by the early behaviourists, this technique established some important theoretical perspectives, such as those outlined in James' *Principles of Psychology*, which in many cases are still of use to modern psychology. With the advent of *behaviourism* in the first part of the twentieth century, introspectionism as a technique became disregarded, but in recent years it has re-emerged to a limited extent within the *phenomenology* school of modern psychologists.

introversion A dimension of personality in which people are quiet, reserved, and find social situations stressful. In the *Eysenck Personality Inventory*, it is the opposite of *extraversion*.

intuitive definitions Definitions that have been adopted or used because they 'feel right' to the person using them, rather than because they have been verified according to extrinsic or objective criteria.

invariants In Gibson's theory of *ecological perception*, these are the properties of the *optic array* that don't change when other aspects do.

invasiveness A term used in *neuropsychology* to refer to whether a measuring technique is located entirely externally, as in *fMRI scans*, or involves adjustments to the internal state of the body (e.g. the ingestion of radioactive isotopes prior to *PET scans*).

inverse problem The problem that results from taking measurements of *event-related potential* at the level of the scalp, and trying to infer the specific neural activity which has produced that result, out of a potentially infinite number of possibilities. See also *dipole modelling*.

involuntary response A reaction or reflex which is produced to a stimulus regardless of the individual's conscious intervention or inclinations. See also *unconditioned response*.

iodopsin A form of light-sensitive pigment found in the *cone cells* of the *retina*, which responds to coloured light by changing the electrical polarity of the cell, and so contributing to an *electrical impulse*.

ionotropic receptors Receptors that open or close in ionic channels in response to the presence of a particular *neurotransmitter*.

Iowa gambling task A problem-solving task used to identify lesions in the *ventromedial frontal cortex*. The task involves a card game in which people have to learn to avoid making risky choices, producing a net loss, in favour of less risky and more rewarding choices.

ipsative Assessed or measured by comparison with the self. Ipsative scales involve the individual using their own values or behaviour as the yardstick by which comparisons and evaluations are made. See also *normative*.

ipsilateral Belonging to, or relevant to, the same side. The prefix 'ips-' usually means 'of one's own'.

IQ See *intelligence quotient*.

IRM See *innate releasing mechanism*.

iteration A complete sequence of processing steps or stages. In data analysis, for example, some procedures for *qualitative analysis* require the analysis to undergo several iterations (i.e. they require the analytical process to be repeated several times, each repetition of the procedure being performed on the information obtained from the previous one). Each full sequence, or iteration, reveals different levels of meaning in the data. See also *grounded theory*.

iterative A procedure in which the same action or procedure is carried out repeatedly, in order to achieve further refinement or the closer approach to a goal. Each round of action gets closer to the objective until it is achieved or sufficiently well approximated.

J

James, William (1842–1910)

Widely considered to be one of the 'founding figures' of modern psychology, James exerted most of his influence through his major textbook *Principles of Psychology*, published in 1890, in which he explored the nature of the human mind. He took the view that consciousness could either come through the 'front door' (i.e. learned from scratch by the individual), or through the 'back door' (i.e. shaped by our evolutionary history). Many of his insights into the nature of experience are still taken as the starting point for the teaching of psychological topics such as emotions (as in the *James–Lange theory*) and infant cognition. His approach to investigation is considered a prototypical example of *introspectionism*, and in later years he became more concerned with philosophy than with psychology itself.

James–Lange theory An early theory of emotion which argued that the experience of emotion arises from the perception of physiological changes in the body, brought about by the emotional stimulus. In other words, the physiological changes occur first, and the emotion is simply the perception of those changes. See also *alarm reaction*, *Cannon–Bard theory*.

jargon aphasia A condition arising from brain damage in which the person's speech is reasonably grammatical, but they have severe problems in accessing the appropriate words for what they want to say. See also *neologism*.

jet lag A syndrome in which the individual's *circadian rhythms* become out of phase with the surrounding environment, as a result of the rapid crossing of time zones during long-distance travel. This produces feelings of extreme fatigue, and in some cases disorientation, sometimes lasting for several days until the individual has fully adjusted to a new time system.

jnd See *just noticeable difference*.

joint attention The sharing of attention between two or more people, all focusing on the same object or location. See also *gaze cueing*, *postural echo*.

judgement In cognitive psychology, the term is taken to mean an assessment of the probability of a given event occurring, which is based on incomplete information.

Jung, Carl Gustav (1875–1961)

Jung was an early disciple and collaborator of Freud, but broke from him in 1913 to investigate the unconscious basis for symbolism and myths, which he believed existed in similar forms in all cultures. He argued that the unconscious keeps contact with ancient insights which were lost to the conscious mind as industrial society developed. Jung's *analytical psychology* was based on the idea of *archetypes* – powerful symbols that are embedded deep in the *collective unconscious* of humankind. Certain everyday occurrences or symbols are invested with powerful significance through *synchronicity* – direct connection with the collective unconscious. Archetypes, Jung believed, exert an unrecognised influence, identifiable through everyday symbols and through dreams. For a time, Jung's theorising led him to an involvement with *parapsychology*, giving him a reputation for mysticism. However, his idea of psychological types was used as the basis for the Myers Briggs Type Indicator – a *psychometric* test that is particularly popular among occupational psychologists. He also developed the concept of introversion–extraversion, which was subsequently adopted by Eysenck (perhaps the least similar psychologist possible).

Jungian Pertaining to the psychoanalytic system developed by Carl Jung, sometimes also referred to as *analytical psychology*.

just noticeable difference (jnd) The smallest change of stimulus that an individual is able to detect consistently for 50 per cent of the time. The amount of the jnd varies as a proportion of the intensity of the stimulus that is changing. For instance, a relatively larger change is necessary before a difference in volume of a loud sound is detected, than for a relatively quiet sound. See also *Fechner's law, Weber's law*.

just world hypothesis The idea that everything works out fairly in the end, so that people, by and large, get what they deserve.

juvenile delinquent A young person who has been convicted of a criminal offence.

K

Kelly, George (1905–1966)

George Kelly founded personal construct theory, which formed the basis of cognitive approaches to *psychotherapy*. Kelly was impressed by the different ways in which different people perceive and understand the same events. He proposed that all cognition is based on *personal constructs*, by which we distinguish between people and events by those distinctions that we have learned are most useful. His concept of 'constructive alternativism' pointed out that we cannot deal in absolute truths, and proposed that we should focus instead on the varied ways in which people make sense of their worlds. Kelly's theory is based around the idea of 'man as scientist' – that we are continually searching for better ways of understanding and prediction. He developed the *repertory grid* as a way of recording constructs, and was rather disappointed that the test became better known than the much more important theory behind it. He pointed out that most psychological theories account for the behaviour of 'subjects', but not for the activities of psychologists, whereas a good theory would be 'reflexive' – both applying to itself and explaining its own existence.

key word method A *mnemonic* technique for learning the meanings of technical or foreign terms. It involves identifying a key familiar word derived from the sound of the unknown one. A visual image is formed linking this key word with the meaning of the word to be learned. The visual image forms a link between the perceived sound of the new word and its meaning.

kibbutz An Israeli community in which property and responsibility are held in common by all members of the kibbutz (kibbutzniks). Many kibbutzim have communal child-rearing systems, which were intensively studied in the 1960s. The then-current theoretical ideas on mother–infant *bonding* implied that children would become psychologically damaged if they were not kept with their mother. Little evidence of this was found among the communally reared children of the kibbutzim. See also *metapelet*.

kin selection A concept put forward in *sociobiology*, kin selection involves the idea that an individual may protect their genes for the future by protecting not just their offspring, but other relatives who share them. Since siblings share on average 50 per cent of their genes, the individual can ensure that a proportion of the genes survive by protecting their siblings. The concept is used to explain behaviour that is apparently altruistic, such as the self-sacrificing behaviour of worker ants. It is open to question how far it has relevance for human beings.

kinaesthesia A form of sensory perception that identifies movement of the body or parts of the body. It involves receptors in the muscles, tendons, joints, and the *vestibular system* of the *inner ear*, some of which are also involved in *proprioception*, but the difference is that kinaesthesia involves the perception of movement while proprioception involves the perception of position.

kinaesthetic To do with sensations of movement.

kinesics The study of human movement patterns and the types of communication that use them. Kinesics is a major area in the study of *non-verbal communication*, involving gestures and changes of posture and gait.

Klinefelter's syndrome A condition in which a man has inherited an extra X-chromosome, having an XXY group of sex chromosomes instead of an XY pair. Such individuals are usually clearly male, but can sometimes show some female *secondary sexual characteristics*.

Kluver-Bucy syndrome A syndrome observed in monkeys after bilateral lesions of the *amygdala*. It consists of unusual calmness and tameness, dietary changes, and an increased tendency to exmine objects with the mouth. It is proposed that these changes arise from objects having lost their emotional connontations for the animal, owing to the lesions.

knowledge-based errors Mistakes or errors that arise from the people concerned having the wrong factual information, and so taking inappropriate actions when an emergency arises.

knowledge effect The tendency to assume that other people possess the same information as you do.

knowledge frame The set of assumptions and information within which a particular problem is located. The knowledge frame defines what counts as relevant information and needs to be taken into account when making decisions, and selecting what information is to be discarded or ignored. See also *decision-making*.

knowledge-lean problems Problems that can be solved without the need to apply specifically relevant prior knowledge.

knowledge-rich problems Problems that can only be solved with the use of considerable background information.

Korsakoff's syndrome A condition acquired by long-term *alcoholics* who have combined heavy drinking with eating too little, resulting in an extended period of thiamine deficiency. Korsakoff's syndrome patients demonstrate severe and apparently irreversible *proactive amnesia*, such that they are unable to retain new information, while still maintaining their repertoire of basic skills. While conversational topics remain on a general level, many Korsakoff sufferers remain undiagnosed. An attempt to retrieve current information often reveals the deficit.

Kruskal–Wallis test A test for statistically significant differences between three or more samples, which can be used when *analysis of variance* is not appropriate. See also *levels of measurement*.

kurtosis How much the scores in a particular sample cluster towards the middle or ends of the distribution. See also *skewed distribution curve*, *positive skew*, *leptokurtic*, *platykurtic*.

L

labelling When a label is applied to someone, there is a tendency for that person to be seen, both by others and often also by themselves, as having all of the characteristics implied by the label, and being nothing more than that. Therefore, labelling someone as schizophrenic or depressive can cause them to be treated as less than a whole person, since all of their behaviour is likely to be interpreted in terms of the illness, as schizophrenic or depressed behaviour. This tendency can be resisted by insisting on referring to 'a person with depression' rather than 'a depressive', but the tendency remains difficult to avoid. The study of labelling and its implications is an important part of *social psychology*, and has been so ever since the discovery of the *self-fulfilling prophecy*. See also *stereotype*.

labile Changeable, or likely to alter rapidly. The term is often used of emotional states or autonomic arousal.

LACS See *Leeds Attributional Coding System*.

LAD See *language acquisition device*.

laddering A technique drawn from *personal construct* therapy, which involves asking questions that become progressively more personal or intense, with each being based on the response to the previous question.

Laing, R.D. (1927–1989)

The psychiatrist R.D. Laing was most famous in applying the philosophical approach of *existentialism* to psychiatry and social psychology. In doing so, he examined some of the less positive aspects of social living such as the mind games or 'knots' that people use to confound and manipulate others emotionally. He developed a major alternative explanation for schizophrenia, in which he asserted that the primary cause of schizophrenia was not medical, but social, arising from disturbed relationships within the family. Although refuted by the medical establishment at the time, and challenged by some later researchers, his work drew attention to the importance of social stressors, and the influences that these exert on vulnerable people. See also *vulnerability model*.

laissez-faire Leaving people to get on with things in their own way. It is used to indicate a *leadership style* in which most of the responsibility for action is left with the group, rather than assumed by the leader. Groups with laissez-faire leadership tend not to be as productive as others, but some findings suggest that they continue to operate better than other groups when the leader is absent.

Lamarckian genetics The theory of genetic transmission proposed by Lamarck at the beginning of the twentieth century. This model proposed that characteristics which an individual acquires during their own lifetime can be passed on to their offspring. For example, it was suggested that giraffes had acquired long necks because they had had to stretch upwards for food, and the elongation caused by stretching had been inherited by the next generation. Although now thoroughly discredited as a model, Lamarckian genetics influenced a number of other theories, most notably Piaget's model of *cognitive development*. See also *genetics*, *Mendelian genetics*.

language The complex system of *communication* that involves the organisation of words into meaningful combinations. Although most people would agree that the use of language is a distinctively human attribute, the lack of a precise definition of what exactly language is makes it difficult to decide whether such phenomena as bird songs, bee dances, or whatever can be taught to chimpanzees in this line, should be called language. However, it is generally accepted that language involves *symbolic representation*, and that there are distinct rules concerning acceptable combinations of the elements of language (usually words) which do not permit all possible combinations to be regarded as meaningful. Language can be studied on a number of levels, which may be broadly classified as lexical (concerning the word units themselves and their referents), *syntactic* (concerning the rules for combining words into meaningful

utterances) and *semantic* (concerning the meaning of what is said). The use of analogy and metaphor in language means that the lexical characteristics of an utterance may not be identical with its semantic characteristics (e.g. describing someone as 'burning' with enthusiasm). Psychologists have also studied social aspects of language use, such as the impact of *accents* or sexist language, and recently much research attention has been devoted to *discourse analysis* (looking at the way in which language is used in complete conversations). See also *paralanguage*, *psycholinguistics*, *sociolinguistics*, *verbal deprivation hypothesis*.

language acquisition A term used to describe how language is learned by small children. The term 'acquisition' is used in preference to 'learning' as a result of heated debates about the precise mechanisms involved. It is considered to be more non-committal.

language acquisition device (LAD) A mechanism proposed by Chomsky to explain the extreme rapidity with which young children develop speech. He proposed that the young infant is born with an innate language acquisition device, which enables it to extract basic rules of grammar from the speech heard around it. Moreover, this occurs as a more or less automatic process – all that is required is that the child hears or experiences language used by others. In view of an increasing body of research indicating that human interaction forms a fundamental part of speech acquisition, later theorists have modified this concept, preferring instead to talk of a language acquisition system, or LAS, which allows for rather more active involvement on the part of the child than simply passive

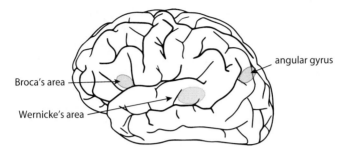

Figure 29 Language areas of the brain

decoding. See also *deep structure, surface structure*.

language areas Specific parts of the *cerebral cortex*, usually (although not always) located on the left hemisphere, and mediating the functions of language. There are generally believed to be three main language areas, although modern research suggests that the actual processes of language are more complex. Nonetheless the three areas are:

(i) *Broca's area*, which is largely responsible for speech production and the formulation of appropriate words;

(ii) *Wernicke's area*, which is concerned with the comprehension of speech; and

(iii) the *angular gyrus*, which receives information concerned with the written word from the *visual cortex* and converts it into sound-equivalent representations for decoding in Wernicke's area (see Figure 29).

larynx The organ in the neck of mammals that is involved in sound production. The larynx is particularly important in human beings as its flexibility offers a wide range of possible *phonemes*, making possible the use of spoken *language*.

Lashley, Karl (1890–1958)

Karl Lashley was one of the first significant researchers into the relationship between memory and the *cerebral cortex* of the brain. His most significant discoveries were the principle of mass action and the principle of *equipotentiality*. The principle of mass action states that with regard to memory, it is the overall amount of functioning cortex that is important rather than specific areas, and the principle of equipotentiality was concerned with how other areas of the cortex could take over memory functions in response to brain damage. Lashley's research was important in highlighting that, although some brain functions were localised, higher ones such as memory and thinking utilised the whole cortex rather than small areas.

late selection models Models of *selective attention* which suggest that any filtering or selection occurs at a late stage in cognitive processing, rather than when the information is first received. See also *filter models*.

latency period In Freudian theory, the period from the end of the Oedipal stage around 6 years, until the onset of *puberty* and the beginnings of genital sexuality. Freud saw this as a relatively calm period of the child's development.

latent Unrevealed and inoperative, but nonetheless present and liable to become active or relevant if situations change. See also *latent learning*.

latent content The underlying and usually hidden meanings in the account provided by a patient in *psychoanalysis*. The term is usually used about dreams, which Freud thought were particularly rich in indications of unconscious processes for anyone who could see past the *manifest content*. See also *dreamwork*.

latent learning A system of *learning*, first demonstrated in 1932 by Tolman, who presented clear empirical evidence that even laboratory rats could form internal, cognitive representations of a complex maze, and that learning need not necessarily be manifested immediately in behaviour, but might remain latent until it was advantageous to use it. Latent learning was important as a concept because it provided a counter to the *behaviourist* argument that learning and changes in behaviour were synonymous (see Figure 30).

lateral On the side, or outer part, of the body or segment. See also *medial, ventral, dorsal*.

lateral fissure A long fissure, found at the side of each *cerebral hemisphere*, which serves as the boundary between the *temporal lobe* and the *frontal lobe*.

lateral geniculate nuclei A group of cells found in the *thalamus*, which receive information carried along the optic nerve from the eyes. The first synapse of the optic nerve is found at this point, and some basic perceptual organisation seems to occur here, namely the sorting of the visual information by means of *simple cells, complex cells* and *hypercomplex cells*, such that hypercomplex cells fire in response to simple patterns and shapes.

lateral hypothalamus (LH) A part of the thalamus that has been shown to affect the intake of food in experimental animals, and is thought to be implicated in human *eating disorders*. Electrical stimulation of the lateral hypothalamus induces eating behaviour in some animals, while its removal or destruction results in the animal ceasing to eat. See also *ESB*.

lateral inhibition The reduction of activity in one *neurone*, caused by the activation of a neighbouring neurone.

lateral inter-parietal area (LIP) An area of the brain that responds to relevant environmental stimuli in the planning of the direction of eye movements. See also *visual system*.

lateral prefrontal cortex A part of the brain that appears to be actively involved in tasks requiring the control or evaluation of neutral stimuli or information. See also *prefrontal cortex, multiple-demand network*.

lateral premotor cortex This is part of the *premotor cortex*. It receives visual information from the parietal lobe, and is particularly concerned with acting on objects in the immediate environment, such as reaching for a cup of tea,

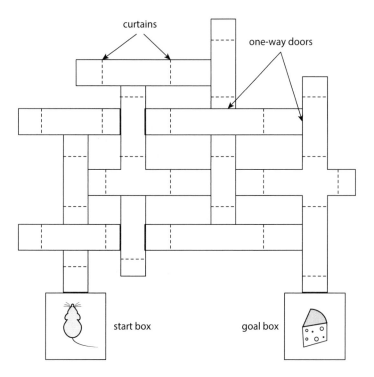

Figure 30 A maze used to test latent learning

or tapping a screen. See also *medial premotor cortex*.

lateral thinking Thinking that involves a 'sideways leap' from conventional attempts to solve a problem, and which reaches a solution by adopting novel tactics or by reformulating the problem in an unusual manner. Lateral thinking has been promoted since the 1960s by de Bono, and involved a search for originality and flexibility in mental operations that would counteract sterile and hidebound problem-solving practices, both in management and in day-to-day *problem-solving*. *Divergent thinking* has a similar meaning. See also *creativity*.

laterality Specialisation of function on one side. The term is used both of *handedness* and of the specialisation of function in either the left or right hemisphere of the brain.

Latin square An experimental design in which the set of conditions is presented as if in a grid, with each condition appearing once in each column and once in each row. Each condition therefore has the same average position in the sequence. Each of four participants experiences a different row of the square, to eliminate *order effects*. However, in the usual form, a Latin square does not avoid the possible effect of one condition on the next (see Figure 31).

Latin square counterbalancing A way of organising the conditions of an

```
A       B       C       D
C       A       D       B
D       C       B       A
B       D       A       C
```

Figure 31 A Latin square

experiment in order to control for order or *practice effects*. It is similar to the ABBA *design*, but suitable for three or more conditions.

Law of Effect The principle, developed by Thorndike, that a response which was followed by a pleasant consequence would be more likely to be repeated. This idea was developed and amplified by B.F. Skinner in his work on *operant conditioning*.

Law of Effort A principle developed as a result of investigations into *imprinting* in ducklings, in which it was observed that the more effort a duckling had to put into following its imprinted 'parent' around, the stronger the *attachment* bond would become.

Law of Exercise The principle of association learning, which stated that a learned connection between a stimulus and a response would be established by the repetition of their association. In other words, if they occurred together often enough, they would become associated together, and learning would have occurred. This concept was later developed more fully by Pavlov in his research on *classical conditioning*.

Law of Mass Action A principle formulated by Lashley as a result of investigations into the role of the *association cortex* in learning. He found that much of the *cerebral cortex* appeared to have non-localised functioning, but instead seemed to function as a mass – the more

there was of it, the more effective the learning; or alternatively, the greater the amount destroyed, the greater the learning impediment. See also *equipotentiality*.

Law of Parsimony See *Occam's razor*.

Law of Prägnanz The principle by which meaningfulness and the organisation of visual stimuli occurs, according to the *Gestalt psychologists*. The Law of Prägnanz is concerned with the ways in which perceptual organisation occurs through the subsidiary principles of proximity, *similarity*, *closure* and 'good Gestalt', such that we see meaningful figures against backgrounds, rather than just a jumbled mass of disparate elements of visual information (see Figure 32).

lay epistemology An approach articulated by Kruglanski, lay epistemology represents an attempt to structure the processes by which *social attributions* and *social representations* become incorporated into the individual's personal knowledge frameworks and used as 'common sense'. One of the distinctive processes identified in studies of lay epistemology is that of 'freezing', in which the person latches on to one specific explanation and then does not change it, even in the face of directly contradictory information.

leadership style Patterns of behaviour by designated group leaders that have been found in empirical studies. One division is between task-oriented leaders whose efforts are directed towards getting the

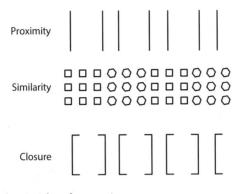

Figure 32 Gestalt principles of perception

job done, and maintenance-oriented leaders who pay more attention to ensuring that the group is working together well. Other forms of leadership are *authoritarian, authoritative* (maintaining authority through example and negotiation), *democratic* (working through persuasion and consensus), and *laissez-faire* (largely leaving the group to find its own solutions). Similar styles have been identified in studies of parenting. See also *child-rearing styles*.

learned helplessness A concept demonstrated experimentally by Martin Seligman. He showed that animals which had received unpleasant experiences about which they could do nothing were less ready to undertake action when in a similar situation where a relatively simple response would avert an unpleasant experience. Instead, the animals would remain passive and do little to help themselves, not even struggling. Seligman drew parallels between the behaviours shown by animals in this condition and the behaviours associated with *depression* in humans. From these parallels, he developed helplessness theory, which proposes that (some) depression may result from a belief of having no control over bad events.

Subsequently, the theory was revised by Seligman and others in terms of *attribution theory*. See also *learned optimism*.

learned optimism A process proposed by Seligman in the 1990s. Having spent several of the previous decades exploring *learned helplessness*, Seligman then turned his attention to positive thinking, and identified a style of thinking characterised by distinctive attributional patterns and a deliberate attempt to identify positive aspects of events. His research showed learned optimism to be mentally healthy and a significant tool in stress management. See also *positive psychology*.

learning A relatively permanent change in knowledge, behaviour or understanding that results from experience. Innate behaviours, maturation and fatigue are excluded. Learning has been claimed to be the core phenomenon of psychology, although in practice the field often seems to have operated by producing a theory and then defining learning as being whatever that theory explains. Specialist areas include *modelling* and *imitation, motor skills, insight*, the formation of *schemata, creativity, habituation* and *conditioning*. The learning of specific skills such as *language* have become areas of study in their own right. See also *connectionism*.

learning curve The graph obtained when a measure of competence is plotted against the number of learning trials the animal or person has had. The learning curve has a characteristic shape, but this is usually achieved rather artificially, by averaging together a large number of learning curves. Individual curves may be much less regular (see Figure 33).

learning difficulty The term used at present to refer to people with limited cognitive ability who would otherwise be said to have *mental handicap*. Often used in the form 'people with learning difficulties' in an attempt to reduce the effect of *labelling*. The term is somewhat unsatisfactory because, by only referring to learning, it understates the difficulties experienced by this group of people and their carers.

learning set A generalised style of learning, or state of preparedness to solve problems in certain ways, which has been acquired through experience with similar types of problems. Possession of a learning set means that the individual is likely to look for that kind of solution in preference to any alternative strategy. Where problems are similar, learning sets may be advantageous, but they may prove a hindrance to the individual faced with a problem that requires a novel approach. See also *insight learning*.

learning theory A theory about how learning occurs. Note that, as discussed under *learning*, the theory is not specifically about what learning is, since that tends to be assumed at the outset, although it may be modified as the theory develops. Some theories, such as *operant conditioning*, are presented as accounting for practically all learning, while others deal with a particular type (e.g. *insight learning*). There are also

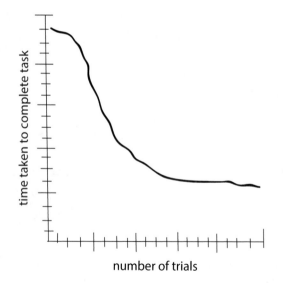

Figure 33 A learning curve

theories for specific phenomena such as *transfer of training* and *modelling*.

Leeds Attributional Coding System (LACS) A technique for *attributional analysis* developed by Stratton *et al*. in 1986, in which *attributions* are analysed in terms of five dimensions: stable/ unstable, global/specific, internal/external, personal/universal, and controllable/ uncontrollable. As an alternative to *covariance* theory, the LACS has been found to be useful in *family therapy*, as well as in other contexts (e.g. the qualitative analysis of the information provided by focus groups).

left brain A commonly used term indicative of a popular misconception about brain functioning. See also *hemisphere bias*.

left hemisphere The left half of the *cerebrum*. The cerebrum is divided into two hemispheres by a deep fissure. In most people, the left hemisphere contains the *language areas*, and is also thought to be concerned with the general functions of logic and numeracy. It is generally referred to as the dominant hemisphere, as functions from the left hemisphere will usually override those from the right hemisphere.

lemma An early, abstract form of a word that has not yet been outputted by the speech system.

leptokurtic A distribution of scores with very few extremes, so the curve appears pointed towards the centre. See also *normal distribution, kurtosis*.

lesbian A female person who is sexually attracted to members of her own sex.

lesion A term used to refer to damage to organic tissue, usually used by psychologists to refer to brain or neural injury. Lesions may be surgical or accidental, and may take the form of cutting of specific fibres or pathways, or of general damage (e.g. damage caused by the impact of a heavy object).

leucotomy A form of *psychosurgery* that involves severing the main connections between the *frontal lobe* and the rest of the brain. Leucotomy was introduced as a less drastic alternative to *lobotomy*, and has been shown to produce difficulty with *decision-making* and a limitation of impulsive behaviour. Still carried out, it is a contentious operation, since its effects: (i) are irreversible; and (ii) can be seen as a form of social control.

levels of analysis Ways of describing a phenomenon, such as a human activity, at different degrees of specificity or generality. For example, an arm movement might be described at the level of muscle or motor nerve actions, or as an aggressive act designed to intimidate. Different levels of analysis cannot readily be converted into each other (see *reductionism*), so several levels of analysis are needed for a full description of human activity.

levels of explanation See *levels of analysis*.

levels of measurement Types of measurement that differ in how far they can be manipulated mathematically. The lowest level of measurement is known as nominal data, which is information that cannot be ranged on a scale, but only organised into different categories. The next level is ordinal data, which are data that can be put into a definable order, and so can be ranked. However, no information can be provided about the size of the difference between any two items. For example, if colours are arranged in order of preference, it is possible to say that one colour is liked more than another, but it is not possible to be precise about how much more it is liked.

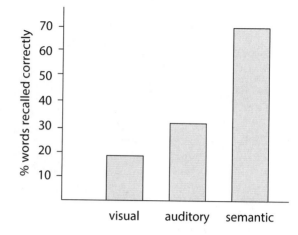

Figure 34 Levels of processing

The third level of measurement is *equal-interval* data, in which the measurements can be ordered on a scale that has equal intervals (e.g. measurements of temperature in degrees Fahrenheit or Celcius). The highest level of measurement is known as ratio data, which is equal-interval data with an absolute zero, such that it is possible to describe one score as a precise proportion of another. Because temperature in degrees Celsius is only an interval scale, there is no sense in which 40 degrees is twice as hot as 20 degrees. However, height is a ratio scale, so 2 metres is twice as high as 1 metre. See also *nominal scale, ordinal scale.*

levels of processing A theory of memory proposed by Craik and Lockhart, which argues that information may be processed at a number of levels depending on how it is organised, linked with other memories, tied in with emotional experience, and so on. Information that has been only superficially processed or accepted passively will be readily forgotten, and this is used to explain the phenomenon of rapid forgetting previously characterised as *short-term memory.* Information that has been processed more deeply will be retained for a longer period of time (see Figure 34).

Lewin, Kurt (1890–1947)

Kurt Lewin was one of the pioneers of social psychology, influencing many future psychologists such as Abraham Maslow, Carl Rogers and Leon Festinger. His field theory argued that social behaviour can only be understood in the context of the social environment operating on the individual: a view which challenged the S–R approach of the behaviourists. Lewin also founded and developed the idea of *action research*, on the grounds that laboratory methods were simply inappropriate for studying social or working experience, and undertook seminal work on *leadership styles* and the processes of psychological change.

lexeme The basic unit of a language, which may be a single word-like sound or a whole word.

lexical To do with words.

lexical decision task A task used in cognitive experiments that requires the research participant to choose between different words.

lexicalisation

(i)   The process of selecting a word based on the meaning that is intended.
(ii) The speech production process of translating a word's meaning into its sound representation.
(iii) How a sound's meaning becomes a base or 'blueprint' for the sound itself, such that hearing the sound automatically links with the meaning. 'Ow' might be an example.

lexicon The set of words generally taken to define a *language*. In the case of artificial languages, such as *Yerkish*, the lexicon is very much smaller than it is for human languages.

LH See *lateral hypothalamus*. Also used as an abbreviation for 'left-handed'.

libido A term originally used by Freud to refer to sexual energy that is derived from the *id* and is available to power mental and physical activity. Later, Freud regarded libido as a general life energy. In common usage, the connotation of sexual energy is still associated with the term.

lie detector See *polygraph*.

lie-scale A subset of questions in a test designed to find out if the person is being honest in their answers. A typical item would be 'I have never told a lie'. Anyone agreeing to this statement is likely to be responding with social desirability as a stronger motivation than accurate self report. More simply, they are almost certainly lying.

life coaching See *coaching*.

life event An event that results in a major change in the life situation of a person. There is evidence that all life events, even those that are fundamentally positive, impose some stress. Holmes and Rahe have produced a 'Life Events Scale', which gives weightings to different events, ranging from 100 for death of a spouse down to 12 for Christmas and 11 for minor violations of the law. The scale can be used to provide a total score for all of the life events experienced during, say, the last year. People who have experienced a lot of change will obtain a high score, and high scores may indicate that a person is at higher risk of illness or accidents. Negative life events may also make some people more prone to *depression*.

life script Cultural expectations or assumptions concerning how major life events are expected to proceed during a person's life.

lifespan The entire period of a person's life. There has been a move within *developmental psychology* to study the whole lifespan rather than restrict the field to childhood. This approach has opened up the adult years from 20 to 65 as an important period within which to study development, but so far the obvious worthiness of the objectives has not been matched by exciting findings or theories.

light adaptation The process by which the photosensitive cells of the retina adjust to changing levels of illumination.

By varying their sensitivity to light, and also by the adjusting of the pupil of the eye in order to maximise light intake in dim conditions, and minimise it when conditions are bright, the individual adjusts their perception to accord with the amount of light available. See also *dark adaptation*.

lightness constancy The experience of a consistent level of illumination in different environments, even though objective measurements of the light available would show them to be widely varied. For example, sitting under electric light in the evening is often perceived as 'full light', and as equivalent to daylight, despite the fact that in reality the light level is several thousand times dimmer than sunlight. See also *perceptual constancy*.

Likert scale A five-point scale commonly used in attitude measurement. Typically, a Likert scale will express variation along a single dimension, such as 'strongly agree – agree – neutral – disagree – strongly disagree'. See also *ordinal scale*.

limbic circuit A loop of brain cell activity particularly associated with reward-based learning. The limbic circuit begins and ends in the *cortex* of the *frontal lobe*, and includes the *amygdala* and *anterior cingulate gyrus* parts of the *limbic system*, the *basal ganglia* and the *thalamus*.

limbic system A term used to refer to a series of small structures buried deep in the centre of the brain, including the *hippocampus*, the *amygdala*, the *cingulate gyrus* and the *mamillary bodies*. The limbic system is generally considered to be involved in relating the organism to its environment, and its structures appear to be involved

in several disparate functions. These include the encoding of memories (the hippocampus), recollective memory (the mamillary bodies) motivation and emotion (the amygdala). and the detection of emotional and cognitive conflicts (the cingulate gyrus). See also *limbic circuit*.

limerence The infatuated emotion often described as romantic love. The concept of limerence was developed by Tennov to distinguish between that emotion and the deeply affectionate companionship often developed in more long-term relationships. The two emotions are quite different, and have very different characteristics, so referring to them both as 'love' can be seriously misleading. See also *loving*.

line of best fit The line in a *scattergram* that has the minimum overall total distance from the data points. It is the line on which the *correlation* is calculated.

linguistic determinism The theory, put forward by Benjamin Lee Whorf, that thinking and perception are determined by the language we have available. The usual example is that Inuit Eskimos, having many more words for different kinds of snow than the English, will be able to make finer discriminations on the subject. The hypothesis has not been validated experimentally perhaps because meaning is embedded in a whole combination of linguistic and cultural practices, and not in single words. The belief that the availability of certain words of phrases influences thought and behaviour remains widespread. It is used in behavioural programmes, such as when training young children to use words like 'also' in order to consider alternative consequences of their actions. It also underlies attempts to change cultural attitudes by making people more aware of the consequences of using words with disparaging implications, such as calling young women 'chicks'. It is an interesting confirmation of the approach that people who wish to resist it have attempted to convert the label of 'political correctness' into an insult.

linguistic intelligence A form of intelligence that is concerned with how competent or skilled the person is at language. See also *multiple intelligences.*

linguistic relativity hypothesis Sometimes also known as the *Sapir–Whorf hypothesis,* this is the idea that thinking is dependent on the language used by the individual – in other words, that the possession of words for a *concept* shapes a person's thought. In the 'strong' form of the hypothesis, words are seen to determine thought entirely, but a 'weak' form has become more generally accepted, which states that the words available serve to facilitate and amplify thought, and to indicate relationships between concepts, rather than actually to determine them. See also *linguistic determinism.*

linguistics To do with *language.* The term linguistics is used to refer to the study of language itself.

LIP See *lateral inter-parietal area.*

lithium The basis for drugs which are an effective treatment for *bipolar depression* in most cases. The effect seems to be to prevent the manic phase, so that the cycle does not continue and so the depressive phase is also prevented. The method of action of the drug is not known. Lithium is an element that is close to sodium and potassium, so it is thought likely that it alters neural transmission in the central nervous system. The drug has to be taken continuously and it is dangerous, with significant side effects even in carefully controlled doses.

Lloyd Morgan's canon The principle proposed by the nineteenth-century physiologist that animal behaviour should never be explained in terms of higher-level mental functioning if it could be explained in terms of a more basic process. This rule was particularly influential with the *behaviourists,* but has led to some remarkably convoluted ways of explaining animal behaviour, as researchers tried to avoid describing processes such as remembering or reasoning, when faced with animals that were clearly doing both. The extremely mechanistic but not very practical applications of Lloyd Morgan's canon are a good example of some of the shortcomings of *reductionism* as an approach.

lobotomy A form of *psychosurgery* in which the *frontal lobes* of the brain are removed. It was originally developed as a method of docilisation for highly aggressive or unstable individuals, but its use was both politically and psychologically suspect. It has been largely replaced by *leucotomy.*

localised functions Functions, usually of the *cerebral cortex,* that have been shown to be located at a particular site. Among the localised cortical functions are motor control, located in an area alongside the *central fissure,* body skin sensation, located on the other side of the central fissure, vision, located in the *striate cortex* or *visual cortex* in the occipital lobe, olfaction (the sense of smell), located in a strip at the base of the *temporal lobe,* and the *language areas.*

location constancy The way in which the perceptual system automatically modifies its judgements and estimations of objects and distance, depending on their location and the location of the perceiver. Objects viewed from an alternative location are not perceived as having changed their position, despite the fact that the background to them has altered. Instead, they are seen as having remained constant. The *perceptual constancies* are often used to illustrate the way in which the received visual image is only a part of perception – what is known on a cognitive or experiential level is an equally important part.

locus of control (LOC) A concept at the core of a social learning theory developed by Rotter in the 1950s. It refers to the belief that a person has about where social reinforcements originate – whether they are internal to the person, or external. Someone with an *internal locus of control* will tend to believe that marks on an essay depend on the amount of effort and ability applied to writing it. Someone with an *external locus of control* will tend to attribute the marks to luck, predestination or the whims of the person doing the marking. LOC can be measured using a variety of short self-report scales, and has been found to relate meaningfully to how people behave in a wide variety of situations. Such evidence supports the *construct validity* of the scales. Writings in the area often imply that an internal LOC is preferable. It is true that an internal LOC is more likely to result in the individual making efforts to improve their situation, but whether this is useful depends on whether events are actually under their control or not. A similar but not identical concept was developed more or less independently in *attribution theory*. See *internal–external scale*.

log-linear modelling A statistical technique for estimating the effect of independent variables on frequencies. The logarithm of the frequencies is used because this has desirable mathematical characteristics. It allows the effects of a number of independent variables to be estimated (where *chi-square* can only cope with one), and the *interactions* between them to be calculated.

logic A set of rules by which conclusions can be reliably deduced from initial statements (propositions). Logic can be applied without regard for the truth of propositions. For example, the statement 'All students work hard and those who work hard pass their exams; therefore all students pass their exams' sounds logical. The fact that it is not true that all students work hard or pass their exams if they do means that the conclusion is not necessarily true. Logic has been of interest in psychology because it can be regarded as perfect reasoning, and is therefore a starting point for analysing how people reason. It turns out that people are much more sophisticated and rather less rigid in their thinking than any logic that has been invented, and there is not too much similarity between the two processes.

logical concepts Concepts that are founded on clear and unambiguous rules, without exception. Logical concepts are quite rare in everyday life. See also *concept*.

logical-mathematical skills Aspects of intelligence that are concerned with how well the person is able to deal with abstract logical puzzles and mathematical or symbolic problems. These skills form part of the *componential intelligence* sector of *triarchic intelligence*. See also *multiple intelligences*.

logistic regression A form of *regression analysis* designed for use when the outcome or *dependent variable* is *dichotomous*. The analysis provides a prediction of how much influence the independent variable will have on the either/or state of the dependent variable (e.g. the effect of alcohol consumption on becoming pregnant, after other aspects of diet have been taken into account).

logogen A cognitive unit of word recognition, sometimes referred to as a 'dictionary unit', and used in theories of *selective attention* and reading.

long-term memory (LTM) A term used to describe memories other than those that remain for a few seconds only. According to the *two-process theory of memory*, any information which is retained for any length of time above a few seconds is deemed to have been stored in LTM, while that which lasts just for a brief interval (such as a telephone number that has just been looked up) is considered to have been stored in *short-term memory*. Many modern researchers question this commonly accepted distinction, arguing that it is unnecessary and that it fails to discriminate between information retained for varying periods of time. One alternative to this approach has been the *levels of processing* theory, which argues that the decisive factor in determining how long information is retained is how deeply it has been organised and processed, and that there is no need to postulate separate memory stores. See also *orthographic lexicon, long-term working memory*.

long-term potentiation (LTP) The way that neurones which are frequently stimulated by their presynaptic neurones show an increase in the probability that they will be activated. This links with *Hebb's theory of synaptic*

learning, in which he proposed that learning occurs through the increased activation of *neural pathways*.

long-term working memory An efficient form of memory storage characteristic of experts' cognition, in which relevant information is rapidly stored in *long-term memory*, but accessed through retrieval cues in *working memory*.

longitudinal study A study that takes place over a period of time, and is concerned with studying some form of development or change. Longitudinal studies have been valuable in challenging many erroneous or commonly held beliefs. For example, longitudinal studies of the relationship between ageing and *intelligence* suggest that intelligence, if used, continues to develop and increase throughout life, rather than declining with age as was once thought. See also *cohort effect, cross-sectional study*.

loss aversion A tendency in *decision-making* to be more sensitive to potential losses than to potential gains.

love need A term used by some humanistic psychologists to refer to the need for affection or *positive regard* from others, which is seen as a fundamental part of human nature.

loving A usually intense and long-term form of emotional positive regard for another person. In psychology, it is often distinguished from the short-term infatuation known as *limerence*.

LSD See *lysergic acid diethylamide*.

LTM See *long-term memory*.

LTP See *long-term potentiation*.

lucid dreaming Dreams in which the dreamer is aware that they are dreaming. Sleep researchers have discovered that it is possible for lucid dreamers to 'control' their dreams, making events happen or characters appear by will. Lucid dreams can be induced in the laboratory by delivering a prearranged stimulus, such as a puff of air or a very mild electric shock, during *REM sleep*.

lysergic acid diethylamide (LSD) A recreational drug that forms a potent *hallucinogen* when ingested, producing visual disturbances, sometimes hallucination, and a heightened or distorted awareness of reality.

M

MA See *mental age*.

Machiavellianism A *personality trait* that involves a manipulative approach to interactions with other people, together with a disregard of moral conventions and principles and an emphasis on self-interest. Machiavellianism is considered to be one of the *Dark Triad* of personality traits.

magical thinking The belief, common in young children, that thinking of something makes it happen or exist.

magnetic resonance imaging (MRI) A *non-invasive technique* in which the brain is studied using a succession of electromagnetic waves, like radio waves, which are passed through the brain. Active brain cells respond to electromagnetic stimulation by producing their own electromagnetic waves, which the MRI scanner detects and records. A computer combines hundreds of these measurements and collates them, building up an image of the electrical activity in different areas of the brain.

magneto-encephalography (MEG) A *brain scanning* technique that is based on recording the electrical fields generated by the brain's activity, by means of electrodes attached to the scalp.

magno cells Cells that form part of one of the major visual pathways in the brain. Magno cells are found in the *visual cortex*, and carry information about brightness and depth. They are thought to have evolved earlier than the complementary *Parvo cells*.

main effect The overall relationship between a class of independent variable and the dependent variable. The term is used mainly in *analysis of variance*.

major hemisphere See *dominant hemisphere*.

majority influence The effect of the opinions or actions of most of the people present or relevant on the actions of a single individual.

maladjustment A poor *adjustment*. The term is used of people, particularly children and adolescents, whose behaviour is judged to conflict strongly with the expectations and requirements of society.

malapropism A common speech error that involves using a word which has a similar phonological form to the intended one, but is inappropriate to the context and intention of the *utterance*. The term derives from the character Mrs Malaprop, in Sheridan's play *The Rivals*.

mamillary bodies A pair of small, round bodies found below the *thalamus* and considered to be part of the *limbic system*. They have connections to the anterior thalamus, and are considered to be important for recollective *memory*.

mania An emotional disorder during which there is elation, talkativeness, impatience with others, overconfidence and an uncontrolled flight of ideas. See also *bipolar depression*.

manic depression An emotional disorder in which there is an alternation between *mania* and *depression*. See also *bipolar depression*.

manifest content The overt content of an account, usually of a dream. Dream interpretation involves seeing beyond the manifest content to understand the underlying meaning – the *latent content*.

manipulative skill A skill that involves direct action with the hands, usually in terms of handling and placing of objects.

Mann–Whitney test A two-sample statistical test used for *ordinal data*, or interval data not deemed suitable for a *t-test*, and independent samples. See also *statistical significance*.

mantra A word or phrase on which a person concentrates as an aid to meditation. Traditionally, the mantra is derived from Hindu scripture and has spiritual power.

marijuana A *psychoactive* drug that induces a feeling of lethargy and relaxation when consumed. Marijuana is derived from the cannabis plant, and may be consumed either by smoking the dried leaves or resin of the plant, or by eating small pieces of the resin. The use of marijuana as a relaxant is extremely common in many areas of the world, including Africa, the Middle East and Central America. It is widely (although often illegally) used as a *recreational drug* in Western industrial societies. Marijuana appears to exert its main effects by increasing the *noradrenaline* levels in the brain.

Marler, Peter (1928–2014)

Peter Marler has been a major figure in comparative psychology through his work as an ethologist and neurobiologist. Among other discoveries, he identified the use of natural concepts in monkeys, and worked with other famous figures on social relationships in the great apes and other primates. Most importantly, Marler contributed significantly to our understanding of the role of neural adaptation in learning, through a lifetime of research, including work that clarified the relationship between environmental and inherited aspects of birdsong, the role of critical and sensitive periods, and the nature of species-specific learning.

Marr, David (1945–1980)

David Marr is best known in psychology for his work in clarifying the way that we process visual information to arrive at our perception of real-world objects, people and animals. His work on the neural and computational stages required to build up a fully three-dimensional representation of the outside world from the neural input represented by the optic array has become the basis of both medical and scientific understanding of visual processing.

masking A term used in cognitive research to refer to suppressing the processing of a response by introducing a second task requiring processing immediately afterwards. There may still be some unconscious processing of the first task taking place, but it is masked by the conscious demands of the second.

Maslow, Abraham H. (1908–1970)

Abraham Maslow is most famous for his theory of the *hierarchy of human needs*. This model distinguished between deficit needs, such as safety, and higher needs, such as *self-actualisation*. Although the theory is essentially only a description, it has been widely used, especially in the personal growth movement and in *occupational psychology*. Its emphasis on the idea that human beings move beyond deficit needs in order to fulfil their human potential made it much more attractive and relevant to the lives of ordinary people than the dominant focus on negative drives such as fear and hunger. Perhaps the main reason for the theory's popularity, however, was the way in which it provided other psychologists with a clear and tangible example of the *humanistic* approach to psychology, at a time when *behaviourism* dominated most psychological explanations for human activity.

masochism Obtaining sexual gratification from personal pain or humiliation. Often associated with *sadism*.

massed practice Extended periods of practice while learning a new skill, taken without breaks. Massed practice has been found to be less effective than *distributed practice*, which allows for consolidation of the learning.

mastery goals Personal goals that are to do with acquiring competence and skills in order to be able to carry out tasks or exercises.

mastery play Play that leads to the acquisition of new skills. This definition leaves open the question of whether children are motivated to achieve mastery, or cannot avoid learning when having fun. See also *play*.

matched participant design A research design in which different people are allocated to each of the experimental conditions, but in which they have been carefully matched on significant factors, so that if one group contains a single high-intelligence individual, then so does the other. The intention is to ensure that *individual differences* will act equally on each of the experimental conditions, rather than affecting one condition more than the others.

matching The name given to ensuring that two sets of experimental materials or research participants are identical in all important respects. A matched task or test has questions carefully selected to ensure that, in each test, the questions are equivalent in difficulty and in the type of problem posed. It is also desirable to select a group of people matched in terms of age, sex and overall intelligence levels, although other criteria may also be used if required for the study.

matching hypothesis The idea that people will tend to form lasting relationships, particularly marriages, with those of similar appearance, or at least a similar degree of attractiveness. The concept is problematic, not least in terms of the use of ratings of attractiveness based on photographs of strangers. It forms part of research into *impression formation*.

materialism

(i)   A theoretical position that assumes that everything can be explained in terms of physical matter. It leads to a *reductionist* position that thoughts, feelings and all manifestations of mind can be accounted for in terms of physiological processes.

(ii)   In everyday language, materialism refers to placing importance on acquiring material possessions.

maternal deprivation A concept proposed by John Bowlby and Rene Spitz to account for the poor development of children brought up in institutions. Of the various disadvantages suffered by these children, the theories of the time (the 1940s) focused on the lack of consistent mothering. Bowlby added other evidence and concluded that any disruption of mothering, especially between the ages of 6 months and 3 years, was likely to have damaging long-term consequences. The belief that infants should never be separated from their mothers became stressed beyond anything Bowlby had claimed. It has been suggested that the concept of maternal deprivation was exploited in order to remove women from employment and so release jobs for men at the end of the Second World War. If so, then similar calls might be expected during any other period of high male unemployment. The concept of maternal deprivation was soon challenged, and much evidence has now been accumulated showing that good development is possible without the consistent presence of a mother or mother substitute. However, the evidence does not show that good development is especially easy under these circumstances. A fair statement might be that, while around 1950 mothering could be thought of as something that the infant either did or did not receive, we now know that the normal processes of mothering provide a great variety of physiological and emotional effects, learning experiences, motivations, practice in social interaction and no doubt much else besides. Substituting for all of these may certainly be possible, but it is likely to be difficult. See also *attachment, maternal privation*.

maternal drive The tendency, usually presumed to be innate, to engage in caretaking behaviours such as nest-building, retrieving and suckling during the infancy of offspring. The tendency is displayed by mothers, and sometimes by fathers, in many species. Use of the term *drive* implies that there is some basic need to be maternal – an assumption that should not be accepted uncritically. The term 'maternal instinct' is sometimes used instead, but this is even more likely to bring in assumptions for which there is inadequate evidence. The most misleading use of the terms arises when meanings that have been developed by studying species such as rats are applied uncritically to humans.

maternal privation Rearing from birth without a mother. Strictly, privation means 'never having', while deprivation means having something taken away. Experiments involving total maternal privation have been carried out on various species, although not with humans. However, these are typically classed as *maternal deprivation* studies, and in practice the term maternal deprivation is used for all variations of a shortage of mothering in the upbringing of young.

MATLAB A commercial computing and programming environment, able to handle complex computations, 3D modelling and many other functions, and designed to interact with a variety of programming languages and symbol sets.

maturation The term used to describe behavioural or physical changes that occur as a direct result of *genetic* action, but which emerge as the animal or human matures or grows older. A clear example of maturation in terms of physical development are the changes that occur at puberty. In the 1920s, Gesell proposed a theory that nearly all development is controlled by maturation and so is independent of practice or experience. Modern approaches tend to take a more interactive stance.

MBD See *minimal brain dysfunction*.

McGurk illusion A striking auditory *illusion* that occurs when an auditory stimulus is combined with a different but matching visual stimulus, resulting in the perception of a third, different event. For example, if someone is given the auditory input of 'baba' while at the same time seeing someone making lip movements of 'gaga', they will report – quite definitely – hearing 'dada'. It is believed that this illusion arises from the way that speech perception is based on the fusion of multiple inputs.

mean The name given to the arithmetic average of a set of numbers, calculated by summing the numbers and dividing this total by the number of figures in the set. The mean is one of the three main *measures of central tendency*, but it can only be used for equal-interval or ratio *levels of measurement*.

means-end analysis An approach to *computer simulation* and other forms of problem-solving in which the solutions are calculated by comparing the final goal state with the current situation, and developing strategies, known as *heuristics*, designed to reduce the gap between them.

measures of central tendency A collective term for all of the statistical measures that provide information about the most typical distribution of scores. The *mean* is the most widely used, but others may be more informative in certain circumstances. For example, when considering the spread of incomes in a particular country, the mean may be unduly affected by a few extremely rich people. The *median* will tell you the income of someone right in the middle of the earning population, while the *mode* will tell you the most common income (see Figure 35).

measures of dispersion A collective term for all of the statistical measures that provide information about the way in which a distribution of scores is spread out. See also *range, standard deviation, variance*.

medial In or towards the middle. See also *dorsal, ventral, lateral*.

medial geniculate nucleus A set of cells in the thalamus that are associated with auditory perception, in particular with locating and identifying sounds. See also *lateral geniculate nuclei*.

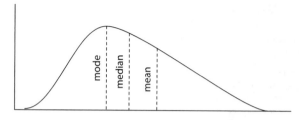

Figure 35 Measures of central tendency

medial pre-optic area (MPOA) A region of the *hypothalamus* that responds to pregnancy-related hormonal change and triggers parental behaviours in many mammals.

medial premotor cortex Often known as the supplementary motor area, this part of the brain, which is located just in front of the *primary motor cortex*, receives strong *proprioceptive* signals, and is associated with dealing with spontaneous, well-learned action sequences that don't require much cognitive processing. Examples might include rapid typing on a keyboard, or (for a musician) playing a familiar tune on a well-known instrument. See also *lateral premotor cortex*.

median A *measure of central tendency* that is calculated as the middlemost score from a given set. Fifty per cent of the scores in a given set will fall at or below the median score, and 50 per cent fall at or above it. The median is appropriate for use with ordinal *levels of measurement* (see Figure 45).

mediators Processes (e.g. *memory*, *perception*, thought) that occur in between a stimulus and a response. The early behaviourists claimed that as mediators cannot be observed directly, they should not form part of scientific psychology. *Cognitive psychologists*, on the other hand, regard them as the main subject matter of psychology. See also *schema*.

medical model An overall approach to abnormal behaviour or personality that assumes an individual organic source of any disorder, mental or physical. This implies that the task of treatment is to diagnose the condition and then cure it. The medical model has been called into question in relation to the less serious psychiatric disorders. One of several problems with the medical model is that it tends to result in *labelling*.

meditation A process of disciplining or training the mind, either to achieve an internal focus or to achieve full *apperception* of an external single stimulus, such as a crystal or a chant. In either case, it involves disregarding and eventually cutting out completely, all distracting thoughts and ideas. See also *mindfulness*.

medulla The lowest part of the brain, formed by an outward thickening from the spinal cord. Also known as the brainstem, the medulla mediates the autonomic functions of breathing, digestion, heartbeat and blood pressure.

meiosis The process of cell division involved in *sexual reproduction*, in the formation of gametes (ova and spermatozoa). Unlike the kind of cell division that is involved in growth and tissue repair (see *mitosis*), this process involves the separation of pairs of *chromosomes*, such that the resulting cells are *haploid* (i.e. they have only half the normal number of chromosomes). In order to form a complete *zygote*, which can develop to form a new individual, these cells must combine with another haploid cell to make up the full complement of chromosomes. In this way, the newly formed individual comes to inherit half of its chromosomes from each parent.

MEG See *magneto-encephalography*.

meme The term given to a unit of culture that is transmitted from person to person (or group to group) according to its perceived usefulness. The term has been popularised by its use in Internet contexts, where it refers to the rapid spread of an idea, phrase or jargon word.

memory The general term given to the storage and subsequent retrieval of information. Memory has been intensively studied by psychologists throughout the history of psychology, and consequently involves an extensive range of theoretical approaches and fields of enquiry. These include the study of *episodic memory*, everyday memory, *levels of processing*, encoding and representation, and physiological correlates of memory. See also *two-process theory of memory*.

memory bias The tendency to retrieve more negative or unpleasant information from memory, than positive or pleasant information. See also *mood congruity*.

memory span A well-known measure of an individual's capacity for retaining small units of meaningless information over a brief period of time. In a typical measure of memory span, a list of digits is read out to someone at a regular pace. On completion of the list, the individual is required to repeat what they have heard, either forward or backward. First observed by Miller, it has been repeatedly observed that the average span available to the individual is of 7 ± 2 digits, and that this can only be increased by some system for *chunking* the information into meaningful units. See also *levels of processing, two-process theory of memory, working memory*.

memory trace In older texts sometimes referred to as an *engram*, a memory trace is a hypothetical 'image' of what is to be remembered, which has been encoded and which is stored for varying periods of time. The term memory trace is usually associated with the *decay* theory of forgetting, which holds that memory traces die away if they are not strengthened by being recalled from time to time. As this approach is not particularly open to empirical investigation, the term fell into disfavour as an explanation of forgetting for many years. However, with the advent of more sophisticated cognitive research, and more expecially of forms of *brain scanning*, which allow observation of the active brain, the term memory trace has returned to general use.

menarche The beginning of *menstruation* during puberty.

Mendelian genetics The currently accepted theoretical model of genetic transmission, Mendelian genetics proposes that this occurs through the passing on of discrete units of inherited information – genes – which are fixed, and which change only through accidental mutation. Individual differences occur because reproductive cells are haploid, containing only half the number of genes required for the complete organism, and so have to combine to produce a new individual. The new individual therefore inherits characteristics from each parent, and is thus different from either of them. The combination of Mendelian genetics with Darwinian evolutionary theory proposes that those combinations and accidental mutations which are favourable to the individual, in terms of helping it to survive, will be passed on because that individual will then become fitter, healthier, etc., and therefore more likely to reproduce successfully. See also *evolution*, *genetics*, *Lamarckian genetics*, *sexual reproduction*.

meninges The layers of membrane covering the brain, between the brain and the skull. Meningitis is inflammation of these membranes.

menstruation The phase of the monthly menstrual cycle in which, if the woman is not pregnant, the blood and other material that has built up in the uterus following ovulation is discharged. Many cultures have beliefs about the dangerousness of women during or around menstruation. The major Western version concerns premenstrual tension.

mental age (MA) A construction developed by Binet in his early work on the measurement of intelligence, mental age refers to the abilities of the individual compared to others of that society. By selecting a series of age-appropriate problems and tasks, a set of age *norms* is developed, allowing each child to be assessed in terms of how far they measure up to these criteria. The level of difficulty of items at which the child starts to fail is compared to the norms. The average age of children who pass the items up to this point is found, and this is regarded as the mental age of the child being tested. Binet's original formulation of *IQ* involved the comparison of mental age with the child's *chronological age* ('real' age).

mental chronometry The study of the time taken to process information in the brain. This is a significant measure in both *cognitive psychology* and *neuroscience*, since it is inferred that a longer time taken to respond to a *stimulus* implies that more processing time has been required, and therefore more complex processing procedures have been involved. See also *information processing*.

mental handicap A general term for people of limited intelligence as measured by *intelligence tests*. The classification of people in these terms raises many difficulties, as it labels them in terms of a particular aspect of human ability. Worse still, it is an aspect that is highly valued in this culture, and it is measured by tests which many regard as unsatisfactory. In particular, intelligence tests are usually standardised on the 'normal' population and they may have less *validity* when applied to other groups. However, people who are mentally handicapped need to be identified so that they can be provided with special resources at an appropriate level and, at present, intelligence testing is the most reliable and accurate way of achieving this.

The term 'mental handicap' is one in a long line of labels that may have been scientifically neutral when first used, but which tend to become unacceptable as they pass into the general language as terms of abuse. For example, an earlier grading of mentally handicapped people was as idiots, imbeciles and morons. The term 'mental deficiency' is sometimes used, particularly for mental handicap that is believed to be due to brain damage. The term's current unpopularity is in part due to a recognition that it is not very productive to attempt to distinguish between organic and non-organic cases. 'Mental retardation' is also widely used, particularly in the American literature. More recently, 'special learning difficulties' has replaced 'mental handicap' as the official term, although this solution also raises difficulties, notably in undervaluing the efforts demanded of those who care for people of very limited intelligence. See also *labelling*.

mental imagery The use of imagined pictures, or other sensory images, such as sounds or smells, to represent information in the mind. Mental imagery involves recreating the apparent sensation, as part of the process of memory or thinking. See also *symbolic representation*.

mental model An internal representation of a situation, event, process or experience. See also *concept, mental representation*.

mental representation The form that information takes in the brain. See also *imagery, memory, schema*.

mental retardation A general term for limited intelligence. The term tends to carry a misleading assumption that the low intelligence is due to either a slowness of mental functioning or slow intellectual development. For a fuller discussion, see *mental handicap*.

mental set A state of preparedness to perform certain kinds of mental operations rather than others. Mental sets may refer to particular kinds of problem-solving (see *learning set*), or to readiness to perceive certain things rather than others (see *perceptual set*), or to a preparedness to remember certain items of information in preference to others.

mentalising The process of inferring a particular mental state to someone else, or attributing mental states to other people. See also *animism*.

mentalism The approach to psychology which attempted to study and describe the mind directly. The main tool of the mentalist approach was *introspection*. The approach was widely used in the early years of psychology but was strongly attacked by early behaviourists such as Watson and lost its popularity. In recent years, it has been gaining influence, mainly through the use of *protocol analysis* techniques in cognitive studies.

mesencephalon Another term for the *midbrain*.

mesolimbic pathway See *reward pathway*.

messenger RNA Also known as *transfer RNA*, this is a form of RNA that carries coding information from the nucleus to the site of protein synthesis. See also *ribonucleic acid, transcription*.

meta-analysis A research technique that involves comparing the outcomes of a number of different studies in the same area, and examining the general themes or trends which can be identified as a result.

metacognition Cognition about cognition (i.e. awareness of one's own cognitive processes and how they work). An overall term used to refer to personal knowledge about how cognitive processes work, which is often highly influential in cognitive development. The study of metacognition includes the study of how people monitor and control their own cognitive activity, such as being aware of cognitive limitations (knowing that you don't know) or abilities (knowing that you can learn certain types of information readily). The act of looking up a word in a dictionary, for instance, is one that would be unlikely to happen without metacognition.

metalinguistic awareness Knowledge about the nature, forms and functions of language. It is possible to be a fully competent language user without meta-linguistic awareness, but the different ways in which people understand how language works are likely to influence how they interact with their world and each other. It is therefore an important area of study for psychologists.

metamemory Knowledge about how one's *memory* works, or what its limitations are. Such knowledge often directly affects behaviour, such as a decision to write a note to yourself to remind you of something, or to adopt a specific revision technique to make remembering easier. See also *metacognition*.

metapelet The name given to a child-nurse or professional carer for children in an Israeli *kibbutz*. Such an individual, rather than the parents, carries the responsibility for the care of the children, and oversees their day-to-day experience and early learning.

metaphor Using a word relevant to one thing when talking about another (e.g. 'The success of cognitive psychology pulled the rug from under behaviourism'). The phrase 'pulling a rug' creates a powerful image that is much richer than if we just said 'weakened'. The use of such figures of speech is such an important part of thinking and language that it has even been claimed that all novel thinking depends on the use of metaphor.

metencephalon A section of the brain consisting of the *pons* and the *cerebellum*. See also *subcortical structures*.

method of loci A *mnemonic* technique in which a mental image is formed that visualises items to be remembered at specific locations. Usually, the locations take the form of landmarks along a familiar walk or journey – something that is already well known to the person forming the image. By subsequently visualising the journey, the individual is reminded of the items to be remembered.

methodology The procedures adopted for creating knowledge. Different schools of thought, including different approaches to research, use their own methodology. Any account of research will need to describe the methodology used in some detail, and will usually contain a justification for the choice of that particular methodology.

micro-electrode recording A means of investigating neural activity by recording the firing of single *neurones*. It consists of a technique whereby microscopic electrodes, sensitive to very small electrical charges, are inserted into the appropriate region of the brain or nervous system. These electrodes record when their target cells fire. By means of this technique, several discoveries have been made, including the processing of visual information in the *thalamus* and the *visual cortex*, and the changes to neurones involved during the *imprinting* process in young chicks. See also *hypercomplex cell*.

midbrain A part of the brain above the brainstem, which includes part of the *reticular formation* and the *pons*, and which seems to be active in the integration of sensory input and motor activity.

middle ear The air-filled chamber of the ear that is separated from the outer canal by the tympanic membrane, and which serves to amplify the received signal, in preparation for its *transduction* in the *inner ear*. The middle ear contains three small bones, known as the ossicles, which form a link from the tympanic membrane at one side of the chamber to the oval window at the other. Each ossicle receives the vibrations in turn, and amplifies them slightly as it passes them on. In sequence, the ossicles are the malleus (hammer bone), the incus (anvil bone) and the stapes (stirrup bone), named in accordance with their overall shapes.

Milgram, Stanley (1953–1984)

One of the most famous of all social psychologists, Stanley Milgram conducted research into a wide range of real-world social behaviours, but is most famous for his studies of *obedience*, in which he showed that, given the right circumstances, even quite ordinary people were able to obey orders to the extent of killing another person. Milgram proposed that we all have two distinct states – the *autonomous state* in which we act as individuals, and the *agentic state* in which we act as agents of others and suppress our own consciences. The fact that all injury was simulated did not prevent a massive ethical debate arising from Milgram's work, resulting in the development and application of strict *ethical guidelines* for psychological research.

mimicry The copying of a specific action or sequence of behaviour, without necessarily any understanding of the goals of the action. Most bird vocalisations are considered to be mimicry rather than *imitation*.

mind-body problem The problem of how the physical, chemical and electrical characteristics of the brain can produce sensations, thoughts and emotions in the mind.

mindblindness The inability of autistic individuals to comprehend that other people have minds of their own, and therefore different viewpoints. See also *theory of mind*, *false belief task*.

mindfulness The practice of bringing one's mental attention to the immediate present, and disregarding extraneous thoughts or stimuli concerned with aspects of living that are more distant in either time or space. Mindfulness as a technique combines Buddhist meditational techniques with approaches used in *Gestalt therapy*, and is often considered to have begun in the 1970s, although it only achieved general popularity in the 2010s. It has been shown to have considerable psychological and physical health benefits, such as dealing with *stress* and *anxiety*, attenuating pain, and assisting in dealing with drug *addiction*.

minimal brain dysfunction (MBD) The preferred choice from a number of terms that have been proposed to account for, or at least label, a set of quite common childhood conditions which include *hyperactivity*, *attention* *deficit disorder* and clumsiness. They are the kind of problems that could arise because of brain damage, but no organic damage can be identified in these children. The conditions were therefore classified as 'minimal brain damage', with the implication that there was damage but it was too minimal to be detected. As psychologists came to realise that invisible brain damage was not really a useful explanation of anything, alternative terms were proposed such as minimal cerebral injury and eventually MBD. It is now becoming recognised that the various conditions have little in common, so the search for a suitable term under which they can all be grouped is likely to be abandoned.

minimal group paradigm An approach to the study of *social identification*, in which minimal indicators of group membership are shown to produce reliable social effects. In a typical example, participants in a minimal group paradigm experiment are allocated to membership of a group according to some arbitrary criterion, such as the toss of a coin. When asked to allocate resources to members of their own or other groups, they then show a reliable tendency to favour their own group above the others. Minimal group studies have generated a number of hypotheses about social identification that have been supported by more realistic investigations, including the tendency to accentuate differences between the in-group and the out-group, and to stereotype out-group members. However, such studies appear to be particularly susceptible to *demand characteristics*, as it is difficult to imagine what other behaviour could be expected of the cooperative participant whose only information is that they belong to either one group or another.

Minnesota Multiphasic Personality Inventory (MMPI) The most famous questionnaire measure of *personality*, consisting of 550 items and providing eight scales or traits. The objective evidence suggests limitations in its use either as a clinical predictor or as a guide to how people are likely to behave in practice. However, it is still widely used in research.

minor hemisphere The name given to the half of the *cerebrum* that does not form the *dominant hemisphere*. In most cases, this is the right hemisphere, but in some people the right hemisphere is dominant and the left one forms the minor, or non-dominant, hemisphere.

minority influence The way that a small group of people can sometimes produce a social or cognitive change even though the majority may be against their ideas. The key aspects of minority influence are consistency over time, clarity and persistence.

mirror neurone A *neurone* that is active in goal-directed actions designed to copy or imitate the action of someone else. Mirror neurones respond to the person's (or monkey's) own actions, and also to the same action seen performed by others (i.e. they appear to disregard the distinction between self and other). They are often tuned to very precise actions, such as grasping, twisting or tearing, and do not respond to robotic actions of the same type. See also *mirror systems*.

mirror self-recognition The ability to recognise oneself in the mirror. This is one of the key comparative techniques for assessing whether a given species has a *self-concept*. It is usually assessed by placing a mark on an individual's face or head while they are asleep, and then seeing how they respond when they see it in a mirror – in particular, whether they attempt to rub it off themselves, or off the image in the mirror.

mirror systems Specialised groups of *neurones* found in the *cerebrum* that appear to reflect, or mimic, input from other people. For example, interacting with someone who is smiling at you produces a 'smiling' response among these neurones, and the neural *node* which is activated when we feel disgusted is also activated when we see someone else expressing disgust. The discovery of mirror systems sets a strong physiological basis for empathy and social sensitivity, and reinforces the importance of the social nature of human evolution. See also *mirror neurone*.

mirroring The process of echoing or sharing other people's emotions or reactions. See also *echopraxia*, *echolalia*, *postural echo*.

misery-is-not-miserly effect The tendency for people who are depressed or sad to be prepared to pay more for a commodity or event than other people would. See also *mood*.

misinformation effect The distorting effect of information presented after an event to eyewitness memory. See also *eyewitness testimony*.

mismatch negativity (MMN) A change in *event-related potential* that happens when an auditory stimulus is different from the prior auditory stimuli which the person has experienced.

missing fundamental phenomenon A phenomenon in *audition*, whereby the fundamental note in a chord or complex sound can be removed, but its absence is not perceived because the brain reinstates it.

mitochondria Small energy-producing structures found inside the cell nucleus. Mitochondria also contain a form of DNA that derives from nurturing in the womb, and therefore maps genetic origins along the maternal line. Mitochondrial DNA has been widely used to map the ancestral origins of the human species.

mitosis The process of cell division that results in each new cell possessing a full complement of *chromosomes* – an identical copy of the genes carried by the parent cell. This is the most common form of cell division, being the type which is involved in tissue growth and repair; it contrasts with the form of cell division involved in *sexual reproduction*, which is called *meiosis*. Mitosis also made possible the development of *cloning*. Since each cell of the body carries the full genetic complement of that animal, given the right medium for cell division and growth, it is possible to recreate an identical animal from a cluster of parent cells.

mixed conditions Research designs that involve a combination of *repeated-measures* and *independent-measures designs*.

mixed error effect A type of error of speech in which the word given is incorrect, but related to the correct one in terms of its meaning and its sound.

MMN See *mismatch negativity*.

MMPI See *Minnesota Multiphasic Personality Inventory*.

mnemonic An aid to memory, which can be achieved in any way, including leaving a note for oneself. Several different kinds of mnemonics have been identified and developed over time. Many of them are concerned with forming of mental images that will help the person to remember connections between items, or lists. Some mnemonics rely on the use of visual imagery, such as the *method of loci* or the *key word method*. Other mnemonics rely on verbal processing, such as first-letter mnemonics, in which the first letter of each item spells out a new word or a sentence, for example 'Richard Of York Gave Battle In Vain' for the colours of the spectrum (red, orange, yellow, etc.). The famous 'knot in the handkerchief' is a mnemonic that combines visual and tactile cues to help the person to remember.

MNI template A 'standard' brain developed by the Montral Neurological Institute, which has been derived from the data from 305 individual brains and is used for *stereotactic normalisation*. See also *Talairach cooordinates*.

mob psychology An approach to crowd psychology that sees members of crowds as reverting to a primitive state in which individual conscience and responsibility are entirely suppresssed, and the person becomes entirely impulsive and emotion-driven. This approach to crowds was extremely popular in the early twentieth century, as it allowed the governments of the day to ignore or dismiss people's grievances. A modern-day equivalent of mob psychology can be found in Zimbardo's theory of *deindividuation*. In Europe, however, crowd researchers have taken rather a different view, and have investigated the perceptions of people in crowds, which turn out to be rather more rational and balanced than might be thought from conventional 'mob' theories.

modal To do with the *mode*. The modal score in a data set is the most commonly occurring value. See also *variation ratio*.

modal model of memory A simplistic approach to memory storage that sees information as passing from STM to LTM by rehearsal and repetition, as put forward by Atkinson and Shiffrin. Generations of students have shown how this is not really a very effective memorising technique. See also *levels of processing*.

mode The most frequently occurring score within a distribution. It is one of the *measures of central tendency*.

modelling Providing an example which can be imitated, such that the imitator is able to learn new styles of behaviour. Modelling is considered to be an important aspect of *social learning* in children, because what is copied is more general than the imitation of a specific behaviour. It is often used explicitly in therapy, to allow adults to vary their styles of interaction with others.

modes of representation Ways of coding information internally. Bruner identified a developmental sequence in representation, arguing that the first mode to develop was *enactive representation*, in which information is stored as 'muscle memories'. As the child's experience widens, and the environment makes increasingly complex demands, more sophisticated modes of representation are required – first *iconic representation* (using images) and then *symbolic representation* (in which information is represented by symbols).

modularity The idea that certain cognitive functions or areas of the brain are limited to the perfomance of particular tasks, and in the information they possess.

molar actions Actions that involve the whole body (e.g. walking, jumping, turning round). Compare *molecular actions*.

molecular actions Actions that involve only part of the body, and in which the rest of the body is relatively stationary (e.g. typing, writing, sewing). Compare *molar actions*.

mongolism See *Down's syndrome*.

monitoring The process of continually checking progress in a task by connecting the information held currently in mind with the task requirements.

monochromatism Seeing in one colour only, usually interpreted as seeing in black and white. In other words, monochromatic individuals are those who are entirely blind to all wavelengths of colour. This is a rare condition, as most *colour blindness* involves lack of sensitivity to a few wavelengths only.

monocular depth cue An indication of how distant something is, which can be detected just as well with only one eye as it can with two. Monocular depth cues include relative size, height in plane, *superposition*, *gradient of colour*, *gradient of texture*, shadow, and *motion parallax* (see Figure 36).

monotropy Bowlby's original idea of the way in which *attachment* develops between the young infant and its mother. Based on ideas from ethological studies of *imprinting*, the theory stated that the relationship which an infant formed with its mother was qualitatively different from any other relationship which it formed with other people, and that if the bond was broken, through separation, during the early years of life, then the child could suffer permanent damage. This led to the *maternal deprivation* debate, and produced extensive research into attachment and *mother–infant interaction*.

monozygotic (MZ) twins *Identical twins* who have developed from the same fertilised ovum which has subsequently split to develop as two independent foetuses. Monozygotic twins are identical genetically, and hence have been used in studies of the relative importance of genetics and environmental influences in development. See also *heritability estimate*.

mood A temporary emotional state that is extended over time, forming an affective baseline for personal responses and reactions. See also *mood congruity*, *misery-is-not-miserly effect*.

mood congruity The observation that emotional material is learned more effectively if the participant's mood matches the affective value of the material to be learned. See also *state-dependent learning*.

mood disorders Mental problems such as depression that manifest themselves as fluctuations or extremes in the person's general emotional state or mood.

relative size

height in plane

superposition

shadow

Figure 36 Monocular depth cues

mood freezing A phenomenon observed by researchers in the 1980s, who gave a *placebo* to participants, informing them that it would make it impossible for them to change their moods. They then put them through a series of frustrating tasks, and identified a number of strategies that participants used instead of reacting aggressively, including leaving the situation, seeking distractions, practicing relaxation techniques, etc. The study particularly challenged the validity of *catharsis*. See also *mindfulness*.

mood-state-dependent memory Memory that is linked with the individual's emotional state or *mood* (e.g. the way that memories about a partner's inadequacies or irritating behaviours are more likely to come back if someone is in an irritable or angry mood, while the same memories are totally fogotten when the person is in a more positive mood). See also *state-dependent learning*.

moral anxiety In Freudian theory, anxiety that arises from a fear of the *superego*. As the superego has incorporated the rewards and punishments of the parents, it is able to inflict pain, and if it becomes too powerful the person may live in a chronic state of anxiety. See also *neurosis*.

moral development This should refer to the development of moral standards and behaviour. In fact, the term has been taken over by a particular approach that concentrates on moral judgement. Piaget analysed tendencies in the developing moral judgement of the child, such as a progression away from a belief in absolute justice. Lawrence Kohlberg developed Piaget's ideas and produced a scheme of six stages of moral reasoning along which the child progresses. While moral reasoning is important, the theory has been criticised both for the ways in which the stages are defined and for appearing to undervalue other aspects of moral development such as moral behaviour. See *autonomous morality*, *conventional morality*, *pre-moral stage*.

moral disgust a form of disgust that comes from a distasteful feeling about the moral standing of a person's attitudes or actions, often in terms of their disposition to engage in acts which are considered to be morally wrong.

moral emotions Emotions that are connected with the propriety or significance of one's own behaviour in relation to others, or others' behaviour in relation to the self or third parties.

moral norms Rules of conduct that are based on social principles of right and wrong, generally deriving from ideas about personal welfare. See also *conventional norms*.

moral realism Another name given to the stage of *heteronomous morality* described by Piaget, in which the child accepts fully the rules that are given to it by society and those in authority. See also *autonomous morality*, *moral development*.

moral therapy An early approach to humane treatment of the mentally disturbed, pioneered by Pinel shortly after the French Revolution. The essence of moral therapy was that mentally disturbed people should be treated not as dangerous lunatics, but with dignity. The therapy involved such measures as discarding chains and constraints, and providing clean living quarters and such work as the patients were able to undertake. It had a remarkably high success rate, and eventually made a significant contribution to the reform of the care of the mentally ill.

Moro reflex A reflex found in newborn babies in which the limbs are closed in to the body and the hands are clenched. The probable function of the reflex can be seen when it is elicited by letting the baby slip while holding it and the Moro reflex causes the baby to cling on to its caretaker (do not try this, take our word for it!). See also *reflex*.

morpheme A unit of spoken language, in which basic speech sounds (*phonemes*) have been combined to produce basic syllables or simple words.

A morpheme is the smallest unit of speech that has any real meaning in communication.

morphology The study of form, or complete units. In linguistics, morphology refers to the study of how *morphemes* are utilised and combined in speech. In biology, it refers to the study of the form and function of parts of the anatomy, or the structure of the living being.

morphosyntax Linguistic rules concerned with word order and the grammatical elements of words.

Moscovici, Serge (1927–2014)

Along with *Tajfel*, Moscovici was a central figure in the development of *European social psychology*. His work in *social representation* theory at the Ecole des Hautes Etudes et Sciences Sociales in Paris began in the early 1960s, with a study of the social role of psychoanalytic theory in French folk wisdom, but was more clearly articulated two decades later, following a series of psychological investigations into the mechanisms of social influence, such as the role of *minority influence* in *conformity*, during the 1970s. Social representation theory became one of the key theories in European social psychology, expressing as it does the way in which cultural and social beliefs can be transmitted and developed through individual and group interaction.

mother–infant interaction The forms of interaction between caregivers (who may or may not be the mother) and infants, particularly in the first few months of life. This interaction has been extensively studied to provide information about the beginnings of *attachment*, and has been found to be very complex. It is often called parent–infant interaction, for obvious reasons.

motherese A simplified form of speech that adults adopt when talking to babies. Also known as *infant-directed speech*,

motherese is characterised by a generally higher pitch, slower expression of elongated vowels, and more pitch variability. Infants respond preferentially to this type of speech, and it has been suggested that it assists their learning of the relevant phonemes for their spoken language.

mothering Providing the physical, cognitive and emotional care and stimulation required by an infant or child. Research indicates that this kind of care can be provided by any adult or older child provided that they have an appropriate commitment, a knowledge of the needs of infants, and an ability to respond to the signals offered by the infant. There is therefore no sound reason to suppose that this care can only be provided by the biological mother or by a woman.

motion parallax The apparent relative movement of objects in the visual field, which occurs when the person doing the perceiving moves around. Objects in the foreground seem to move more than objects in the background, so that when a perceiver moves, such objects appear to change their relative position in the visual field. See also *depth cue*.

motivated forgetting A term for the forgetting of information as a result of an *unconscious* unwillingness to remember it (e.g. the forgetting of an impending dental appointment, because you don't want to go). According to Freud, all forgetting is motivated forgetting in some way, either because it could lead to the recall of deeply buried childhood traumas, or because the forgotten information is symbolic of such trauma. Other researchers have identified alternative explanations for many kinds of forgetting, but motivated forgetting is still considered to be valid as an explanation for some instances of failure to recall information.

motivation The general term given to an inferred underlying state that energises behaviour, causing it to take place. There has been extensive physiological research into the neural mechanisms involved in motivational states such as hunger, thirst, the need for sex, exploration of novelty, and so on. In addition, much research has emphasised the social aspects of motivation – the need for *positive regard* from others, or the way that specific forms of behaviour may occur as a result of the need to communicate or interact in meaningful ways with other people. While the majority of psychology textbooks limit discussions of motivation to physiological factors and need or *drive* theories, a more comprehensive formulation of human motivation might incorporate a wider range of motives. These would include motivations arising from cognitive processes, such as *cognitive dissonance* or *personal constructs*, factors involved in motivating personal action such as *self-efficacy beliefs*, *locus of control*, *attributions* and *learned helplessness*, affiliative motivators such as *empathy* or *positive regard*, and sociocultural motivators such as *social identifications* and *social representations*.

motivators Specific incentives or aspects of the environment that can induce certain forms of behaviour in the individual. The term has been commonly used in management theory, where it includes such items as the provision of personal career development for individuals at work, or bonus payments which would encourage those in employment to work harder. See also *Hertzberg*.

motive A specific inferred reason put forward to explain the likelihood of a particular behaviour occurring. See also *motivation*.

motor Referring to movement.

motor aphasia A disorder of speaking (see *aphasia*) that is due to problems with the muscles of the tongue, lips, etc.

motor end plate The part at the very end of a *motor neurone* where the *axon* divides into small *dendrites*, which spread out and make synaptic connections with *receptor sites* in the muscle fibres. The *neurotransmitter* involved at the motor end plate is *acetylcholine*.

motor neurone A nerve cell that transmits information in the form of electrical impulses from the *central nervous system* to the muscles of the body. This information forms a signal for muscular contraction, resulting in movement of the limbs or body. Motor neurones tend to have their cell body located within the *grey matter* of the central nervous system itself, surrounded by dendrites that receive information from many other neurones. The *axon* is elongated, and reaches from the central nervous system to the muscle fibre itself, where it spreads into *dendrites* to form the *motor end plate*. Motor neurones are usually *myelinated*, which speeds up the passage of the impulse along the axon and allows more accurate timing. See also *connector neurone, sensory neurone* (see Figure 37).

motor program Stored action routines that conform to pre-established patterns.

motor projection area The part of the *cerebral cortex* that is directly concerned with the mediation of physical actions. Also known as the *primary motor cortex*, this area forms a strip running alongside the *central fissure*, on the side of the *frontal lobe*. It runs directly parallel to the *somatosensory projection area* and, in a manner similar to that of the organisation of the somatosensory area, different parts of the strip mediate activity in different parts of the body. The most mobile parts of the body, such as the hands, have a large proportion of surface area representing them in the motor area. See also *homunculus, premotor cortex*.

motor skill A skill that is physical, as opposed to a *cognitive skill*. The word 'motor' in this context implies muscle movement. The study of motor skills involves looking at the influence of practice, feedback, and the development of smooth muscular coordination, and it was the main area for studying the acquisition and operation of skills. The area was strongly influenced by Cambridge psychologists who became fascinated with the skills involved in playing cricket and the training of fighter pilots during the Second World War. Other major landmarks include a study of cigar makers in Cuba, which discovered that performance improved for at least the first 250 million cigars rolled, and that the improvement followed a *power law*. See also *automatisation*.

MPOA See *medial pre-optic area*.

MRI scans See *magnetic resonance imaging*.

MS See *multiple sclerosis*.

MT An abbreviation for the middle temporal area of the *visual cortex*, also known as V5.

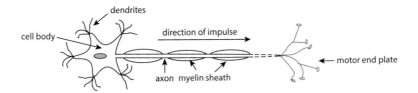

Figure 37 A motor neurone

mu oscillations A pattern of EEG variations that are found across the *sensory* and *motor cortex*, and are most common when the person is at rest.

mu suppression The way that performing actions involves a decrease in *mu oscillations* in the brain.

mu waves see *mu oscillations*.

Müller–Lyer illusion A well-known *geometric illusion* that consists of two equal lines, one with 'arrowheads' and the other with lines forming 'fishtails' at the ends. See also *visual illusions*.

multi-cell recordings The combined activity of many neurones, recorded individually at one electrode. Multi-cell recordings are usually measured by the number of *action potentials* per second.

multi-voxel pattern analysis (MVPA) A method of analysing *fMRI* data in which the patterns of activity across the cortex are linked to cognitive processes.

multicultural Involving characteristics and aspects of several different cultures simultaneously. The term is usually used to refer to modern societies in which members of several cultural groups live, each bringing aspects of their previous culture to bear on the life of the society.

multimodal Having more than one mode.

multiple-demand network A set of brain regions, mainly in the prefrontal cortex, that are shown by *fMRI* scans to be activated in a wide range of tasks involving cognitive control. The network also includes regions of the *lateral prefrontal cortex* and the *anterior cingulate gyrus*.

multiple intelligences A theory of intelligence put forward by Gardner, which held that intelligence actually consists of seven distinct and independent abilities, each of which should be assessed and evaluated separately. The seven intelligences are: *linguistic intelligence, musical intelligence,* mathematical-logical intelligence, *spatial intelligence, bodily-kinaesthetic intelligence,* interpersonal intelligence and intrapersonal intelligence. See also *triarchic intelligence, emotional intelligence*.

multiple mothering Childcare that is carried out by a number of different people, usually in succession. Infants in institutions were often exposed to a succession of caregivers, and it is widely accepted that this form of *maternal deprivation* resulted in long-term difficulties in forming relationships. These days, considerable efforts are made to avoid the repeated making and breaking of *attachments* in children who have to be brought up in care.

multiple personality A rare condition in which a person functions with two or more distinct *personalities*. The personalities may alternate and may appear to be quite unaware of each others' existence. Multiple personality is not a form of *schizophrenia*, but a development of a phenomenon that is quite common and normal in childhood. See also *dissociation*.

multiple regression A statistical technique by which the contribution each *independent variable* makes to the criterion variable is calculated. For example, we might have a criterion score of the number of friends each person has, and want to know the relative contribution of factors such as attractiveness, wealth and age. Because these variables are themselves correlated with each other, it is difficult to say how important each is on its own. In multiple regression, the strongest correlate of the criterion

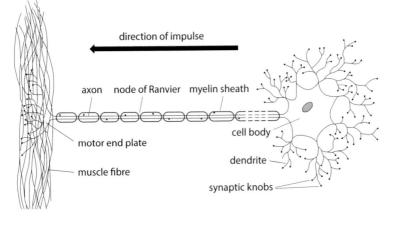

direction of impulse

axon   node of Ranvier   myelin sheath

motor end plate

muscle fibre

cell body

dendrite

synaptic knobs

Figure 38 A motor neurone

is identified and then the scores on all the other variables are rescaled to eliminate their statistical *association* with that variable. The next strongest correlate is then selected, and the two variables combined to generate a multiple regression coefficient. All variables are now rescaled to eliminate their correlation with this coefficient, and so the process goes on until a score is available for all of the variables. At this stage, the correlation of each variable with the criterion is completely independent of its correlation with the other variables. So in our example, the correlation of age with number of friends is no longer potentially boosted by the fact that older people tend to be more wealthy, or reduced if, in this sample, they are perceived as less attractive. The multiple regression coefficient is a measure of how well the chosen set of independent variables predict the criterion, and the calculation also shows how much each measure independently contributes to the prediction. A major use of multiple regression is in constructing tests that predict the criterion. In our example we will be able to predict (for this sample) the number of friends we will find by choosing certain combinations of the independent variables.

multiple resource theory The idea that cognitive processing depends on several different processing resources, such as visual or semantic processing, which are limited but work together.

multiple sclerosis (MS) A progressive degenerating illness that results in the person gradually losing motor coordination and control. MS is produced by the destruction or degeneration of the *myelin sheaths* covering the axons of nerve cells in many parts of the brain, thus slowing down the transmission of information from one part of the brain to another. The process by which this occurs is not yet fully understood.

multipolar neurones See *connector neurones*.

multitasking Carrying out several tasks at the same time – or, in neurological terms, in rapid succession. Multitaking requires both *task switching* and an ability to retain awareness of future goals while dealing with immediate ones.

multivariate analysis A general term for statistical techniques such as *multiple regression* and *factor analysis* that processes the correlational relationships between several variables.

musical intelligence A form of intelligence put forward by Gardner that is concerned with musical comprehension and appreciation as well as musical ability. See also *multiple intelligences, interpersonal intelligence.*

mutation A spontaneous or relatively sudden change in genetic structure that, because it is genetic, may be passed on to offspring.

MVPA See *multi-voxel pattern analysis.*

myelin sheath An insulating fatty substance that is wrapped around the *dendrons* and *axons* of neurones in the central nervous system. The myelin sheath is formed by *Schwann cells*, which coil themselves round the axon, thus preventing ionic transfer between the inside of the neurone and the surrounding fluids. A small gap between each Schwann cell is known as the *node of Ranvier*, and it is at these points that ionic transfer takes place. Because of this arrangement, the *electrical impulse* travels along the *neurone* in a series of jumps, which forms a much faster method of

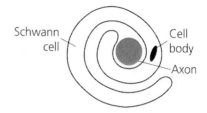

Figure 39 Eysenck's version of the theory of the humours

passing information the length of the neurone than would a steady progression. This system is particularly utilised in the central nervous system itself, and in the receipt of sensory information and the transmission of motor impulses. In cases where a slightly slower progression is not a disadvantage, as for example in the *autonomic nervous system*, neurones tend to be unmyelinated. The *white matter* of the central nervous system consists of packed masses of *myelinated* nerve fibres (see Figure 39).

myelinated Covered with a *myelin sheath*.

myelination The process of covering the axons of neurones with a *myelin sheath*, which speeds up neural transmission. In human infants, myelination can continue for some years after birth.

myside bias The tendency for people to evaluate statements or ideas in terms of their own beliefs.

MZ twins See *monozygotic twins*.

N

n-back This is a performance task that is often used as a measure of *working memory* capacity. The person is presented with a continuous sequence of stimuli, and asked to identify when a new stimulus is the same as one that is a fixed number of items (*n*) back in the list. The value of *n* varies, and the higher it is, the more difficult the task. A variant of this task is the dual *n*-back, in which two different sets of stimuli are presented together – usually one *visual* and one *auditory*. The task requires considerable concentration, and in fact a variant of it was the central task in the board game of that name.

N170 A distinctive variation in the *event-related potential* pattern that happens when the person is looking at faces rather than at other types of visual stimuli. See also *face recognition*.

N400 This is a response pattern appearing in *EEGs* when a word meaning appears unexpectedly, or out of context.

naive Inexperienced or without previous exposure to the particular tasks or experiences being used in a specific research project.

naming task A cognitive processing task in which the person is presented with a rapid sequence of words, visually, and asked to pronounce them.

nano- One billionth. One nanometer (nm) is a billionth of a metre and is used as a measurement of the wavelength of light. One nanosecond (ns) is a billionth of a second and is most likely to be encountered in measurements of the speed with which a computer can perform its simplest operation (known as the cycle time).

narcissism A love of the self. The more puritanical approaches to therapy regard narcissism as always undesirable, and when most of a person's affections are fixated upon themselves, this must be so. However, there is plenty of evidence that a healthy degree of affection for the self is essential for maintaining *self-esteem* and productive functioning. In personality assessment, the trait of narcissism is one of the *Dark Triad*, characterised by *egotism*, pride, grandiosity and a lack of *empathy*.

narcolepsy A condition in which the person is subjected to sudden, short, uncontrollable episodes of deep sleep. It is much more extreme than the tendency to sleep during psychology lectures, and also much rarer.

narcotic Drugs that have both sedative (encouraging sleep) and analgesic (pain-relieving) properties. They are usually of the opiate family, such as *morphine* or *heroin*.

narrative review A literature review, either introducing a piece of research or published in its own right, that picks out interesting features in the literature and discusses them.

nativism A school of thought which holds that the important determinants of development are directly inherited through genetic transmission. The name implies that the emphasis is on qualities which are inborn. Although nativists do recognise that environmental factors may have an effect on development, they consider such effects to be minimal, with the main explanation for individual differences being the *genotype* of the individual. The maturational theory of Gesell is an example of a nativist position. See also *empiricism*.

natural categories Types of concept identified by Rosch, which seem to fit with everyday behaviour or activities, and so form a useful and unremarkable way of grouping objects together. They may have superordinate or subordinate concepts, but the central concept is one that relates to something which human beings do. For example, the concept of chair has a superordinate concept of furniture, and many subordinate concepts, such as armchair or stool. However, all chairs share the same property, of being things that people sit on, and in this respect 'chair' is a natural category. The comparative psychologist Peter Marler suggests that natural categories may even predate and form a precursor to language.

natural concepts Concepts that appear to emerge purely as a result of the animal or human's interaction with their world. See also *concept, concept formation*.

natural experiments Experiments in which variables vary, and opportunities exist to study their consequences, but as a result of social, biological or economic circumstances and without deliberate manipulation by the experimenter.

natural science paradigm A framework for scientific inquiry based on the natural sciences of physics, chemistry and biology.

natural selection See *evolution*.

nature–nurture debate The name given to two opposed theoretical stances common within psychology. One stance emphasises 'nature', the inheritance of abilities or characteristics, while the other emphasises 'nurture', learning or the effect of environmental influences. Nature–nurture debates represent a convenient way of organising some theoretical issues within psychology, but can often be deceptive in that they may present a false dichotomy, since almost every feature of human psychology has both a genetic and an environmental component. See also *empiricism, nativism, dialectics*.

naughty teddy A semi-legendary character introduced to modern psychology during a series of investigations of the effects of context in Piagetian *conservation* tasks. In investigations by McGarrigle, the changes in shape of the experimental substances were caused by a small teddy bear who 'lived' in a box on the experimenter's table and would periodically emerge to alter the experimental materials. The small children being tested had little trouble recognising that the materials had, in fact, conserved their volume or number despite the actions of the toy bear. The studies were interpreted as throwing some doubt on the basic Piagetian assumptions concerning children's logical capacities. It was argued that the Piagetian findings resulted from the abstract nature of the conventional tasks and their lack of context, rather than from the child's inability to reason.

near-infrared spectroscopy (NIRS) A system for measuring the level of oxygenation in the blood. Areas of high blood oxygenation in the brain are considered to represent a higher degree of neural activity.

Necker cube A reversing figure, which appears to change its orientation irrespective of the intentions of the observer. The Necker cube was cited by Gregory as an example of *hypothesis testing* in perception. Without perceptual cues to indicate which way round the figure should be seen, the brain alternates from one plausible interpretation to the other (see Figure 40).

need A state of physiological deficit. Many needs, such as thirst, are associated with a drive or motivation, but others, such as a need for vitamin C, are not. The term has been extended to non-physiological needs such as *affiliation* and *achievement motivation*. See also *hierarchy of human needs*.

need for achievement A proposed psychological need, sometimes called N-Ach. See also *achievement motivation*.

negative aftereffects *Illusions* that occur immediately after continuous or very intense stimulation of the visual system with the same sensory information. Possibly as a consequence of the *habituation* of *sensory neurones*, the opposite experience to the previous

stimulation is experienced. The best-known negative aftereffects occur as a result of looking at something very bright, such as a light bulb or the sun. For some minutes afterwards, the shape is perceived as a closed figure in the field of vision, and it is usually of the opposite colour to that which was seen. Colour aftereffects can also be induced by staring at a brightly coloured object for a couple of minutes, and then transferring the gaze to a plain background. Negative aftereffects also occur with movement. The *waterfall effect* occurs when a subjective impression of reversed movement is experienced after continuous exposure to movement in just one direction.

negative correlation A measure of the consistency with which an increase in one *variable* is accompanied by a decrease in a second variable. For example, cognitive capacity correlates negatively with number of units of alcohol consumed. A relationship in the opposite direction is called a *positive correlation*, and the measure of such relationships is the *correlation coefficient*.

negative feedback Information which is fed back within a system in such a way that it reduces the distance from a goal. Whereas positive feedback (e.g. when a microphone picks up from the speakers and the sound gets louder and louder) can make a system go out of control, negative feedback is essential for keeping a system within limits and on target. A common example is a central heating system in which a higher temperature causes the boiler to shut down. In this technical sense, an essay mark is only negative feedback if it helps to make subsequent essays move closer to the desired form.

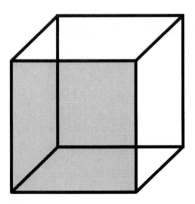

Figure 40 The Necker cube

negative incentive An object which has the opposite effect to an *incentive*, so that the organism works to avoid or prevent it.

negative priming When an object that has previously been ignored suddenly becomes the focus of attention. Negative priming of this kind produces slower recognition and response rates. See also *priming*.

negative reinforcement Reinforcement that involves the withdrawal or avoidance of something unpleasant or aversive. Behaviour that has been strengthened by negative reinforcement – especially in the case of avoidance learning – is extremely resistant to *extinction*. The term is often wrongly applied to punishment. Negative reinforcement, like all reinforcements, strengthens the probability of a behaviour, whereas punishment reduces or suppresses the target behaviour.

negative skew A distortion of a *normal distribution* in which more of the scores are higher, so that the peak of the curve is shifted towards the right. In a negatively skewed distribution, the *mode* will be higher than the *median*, which in turn is higher than the *mean*.

negative state relief theory The idea that helping behaviour originates in our seeking to alleviate the personal distress we feel as a result of seeing others in need.

negative triad A way of describing characteristically 'depressive' negative beliefs. The triad consists of beliefs about the self, the future and the world in general. Depressive individuals characteristically hold negative views on all three of these. See also *attribution*.

neglect

(i) A standard category of *child abuse* indicating a substantial failure to provide what the child needs. Neglect is a form of passive abuse, and may involve poor physical care, a lack of cognitive stimulation or inadequate emotional warmth (see *attachment*). Neglected children are often also actively abused.

(ii) In neurological contexts, neglect refers to the brain's failing to recognise or acknowledge the existence of part of the visual field, despite receiving information about it. See also *hemispatial neglect, extinction*.

Neisser, Ulrich (1928–2012)

Ulrich Neisser was a major influence on the development of cognitive psychology during the second half of the twentieth century. He challenged the mechanistic, linear processing models of cognition which were common at that time, and developed a cognitive model which was much more concerned with how people analyse and deal with the real world (see *anticipatory schema*). He also undertook important research into human memory, showing how time and social influence distort the details of factual memories, but do not necessarily change their social or human meaning.

NEO A term used to summarise the first three traits to be identified using a combination of *meta-analysis* and factor analysis. The letters stand for *neuroticism*, *extraversion* and *openness to experience*. See also *five-factor theory*, *EPI*, *personality trait*.

neo-behaviourism A revised form of behaviourism in which it is recognised that cognitive processes do play some role in determining behaviour.

neocortex Another name for the *cerebral cortex*, which refers to the fact that it is the latest part of the brain to have evolved.

neocortical substrate The layer of neurones immediately below the surface of the *cerebral cortex*, which carries information between different parts of the cortex.

neo-Freudians A term used to describe psychoanalytic theorists who accept Freud's basic ideas, but have developed them further, often emphasising social and cultural factors in psychodynamic processes. The British neo-Freudians have concentrated on *object relations theory*, which in turn has made the study of *attachments* an important part of developmental psychology.

neologism Made-up words. In neurological contexts, the word is often used to describe the words made up by people suffering from *jargon aphasia*.

neonate A newborn. For humans, the neonatal period is usually taken to extend from birth to 1 month. Recently, it has been recognised that the first major change in functioning occurs at around 8 weeks, and it has been suggested that the neonatal period should be extended up to the time when these changes start.

neoteny The evolutionary model, proposed by the biologist Stephen Jay Gould (among others), which argues that human infants are born 'prematurely' in the sense that they are far more helpless than most other young animals, and thus have a long period of dependency before they are capable of independent existence. This extended dependency period allows biologically for more extensive brain development, and psychologically for an extended learning period, so providing the human being with both the ability to adapt to numerous different types of environment, and a highly developed capacity for learning. See also *evolution*.

nerve A fibre or system of fibres that conveys sensory information from the sense receptors to the *central nervous system*, or motor impulses from the central nervous system to muscle fibres. Afferent nerve fibres consist of the *axons* or *dendrons* of *sensory neurones* bunched together to form a thread-like structure, while efferent nerve fibres consist of the axons of *motor neurones* arranged in a similar manner.

nerve cell See *neurone*.

nerve growth factor (NGF) A stimulating protein that can be produced by the body in some circumstances, and encourages the development or regrowth of neural fibres. See also *synapse*, *synaptogenesis*.

nervous breakdown A nontechnical term for a more or less complete loss of ability to cope with day-to-day living, showing itself in changes from the person's normal behaviour, such as extreme weepiness or anxiety, and general loss of psychological well-being.

nervous system The network of nerve fibres that run throughout the body, which includes the two main structures of the *central nervous system* – the *brain* and *spinal cord*.

nested territories Territories that are located as smaller areas within larger ones. For example, the female American jaçana maintains a large territory during the mating season, and several males occupy smaller territories nested within it, with the female mating with all of them. The female defends her large territory against other females, and the males defend theirs against one another.

neural To do with *neurones*.

neural impulse The small burst of electrical activity that is generated when the neurone receives sufficient *neurotransmitters* into its *receptor site*. Also known as the neurone's *action potential*. See also *myelin sheath*.

neural network A group of brain cells, or *neurones*, interconnected in such a way that they are all involved in some neurological function or process. The term is also used by researchers in *artificial intelligence* to refer to an interconnected group of decision-making computational nodes, forming a network that is involved in a particular function or process, although it is more accurately referred to as an *artificial neural network* (ANN) in that context. See also *connectionism, parallel distributed processing*.

neural pathways The routes through the brain taken by sequences of *neurones* and the activation of *nodes*. Different neural pathways have been linked with different aspects of experience (e.g. visual pathways or reward pathways). See also *population vector*.

neural plasticity The ability of nerve cells and brain tissue to adapt their functioning as they recover from injury or trauma. Neural plasticity is particularly strong in children, who often recover from substantial brain damage with little long-term effect, as the remaining brain tissue takes over the functions of the damaged parts. Adults can also show surprisingly high levels of neural plasticity, but this is complicated by the extremely high levels of motivation required for the effort of recovery, and the way in which many adults experiencing such injury see themselves as being permanently damaged, and therefore fail to make the required efforts.

neural substrate A term used to indicate those parts of the nervous system that are concerned with a particular psychological state or behaviour.

neural tube A primitive type of spinal cord, which consists of nerve fibres running the length of the body, with a hollow space in the centre. It is found in simple organisms such as flatworms, and is thought to have been one of the first stages in the evolution of the *brain* and *nervous system*.

neuroanatomy The study of the structure and composition of the nervous system. See also *functional neuroanatomy*.

neuroblast A form of *stem cell* that will develop into a *neurone*.

neurochemistry The study of the chemical aspects of the nervous system, which includes the study of specific *neurotransmitters* and of ionic transfer within the *neurone*.

neuroconstructivism The term used to describe the interaction between brain capacity and the demands of the environment, which leads to increased neural development and the development of mature cognitive systems.

neuroeconomics The use of methods and theories derived from neurological research to account for economic *decision-making*.

neuroethics The application of neurological findings to *ethical issues*.

neurogenesis The process of generating new nerve cells in the brain. See also *neuroblast*.

neurogenetic determinism The *reductionist* idea that human life and experience is entirely caused by genetic and neural factors, rather than seeing them as contributing towards experience through a dynamic interaction with society and the environment.

neurogenetics The study of the relationship between neural development and genetic factors.

neuroimaging The use of scanning techniques to develop images of the structure of, and changes to, the brain. The advent of improved *brain scanning* has resulted in the rapid development of neuroimaging as an area of research.

neuromuscular junction The synapse where nerve messages communicate with muscle fibres. See also *motor end plate*.

neurone A cell that receives or relays information within the nervous system. The information takes the form of *electrical impulses*, which are passed from one cell to another by means of *synaptic transmission*. There are generally considered to be three main kinds of neurones:

(i) *sensory neurones*, which receive information from the sense receptors and pass it to the central nervous system;

(ii) *motor neurones*, which transmit information from the central nervous system to the muscles, thus affecting actions; and

(iii) *connector neurones*, which are mainly found within the central nervous system, and which relay information to and from several neurones.

See also *neurotransmitter*.

neuropsychology The study of brain processes, especially when damaged or faulty, to give an understanding of behaviour, capability and consciousness. See also *clinical neuropsychology*.

neuroscience The scientific study of the components, structure and function of the *brain* and *nervous system*.

neurosis A broad category of psychological disturbances that are not believed to have an organic origin and which are not *psychoses*. The major neuroses are *depression*, *hysteria*, *obsessions* and *phobias*. Usually the sufferer maintains contact with reality, recognising that the symptom is irrational but still unable to modify it. The term has gone through several meanings since the eighteenth century, when it referred to a disease of the nervous system. The usage indicates a belief about the source of the problem, and today neuroses are expected to have psychological causes, whether in the remote or recent past or in the present.

neuroticism A *personality trait* indicating a tendency to be anxious. It is the opposite of psychological stability, and forms one of the central traits in the *five-factor theory* of personality.

neurotransmitter A chemical involved in *synaptic transmission*. There are many different chemicals that serve as neurotransmitters, of which the best known are *serotonin*, *acetylcholine*, *dopamine*, *noradrenaline*, *endorphin* and *enkephalin*.

Neurotransmitters are highly influential in subjective experience as well as in more general brain functioning, and many of the *psychoactive drugs* exert their effect either by blocking the uptake of specific neurotransmitters or by preventing their dispersal and causing a build-up of the substance within the *synaptic cleft*.

new paradigm research An alternative framework for research, based on *hermeneutics* – in other words, emphasising the importance of social experience and social meaning. Traditional psychological methodology in the 1970s was seen as deterministic, tightly controlled and often artificial, resulting in socially meaningless information. New paradigm research involved a rethinking of the relationship between the psychologist and the person or persons who are the subject(s) of psychological enquiry. In new paradigm research, people are seen as active collaborators or participants in the study, whose opinions and experiences have value. This stands in direct contrast to conventional psychological methodology, which tended to assume that its 'subjects' were there to be manipulated or tricked by the experimenter, and that good empirical investigation consisted of 'controlling', or preventing, any human influences from individual subjects from affecting the research.

New paradigm research is therefore closely linked to the growing interest in *ethical issues* in psychology, and to the approach to social enquiry known as *ethogenics*. It tends to involve non-experimental methods of investigation, such as interviewing people and asking them about their experiences, or the dynamic real-world approaches exemplified in *action research*. It also tends to involve methods of analysis that are directly concerned with identifying the social meaning in the material, rather than with simple quantification. See also *qualitative analysis*.

NGF See *nerve growth factor*.

nicotine Sometimes described as one of the most addictive drugs ever known, nicotine is one of the most popular *recreational drugs* taken in industrial society. It is usually smoked, but sometimes chewed, and has been clearly implicated in lung and mouth cancers, and in heart disease. Its psychological effects include a slight sedative effect. Nicotine is picked up in *receptor sites* in the motor end plate of the muscle fibres, thus reducing the uptake of *acetylcholine*. Consequently, nicotine withdrawal often leads to increasingly restless sensations, as the muscles become more receptive to acetylcholine, and to increased lability of the *autonomic nervous system*, accentuating both positive and negative emotional reactions.

NIRS See *near-infrared spectroscopy*.

nociception The perception (and experience) of pain.

nocturnal To do with or taking place during the night-time. For example, nocturnal enuresis is bed-wetting that occurs at night, and nocturnal animals are those that are active at night.

node of Ranvier The small spaces that occur between the *Schwann cells* forming the *myelin sheath* along the *axon* of the *neurone*.

nodes The basic units in *neural network* models, nodes are groups of *neurones* that are activated in response to activity from other parts of the network.

noise Stimulation that does not carry any information. Often this will be a sound, but noise can occur in any sensory channel. Noise is of most interest when it accompanies information (which would tend to be called the signal), and therefore makes it more difficult to detect or interpret the signal accurately. A measure of detectability of a stimulus is to divide the strength of the signal by the amount of noise – the *signal-to-noise ratio*. The term is also used within psychology in its more usual sense of a strong auditory stimulus that may be of interest as a source of stress or of deafness.

nominal scale See *levels of measurement*.

nomothetic Concerned with the formation of general laws, usually of behaviour. Nomothetic principles are concerned with that which is abstract, universal or generally applicable to humankind. See also *hermeneutic*, *idiographic*.

nomothetic tests Tests that are constructed in order to make comparisons between people. Compare *idiographic*.

non-common effects Effects that are specific to a particular behaviour or circumstance, rather than representing more general or widespread outcomes.

non-contingent reinforcement *Reinforcement* that is not dependent on a particular action or response from the organism involved. Such reinforcement is often involved in *superstitious learning*.

non-declarative memory Memories that are used but not consciously processed (e.g. the *procedural knowledge* involved in having a bath or drinking a cup of tea).

non-directive therapy The group of therapies and counselling techniques that consistently avoid making value judgements about what the client has done, is doing, or should do. See also *client-centred therapy*.

non-invasive techniques Approaches to the study of the body or brain that do not involve penetrating the skin. See *EEGs*, *CAT scans*, *MRI and PET scans* for examples of non-invasive methods used in brain research.

non-modal scores The scores in a data set that are not *modal*. See also *variation ratio*.

non-parametric statistics Statistical techniques such as *rank correlation* and the *Mann–Whitney U-test* which do not require that the data should fit requirements such as *interval scaling* and *normal distribution*. Because they use less of the information in the data, they are usually less powerful than *parametric statistics*. The corresponding advantage is that they make fewer assumptions about the nature of the data and so are less likely to give misleading results. In principle, non-parametric tests are preferable if they are able to demonstrate a result. In practice, parametric tests are treated as if they have higher status and are widely used even when the assumptions are known to be violated. See also *levels of measurement*.

non-participant techniques A term that used to be applied to observations in which the observer (researcher) takes no part in the activity which is being observed. The term has become obsolete since the word 'participant' is now used to refer to the people taking part in the study.

non-technological society A term used to describe societies that maintain their traditional economic systems and cultures, such as are found in some parts of Africa, Australia and South America. In colonial times, such cultures were often referred to as 'primitive', but a deeper knowledge of them has shown that their levels of sophistication are extremely high, but that they centre around a more ecologically balanced style of living, rather than around technological development. Consequently, the term non-technological societies is increasingly used as providing a more accurate description.

non-verbal communication (NVC) Communication through signals other than those used in language (e.g. *posture*, appearance, smell, and a range of specific behaviours such as *pupil dilation*, *facial expression* and the pattern of *eye contact*). Extensively studied by Michael Argyle, non-verbal communication takes place through a number of different *non-verbal cues*, which can be combined in various ways. Some researchers have estimated NVC as being more than four times as powerful as *verbal communication*, although one could imagine that trying to teach the psychology syllabus non-verbally would be rather laborious. An understanding of the cues and use of non-verbal signals forms the basis of most social skills training.

non-verbal cue A signal that conveys some kind of communication to an observer without involving the use of language. Non-verbal cues are usually considered to be of seven main types: *paralanguage*, *proxemics*, *posture*, *gesture*, *facial expression*, *eye contact* and dress. Some theorists consider that *ritual* and ritual symbolism should also be regarded as an important medium of *non-verbal communication*.

noradrenaline A *neurotransmitter* and *hormone* that is commonly involved in emotional reactions as a main transmitter of the *sympathetic division* of the *autonomic nervous system*, as well as within the brain itself.

norepinephrine The American name for *noradrenaline*.

norm The range of values within which the members of a particular population can be expected to function. *Psychometric* tests will list different sets of standardised norms for various groups of people (e.g. '45-year-old women' or '6-year-old boys'). Users of the tests can then compare their results with the norms for a comparable population. Within developmental psychology, norms are used to determine whether a child is performing so far out of the normal range as to require special treatment. See also *social norms*.

normal curve The bell-shaped curve that is produced when data from a population with a *normal distribution* are plotted as a frequency distribution.

normal distribution When Francis Galton began measuring a number of human characteristics, he found that they could be plotted as a frequency distribution which consistently took the form of a normal distribution curve. Many of the sources of data that psychologists deal with fit a normal distribution either because the population has that form or because the measure has been constructed deliberately to provide it (e.g. intelligence tests). The normal distribution has therefore been an important basis for many *parametric* statistical tests, such as *t-tests* and *analysis of variance*. Because it is mathematically clearly defined, it can easily be used to define aspects of a set of scores, particularly to indicate the probability or the implausibility of any specific score. Once the mean and the standard deviation of a normal curve are known, the frequency with which scores will be found a given distance away from the mean can be accurately computed. These frequencies are given as tables of *z-scores* in statistical texts. The values of most interest to psychology are those that will occur no more than 5 per cent or no more than 1 per cent of the time, as these are the conventional levels that count as evidence against the *null hypothesis*. It is also a feature of the normal distribution that the *mean*, the *mode* and the *median* have the same value.

Problems with the normal distribution arise because many sets of data are not actually distributed precisely, or even approximately, in this way. Yet the convenience of tests based on the distribution means that they are often used in any case, and we can usually only guess at how much influence this has on the results of the studies. Tests that do not assume a normal distribution are known as *non-parametric statistics* (see Figure 41).

normality A state that is usually considered to be unremarkable – the opposite of abnormal. In attempting to identify normal and abnormal behaviour for the purposes of psychological classification, three alternative approaches are often specified. First, normality is taken to be behaviour that is accepted as usual, or as frequently occurring. Abnormal behaviour is then regarded as behaviour that is uncommon, or at least which is infrequently acknowledged. (In some cases, such as the imagined 'seeing' of a recently dead relative, the experience may actually be very common, although not often openly acknowledged.) A second definition of normal behaviour is behaviour that conforms to accepted norms or social demands. In this event, social consensus becomes a major factor in decisions concerning normality and abnormality. The third approach concentrates on statistically common behaviour, irrespective of consensus. This approach rests on the assumptions of the Gaussian (*normal*) *distribution*. The problem with this approach is that people who are statistically uncommon in a highly valued direction (e.g. of extremely high IQ) are also defined as *abnormal*.

normative To do with, or expressing, the *norm*.

normative social influence Social influence that 'pushes' the individual towards conforming to the generally accepted social norm.

normativism Judgements of the 'correctness' of a way of thinking that depend on how well it conforms with particular *norms* or standards.

NREM sleep Non-rapid eye movement sleep – the stages of sleep in which *rapid*

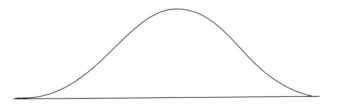

Figure 41 A normal distribution curve

eye movements do not occur. See also *orthodox sleep, sleep cycles.*

nuclear family A family consisting of two parents, usually one of each sex, and their offspring. The nuclear family has been treated as the basic family structure on which Western society is based, so people have been concerned to discover that it is much less common than had previously been supposed. In fact, there are grounds for supposing that it never was as common as had been assumed.

nucleotides The four base chemicals that make up *DNA.*

nucleus A dense area within the cell body that contains structures necessary to the life and development of the cell, including *chromosomes* and messenger *ribonucleic acid.*

null hypothesis A prediction in a research study that the outcome of the study could have been simply a consequence of chance factors, and not a result of the experimental conditions. The null hypothesis can never be totally ruled out, which is why it is wrong to make statements such as, 'The t-test is significant so the hypothesis is true'. Instead, the amount of confidence that can be placed in the results of a study is expressed in terms of how low the probability (p) is that the null hypothesis is correct. This is known as the significance level, or confidence level. In most student experiments, the acceptable level of significance is set at $p < .05$. In other words, if the probability that the null hypothesis is correct is less than .05, or 1/20, the results will be accepted. For research with more potentially damaging consequences, more stringent significance levels are used. A slightly more accurate way of describing the null hypothesis is to say that the results occurred through sampling error. This refers to whether the sample of subjects in the study accurately represents its parent *population.* See also *normal distribution, statistical significance, statistics.*

number neurones Neurones that are most likely to respond to numbers or sizes.

NVC See *non-verbal communication.*

obedience Within social psychology, obedience has been studied as the social phenomenon that enables an individual to perform actions when instructed to do so by someone else, and which they would not consider when acting independently. Its study was largely initiated by an attempt to understand the behaviour of German troops and civilians during the Second World War, and was given an impetus by the work of Milgram. His study of obedience shows how the *demand characteristics* of a situation appear to enable people to suspend their own conscience, and to perceive themselves as having had no option but to obey. See also *autonomous state, implacable experimenter*.

obesity Excessive weight. Obesity is usually defined in terms of body weight being a certain percentage above the ideal weight for that person's age, sex and height. The percentage varies, but is often either 15 per cent or 30 per cent. This vagueness is not crucial, as there is no absolute standard for 'ideal weight', which is largely a cultural judgement.

object concept The idea that objects have a continuing existence, whether the individual is paying attention to them or not. Although this has been disputed by philosophers, the operational concept is an important one for the young child to develop in their interactions with the world, and the way in which this happens has been extensively studied as part of *cognitive development*.

object constancy The perceptual process by which adjustment is made to the fact that objects have a continuing existence even when they are not being attended to. See also *object concept, shape constancy, size constancy*.

object orientation agnosia An inability to identify the orientation of an object (e.g. which way up it is), even though the person can recognise and identify the object itself. See also *object constancy*.

object permanence See *object concept*.

object relations theory A *psychoanalytic theory* developed primarily by Melanie Klein and W. Ronald Fairbairn in Britain as a reaction against Freud's concentration on instincts. Objects are the people, parts of people or things to whom the individual relates. Infants are believed to relate only to separate parts of people, such as the mother's breast. The ability to perceive the parts as belonging to a whole person, with both their good and bad aspects, has to be learned. Only a whole person can be recognised as having their own feelings, needs, etc., which ought to be respected, so only a whole person can be the object of a mature relationship. Psychological disturbance in adults is believed to result from problems in object relations in childhood, with the more severe conditions reflecting problems earlier in development – hence the emphasis by Klein on the breast as the first, crucial, part object. Therapy is directed towards resolving the relationship with bad or persecutory objects internalised by the patient, so that they can make mature relationships with people and not just use them as vehicles for their own gratification.

objectification A process of *social representation* theory in which an idea becomes associated with a specific object, category, person or item. Objectification using an object, category or item is known as *figuration*, while that using people is known as *personification*.

objective test A test that can be marked without any need for subjective judgements. For example, multiple-choice tests and intelligence tests are regarded as objective by most psychologists.

objectivity The attempt to stand outside the research process so that no personal feelings or beliefs will influence the results.

observable behaviour Behaviour that is visible and can therefore be used in an *observational study* or a *behavioural assessment*. Observable behaviour is mainly distinguished from internal psychological processes.

observational learning *Learning* that occurs as a result of observing the behaviour of others. As such, observational learning includes the two processes of *imitation* and *identification*, and is an important component of *social learning theory*.

observational study A study that involves watching what happens, in a given context, rather than intervening and causing changes. Observational studies may take place in a variety of conditions, ranging from a highly controlled laboratory setting to uncontrolled 'field' conditions. Similarly, the observation itself may be undertaken in a number of ways, ranging from the use of electronic equipment, to the presence of a human observer, to the active participation of the observer in the interaction under study. No matter how well controlled they are, observational studies can only provide *correlational*

data, as without the direct manipulation of variables, such as occurs in an *experiment*, causality cannot be inferred. The major methodological problem is that the presence of the observer, particularly if filming is used, is likely to influence the behaviour being observed. See also *participant observation*.

obsession An idea or image that persistently enters thought despite being unwanted and recognised as abnormal. See also *compulsion*.

obsessive–compulsive disorder A neurotic disorder in which the person is unable to resist spending a lot of time in *obsessional* thoughts that are usually absurd and/or obscene, and carrying out pointless rituals – *compulsions*. The condition is extremely distressing and associated with a high level of anxiety. Psychoanalysis regards it as a *personality disorder* in which tremendous efforts have been made to suppress and control emotions, with the obsessions and compulsions being the denied aspects of the self that are breaking through the defences. In extreme cases, the person may spend so much time on the ritual thoughts and acts that they are unable to do anything else at all. Behavioural approaches view this as an outcome of *conditioning* processes in which the ritual is reinforced because it provides temporary relief from the anxiety of tackling some real task.

Occam's razor A scientific principle which states that, given a choice between two possible solutions or theoretical explanations for a given problem, the simpler one of the two should be adopted. It is also known as the law of parsimony.

occipital face area (OFA) An area of the *visual cortex* that responds preferentially to faces, but does not process facial identity. See also *fusiform face area*.

occipital lobe The lobe of the brain that is found at the back of the head. The occipital lobe contains the *visual cortex* of the *cerebrum*. See also *frontal lobe*, *parietal lobe*, *temporal lobe*.

occupational psychology The use of psychological knowledge and principles in the study of people at work, or in any productive occupation. Occupational psychology and *industrial psychology* are closely linked, but occupational psychology has a wider range than just the study of people in industrial situations, as it includes such occupations as that of housewife, novelist and unemployed person. See also *organisational psychology*.

ocular dominance columns Arrangements of cells in the *visual cortex* of the brain, identified by the Nobel prizewinners Hubel and Wiesel. They found that cells dealing with the same elements of visual stimulation (see *simple, complex* and *hypercomplex cells*) were arranged in columns running perpendicular to the surface of the brain, and that these columns alternated in a highly regular fashion between those receiving visual information from the right eye and those receiving information from the left eye. It is thought that this arrangement helps the brain to compare the different images from the two eyes – using *binocular disparity* as a *depth cue* (see Figure 42).

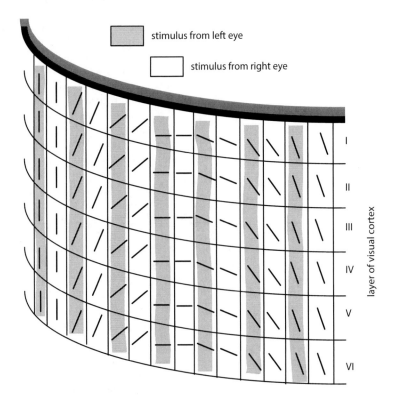

Figure 42 Ocular dominance columns

oculomotor cues *Depth cues* that are generated by the slight movements of the eye muscles as the eyes change their focus. Detection of these slight movements is an example of *kinaesthesia.*

oedema A blood clot occurring among the neurones of the *central nervous system*, which can produce a *stroke* or *aneurism.*

Oedipus complex In Freudian theory, a process occurring during the *phallic stage* (around 3 to 5 years) in which the child wishes to possess the parent of the opposite sex, and so sees the same-sex parent as a rival. As this parent is also powerful and successful, the child will feel threatened, but also tends to resolve the conflict by identifying with the rival parent. Neo-Freudians, particularly of the *object relations theory* school, have shifted the emphasis on to earlier relationships with the mother, so that Oedipal conflicts have come to be seen either as occurring at a younger age, or as less important as a source of psychological disturbance. The Oedipal process is regarded as applying just as much to girls as to boys.

OFA See *occipital face area.*

olfaction The sense of smell.

olfactory cortex A strip of the *cerebral cortex* that runs along the base of each *temporal lobe* and receives information from the scent receptors in the nose. This area is concerned with the analysis and interpretation of smells.

olfactory epithelium An area in the higher part of the nose that detects the minute chemical particles conveying smell information. Nerve cells present in the olfactory epithelium pass this information on to the *olfactory cortex.*

omission bias A general preference for risking harm through inaction rather than risking harm through action.

one-tailed test The use of statistical tests when a hypothesis clearly predicts only one direction of outcome. Suppose the research hypothesis is that distraction by loud noise will reduce the amount remembered. When you examine the memory scores of the distraction group, you merely need to test whether they are significantly lower than the mean for the control group. This may amount to a *significance level* of $p < .05$, meaning that their mean falls within the lower 5 per cent of the normal distribution of possible outcomes. Compare this judgement with that for a *two-tailed test.*

one-trial learning A very rapid form of learning, through *classical conditioning*, in which just one experience is sufficient for a lasting learned association to occur. Most examples of one-trial learning are concerned with food or pain, and are thus regarded as being linked to very basic survival mechanisms. If consumption of a specific food is followed by vomiting, or if contact with a specific stimulus is followed by a painful experience, then a strong avoidance behaviour will result which is highly resistant to *extinction.* Forms of one-trial learning that are specific to the species and which seem to have a biological basis are examples of *prepared learning.* One-trial learning has also been associated with instances of *superstitious learning.*

one-way ANOVA An *analysis of variance* carried out on the scores on a single variable of a number of groups (e.g. the exam results of four sets of students). It compares the variance within the groups with the variance between the means of each group to calculate an F ratio. This calculation can indicate whether the group means differ significantly more than would be expected from just the variation between individuals.

ontogeny The origins and development of the individual. The most well-known use of the word is probably in the phrase 'ontogeny recapitulates *phylogeny*', which is a biological principle that was popular at the beginning of the twentieth century, stating that the stages of growth of each individual member of a species mirror the evolutionary development of the species itself. For instance, much was made of the idea that the human foetus in its early stages had structures which resembled gills, a tail, etc. Although this idea is now regarded as contentious, or even dubious, it was highly influential at the time. For example, Piaget's study of *cognitive development* in the child was undertaken because of his interest in the evolution of abstract thinking and formal logic. By looking at how children developed logical processes, he hoped to identify the evolutionary stages by which rational thought had evolved.

ontological To do with individual development. See also *ontogeny*.

ontology The branch of physiology concerned with the existence of things and how they have come to be as they are. Compare *ontogeny*.

OOB see *out-of-body experience*.

open field test A measure of anxiety and/or independence, used mainly with animals but sometimes also with small children. It involves a wide open, unprotected area in which the animal or child is placed, and symptoms of anxiety (clinging to mother or toys, droppings, etc.) are recorded.

open questions Questions that may be asked during a research or a therapeutic interview that are phrased so that a detailed answer is required. An example would be: 'Can you tell me about any ways that studying psychology has helped you gain insight into your own behaviour?' Such questions invite the participant to respond in terms of their own thinking and so are likely to be more productive than *closed questions*.

open system A system that is open to receive energy or information. Open systems are therefore able to develop, and will tolerate new structures within them, in contrast to closed systems.

openness to experience One of the main factors in the *five-factor theory* of personality, which reflects a tendency to welcome new experiences and to be ready to change impressions.

operant Any unit of behaviour that has an effect (of any kind) on the environment. Also known as operant behaviour, it is the basis of the conditioning of voluntary behaviour. Unless behaviour that has some kind of effect in the environment is produced spontaneously, the *Law of Effect* cannot come into play, and the behaviour will continue to be emitted more or less randomly.

operant conditioning A process of stimulus–response learning of voluntary behaviour, which occurs through the consequence of actions produced by an organism (an animal or human being). The idea is that the learning of an appropriate action or operant is likely to be reinforced (strengthened) if the action is followed by a pleasant consequence (see *Law of Effect*). This increases the probability that the action will occur again. Reinforcement in operant conditioning can be positive or negative. If it is positive, the action is directly rewarded; if it is negative, it is indirectly rewarded by the removal or avoidance of something unpleasant. The other major class of conditioning is *classical conditioning*. See also *partial reinforcement, primary reinforcement, secondary reinforcement, reinforcement schedule*.

operant strength This is a term used to describe how strongly a response acquired through operant conditioning has been learned. There are two main measures of operant strength – *resistance to extinction* and *response rate*.

operation span the maximum number of items on a list that a person can recall accurately more than 50 per cent of the time. See also *digit span*.

operational definition A definition that identifies something by its effects. An operational definition may not form an ideal definitive statement, expressing all aspects of the topic being defined, but it needs to be good enough to allow some *empirical* investigation of the topic. For instance, systematic work on *sustained attention* only became possible when researchers adopted the operational definition of attention as being the detection of relatively small changes in stimuli from within a varied background (e.g. picking out one particular signal on a radar screen). Failures to detect the target stimuli were accepted as evidence of failure to attend. Although this was not an ideal definition of attention itself, it served as a useful operational definition. Apart from giving clear rules by which the phenomenon can be identified, the definition also has to be close enough to the accepted meaning to be acceptable to most researchers. See also *signal-detection task*.

operations Manipulations of objects or concepts. The major use within psychology is in Piaget's theory, which is largely about the different kinds of cognitive operations, particularly logical manipulations, which are carried out by children at different ages. See also *concrete operational stage, formal operational stage*.

opiates Drugs that have both analgesic (pain-relieving) and *narcotic* (sleep-inducing) effects. Opiates include naturally occurring drugs such as opium and morphine, drugs synthesised from those natural substances, such as heroin, and some synthesised chemicals that have the same properties. There are also several naturally occurring opiates, of which the most well known are the *endorphins* and *enkephalins*, which act as *neurotransmitters* in the brain. Some foodstuffs (e.g. milk) contain small amounts of naturally occurring opiates. Opiates are widely used both as clinical and as recreational drugs, and in general are highly addictive.

opponent processing A theory originally proposed by Hering as an explanation for *negative aftereffects* – especially those concerned with colour. Hering located opponent processing as occurring in the *rod* and *cone cells* of the *retina*, although more recent research indicates that it takes place in the second retinal layer of bipolar neurones. The idea is that cells, or groups of cells, have two different and complementary modes of operation. One group of cells responds to red stimuli when in one mode, and to green stimuli when in the other, a second group responds to blue or yellow stimuli, and a third group responds to light or dark. Overstimulation of any one system through continuous presentation of just one of the paired stimuli results in compensation when the stimulation stops – the opposite stimulus is experienced as the cells gradually return to normal functioning. See also *negative after-effects*.

opportunity sampling An approach to *sampling* (it is hardly a method) in which research participants are taken into the research as they become available. Opportunity sampling is liable to produce a highly biased sample, but this may not matter for certain research objectives.

oppositional defiant disorder (ODD) A pattern of behaviour in children in which they react negatively to authority and to attempts to control them. It is not as extreme as *conduct disorder*, but is sufficiently problematic for caregivers to have been classified as a disorder rather than ordinary childhood tendencies to test out rules and follow their own wishes. It has been suggested that much of the problem arises because parents are showing the characteristic ODD pattern in relation to their partners and their children, but this idea has not been taken up enthusiastically by the adults concerned – or it may just be that doing something harmless and pleasant does not need controlling.

opsins Light-sensitive receptors.

optic To do with the eye and vision.

optic apraxia A variant of *simultanagnosia* in which the person has difficulty using vision to guide actions, such as hand movements, because they have problems with the motor planning involved in moving eyes and hands simultaneously. See also *ataxia*.

optic array The way in which the contents of the visual field are represented on the retina of the eye. The *photoreceptor* cells of the *retina* can be visualised as a series of dots, forming an image like that on a TV screen. The optic array is the way in which those dots

are responding to information entering the eye from the outside world. Strictly speaking, it is the pattern of light reaching a single point on the retina, from all directions, but the term is generally used to refer to the broader image.

optic ataxia This is the inability to use vision to accurately guide action, even though the person may not have any particular visual or voluntary movement deficits. Effectively, they fail to coordinate their muscular actions, and so do not make the appropriate adjustments to their eye movements at the right time. It is generally considered to result from damage to the occipitoparietal junction. See also *optic apraxia*.

optic chiasma A point within the brain where the optic nerves from each eye meet. At this point, nerve fibres carrying messages from the left side of each *retina* combine, and pass on the left side of the *thalamus* and then to the *visual cortex* on the left hemisphere. Those carrying messages from the right side of each retina combine and pass on to the right side of the brain. This crossover and recombination of nerve fibres is thought to be instrumental in *depth perception*, specifically in the process of *binocular disparity*, in which the image from each eye is compared.

optic flow The way that aspects of the visual field change their relationships as the person moves around their environment. An important feature of Gibson's *ecological perception*, optic flow (aka visual flow) removes the need for *hypothesis testing* in, for example, *depth perception*. See also *optic array*.

optic nerve The *axons* of the *ganglion cells* in the *retina*, which bunch together and carry visual information from the eye to the *lateral geniculate nuclei* of the *thalamus*. The place where the optic nerve leaves the retina is the *blind spot*.

optimistic bias A characteristic belief that bad things will happen to other people rather than to ourselves.

oral To do with the mouth. Oral functioning is particularly important for the young infant, and seems to be a major source of pleasure. The oral region is quite mature in good time for birth, and the newborn is able to coordinate sucking, swallowing and breathing. In Freudian theory, the oral stage is the first of the psychosexual stages, and fixation at the oral stage is said to produce adult tendencies such as greed, mania and depression, and a tendency to engage in oral behaviours such as smoking and lecturing.

orbicularis oculi The muscle in the face that closes the eyelids, and is the muscle stimulated when using the *eyeblink response* measure.

orbitofrontal cortex An area on the ventral surface of the *frontal lobes*, above the eye sockets, which has reciprocal connections with the main parts of the *limbic system*. It is concerned with the immediate motivational value of rewards, adjusting the value of rewards according to their context and immediate relevance.

order effect An experimental effect that arises as a result of the order in which two tasks are presented. Order effects are of two main kinds:

(i) *practice effects*, where the research participant becomes more skilled at a given task as a result of practice, and so performs better in later conditions of the experiment; and

(ii) *fatigue effects*, where the research participant becomes tired or bored as the study progresses, and so performs worse in later experimental conditions.

See also ABBA *design, counterbalancing.*

ordinal scale A system of measurement in which the basic units can be ranked. See also *levels of measurement, rank.*

ordinate The vertical or *y-axis* on a graph. By convention, this axis usually carries the measure of outcome, or dependent variable (see Figure 43). See also *abscissa.*

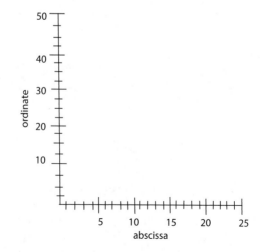

Figure 43 The ordinate and abscissa of a graph

orectic To do with desire or appetite. The term is only likely to be encountered as opposite of *cognitive*.

organ of Corti The structure in the *inner ear* that affects the *transduction* of vibration into electrical impulses, which are then transmitted to the brain for interpretation. The organ of Corti consists of two membranes – the *basilar membrane* and the tectorial membrane, between which are hair cells that trigger off an electrical impulse when vibrated. This then passes to the fibres of the auditory nerve, which are embedded in the basilar membrane. See also *frequency theory*, *place theory*.

organic disorder A disorder that is known, or at least believed, to be due to a physiological or organic malfunction. The extent to which psychological disorders result directly from organic brain dysfunction is one of the major controversies in the field. Psychiatrists are more likely than psychologists to believe that disorders are organic. The term is sometimes used as a contrast (e.g. to distinguish organic *psychoses* from those that are better understood psychologically, and are called 'functional' psychoses).

organism A term used during the *behaviourist* era of psychology to describe animals and human beings when talking in terms of simple (stimulus–response) learning processes or motivational states, such as hunger or thirst drives. The use of the term in preference to 'animal' or 'person' was intended to signify:

(i) the way in which stimulus–response learning applied to all active creatures alike, as the basic building block of behaviour; and

(ii) the dispassionate objectivity of the scientist, whereby people were to be regarded simply as units which emitted behaviour, irrespective of sentimental human values.

See also *social responsibility of science*.

organisational culture The set of implicit beliefs, customs and conventions that are typical of a particular organisation, and which distinguish it from others. In psychological terms, organisational cultures can be seen as *social representations*, closely linked with the social identifications of the working groups within the organisation, and gaining their strength from the extent to which the shared beliefs and social representations in different working groups overlap with one another.

organisational psychology The study of how people act and interact in organisations. Although sometimes regarded as a part of *occupational psychology*, organisational psychology is increasingly accepted as an area of study in its own right. It is distinguished from *industrial psychology* in that it includes public sector and voluntary organisations.

orgone energy A basic energy proposed by Wilhelm Reich to be the activating universal life force. Although it bears some similarity to Freud's concept of the libido, Reich took his ideas very much further, arguing that orgone energy is a physical energy which can be accumulated by special devices, and which can be utilised directly for therapeutic purposes. Orgone energy, he argued, is the source and motivation of all life and is generated by free sexual expression, among other things. Many members of the psychological community at the time (the 1940s to 1950s) found Reich's claims extreme; the state saw them as directly fraudulent and prosecuted Reich accordingly.

orientation The angle at which something is arranged or exists. When used to refer to an individual's theoretical stance, it means the attitude or position which that individual adopts towards a specific theory or school of thought.

orienting Changing attention from one focus to another. See also *covert orienting*, *orienting reflex*.

orienting reflex A set of physiological and behavioural changes that occur in response to an unexpected stimulus which attracts the attention of the individual. The orienting reflex includes a positioning of the body towards the sound or other stimulus, keeping the body very still, a dilation of the blood vessels in the head, *EEG* changes, and alterations to muscle tone, heart rate and breathing. This combination of physiological changes means that the individual is more prepared to receive the stimulus. The opposite pattern, when a stimulus is being excluded, is called the defensive reflex. See also *attention*.

orofacial dyspraxia An impairment of speech that involves a problem in carrying out the coordinated movements involved in speaking. See also *dyspraxia*.

orthodox sleep Ordinary, quiescent sleep that does not involve *rapid eye movements* (REM) or the experience of *dreaming*. Orthodox sleep occurs at four levels or stages, which correlate with the subjective experience of being lightly or deeply asleep, and which each show characteristic *EEG* patterns. Stage 1 sleep is entered first, and is the lightest form of sleep, with a fairly regular EEG pattern. Some dreaming may take place during this stage. The sleeper then progresses through the stages to the deepest level of stage 4, in which the EEG is very irregular with large spikes. In this stage, it is very difficult to awaken the sleeper, and in children bed-wetting, night terrors and sleepwalking may occur. The pattern changes through the period of sleeping (see *sleep cycles*). Orthodox sleep is also called *NREM (non-rapid eye movement) sleep*. See also *paradoxical sleep*.

orthographic lexicon The part of *long-term memory* that stores word spellings.

orthographic neighbours A term used in cognitive research to refer to the number of words that can be formed from a target word, by changing one of its letters.

orthography A system of writing.

osmoreceptors Although not empirically established, osmoreceptors are thought to be receptors in the brain that respond to changes in fluid composition in brain cells, and so are thought to act as signals to the brain for the experience of thirst.

osmotic thirst See *hypovolemic thirst*.

other-race effect The finding that memory for people of a similar ethnic background to the observer is generally better than memory for the faces of people of different ethnic backgrounds. See also *face recognition*.

otoliths Small particles of a bony substance that float in the fluid-filled semicircular canals of the *inner ear*. The canals are lined with hair cells, which produce an electrical impulse when the otoliths come into contact with them. In this way, movement and turbulence of the fluid in the semicircular canals are detected, which is an important factor in the sense of balance.

out-of-body experience (OOB) The subjective experience that the person is floating outside of their body, and only connected to it very loosely. Sometimes experienced during *dreaming*, OOBs are also characteristic of near-death experiences. In *parapsychology*, they are believed by some to enable remote viewing of real-world objects.

outcome variable See *dependent variable*.

outer ear The part of the ear that is in direct contact with the outside world. It includes the pinna and the lobe (the two external parts of the ear itself) and the auditory canal. The pinna and lobe serve to direct sound waves into the auditory canal, and they pass along it in the form of waves of changing air pressure until they come into contact with the eardrum, or tympanic membrane. This marks the boundary between the outer ear and the *middle ear*, and vibrates in response to the air pressure. See also *inner ear*.

outliers Scores or results which are so very different from the mean or other *measure of central tendency* that they stand out from most of the other scores.

overcompensation An excessive response in attempting to overcome a disadvantage or difficulty. There is usually an implication that the person who does this is abnormally affected by the original problem. For example, a short person who goes to exceptional lengths to disguise or compensate for their height would be judged to be excessively sensitive about it. The term is more often used as a derogatory expression in lay language than in psychology, where it has no technical meaning. See also *compensation*.

overextension The tendency, found particularly in young children acquiring a language, to apply words too widely (e.g. calling all animals 'doggy'). See also *overgeneralisation*.

overgeneralisation The situation that occurs when findings from research are extended beyond their implications (e.g. when the extent of drug use in a small group of students is used to make claims about drug usage in the general *population*). The term was also used by Piaget to identify a characteristic of the *preoperational stage*, which was that young children would overgeneralise rules that they had learned and apply them inappropriately. Piaget argued that the characteristic disappeared as the child matured, but this may not be as clear-cut an issue as he assumed.

overt Apparent or obvious to the observer.

overt orienting The visible sign that someone's attention has been drawn to an object or phenomenon, shown by movements of the eyes, head or body. See also *orienting reflex*.

ovum An egg. The female contribution to reproduction that requires fertilisation by a male sperm. See also *zygote*.

own-age bias A phenomenon observed in *eyewitness testimony*, whereby people are more likely to identify someone round about their own age as the culprit, rather than much older or younger people.

own-race effect The finding that people are more able to recognise faces of people from their own ethnic group than they are of those of another ethnic group. This has been taken by some social theorists as evidence of implicit *racism*, but, apart from in known racist individuals, there is no neural indication that this effect is also linked with negative affect. See also *own-age bias*.

oxytocin A peptide *hormone* released by the *pituitary gland*, which is involved in *attachment* formation and is also involved in orgasm, lactation, and uterine contractions during labour. See also *vasopressin*.

P

P value The probability of a statistical outcome like the one that has been observed, if the *null hypothesis* is correct.

P600 An *event-related potential* that occurs in the *temporal lobe*, and seems to be associated with the processing of grammatical anomalies. It implies that *syntactic* structure is as important in language processing as *lexical* knowledge, although not the same.

paedophilia A condition in which an adult is sexually attracted to children and can only achieve sexual arousal with them. See also *sexual abuse*.

pain A state of acute discomfort brought about by stimulation of pain receptors in the nervous system. Pain can take several forms, and may be chronic or acute. See also *phantom limb*.

pain anxiety Fear or nervousness that pain will be likely to occur. There is a model of pain perception bearing the same name which states that some people become hyper-vigilant and over-anxious about pain, because they have developed what amounts to a phobia about it. As a result, these people tend to interpret ordinary states of discomfort as more painful than another person might.

pair bonding A long-enduring *attachment* with a single individual partner.

paired-associate learning A learning task that involves the association or linking together of two stimuli, usually words. This form of learning task was extremely popular in the study of *memory*

throughout the 1950s and 1960s, but in more recent times has been heavily criticised for its artificiality.

pairing Presenting two stimuli in such a way that they always occur together.

PALS An acronym used in some psychology syllabuses indicating Psychological Applied Learning Scenarios (i.e. aspects of real-world experience that are used to demonstrate the operation of psychological processes).

pandemonium model A hierarchical model of cognition, first proposed in the late 1960s, which forms an interesting example of *bottom-up processing*. It was mainly concerned with feature recognition in perception, and how the identification of features can be combined to result in meaningful percepts. The model proposes a hierarchical organisation of 'sub-demons', 'cognitive demons' and 'decision demons'. There are myriads of sub-demons, each of which is tuned in to detecting specific aspects of a stimulus, such as the specific letters in a word. When a stimulus occurs, the appropriate sub-demon shrieks. The more similar the stimulus is to the demon's template, the louder it shrieks. The decision demon at the next level in the hierarchy is faced with the task of deciding which of the shrieking sub-demons best represents the stimulus, taking into account other shrieking sub-demons responding to subsequent stimuli (hence the name 'pandemonium model'). As the overall picture becomes more complex, general cognitive demons come into action, which operate at a higher level, and represent complete concepts or *schemata*. Because of the idea of competition between the demons at each level, this model is well able to cope with the explanation of our response to ambiguous stimuli, but some consider it to be less satisfactory in explaining some of the more general aspects of active cognition.

panic attack An *anxiety disorder* in which the person experiences sudden and unpredictable attacks of acute anxiety or terror that have no organic cause, and which are not a response to any threat in the environment. The anxiety is increased by the fact that the person does not know when another attack will happen, and cannot make any sense of what is happening to them.

Papez circuit A neural pathway based in and around the *limbic system*. It was originally thought to be the source of feelings of emotion, but this idea has not been supported by more recent neurological observation.

paradigm The framework of assumptions or beliefs within which a particular item of knowledge is located. Literally, a paradigm is a set of beliefs that are shared by a scientific community, and which are used to interpret factual information. Perhaps the clearest example of the power of a paradigm can be seen in the school chemistry syndrome in which, despite rhetoric about learning from direct observation, thousands of children fail to obtain the 'correct' results from their project work, but what is actually written up is the result that the scientific community believes should have happened, rather than the one which actually did.

paradigm specificity This occurs when the findings from a piece of research

cannot be replicated unless all of the assumptions and conventions of explanation and procedure are also adopted by the would-be replicator. In other words, the findings apply only within one specific knowledge *paradigm*, and cannot be generalised outside of thhat context.

paradox A situation in which two or more rules combine to give an impossible outcome, such as the Cretan who said 'all Cretans are liars'. Paradoxes have been much studied in logic and mathematics, but for psychologists the chief interest is in those that trap people into apparently crazy behaviour (see *double bind* for an example). Some therapists believe that many symptoms result from paradoxes in the person's life and so are best treated with a 'counter-paradox' designed to free them. A common example would be to instruct the person to have their 'uncontrollable' symptom at a particular time. If they have the symptom, then it shows that they can control it. If they do not have the symptom, this shows that the symptom can be prevented (i.e. it is controllable). As with any other powerful therapeutic technique, paradoxical injunctions can be ineffective and potentially harmful unless they are used with respect and sympathetic understanding for the patient.

paradoxical sleep A name given to the type of sleep in which rapid eye movements occur (it is also called *rapid eye movement [REM] sleep*), and during which *dreaming* takes place. It was named 'paradoxical' in the 1960s, as a result of the discovery that EEG patterns shown in this type of sleep suggested that the sleeper was only sleeping lightly and would wake easily, whereas in reality they proved very difficult to wake by some stimuli (e.g. loud noises) but easy to waken by more meaningful events (e.g. having their name spoken). See also *orthodox sleep, sleep cycles*.

paralanguage The *non-verbal cues* that are used during speech, and include speech sounds, such as 'er' and 'um', the timing of utterances or inflections and accents. Paralanguage is an important part of communication through speech, but provides information independently of the actual verbal aspects of the communication. A measure of the importance of paralanguage to speech is the way that in written language, punctuation is needed to substitute for the additional information normally added through tones of voice or pauses.

parallax See *motion parallax*.

parallel distributed processing (PDP) A *computer simulation* system which works on the principle that human reasoning often involves the simultaneous operation of more than one sequence of argument. Consequently, PDP involves simulation programs that operate several different logic chains simultaneously, with considerable cross-linking between them. The particular value of this approach appears to be that it is capable of producing novel or unexpected outcomes in computer problem-solving. The general approach to computer simulation expressed by this technique is also known as *connectionism*.

parallel play A form of *play* in which two or more children play alongside each other without direct interaction. It is common in young children before social play becomes usual.

parallel processing The processing of information in such a way that more than one set of *operations* is happening simultaneously. Models of parallel processing were introduced to *cognitive psychology* in an attempt to account for the extremely rapid ways in which people can search for information, taking several features into account apparently all at the same time.

parameter A mathematical measure of some characteristic of a population, such as the mean. The same measure in a sample is called a *statistic*.

parametric statistics Statistical techniques that which have been developed on the assumption that the data are of a certain type. In particular, the measure should be an *equal-interval scale*, the scores should be drawn from a *normal distribution*, and different samples should be independent of each other – the choice of items or scores in one sample should not have affected the choice of items or scores in another. Because construction of the tests is based on these assumptions, using them on data that do not fit the assumptions can give misleading results, although there seem to be no clear answers about how serious a problem this is. Parametric statistics are usually preferred because, by using more of the information available in the data, they are more powerful in detecting significant effects. The alternative is to use *non-parametric statistics* that do not make the same assumptions about the data. However, apart from the loss of power, there are not always non-parametric versions of techniques such as *analysis of variance* and *factor analysis*. See also *levels of measurement*.

paranoia A disorder in which the person is dominated by thoughts of persecution, grandeur and sometimes jealousy. Intellectual functioning is not impaired, and great ingenuity may be shown in interpreting every event to fit with the paranoid belief.

paranoid schizophrenia A schizophrenic condition of which the main feature is paranoia, but the consistency of the beliefs found in paranoia is missing. See also *schizophrenia*.

parapsychology The study of phenomena that resemble psychological or physical events, but cannot be explained by accepted principles or mechanisms. Parapsychologists investigate instances of apparent *clairvoyance*, *psychokinesis*, *ESP* (extra-sensory perception) and *telepathy*. A considerable amount of their work is also devoted to the study of deception (i.e. how fraudulent 'psychics' manage to persuade people to believe in clairvoyance, ESP, etc.).

parasympathetic division The division of the *autonomic nervous system* that comes into action during the quiescent emotions, such as contentment or sorrow. The parasympathetic division is also concerned with processes for restoring and conserving bodily resources such as digestion, and storing glycogen and other reserves that have been depleted by the action of the *sympathetic division* of the autonomic nervous system.

parenting A term used instead of *mothering* either to emphasise that any adult could be providing the care, or to refer to a specific aspect of care of the young that is undertaken by either parent.

parietal lobe The large area of the *cerebrum* located behind the *central fissure* and above the *occipital lobe*. See also *frontal lobe, temporal lobe*.

Parkinson's disease A progressive neural disease that affects older people, producing gradual loss of motor control, noticeable trembling of the limbs, and eventually resulting in paralysis. Parkinson's disease is known to be caused by *dopamine* deficiency in the brain, and the symptoms can sometimes be alleviated by treatment with a drug known as L-dopa, which is converted into dopamine in the brain itself. Unfortunately, this form of treatment also has distressing side effects, so it is not regarded as a fully satisfactory method of managing the disease. Long-term use of many antipsychotic drugs can produce a set of symptoms similar to Parkinson's disease, known as drug-induced Parkinsonism. See also *hypokinetic*.

parsimonious Parsimonious explanation is the form of explanation that is the most efficient, or requires the fewest number of adjustments, conditions or iterations to be complete. See also *Occam's razor*.

parsimony principle See *Occam's razor*.

parsing The process of analysing sets of words or sentences to identify the *syntactic* structures that determine how they are grouped.

part-whole effect The way that a facial feature is more easily recognised if it is presented as part of a whole face, than if it is presented on its own. See also *face recognition*.

partial correlation A calculation of the correlation between two variables which is adjusted so that the influence of the correlation of each of them with a third variable is eliminated. For example, in a given sample, physical health and IQ might correlate, but it may be that each of these variables correlates with quality of diet. Once the correlation with diet is 'partialled out', the partial correlation between health and IQ may be much reduced.

partial reinforcement Reinforcement in an *operant conditioning* process that is not given every time the desired behaviour is shown, but only some of the time. This is also known as *intermittent reinforcement*, and produces a somewhat slower but stronger form of learning that is more resistant to *extinction*. See also *reinforcement schedule*.

participant The title given to someone taking part in research who is not the researcher. It has replaced the term 'subject', which was felt to imply (or recognise) that there was a one-way process in which researchers operated on passive subjects who had less awareness or control of what was happening. Using the term 'participant' reminds us that research is a mutual venture in which everyone involved has hypotheses about what is happening, and intentions about what should happen.

participant observation A research technique in which the researcher takes a full role in the group being studied, often without the other members being aware of the research. In this way, the distortion produced by the presence of an observer is minimised, and the researcher can obtain a fuller appreciation of the experiences of the group. See also *action research, observational study*.

particularistic meanings Meanings of words or phrases that are entirely dependent on the context in which they are uttered. See also *universalistic meanings*.

Parvo cells Cells that form part of a major visual pathway in the brain. Parvo cells are found in the *visual cortex*, and carry information about colour and fine detail. They are thought to have evolved more recently than the complementary *magno cells*.

pattern perception The way in which different perceptual features of shapes or figures are recognised as belonging together and forming a pattern of stimuli, rather than being separate and discrete. Without pattern perception, our subjective experience would simply be of patches of light and dark, or of patches of colour, without any linking of the stimuli into meaningful units. The basis of pattern perception is *figure-ground organisation* (i.e. the inherent tendency for our perceptual system to organise sensory data into meaningful figures set against backgrounds). This organisational principle results in pattern perception, and is evident in the *perception* of other sensory modes, such as music or speech perception, which involve pattern perception in linking and distinguishing the different components of the information.

pattern recognition The ability to identify or recognise two-dimensional patterns, such as fingerprints or cartoon images. See also *pattern perception*.

Pavlov, Ivan P. (1849–1936)

Despite his personal identification as a physiologist, Pavlov became one of the most well-known figures in psychology's history. His discovery of *conditioned reflexes* while studying digestion in dogs led to a systematic investigation of learning processes, and established the principles of *classical conditioning*.

These were taken as a foundation of *behaviourism* by J.B. *Watson*, and so influenced the development of psychology throughout the twentieth century. He was Professor of Physiology at the Institute of Experimental Medicine in St Petersburg for nearly 50 years, between 1890 and 1939, and remained in post under Lenin despite being an outspoken opponent of the Bolsheviks. There are sometimes advantages to being an internationally recognised, prestigious scientist.

Pavlovian conditioning See *classical conditioning*.

payoff matrix In *game theory*, this is a matrix that lists the costs and benefits to the players which are involved in the differing decisions of players.

PDD-NOS This stands for 'pervasive developmental disorders not otherwise specified' (i.e. problems developed in childhood that appear to fit the category of *autistic spectrum disorders*, but don't have a clear label or reflect a known grouping of symptoms).

PDP See *parallel distributed processing*.

peak experience The rare experience of feeling for a moment complete and at one with oneself and the world. Maslow regarded peak experiences as important, but not essential, aspects of *self-actualisation*.

Pearson's product–moment correlation (r) A measure of *correlation* that uses interval data (see *levels of measurement*). It is thus a *parametric* test and makes the standard assumptions about the data. It is the preferred measure of correlation if the data are suitable. If not, then *Spearman's rank–order correlation coefficient* may be used. See also *statistics*.

pecking order An idea taken from the observation that chickens seem to have a social hierarchy in which anyone can peck those below them, but not those above. The unfortunate character at the bottom is under attack from all of the others, and is literally 'henpecked'. The term has been extended to describe any social hierarchy in which there is a clear and specific definition of the order in which people or animals are dominant. This is more technically known as a *dominance hierarchy* and turns out to be surprisingly rare in the animal kingdom.

peer group A group composed of people from similar backgrounds and of equal status. The term is most commonly used to indicate that the group is composed of children of equal age.

penis envy In *psychoanalytic theory*, the envy that girls are claimed to feel about the fact that boys have a penis and they do not. Freud believed that women experience penis envy throughout their lives, but this is now a deeply unfashionable point of view for which Freud has received his fair share of *interpretations*.

percept The impression which the person receives of that which is being perceived. The percept is the subjective or internal experience that represents an object or event in the external world.

perception The process by which we analyse and make sense of incoming sensory information. Perception has been studied extensively by psychologists, and now forms part of *cognitive psychology*. Perception can be distinguished from *sensation*, which concerns the stimulation of sensory receptors and may also be restricted to the earlier stages of processing incoming information. However, there is no fully agreed definition. Some theorists, such as Ulric Neisser, regard perception as identical to the rest of cognition, and so would make little or no distinction between the two. Perception includes several distinct areas, such as *visual perception*, *person perception*, auditory perception, and the perception of other forms of information such as nociception, or gustatory, *tactile* or olfactory *stimulation*.

perceptual constancy The way in which a person's perception adjusts itself so that the world is seen as constant, despite the changes in stimulation detected by the sense organs. The perceptual constancies enable us to perceive events more accurately in terms of their meaning (e.g. people are seen as the same size, however far away they are). There are many forms of perceptual constancy, of which the most studied have been *size constancy*, *shape constancy*, *colour constancy* and *location constancy*.

perceptual cycle See *anticipatory schema*.

perceptual defence The idea that the perceptual system has higher *thresholds* for perceiving information that is psychologically threatening to the individual, meaning that such information is less likely to be detected or recognised. See also *defence mechanism*.

perceptual organisation The structuring of visual information, in such a way that it becomes possible to detect figures against backgrounds, and patterns.

perceptual set A state of readiness or preparedness to perceive certain kinds of information rather than other kinds. Perceptual set is a powerful phenomenon

that links closely with *selective attention* and which can be affected by a range of circumstances, such as prior experience, emotion, motivation, culture and habit.

perceptual span The field of view in reading. It has been shown that expert readers have a wider visual span than novice readers (i.e. they can take in more words before and after the word they are focusing on at a given glance).

perfect correlation An exact, one-to-one correlation, in which one variable always increases or decreases exactly in proportion to the amount that the other variable increases. Perfect correlations may be either positive or negative, and have a numerical value of 1.

performance A term used in experimental psychology for the level of competence that a person or animal achieves on a particular task.

performance decrement A measure of the increase in the number of failures or misses achieved by a research participant on a particular task, over a specified period of time – in other words, how much worse they get at doing the task.

periaqueductal grey *Grey matter* in the *midbrain* that has been shown to be involved in *nociception*.

peripheral dyslexia A form of disruption of the reading process resulting from spatial and attentional disturbances, and also disruption of the ability to compute word forms. *Pure alexia* is an example of peripheral dyslexia. See also *dyslexia*.

peripheral nervous system A term for those parts of the nervous system that are not included in the *central nervous system* (the brain and spinal cord). The peripheral nervous system accordingly includes the *autonomic nervous system* and the *somatic nervous system*, which is composed of *motor* and *sensory neurones* carrying information to and from the central nervous system.

peripheral traits *Personality* or attitude *traits* that are not particularly fundamental to the person's sense of self or identity, and can therefore be fairly easily changed.

permastore Another name for *long-term memory* storage.

perseveration The failure to change focus in a task, or to act differently from a previous response when asked – typical of those with *prefrontal cortex* damage. See also *Wisconsin card-sorting test*.

person identity node (PIN) An abstract level of representation proposed as part of the ways that we recognise people. The idea is that the person identity node links with *face recognition units* and with other stored *semantic memory* about that person, and is activated when the person, or information about them such as their name, is encountered.

person perception The application of methods of studying and understanding perception to the perception of people. Person perception is fundamental to the process of understanding other people and often, by implication, ourselves. It has been found to have the usual features of perception when it is operating in conditions in which the object is complex and the conditions are difficult. That is, it is highly influenced by *set* and expectations, and by the needs, fears and wishes of the observer. Person perception is an active and highly researched area within psychology, involving the study of *attribution*, *non-verbal communication*, interpersonal *attitudes* and social *memory*.

personal attributions *Attributions* which are seen to apply just because that particular person was involved. They therefore tend to relate to some unique or identifying characteristic of that person. For example, passing a very high-level music examination on the cello would be likely to be attributed to the special characteristic of exceptionally high talent. If the attributed causal sequence would have happened whoever was involved, it is classed as 'universal'. Some writers, such as Seligman, treat personal attributions as being the same as *internal attributions*.

personal constructs A unique set of ideas about the world and the people in it, which each individual develops and uses to make sense of the world and to function effectively in it. Personal constructs were proposed by George Kelly as the individual theories that people use to generate hypotheses in order to explain their experience. Kelly's model of the person was of 'man-as-scientist' – that the person was actively making sense of the world by formulating hypotheses about it, and then testing them, much as a scientist investigates their chosen subject area. By identifying the special, personal set of constructs that the individual uses, a therapist would be far better placed to understand that person and to assist them with their problems in living. Kelly's was thus an *idiographic* theory, concerned with the uniqueness of the individual and how he understood his world. The form of assessment known as the *repertory grid*, which Kelly developed, allows the therapist to utilise the individual's own constructs in analysing their experience. See also *laddering*.

personal growth The development of character and personal qualities such as tolerance or *self-efficacy* as the person becomes more mature. According to Carl Rogers, personal growth is another way of describing the process of *self-actualisation* – the development and making real of one's talents and abilities. Personal growth may occur in response to life events, or as a result of therapy. See also *post-traumatic personal growth*, *client-centred therapy*, *actualising tendency*.

personal space The distance that people keep between themselves and others during everyday activities. This distance will vary depending on the individual's culture, the circumstances, and their relationship with the other person – we tend to position ourselves more closely to intimate friends than we do to strangers. Personal space is a manifestation of *proxemics*, and an important *non-verbal cue*. It is often described in terms of *territoriality*.

personalism The degree to which the actions of others are perceived as directed particularly towards yourself. There is evidence that we tend to overestimate the extent to which this happens (i.e. we over-personalise). See also *attribution*, *hedonic relevance*.

personality Those relatively enduring features of an individual that account for their characteristic ways of behaving. We put this forward as a useful definition, but many alternatives would be possible. The differences are not a matter of accuracy, but of deciding which approach to the subject is most likely to be productive. Some uses of the term 'personality' refer to patterns of behaviour rather than their causes or, more narrowly, to the social *roles* that a person adopts. Some theories are concerned with the way in which the structures underlying personality are formed (e.g. Freud), and in general

the *psychodynamic* approaches stress personality as an integrated whole, more than the sum of its parts (see *personality dynamics*). Other theories are trying to attain a biological basis (e.g. Eysenck's *type theory*). Another approach is to measure different aspects of people on the assumption that their behaviour is the product of many *traits*. Type and trait theory are coming together with the *five-factor theory*. Completely different is the line taken by many psychologists, such as Walter Mischel, who claims that there is little evidence of stable structures within people that cause them to behave in certain ways. Instead, he suggests that, as far as human behaviour is consistent at all, it is consistent because people tend to spend their time in particular kinds of environments and so behave in recognisable ways. Mischel would claim that there is no such thing as personality as defined above.

personality assessment A system for measuring the personality characteristics of different people. Personality assessments may utilise the format of objective testing, as in a *personality inventory*, or of *projective tests* such as the *thematic apperception test* or the *Rorschach inkblot test*, or they may be tests based on *phenomenology*, such as the *repertory grid* or the *Q-sort*.

personality disorder A term for the very broad class of psychological disorders that seem to arise from long-term characteristics of the person. Roughly speaking, the term applies to conditions that reflect what the person is, rather than how they behave (*behaviour disorders*). Examples include *psychopathic personality* and *paranoia*.

personality dynamics An approach to understanding behaviour in terms of the active interplay of aspects of the personality structure. Freud's account of personality in terms of interactions between the *id*, *ego* and *superego* is the classic example.

personality inventory A personality test that takes the form of a set of straightforward questions about the individual's behaviour, which is used to build up a *personality profile* or to assess *personality traits* quantitatively according to a predetermined set of criteria. See also *trait theory*.

personality profile A system for describing the outcome of a personality test that assesses the individual in terms of predefined *traits*. Rather than just providing a single score as the outcome of the test, an image of how the individual has scored on each of the set of traits is given, usually graphically.

personality trait A dimension of personality, such as affability or introversion. Trait theories of personality tend to assume that traits are (a) stable and (b) inherited, although not all trait theorists hold these beliefs to the same degree. Personality tests are usually based on trait theories, although they vary in the actual traits they attempt to measure.

personification A form of *objectification* in which the idea becomes associated with a particular individual (e.g. the identification of a particular economic ideology as 'Thatcherism', or of a moralistic and overprotective approach to society as 'Rantzenism').

persuasion The social process of encouraging a person to act or think in a particular way or towards a specific goal. See also *attitude*.

PET scans See *positron emission tomography*.

PGO waves A characteristic waveform of electrical activity in the brain, often found in *REM sleep*. They get their name because they originate in the *pons*, go through to the *lateral geniculate nuclei*, and then pass on to the *occipital cortex*.

phallic stage The third *psychosexual stage* in Freudian theory, in which the child's interest focuses on the penis. Having based a significant part of personality development on something possessed by only half of the species, Freud's theory ran into all kinds of complications, and some accusations of male chauvinism, about this stage. The phallic stage ends with the *Oedipus conflict*, and is generally concerned with issues of potency. The term 'phallic' is used when the emphasis is on symbolic aspects of the penis.

phantom limb The experience, by people who have had a limb amputated, of sensations as if they still had the limb. It is of interest to psychologists because it is informative about how the *body image* is maintained.

pharmacodynamics The biochemical and physiological effects of drugs on the body.

pharmacokinesis Muscular movements or spasms that result from the actions of drugs rather than originating with a disorder. The spasms characteristic of *Parkinson's disease*, and once thought to be an inevitable symptom, have now been shown to be pharmacokinetic in nature.

phenomenal consciousness The content of immediate awareness, sometimes also described as the 'raw', or unprocessed, feeling of sensation.

phenomenal field A term used by perceptual theorists to describe the totality, or complete picture, of what is being perceived.

phenomenology The position that the only reality of which we can be directly aware is conscious experience. It therefore attempts to study the ways that consciousness develops and operates. Phenomenology was initiated within philosophy and has had its main application within sociology. In psychology, it provided the impetus for *constructivist* theories.

phenotype The developed organism that results from the interaction of the genetic characteristics which were inherited from the parents, and the environment in which development occurs. Although the term carries an idea of an end product, the phenotype is a dynamic rather than a static phenomenon that, as both genetic and environmental influence continue throughout life, is constantly developing and changing. See also *genotype*.

phenotype-first An approach to genetic analysis that involves comparing many different phenotypes in order to explore or identify genetic differences. See also *genotype-first*.

pheromones Chemicals that are released into the atmosphere from the body and which provide a form of communication, as they are detected by other members of the species. Many species release distinctive pheromones to signal sexual receptiveness, and synthesised pheromones are often used by animal breeders to facilitate mating of their animals. Although pheromone detection appears to be linked to the sense of smell, it is not identical to it, as many pheromones seem to exert a direct effect on hormone balance.

phi phenomenon An illusion of movement brought about by the sequencing in illumination of adjacent lights. If one light comes on when the other goes off, and the light next to it goes on when that goes off, what is perceived (assuming it happens reasonably quickly) is an impression of one light moving across from the location of the first one to the location of the last. This phenomenon is widely used in illuminated advertising signs, and can sometimes be very convincing. Should the lights be arranged in a circle, the perceived circular motion is seen as describing a circle of smaller diameter than the actual arrangement of the lights. It is thought that the phi phenomenon is a manifestation of the Gestalt psychologists' *principle of closure* occurring with dynamic stimuli rather than with static ones.

phobia A neurotic disorder in which there is a strong and persistent fear of objects or situations that is not justified by any danger that they pose. The sufferer will be aware that the fear is irrational, but will make strenuous attempts to avoid the feared situation. Often the symptoms can best be seen as attempts to avoid the (very unpleasant) sensations of anxiety, rather than being closely tied to the feared object. Phobias may be attached to a wide range of situations, and particular forms are indicated by putting the appropriate term (usually in Latin or Greek form) in front of the word, as in *agoraphobia* and claustrophobia. Specific phobias can usually be treated effectively by *behaviour therapy*, but many of them, such as agoraphobia, incorporate a fear of social interaction, and are more difficult to treat.

phobic disorder The standard term used to cover all of the *phobias*.

phobic reaction The full range of behaviours shown by a person suffering from a *phobia*.

phoneme A basic unit of spoken language – a speech sound. Phonemes are not the same as syllables. A one-syllable word such as 'cat', for instance, is made up of three distinct phonemes that are combined to produce the syllable, or *morpheme*.

phoneme restoration The way that a listener will often 'fill in' a missing phoneme in order to make cognitive sense of the utterance that they are listening to.

phonemics The study of regularities and distinctive patterns in the combination of *phonemes* in spoken language.

phonetic spelling Methods of spelling that are exactly equivalent to the sounds of the spoken words. In English, therefore, phonetic spelling bears very little resemblance to written English.

phonetics The study of speech sounds in terms of their physical properties rather than their use to create meaningful speech (*phonemics*).

phonological To do with the perception of words as sounds.

phonological dysgraphia A condition in which familiar words can be read easily, but non-words cannot. See also *dysgraphia*.

phonological dyslexia The ability to read real words more easily than non-words. See also *dyslexia*, *peripheral dyslexia*.

phonological lexicon The abstract speech sounds that make up known words. The phonological lexicon is sllightly, or sometimes considerably, different for each language.

phonological loop A part of the *working memory* model that stores verbal information as temporary auditory images.

phonological mediation The idea that reading for understanding is dependent on converting the visual input of the word to its speech equivalent. The alternative view is that the processes of understanding written words and transcoding text into speech are two separate, but interlinked, cognitive tasks. Both theories have led to proposals for improved teaching of reading in schools, with varying outcomes. See also *dyslexia*.

phonology The study of fundamental speech sounds, how they differ in their use within a language and between different languages.

photopsin A light-sensitive chemical in the *retina* that responds to coloured light. There are different types of photopsin, responding to different wavelengths. See also *rhodopsin*.

photoreceptors Cells in the *retina* that respond to light and so are necessary for vision.

phrenology The theory, popular in the nineteenth century, that if someone had a particular ability, then the relevant area of their brain would be larger, and would affect the shape of the skull. Phrenologists aimed to map the bulges in the skull caused by this greater brain development, and believed that mental faculties could be measured in this way. The belief was so widely shared that phrenological evidence was even accepted in law courts. In fact, a whole industry developed in which the technology of skull measurement and pictorial representation of the recordings received much greater attention than the *validity* of the results. Many psychologists claim that current personality assessment does not make the same mistake.

phylogenetic scale An approximate scale that attempts to chart an evolutionary progression through different types and groups of species to human beings. Species are ranked in order of approximate similarity to humans, with primates being closest and thus seen as higher up the phylogenetic scale, and with fish and reptiles being seen as significantly lower down. The concept of the phylogenetic scale is an inherently misleading one, implying as it does that evolution proceeds in a linear fashion, and that other species can be seen as steps towards an ultimate goal, but the concept of species similarity which it contains is sometimes useful in evaluating studies in *comparative psychology*. If we want to generalise to human behaviour, it makes more sense to take examples from other primate groups, or at least mammals, than it does to take them from species that are far less closely related, such as birds, insects or fish.

phylogeny The evolutionary processes by which a species develops its characteristics. See also *ontogeny*.

physical punishment Punishment that involves some identifiable material consequence, such as keeping a child in after school, or loss of pocket money. Although corporal punishment is included in this category, the term physical punishment is used to describe a wider range of punishments than simple physical chastisement. Compare *psychological punishment*.

physiological arousal A general concept used to describe a combination of physical and physiological reactions to threat, excitement or sexual stimulation. There is dispute among researchers about the extent to which a general concept of 'arousal' is useful, since there are many different forms of arousal for different states. Nonetheless, there are generally considered to be several commonly shared characteristics, such as increased heart rate and sweating, dilated pupils, and other adjustments to bodily function that provide the body with additional energy, strength or responsiveness. See also *alarm reaction, autonomic nervous system, galvanic skin response*.

physiological correlate A physical change that accompanies a behavioural or psychological response. The term is used to avoid making assumptions about causality. It may be recognised, for instance, that a cognitive event such as concentration or sleep is accompanied by physiological changes in the body. However, the relationship between the physiological change and the event itself is not a simplistic causal one, and so the term 'physiological correlate' is adopted as a description.

physiological determinism The belief that psychological processes are directly caused by physiological processes. See also *determinism*.

physiological needs Identified by Maslow as being the lowest level in his *hierarchy of human needs*, physiological needs are the requirements for physical functioning, such as the needs for food, water, etc.

physiological psychology The study of the way in which human behaviour and cognition is influenced or performed by processes that take place physically within the body. The term 'physiological' is preferred to 'biological' because such influences are usually exerted by whole systems of physical functioning operating together, as is demonstrated, for example, in the *fight or flight response*, or the sensory information-processing systems. Physiological psychology is often seen as being inherently *reductionist* as it explains behaviour in terms of the actions of neurones and chemicals, but many physiological psychologists maintain an *interactionist* approach to the subject, in which physiological factors are seen as contributing to or influencing behaviour, but not necessarily determining it.

physiological reductionism The claim that the best way to understand psychological processes is to reduce them to the underlying physiological mechanisms, and to study the latter. This approach assumes that *physiological determinism* operates, and usually takes the form of attempting to explain all psychological processes in terms of brain function. See *reductionism*.

physiology The functioning of physical systems in the body, such as the regulation of blood flow, digestive processes, etc. 'Physiology' used on its own usually refers to the workings of the body as a whole, living unit.

pie chart A diagram that presents frequency data in the form of a circle divided into 'slices'. The size of each slice indicates the proportion of the complete data set that the variable makes up.

Piaget, Jean (1896–1980)

Piaget started his psychological studies wanting to understand how mathematical and scientific thinking had developed in human culture. His concept of *genetic epistemology* ('genetic' refers to development, not genes) led him to begin his explorations of the nature of human knowledge by studying how thinking develops in the child. Sixty years, 50 books and 500 papers later, he was still working on this. Piaget's theory is based on the idea that cognitive development occurs through the reduction of *egocentrism*, and through *equilibration*, dealing with new experiences by the processes of *schema* development through *assimilation* and *accommodation*. Like most of the classic developmental theories, Piaget's was based on stages, in this case of cognitive functioning – the *sensorimotor stage*, the *preoperational stage*, the *concrete operational stage* and the *formal operational stage*. Piaget insisted that children's logic is appropriate to their stage, and not just an inadequate version of adult thinking. Piaget's theory continues to be extremely influential, especially in education, but he underestimated the abilities of the child by concentrating on reasoning about the physical world – it is now recognised that the child's social reasoning is more sophisticated. See also *adaptation, conservation, moral development, naughty teddy, operation, reversibility*.

---

pilomotor response The response of the hair of the body standing on end at times of extreme fear or rage. In many animals, this forms an impressive signal, resulting in the animal looking much larger and, presumably, more fearsome to a would-be attacker. It is also sometimes used to fluff up the hair to provide added protection from cold. In human beings, owing to the shortness and near invisibility of much body hair, the pilo-motor response simply results in the skin appearance known as goose pimples, as the contraction of the small muscle at the base of each hair pulls the surround-ing skin into a small bump.

pilot test The testing of an initial ver-sion of a questionnaire by administering it to a smaller sample of respondents. The idea of piloting is to identify prob-lems with the questions or with the analysis.

PIN See *person identity node*.

pineal gland A gland situated centrally in the brain, which was once thought to be the seat of the soul. The pineal gland is known to be involved in the hormo-nal changes which signal the onset of puberty, and some recent research has indicated that it may also be involved in *diurnal rhythms* and seasonal hormonal variation, although the precise function-ing of the gland is far from established.

pitch The property of sound that relates to the frequency of the sound wave, and allows different sounds to be experi-enced as ranging from low to high. High pitches have more vibrations per second (*hertz*) than low pitches, and the gen-eral range of perception of sounds by the human ear spans from 20 Hz to 20,000 Hz. Other animals can perceive sounds outside this range (e.g. elephants are able to detect very low-pitched sounds, while bats notably perceive sounds that are pitched at higher levels than humans can detect). See also *frequency theory, place theory*.

pituitary gland The main or 'master con-trol' gland of the endocrine system. The pituitary gland has a direct link with the *hypothalamus*, and secretes *hormones* that carry signals to all of the other glands, stimulating their operations.

pity A form of concern about some-one else's situation, which involves an indication of awareness of the negative aspects of it.

pivot words Words that children seem to use in the earliest stage of *language* acquisition, as a base to which a large number of other words (called open words) can be attached (e.g. 'allgone car', 'allgone Daddy', 'nasty allgone'). Pivot words were once thought to be the basis of *grammar*, and it was hoped to extend the concept to utterances of three or more words. The idea is no longer widely used in theories of lan-guage development.

pixel A minimal spatial unit (e.g. a dot on a computer screen). See also *voxel*.

PK See *psychokinesis*.

place cells Neurones in the *hippocampus* that are closely linked with location in space. They respond when a person or animal is in a particular location in *allocentric space* (i.e. in response to their own movements).

place theory The idea that the pitch or frequency of a sound is identified by the brain in terms of the specific region of the *organ of Corti* that is stimulated, with high tones triggering off the hair cells nearest to the oval window, while lower tones stimulate hair cells further along the cochlea.

placebo A fake or dummy form of medi-cation that is given during experimental trials investigating the effects of drugs. A placebo resembles the drug under study, but has no measurable effect on the body. By comparing the results of those people who have had the drug and those who have had the placebo, experimental effects such as the influ-ence of beliefs are controlled. In most such studies, a *double-blind control* will be used, such that *experimenter effects* are also controlled, as the experimenter is not aware who has taken the placebo and who has taken the drug.

planum temporale A part of the *auditory cortex* that allows sounds to be integrated with non-sound information (e.g. to distinguish between two sounds coming from different directions).

plasticity This refers to the brain's ability to change as a result of experience. It used to be thought that neural plasticity only lasted until puberty, but it is now clear that some degree of plasticity remains throughout the whole lifespan. However, while neural plasticity (as in recovering from brain damage or ablation) happens virtually automatically in children, plasticity in later life is strongly related to effort and persistence.

platykurtic A distribution of scores with many examples of extremes, such that the normal distribution curve appears flattened. See also *kurtosis*.

play There is no satisfactory definition of play. Either it is defined by exclusion, which amounts to saying it is not work, or the definition makes assumptions that fail to capture the appropriate range of activities. Such a situation is usually an indication that there is no adequate theory. Our ignorance about play comes under two headings – functions and cause. Function is concerned with the role that play has in the development of the individual, and how it came to be present in the species. Theories here concentrate on the fact that much play results in the development of skills that will be useful later in life, but that play is uncoupled from serious consequences, and so can be indulged in safely by the immature organism. The issue of cause – whether a particular child will play in a particular situation – is even less well understood, with most work having been done under the heading of *exploration*. Clues to both function and cause can be found by studying the forms that play takes. Most of this research has concentrated on preschool children, as many of their activities involve play. See also *fantasy*.

play therapy A range of techniques in the diagnosis and treatment of children that exploit the child's tendency to play. Often materials such as puppets, dolls or just a piece of string may be provided and kept for the child between sessions. In play, the child will explore concerns that cannot be expressed in words, and the therapist both learns about the child's problems and can help the child to find ways of dealing with anxieties and difficulties.

pleasure centre A part of the brain that may not really exist, interest in this area resulted from studies in the 1970s showing that stimulation of an area of the *limbic system* created sensations of pleasure. More recent neurological investigations indicate that these outcomes resulted from a complex *reward pathway* rather than a single 'pleasure centre'. See also *ESB*.

pleasure principle In Freudian theory, the basic function of the *id* is to pursue pleasure. In infancy, with a high degree of *dependency* on *caregivers*, and before the *ego* with its *reality principle* has developed, pleasure must be achieved either through dependency on caretakers or through *fantasy*. In this context, Freud wrote of pleasure as the reduction of tension, as if all stimulation or arousal, at least for the infant, is unpleasant.

pluralistic ignorance This occurs when everyone in a group believes something but no one expresses it, and so each person thinks they are alone in their belief. Cases of *bystander apathy* and crowd behaviour may depend at least partly on pluralistic ignorance combined with *conformity* to the presumed beliefs of the rest of the group. The concept also informs the idea of a 'silent majority'.

point of subjective equality (PSE) The value of a continuously variable stimulus at which it appears to be identical to a standard stimulus. It is not usually measurable directly, but derived by a variety of *psychophysics* techniques. For example, judgements may be obtained from a research participant about whether a series of lines are larger or smaller than the standard line, and the point at which they switch from larger to smaller is called the point of subjective equality.

polygenic Resulting from the action of many genes. For example, the genetic element in overall body height results from the action of several genes contributing to the development of different parts of the body. Phenotypic characteristics that are polygenic show continuous variation in the population, as height does.

polygraph A device used to measure autonomic arousal that takes measurements of a number of different indices, and provides a multiple read-out ('poly' is from the Greek, meaning 'many'). Typically, a polygraph will take measurements of blood pressure and heart rate, *EEG*, *galvanic skin response* and muscular tension. By such means, it is possible to tell when an individual is under stress, and so polygraphs are often used as *lie detectors*. A considerable amount of controversy surrounds their use in criminal investigation, as it is not possible to distinguish the stress produced by telling lies from that produced by other factors (e.g. anxiety on behalf of someone else, or physical pain).

polymorphism The process of occurring in several different forms.

pons A region in the lower part of the brain that serves to connect the two halves of the *cerebellum*, and which may also be involved in mediating *dreaming* sleep.

Ponzo illusion A *geometric illusion* consisting of two equal-length horizontal lines, arranged one above the other, and flanked by two straight lines that are angled towards one another at the top. The line in the narrower gap appears longer. The illusion is thought to work as a *visual illusion* because it resembles the perspective produced by looking straight at parallel tracks such as railway lines.

pop-out The way that a single disparate object among a set of others appears to stand out from the rest, by comparison with the way that a number of such features scattered among others seem to have much the same visual qualities, and merge into the whole pattern.

population All of the cases within a given definition (e.g. all of the women in the UK, all of the schools in Huddersfield or all of the people in a given laboratory class). Psychological research is nearly always only able to take a *sample* from a large population, although researchers will often want to generalise their results to the whole of the population.

population norms A set of scores which describes the proportions of a *population* that are expected to achieve particular scores on a test or some other measurement. For example, every *intelligence test* has a set of population norms that describe the proportions of the population who would score at or above different levels on the test. The norms can be used to predict the numbers in a representative sample who will score above the level of interest, or to judge whether an individual is scoring within the normal range. See also *norms, standardisation*.

population vector A calculation of how *neural impulses* come to be channelled along *neural pathways*, given the amount and direction of the firing of the neurones concerned. It is arrived at by summing the preferred directions of firing (vectors) of a large group of particular neurones (i.e. a population).

positive correlation A measure of the consistency with which an increase in one *variable* is accompanied by an increase in a second variable. For example, reaction time correlates positively with number of units of alcohol consumed. A relationship in the opposite direction is called a *negative correlation* and the statistic describing such relationships is the *correlation coefficient*.

positive psychology A relatively recent innovation in psychology introduced by Martin Seligman in 1999. The movement proposes that psychology has been limited by its focus on negative states, and should now develop ways of cultivating positive aspects of human life. It is said that, on a happiness scale, we have become quite good at moving people from –5 to –2, but have not developed any ways of moving people from +2 to +5. Michael Argyle and Abraham Maslow could be seen as pioneers with their work on *happiness* and *self-actualisation*, respectively.

positive regard Liking, affection or love for another person. The term was used by Carl Rogers to describe what he considered to be one of the two basic needs of the human being – the need for positive regard from others. This, he believed, could either be conditional upon appropriate behaviour or unconditional, but as a basic need it would have to be satisfied. Rogers' form of therapy requires that the therapist provides the client with *unconditional positive regard*. See also *self-actualisation*.

positive reinforcement *Reinforcement* which provides something that the organism wants, likes or needs – a reward of some kind. It is the essential component in *operant conditioning*. See also *negative reinforcement*.

positive skew A distortion of a *normal distribution* in which more of the scores are lower, so that the peak of the curve is shifted towards the left. In a positively skewed distribution, the *mode* will be lower than the *median*, which in turn is lower than the *mean*.

positivism A belief that reliable information can only be obtained about events that can be observed directly. It therefore claims that science should only deal with observables and not with hypothetical constructs. *Behaviourism* in its more primitive forms has been the clearest example of a positivistic approach within psychology. An even more restrictive version, called logical positivism, claims that a hypothesis can only be regarded as scientific if there is a way in which it can potentially be disproved by empirical observation. Logical positivism has been largely abandoned or superseded, but it was always more popular among philosophers of science than among psychologists, who mostly just got on with the job of studying hypothesised psychological processes such as *motivation*.

positivity bias A tendency in human decision-making to focus on positive statements rather than negative ones. In social psychology, it refers to a tendency to evaluate individuals more positively than groups or things.

positron emission tomography (PET) A non-invasive technique for investigating brain functioning, PET scans work by detecting the blood supply to different regions of the brain. Each time a nerve cell fires, it depletes its reserves, and must be replenished from nutrients carried in the bloodstream. Blood vessels respond by increasing the blood supply to that area. PET scans detect radioactive glucose introduced into the brain's blood supply, using receptors placed on the scalp. The receptors feed information about the distribution of the blood in the brain to a computer, which combines the information to produce an image of the currently active parts of the brain.

posterior Towards the back, or behind. See also *anterior, superior, inferior*.

post hoc tests Tests carried out after an *analysis of variance* (ANOVA) test, in order to find out what the results of the test actually mean.

post-hypnotic amnesia The forgetting of information as a result of a suggestion made while the subject was under *hypnosis*, and which occurs after the hypnotic state has finished. Post-hypnotic amnesia is commonly described by subjects as feeling like *tip-of-the-tongue phenomenon* forgetting, and can often last for several days.

post-hypnotic suggestion A suggestion made to someone while they are in a hypnotic state, which concerns behaviour that they will undertake once the hypnotic fugue is over. In the case of relatively trivial forms of behaviour, this is often performed by the participant, who typically says that they 'just felt like doing it'. Post-hypnotic suggestion has sometimes been presented by Hollywood film-makers as being so powerful that it could force a subject to act against their will, but this represents part of the Hollywood mythology of hypnotism, which bears little resemblance to the real thing. It is not possible to force someone to do anything against their will, either during hypnosis or through post-hypnotic suggestion – the state of *hypnosis* itself necessarily involves the willing cooperation of the person throughout.

postmodernism An *epistemological* approach that developed as a reaction to the modernist theories dominating society, art and architecture in the first half of the twentieth century. In psychology, it took the form of opposition to *determinist* approaches such as *behaviourism*, which emphasised objectivity to the exclusion of all else. Postmodernist psychology rejected the objective ideal, arguing that it was (i) unattainable and (ii) unrepresentative of human experience, and emphasised the importance of relative viewpoints and the social construction of reality. See also *social constructionism, discourse analysis*.

postpartum depression Depression in a mother within a few months of the birth of her baby, to be distinguished from 'the blues', which is very common around the third day after the birth, but which is not depression and does not persist. Some evidence is beginning to emerge which suggests that depression in women is no more common following birth than it is in other women of the same age. If this turns out to be the case, then there will be little reason to suppose that postpartum depression is in any way caused by the pregnancy or birth.

post-synaptic potential (PSP) The temporary depolarisation of a *neurone* after it has fired – in other words, how ready a neurone is to fire again, after it has just done so. Some PSPs are excitatory, meaning that the probability of firing is higher, whole others are inhibitory, making further firing less likely. See also *excitation, inhibition, synapse*.

post-traumatic amnesia *Amnesia* which results from some kind of accident, such as that resulting from a blow to the head or from severe brain damage.

post-traumatic growth The observation that experiencing traumatic events such as a major disaster or personal tragedy can sometimes result in increased *personal growth*, as the person re-evaluates their life and values and develops new and more positive ways of interacting with the world. See also *post-traumatic stress disorder*.

post-traumatic stress disorder (PTSD) A set of symptoms commonly found following any kind of extremely disturbing experience. Recent research on concentration camp victims indicates that the disorder may persist over many years. It has been found to be a common response in victims of rape, political torture and major disasters. It can also be substantially reduced by therapy.

postural echo A non-verbal signal which often indicates friendliness or that two people are in substantial agreement. While the participants are engaged in a social exchange (such as a conversation), they may be seen to be adopting (usually *unconsciously*) the same posture, or mirroring each other's posture if they are face to face. Postural echo may be used consciously by therapists and salesmen to produce a feeling of rapport in the client. See also *chameleon effect*.

posture A powerful *non-verbal cue* that is commonly used to indicate attitudes or emotions. It is about the positioning of the body and the relative arrangement of the limbs. Posture is commonly, although usually unconsciously, taken as a communicative signal, and may make a considerable difference to how a verbal message is understood (see Figure 44). See also *non-verbal communication, postural echo*.

Figure 44 Posture

power

(i)   In social terms, the ability to direct, command or control social resources, and thereby the behaviour of other people. Power has always been a significant sociopolitical *motivator*, and almost the whole of human history can be viewed in terms of the use and/or abuse of power. See also *status*.

(ii)   When applied to a statistical test, this refers to the ability of the test to identify an effect, or reject the null hypothesis, when an effect is present. In any test, the power increases as the sample size is increased, but some tests are intrinsically more powerful than others. In general, tests that use more of the information in the data are more powerful. So a *t-test*, which calculates the amounts by which scores differ, is more powerful than a *sign test*, which merely uses information about whether scores are larger or smaller. *Parametric statistics* are more powerful than *non-parametric statistics* for this reason.

power law A law propounded by Stevens which states that the subjective strength of a stimulus is equal to the physical strength of the stimulus raised to a power (squared, cubed, etc.). Like *Fechner's law*, the power law relates to the fact that as a stimulus becomes stronger, larger changes are required in order to achieve the same psychological effect. The power law differs from Fechner's law in the mathematical expression of the relationship.

practical intelligence A form of *intelligence* that is characterised by the ability to deal effectively with real-world

problems and difficulties as they arise. It does not necessarily correlate with more abstract forms of intelligence. See also *triarchic intelligence*.

practice effect An experimental effect in which apparent changes in the *dependent variable* occur as a result of the person gaining practice in the task during the course of the experiment, and therefore improving their performance. Practice effects are usually controlled by *counterbalancing* the order of presentation of the conditions of the study.

pragmatics An approach to studying *language* that concentrates on the functions which language performs, rather than on the structure of the language itself (*linguistics*).

precocial animals Animals that can move about as soon, or almost as soon, as they are born or hatched. Research into *imprinting* has traditionally centred around work with precocial animals, as they show the phenomenon in a clear and unambiguous form.

precognition A knowledge of future events that is not based on judgement, but on direct and certain perception of them. As a branch of *parapsychology*, precognition requires more than the certainty that dinner will be provided this evening, and implies a special form of knowledge, different from any that is understood by psychologists. Anyone who could operate precognition reliably would presumably be either very rich or very depressed.

preconscious Thoughts and knowledge that are not at present in the conscious, but which are not repressed and so can be brought into consciousness at will. Freud proposed that the preconscious lies between the *unconscious* and the conscious mind, which it more closely resembles.

predictive validity See *validity*.

predictor variable An experimental variable that appears to be able to predict an outcome.

preferential looking An *observational* approach in the study of infant *cognition*, in which two stimuli are presented simultaneously and the amount of time the infant spends looking at each of them is recorded.

prefrontal cortex This is the area on the *frontal lobes* that is located in front of the *premotor cortex*. The prefrontal cortex is involved in planning and higher-level controls of action. So, for instance, the prefrontal cortex would be involved with selecting relevant actions to satisfy intentions, while the premotor cortex prepares those actions in response to internal or external situations, the *motor cortex* initiates the activity itself, and the *cerebellum* coordinates the smooth movement of the action. See also *contention scheduling, FAS test, dysexecutive syndrome*.

prejudice Literally meaning 'prejudgement', prejudice refers to the maintenance of a prior attitude irrespective of new or contradictory information. It is commonly used in connection with negative or discriminatory social attitudes, such as *racism* or *sexism*. It may also refer to a predetermined favourable judgement by which the individual ignores relevant negative information. See also *stereotype*.

prelinguistic thought The forms that thinking takes in children before they have developed language abilities. Knowing about prelinguistic thought may help us to understand the extent to which adult thought may be independent of language.

premature Describing babies who are born before *gestation* is complete. New obstetric techniques mean that premature babies now survive from a much earlier stage of development than was previously thought possible. Psychologists are concerned about the effects on the immature baby of being exposed to intense environmental stimulation at a time when the nervous system is biologically adapted to the protective environment of the womb.

pre-moral stage The first of Kohlberg's three stages of *moral development*, in which moral judgements are seen entirely instrumentally, in terms of whether or not the individual is likely to be detected and/or punished.

premotor cortex This is the area immediately in front of the *motor cortex*, and it is important for linking actions with information from the environment. The *lateral premotor cortex* links actions with visual objects; the *medial premotor cortex* deals with self-generated actions using *proprioceptive* input.

preoperational stage The second of Piaget's stages of cognitive development. During this stage children are unable to think in terms of logical concepts such as *conservation* or *reversibility*, and they are dominated by perceptual features of their world. The stage starts from about 2 years of age, at the end of the *sensorimotor stage*, when *object permanence* is first seen. It ends at about 7 years when the child starts the *concrete operational stage*.

prepared learning The finding that, to some extent, organisms are biologically prepared to learn certain *associations* very easily. The most common example is that animals which experience nausea will associate this sensation with whatever they last ate, rather than with other kinds of stimuli, even if these were more intense and more recent. It is sometimes called the 'Garcia effect' after its discoverer, but is also known as the 'sauce Béarnaise phenomenon' after an account by Martin Seligman of an experience of being sick, due to a stomach virus, after eating a steak with his favourite sauce, and being unable to face eating it ever again. In fact, the effects can be overcome, and Seligman has had a lot of free meals while people have tested the phenomenon's permanence. See also *one-trial learning*.

pre-processing A term used in *fMRI imaging* to describe the stages in between the initial data colllection and the analysis of that data.

presenting symptom A patient will usually come into therapy on the basis of a complaint about a particular symptom. This is called the presenting symptom – a reminder that some other symptom may be the real problem, which may only emerge in the course of therapy. A major dispute about evaluating different forms of therapy is based on the issue of whether resolving the presenting symptom counts as a success. Many *behaviourists* will work only on the presenting symptom and end therapy once it is eliminated. *Psychodynamic* therapists are more likely to see the presenting symptom as a kind of ticket that enables the patient to get into therapy so that they can then start to deal with underlying problems.

presumptive consent A technique used when it is not practical to obtain informed consent from participants in a specific research programme. A large set of people are asked to give their views on the acceptability of the proposed procedure. Although the people giving their views will not be taking part in the actual research, it is assumed that their views are representative of the general public, so if they deem the procedure to be acceptable, it can be used. See also *ethical issues*.

primacy effect An effect of the presentation of stimuli, whereby those items that are presented first tend to be recalled more readily than those that are presented later on. Primacy effects do not only occur with simple memory tasks, but have their counterparts in *person perception*, too, whereby those characteristics of a person that are first encountered tend to be applied more readily than any characteristics which emerge or are learned later. In *memory* studies, the primacy effect is part of the serial position effect. See also *serial position curve*.

primary abilities The fundamental mental abilities that were suggested by Thurstone as forming the basis of *intelligence*. There were considered to be seven of these: memory, verbal ability, word fluency, number, spatial awareness, perceptual discrimination and reasoning.

primary appraisal An initial assessment (e.g. of how strong a stressor is). See also *transactional model of stress*.

primary auditory cortex The area of the *cerebral cortex* that is responsible for processing hearing. See also *auditory cortex, sensory projection area*.

primary drives Drives that satisfy a fundamental physiological need, such as the need for food or water. See also *secondary drives*.

primary motor cortex The area of the *cerebral cortex* that is responsible for carrying out voluntary movements of the body. See also *motor projection area, sensory projection area*.

primary process In Freudian theory, the more primitive kind of mental process that is present in the functioning of the *id* from birth. It is seen as the way in which the *unconscious* operates later in life, being governed by the *pleasure principle* and not following the same laws as conscious or *secondary process* thinking. For example, primary processes take no account of time and space, so unconscious memories of frightening childhood events are just as real, powerful and present as current *perceptions*.

primary reinforcement A *reinforcement* that satisfies a basic need or drive in the organism. See *operant conditioning, secondary reinforcement.*

primary sexual characteristics Those signs of someone's gender that are directly concerned with reproduction. These include the genitalia – the penis and testicles in the man and the vagina and clitoris in the woman. See also *secondary sexual characteristics.*

primary visual cortex (V1) The area on the *cerebral cortex* that receives visual imput from the *lateral geniculate nuclei*, and begins to combine simple visual features into more complex ones. See also *visual cortex, simple cell, hypercomplex cell.*

primer question A question asked to introduce a topic, whose function is really to prepare the respondent for the questions that will be following.

priming Generating a state of readiness or preparedness to receive or respond to certain types of information. See also *associative priming, primer question.*

principle of closure Probably the most powerful of the *Gestalt principles* of *perceptual organisation*, the principle of closure refers to the perceptual tendency towards complete forms and shapes. Thus, a set of disconnected lines is likely to be seen as indicating an incomplete shape if this is at all possible, rather than simply being taken as independent stimuli. The principle of closure also extends into the perception of movement, in the form of *stroboscopic motion* and the *phi phenomenon.*

principle of parsimony See *Occam's razor.*

principle of proximity One of the *Gestalt principles* of *perceptual organisation*, which states that stimuli which occur close to one another will tend to be perceived as being grouped together, all other things being equal.

principle of similarity One of the *Gestalt principles* of *perceptual organisation*, which states that similar stimuli will tend to be perceived as being grouped together, all other things being equal.

principle of truth The idea that our *mental representations* of assertions or their implications are generally only concerned with what is true, and tend to disregard or ignore false information.

prior general consent When a large pool of research participants are given a general briefing before a study, which includes the fact that they might be misinformed about its true purpose, or experience some emotional stress during the procedure. Those who consent to this form the group from which the actual research participants are drawn. The assumption is that there will be full *debriefing* after the procedure has been completed. See also *ethical issues, informed consent.*

prisoner's dilemma A classic game used to identify strategic choices, in which the person is required to choose between the best collective strategy, which is cooperation, and the best individual strategy, which is non-cooperation. See also *game theory*, *payoff matrix*.

privation A lack, throughout development, of some requirement. Privation should be distinguished from deprivation, in which the requirement was available for a period and then removed. Experiments in which animals are raised with no contact with a mother are privation studies, even though they are often referred to as *maternal deprivation*.

proactive amnesia A disorder of memory in which the person is unable to store new information. See also *anterograde amnesia*.

proactive interference The situation that occurs when information which has already been learned interferes with the learning of new material. Proactive interference is particularly common when someone is trying to learn a set of similar tasks within a relatively short period of time. It may account for the *primacy effect*.

probabilistic concept A concept that involves a set of characteristics which its members are likely to share, but need not necessarily do so. For example, 'chair' is a probabilistic concept in that one of its distinctive features is that chairs usually have four legs. However, there are many styles of chair which do not fit into that category – it is probable, but not necessary. In practice, most concepts used by human beings are probabilistic in nature. See also *classical concept*, *natural categories*, *prototypes*.

probability The likelihood that an event will occur. Formally, the probability is calculated by dividing the number of ways the event could occur by the number of all possible events. For example,

the probability of getting a red apple out of a barrel on a single trial is given by the number of red apples divided by the total number of fruits (e.g. red apples + green apples + oranges) in the barrel. The probability of getting a red apple ranges from 0 (no red apples, so zero probability of getting one) to 1 (nothing but red apples so you are certain to get one). Most use of statistics in psychology amounts to assessing the probability of a result. If the probability is very low, then the assumptions are unlikely to be valid. See also *binomial distribution*, *null hypothesis*, *statistical significance*.

probe A stimulus, such as a word or a digit, which is used to explore something (e.g. how much information is retained in *short-term memory*). In this example, the research participant would hear a sequence of digits read out, and would then be told a specific number and asked if that had been included in the list. The number would be acting as the probe.

probe question A tentative question in an *interview* designed to introduce a particular topic and test whether it would be worth following up with more detailed questions.

problem-solving The study of the various strategies used by people, computers and sometimes animals to achieve solutions, usually of highly specified puzzles. By having the problem clearly specified, it is hoped that the detailed cognitive processes involved in problem-solving will become apparent. However, it is not clear whether the findings from such research have applications to more complex human problems, such as how to pass an examination or pay the mortgage. See also *brainstorming*, *creativity*, *Einstellung*, *functional fixedness*, *groupthink*, *Stroop effect*.

problem space The name given to the difference between the desired outcome or solution to a problem, and the point that the problem-solver has currently reached. Early *computer simulations* of problem-solving involved using *heuristics* to reduce the problem space, and so bring the solution nearer.

procedural knowledge Knowledge of processes or action sequences (e.g. how to make a cup of tea). Procedural knowledge appears to be stored in a different way to *declarative knowledge*, as is shown by the fact that it is rarely affected by brain damage producing *amnesia*.

product–moment correlation See *Pearson's product–moment correlation*.

programmed learning A technique for applying operant conditioning to classroom learning. The information is broken down into small units and presented to the student in such a way that one unit leads naturally on to the next. Each unit involves some kind of simple test question. If the student gets it right, they move on to the next stage; if they get it wrong, they go back over the relevant material again. The idea is that this approach maximises *positive reinforcement* (knowledge of correct answers) for the student, thus maximising interest in and application to the learning process. As an example of pure operant conditioning, programmed learning has been criticised on the grounds that knowledge of results is a cognitive rather than a behavioural reinforcement. In classroom practice, the absence of social interaction between student and teacher has often presented its own difficulties, and programmed learning has tended to be introduced in a manner that is far more limited than Skinner originally envisaged.

progress monitoring The name given to a general heuristic in which very slow progress towards a goal triggers a change of strategy. In everyday terms, it might be referred to as impatience.

projection One of the ego-defence mechanisms identified by Freud, which involves the individual attributing their own *unconscious* motives and ideas to another person, or to an ambiguous situation. For example, a person who has not come to terms with their own sexual drives might come to believe that many other people engage in 'bad' sexual practices. Like other *defence mechanisms*, this is an unconscious process, but it is often a useful signal to a therapist of issues that particularly concern the client.

projective test A form of personality assessment that involves presenting people with ambiguous stimuli, and requiring them to indicate how they would interpret each stimulus. The idea is that the reply will indicate some of the concerns of the individual's unconscious mind – themes and events that particularly concern them at a subconscious level will be projected on to the ambiguous material. Well-known examples of projective tests are the *Rorschach inkblot test* and the *thematic apperception test*.

proper name anomia Serious and recurrent difficulty in retrieving proper names (e.g. of people or cities).

proprioception The perception of the positioning of the limbs, and of movement. Proprioception and *kinaesthesia* are commonly considered to represent a sixth and seventh basic sense, which deal with internal rather than external sensory information. See also *proprioceptors*.

proprioceptors Sensory neurones in the muscles, joints, tendons and *inner ear* that convey information to the *central nervous system* about body position.

prosocial behaviour The opposite of antisocial behaviour. The term 'prosocial' is used to refer to behaviour that involves helping others or making a positive gesture towards them in some way. It is commonly used in discussions of *bystander intervention* and *altruistic behaviour*.

prosopagnosia A form of *agnosia* that is specific to an inability to recognise faces.

prospective memory The type of memory that is concerned with remembering to do things – in other words, memory for things which have yet to happen, such as a dental appointment. See also *event-based prospective memory*.

protocol A plan of the steps or stages involved in the solution of a problem, also used to refer to spoken reports of such stages. See also *algorithm*.

protocol analysis A form of *qualitative analysis* used by cognitive psychologists, in which the research participant attempts to verbalise the protocols or steps involved in a specific procedure (e.g. making a decision, or composing a piece of music). Protocol analysis has stimulated renewed interest in *introspection*, and also in how subjective experience often differs from the cognitive processing itself – in other words, how what people think they have been doing is often quite different from what they actually have been doing.

proto-declarative pointing Pointing that elicits *joint attention* (e.g. indicating

that the other person should look at the thing the pointer is pointing at).

proto-imperative pointing In childhood, pointing which implies that the child wants something. See also *proto-declarative pointing*.

proto-themes Early ideas about themes, which may possibly emerge from the data during the course of a *grounded theory* analysis.

prototypes Specific examples of a concept or a category that are considered to be, or designed to be, typical of that concept or category. Prototypes need to have all of the salient features of the category, but should not have additional features. For example, a prototypical chair would have four legs, a seat and a back, but would not include arms, footrests, or other non-essential features.

proxemics The study of *personal space* and the use of touch as *non-verbal cues* in communication.

proximo-distal A sequence of development identified by Gesell in early studies of infant development of motor coordination, and incorporated into his theory of *maturation*. Gesell observed that motor control appeared to be acquired over the more central regions of the body first, and only later did the extremities (hands and feet) become coordinated. From this, he argued that development proceeded in an orderly direction, which he called proximo-distal ('from near to far'). See also *cephalo-caudal*.

Prozac An *antidepressant* drug which works by blocking the breakdown of the *neurotransmitter* serotonin in the *synapse*, causing a build-up so that there are higher levels available than normal.

PRP See *psychological refractory period*.

PSE See *point of subjective equality*.

pseudomutuality A process that occurs in families whereby everybody pretends to be in agreement and everyone denies that there is any conflict. Their commitment to keeping up this appearance prevents them (or the family therapist) from tackling the real problems in their relationships.

pseudo-neglect Increased attention being given to the left side of the space that the person is in, despite the lack of any lesion or brain abnormality which might produce that effect. See also *neglect, hemispatial neglect*.

pseudowords Strings of letters that can be pronounced as if they were real words (e.g. froom, struglich).

psi The ability to perform paranormal tasks. See *parapsychology*.

PSP See *post-synaptic potential*.

psyche The mind. Psychology was originally defined as the study of the mind.

psychedelic drugs Drugs that induce *altered states of awareness*, commonly resulting in heightened perceptions of colour and sensory imagery. Psychedelic drugs have been used as *recreational drugs* for centuries, but were named 'psychedelic' during the 1960s, as a result of their association with a particularly vivid form of visual art involving massed swirling of colours and similar imagery. Drugs classified as psychedelic include the *hallucinogens* (e.g. mescaline, *LSD* and psilocybin).

psychiatry The medical treatment of abnormal behaviour or of mental disturbance. Psychiatrists are always medically qualified, and therefore, unlike clinical psychologists, may prescribe drugs. Approaches used by psychiatrists range from a concentration on physical methods of treatment (such as chemotherapy) through to *psychotherapy* approaches, in which they may work in very similar ways to some clinical psychologists. Within the National Health Service, psychiatrists have a statutory responsibility to deal with all of the cases sent to them. Psychologists do not have this requirement, and may therefore be able to spend more time on fewer patients.

psychoactive drugs Drugs that affect psychological experience such as moods, consciousness or awareness. Although this is a very general term, it is most often applied to the groups of drugs commonly used for psychological purposes, such as anti-anxiety drugs, *sedatives, tranquillisers, antidepressants, stimulants* and *hallucinogens*.

psychoanalysis The method of psychological treatment originated by *Freud* and developed by various of his followers, the *neo-Freudians*. The major features of psychoanalysis are the use of *free association* to uncover *defence mechanisms* that may then be interpreted by the psychoanalyst in order to bring *unconscious* material into *consciousness*. One of Freud's major insights was that *transference* and *counter-transference* are not obstructions to therapy, but should be a fundamental part of the process. The term is not applied to the methods of those such as Carl Jung, who broke away from Freud and whose approach is called *analytical psychology*.

psychoanalytic theory The theory of personality development and human functioning developed by Freud. Psychoanalytic theory was continually elaborated and refined by Freud during his lifetime, and the process has continued since his death, so there is no single 'psychoanalytic theory', but many. However, they usually contain the ideas of the *unconscious* with its effects on everyday behaviour, *psychosexual* stages of development, and the personality structure of *id*, *ego* and *superego*. Freud gave the theory a strong biological flavour, and the assumption that adult behaviour is powerfully influenced by childhood experiences remains fundamental. One major development of the theory came from *object relations theory*, which emphasised the importance of experiences from very early infancy. Psychoanalytic theory has had an extremely wide influence on Western culture (e.g. in the understanding of art and literature). Many of Freud's original insights such as those concerning *defence mechanisms* are now regarded as common sense. The theory has been attacked as unscientific, on the grounds that it does not make claims which can be tested empirically. It has also been attacked on the grounds that several of its claims have been empirically disproved. See also *continuity hypothesis*.

psychobiology See *biopsychology*.

psychodrama A set of therapeutic techniques, originally introduced by Jacob Moreno in 1925, in which people are helped to act out troublesome emotions or situations. Regarding the situation as a play, and helped by the therapist and usually other group members, the patient can try out alternative ways of responding in safety and can come to understand the problem better.

psychodynamic Describing all of the theories of human functioning that are based on the interplay of unconscious drives and other forces within the person. *Psychoanalytic theory* is the clearest example, and the term 'psychodynamic' is often used to refer specifically to this class of theories.

psychogenic Having a psychological origin or cause. The term is used particularly of disorders for which no organic cause can be identified, so it can be assumed, by default, that the cause is psychological. See also *organic disorder*.

psychokinesis (PK) Bringing about a physical effect at a distance by psychological or, more accurately, *parapsychological* means.

psycholinguistics The study of psychological aspects of language and the relationships between *language* and other psychological processes. Psycholinguistics deals with such questions as the interdependence of language and thought, language acquisition, and the ways in which social experience and language acquisition interact, reading and *pragmatics*. Psycholinguistics is therefore a much broader field than *linguistics*, which is concerned with the origins and form of language itself.

psychological assistant A career grade in the UK that allows psychology graduates to work in *clinical psychology* departments. They undertake routine psychological tasks such as the scoring of *psychometric* tests, research, or the organising of therapeutic events.

The grade is frequently used to gain appropriate experience before training as a clinical psychologist.

psychological determinism The idea that all psychological processes have been directly caused by something, whether that be unconscious motives or fixations, as suggested by *psychoanalytic* theorists, or the patterns of firing of nerve cells in the brain brought about by conditioned responses to stimuli.

psychological punishment Punishment that does not necessarily involve an explicit penalty, but which is more concerned with the communication of social expectation and the disappointment/sadness of people for whom the miscreant cares. Psychological punishment typically requires some form of act of atonement, such as an apology or an attempt to right the wrong. Some research has indicated that psychological punishment is more influential than *physical punishment* in changing behaviour and in developing strong consciences in children.

psychological refractory period (PRP) The name given to an effect observed in cognitive research whereby the person takes longer to respond to the second of two stimuli than to the first, if the two are presented close together in time.

psychological technician Another term for a *psychological assistant*, but also used for a psychology graduate working in non-*clinical psychology* departments.

psychology Psychology has been defined in various ways, depending on the inclinations of researchers at the time when the definition was formulated. It has been variously defined as 'the study of the mind', 'the study of behaviour', 'the study of human experience' and 'the study of mental life'. It is difficult to produce a definition which will satisfy everyone, although we can state that it involves the study of human and animal behaviour and experience, examined from a number of different viewpoints and using a variety of techniques, most of which emphasise the importance of empirical evidence in support of explanatory theory. The field of psychology is divided, often somewhat arbitrarily, into different areas, each of which has its own style. Some qualifiers of the term, such as *developmental, social* and *comparative psychology*, refer to particular kinds of subject matter, with newer areas (e.g. *community psychology*) being added as the discipline expands. Some refer to basic psychological processes such as *cognitive psychology, perception* and *motivation*. Some define scope or indicate a theoretical or empirical approach to the study, such as *neuropsychology* and *experimental psychology*, respectively. Other titles – *clinical, educational, occupational* – refer to the psychological professions, while the term *applied psychology* refers to a general orientation that cuts across the whole field.

psychometrics The measurement (usually through questionnaires or inventories) of psychological characteristics – 'mental testing'. Psychometric tests include *intelligence tests, personality assessments, creativity* tests, and a whole range of other tests used for personnel selection, such as *vocational guidance tests*.

psychomotor retardation The slowing down of speech and movement found in severe depression.

psychopathic personality A form of personality disorder in which the person lacks anxiety and guilt, disregards society's laws and conventions, and has no concern for other people. They may also be impulsive and aggressive. The condition does not fit readily into psychological classifications, but the term is extensively used in legal situations and allows certain kinds of offender to be treated in special hospitals. It is also sometimes called 'antisocial personality disorder'. See also *psychopathy*.

psychopathology The study of deviation from 'normal' behaviour or psychological functioning.

psychopathy A condition of personality that involves high levels of aggression which are not tempered by any sense of guuilt or empathy with the victim. In *personality assessment*, psychopathy is a trait incorporating selfishness, callousness, impulsivity and antisocial behaviour. It is considered to be one of the *Dark Triad*. See also *psychopathic personality*.

psychopharmacology The study of the psychological effects of drugs. See also *psychoactive drugs*.

psychophysics The study of the relationship between the experience of physical stimuli and the physical stimuli themselves (e.g. the study of the relationship between perceived levels of sound, and levels of sound as measured by physical instruments). See also *Fechner's law, power law*.

psychophysiological disorder See *psychosomatic illness*.

psychophysiology Sometimes used with the same meaning as *physiological psychology*, but usually having a more restricted meaning. In its restricted use, the term refers to studies that use non-intrusive methods of monitoring physiological processes (e.g. surface electrodes) to provide information about psychological processes. See also *physiological correlate*.

psychosexual stages In Freud's theory of personality development, the progression of bodily aspects through which pleasure is sought and towards which biological drives are directed. The stages are the *oral stage, anal stage, phallic stage, latency period* and *genital stage*. As with any *stage theory*, each stage must be completed more or less satisfactorily in order for the next to be tackled. Failure to complete a stage implies that a significant part of the person's resources will remain invested in that primitive source of gratification, and their personality will show relevant tendencies, such as *fixation*, throughout adult life.

psychosis A term used to cover the most severe mental disorders, such as *schizophrenia* and *bipolar depression*. The person in a psychotic state loses contact with reality (see *reality testing*), has severe disturbances of thought and emotion that are not open to being changed by contrary evidence, and has little or no insight into their condition. Compare *neurosis*.

psychosocial stages The term given to the eight life stages proposed by Erikson. Each stage involves a basic conflict that the individual needs to resolve, and which in turn provides a foundation for the later stages. In brief, the eight conflicts are as follows:

   (i)   trust/mistrust;
   (ii)   autonomy/doubt;
   (iii) initiative/guilt;
   (iv)   industry/inferiority;

(v)   identity/role confusion;
(vi) intimacy/isolation;
(vii) generativity/stagnation; and
(viii) integrity/despair.

These basic conflicts arise at different stages throughout the individual's life, right up to old age, and present the individual with a set of age-specific challenges to tackle.

psychosomatic illness An illness that has its cause in psychological factors. Although the symptoms and discomfort of psychosomatic illness are genuine, and often highly distressing to the patient, the illness itself does not originate from a physical disorder of the body, but from some kind of mental disturbance or discomfort, often *unconscious* in nature.

psychosurgery The use of surgical intervention in the brain to control behaviour. The most well-known form of psychosurgery is the operation known as *lobotomy* – the removal of the *frontal lobe* of the brain in order to induce quiescent behaviour in highly agitated, aggressive or psychotic individuals. A similar operation, *leucotomy*, involves the severing of the connections between the frontal lobe and the rest of the brain, leaving it in place, and produces similar effects. Although largely discredited as a technique by neuropsychologists, in some areas psychosurgery is still performed to control *psychotic behaviour*. It is one of the more contentious aspects of *psychiatry*.

psychotherapy Usually, this term covers the whole range of psychologically based treatments by which trained practitioners help people who have psychological problems. Sometimes the term is used in a more restricted way, most commonly to refer to forms of treatment in which a psychotherapist and a single client tackle the client's problems by talking. Specific forms of psychotherapy may be identified by additional terms. For example, *psychodynamic* psychotherapy covers forms of psychotherapy that have been based on one of the psychodynamic theories. Some other forms include *non-directive therapy*, *cognitive therapy* and *rational–emotive behaviour therapy*. See also *counselling*, WEG.

psychotic Suffering from a *psychosis* or showing some psychotic symptoms. However, the term is more commonly used to refer to the *personality trait* named by H.J. Eysenck, which he claimed as a third dimension of personality, complementing *extraversion* and *neuroticism*.

psychotic behaviour Behaviour which is comparable to that shown by a person suffering from a *psychosis*.

psychoticism An item on the Eysenck Personality Questionnaire indicating a tendency to be solitary, hostile, and lacking feelings for other people.

psychotropic drugs This term literally refers to drugs that will promote or effect psychological growth. It was first used to describe the 'mind-expanding' *hallucinogens* such as mescaline, psilocybin and LSD. The term is in common misuse nowadays, referring to any drug that has an effect on mood, such as tranquillisers, which are more properly referred to as *psychoactive drugs*.

PTSD See *post-traumatic stress disorder*.

puberty The stage of physical growth during which the child becomes capable of reproduction. The occurrence of puberty is genetically controlled and so is a *maturation* process. In girls, it is taken to start at the onset of menstruation, and in boys at the first presence of live sperm in the urine. As this sign is not readily visible, the growth of pubic hair is more commonly used. Although puberty is regarded as a period preceding *adolescence*, there is no clear definition of its end. It can be taken as lasting until the basic physiological structures required for reproduction have achieved a form recognisably similar to the adult state. Substantial psychological adjustments are required during puberty to cope with changing body shape and appearance, novel hormonal balances and associated emotional changes, and changing sexual identity. Because the early stages of puberty are so visible, the substantial variations in age of onset (roughly from 10 to 14 years) can cause problems for both early and late developers. The average age of onset of puberty seems to have decreased by several years over the last century, which suggests that adjustments are being demanded at an earlier stage of psychological maturity.

punctuated equilibrium An approach to the understanding of evolution which argues that evolutionary development is not inevitably slow and continuous, but can sometimes consist of long periods of relative stability, followed by periods of sudden and rapid change which occur as a result of altered environmental demands.

punishment The application of some kind of penalty or unpleasant event in order to suppress an unwanted form of behaviour. Although punishment is commonly used as a means of behavioural control, there is some evidence to suggest that it is of limited value

by comparison with more directive approaches such as the direct rewarding of desired behaviour which occurs in *operant conditioning*. Note that punishment is not a form of *negative reinforcement*. See also *physical punishment*, *psychological punishment*.

pupil dilation The enlarging of the pupil of the eye. This happens mainly:

(i)   in darkness, or dim lighting, when the pupil enlarges so as to allow more effective vision;

(ii) under the influence of certain drugs, in particular *amphetamines* and *narcotic* drugs (see also *belladonna*); and

(iii) when the individual looks at someone or something which they like or are fond of.

As such, pupil dilation is a very powerful *non-verbal cue*, indicating interpersonal attraction or empathy, and several studies have shown that people will respond more positively to others with dilated pupils (one reason for the low lighting that is common in many restaurants and nightclubs).

pure alexia A form of reading difficulty in which the time taken to read a word increases in direct proportion with the length of that word. See also *alexia*.

pure deletion The assumption that removing a component from a cognitive processing task will not affect the processing of other items in the sequence. See also *pure insertion*.

pure insertion This is an assumption sometimes made in neuro-cognitive research that adding an extra component to a task (e.g. an extra word in a word list) does not affect how other items in the sequence are processed.

pure word deafness A form of *auditory agnosia* in which the person can identify sounds around them and music, but is unable to make sense of spoken words.

pyramidal motor system A set of connections or pathways in the brain that is particularly concerned with the control of movement.

Q

Q-sort A test often utilised in conjunction with *client-centred therapy* to evaluate the individual's self-esteem in their own terms. The Q-sort consists of a set of cards, each of which provides a short statement about character or personality that may be positive, neutral or negative. Clients are asked to sort the cards into piles that express how closely the statements fit with their own *self-concept* (e.g. 'very like me', 'unlike me', etc.). When all the cards have been sorted, the client is asked to sort them again, but this time in terms of their ideal self – 'myself as I would like to be'. The similarity or otherwise between the two sets of card-sorts provides a *correlation coefficient* indicative of the individual's self-esteem. Among other uses, the Q-sort has been employed in studies of the efficacy of client-centred therapy.

quadrantanopia A form of cortical blindness that is restricted to a quarter of the visual field. See also *scotoma, hemianopia, blindsight*.

qualitative analysis An approach to the analysis of psychological information which takes as its starting point the idea that the meaning of the information is the most important thing. Qualitative analysis is therefore not concerned with reducing psychological information to numerical data (*quantitative analysis*), but is concerned with identifying ways of extracting meaning in a systematic and reliable manner. See also *account analysis, ethogenics, thematic qualitative analysis*.

qualitative data Data that are acquired in natural forms such as images, speech or text, rather than as numerical scores.

qualitative difference A difference in kind, not simply in amount. If two things are qualitatively different, this implies that arithmetic comparisons between them are not appropriate – that they are of a different nature, like chalk and cheese. See also *quantitative difference*.

qualitative–quantitative distinction A division that has opened up within psychology over a question of whether true psychological research should be quantitative or qualitative. *Quantitative* research can be considered the dominant paradigm, with a long history from the beginnings of psychology and claiming to be closest to the methodologies of the physical sciences. *Qualitative research* can lay claim to the newer paradigms such as *social constructionism* and the ability to connect to disciplines such as sociology and anthropology. In order to preserve the divide, quantitative researchers must disparage qualitative for its lack of statistical reliability and generalisable findings. Meanwhile, qualitative researchers must disparage quantitative for its lack of *ecological validity* and being limited to finding out what the researcher could specify before doing the research. It is to be hoped that the conflict will be productive in making each approach address its limitations before the inevitable realisation that psychology needs research that genuinely combines the benefits of both approaches.

qualitative research Techniques for obtaining psychological information which assume that the meaning of the information is the most important thing. The most common techniques used in qualitative research are *interviews* and *case studies*. These methods allow greater freedom for the person who is the target of such research to determine what information is generated, so the quality and richness of information is greater, but at the cost of making *reliability* difficult to achieve. See also *account analysis, discourse analysis, grounded theory, hermeneutics, new paradigm research, observational study.*

quantitative To do with numbers and quantities. See also *qualitative–quantitative distinction.*

quantitative analysis An approach to psychological information that is primarily concerned with obtaining numerical information, which can then be analysed using *statistics*. Quantitative methods require the researcher to define the items to be measured in advance, and to control the situation so that only that information is recorded. The result is that high levels of *reliability* can be obtained and measured, but there are frequently problems with *validity*. Although traditional psychology has often tended to assume that only quantitative analysis is worthwhile, recently many psychologists have become increasingly concerned with the *qualitative analysis* of information, in addition to quantitative techniques. See also *psychometrics.*

quantitative data Data that are acquired as numerical scores rather than images, speech or text.

quantitative difference A difference in amount, rather than a difference in kind. See also *qualitative difference.*

quartile A point marking out a segment of a data set, representing one-quarter of the total number of scores. See *statistics.*

quasi-experiments Experiments in which the independent variable has more than one condition, but these have not actually been manipulated by the experimenter. Examples include experiments in which men form one participant group, and women the other.

questionnaire A research tool that involves presenting series of questions to participants, in a form which can be answered physically on paper, electronically, by computer or app, or verbally by a researcher. While it appears to be a relatively simple way of collecting data, designing a good questionnaire is much more complex than it seems: it requires in-depth consideration of how answers will be analysed and conclusions drawn at the early planning stage, and also avoiding collecting additional information that will not ultimately serve the research. The longer the questionnaire, the less likely people are to respond to it. See also *questionnaire fallacy, response rate, response bias.*

questionnaire fallacy The belief that providing people with boxes to tick in a questionnaire will enable you to find out what they actually do. The main problem with this delusion (apart from its consequences) is the way that people will always find a box to tick, even when their behaviour is entirely unrepresented by the options. There are other problems, too, such as the fact that people generally lie to questionnaires (because the questions don't fit their own circumstances), and the way that boxes make issues appear to be discrete categories, whereas real life is a great deal more fuzzy.

quota sampling A system of obtaining a *sample* for a study that involves identifying a set of representative subgroups within the *population*, and taking a number of research participants from each of these subgroups. The size of each subgroup in the sample depends on its proportional size in the original population. For instance, in a study of student attitudes to their college, the sample would be picked to represent the same proportions of different types of students as were found in the college as a whole – if 10 per cent of the students were on day-release courses, then 10 per cent of the sample would be drawn from the day-release students. See also *sampling procedure*.

R

race differences Group differences between different races identified by the use of *psychometric* tests. Because these tests usually measure something valued by European culture, and because their objectivity has been overestimated, findings of lower scores (e.g. on *intelligence tests*) by ethnic minority groups have been used as the basis for claims of racial superiority. These claims have then led to a rather more careful inspection of the evidence, and it is now recognised that neither race nor intelligence can be defined or measured with enough accuracy to justify claims about the relationships between them.

racism Discrimination, *prejudice* or unfair practice towards someone that occurs purely on the basis of their ethnic group or skin colour. See also *authoritarian personality*, *own-race effect*.

radial glial cells Cells that support and guide neurones in the developing nervous system from the *neural tube* to their final destination.

random assignment A research procedure in which participants are assigned at random to different research conditions. Usually, random assignment prevents bias through having participants with different characteristics in groups that are to be compared. However, random assignment can produce groups with unequal characteristics, especially with small samples, so it is always worth checking and reporting the final composition.

random sampling The process of selecting a *sample* for an experiment or other empirical study in such a way that any member of the *population* has an equal chance of being selected. Random sampling, when carried out appropriately, is considered to be the strongest sampling technique for avoiding bias in participant selection. If all members of the population have an equally likely chance of being selected, then if the sample is large enough it should reflect all the characteristics of its parent population.

randomisation A process of sorting participants or experimental conditions into a random order so that no consistent pattern will be operating. For example, if you recruit 20 volunteers from a class, the first 10 to volunteer may differ in motivation or altruism from the last 10. It would be important to randomise the order of these people in an experiment, rather than just putting the first 10 research participants to volunteer into the first condition and the rest into the second. See also *counterbalancing*.

range The difference between the highest and lowest values of a set of scores. The range is the simplest and crudest *measure of dispersion*.

rank To put a set of scores into order by size. The word can also mean the position of an item within a set of ranked scores. Ranking provides no information about how far apart adjacent scores

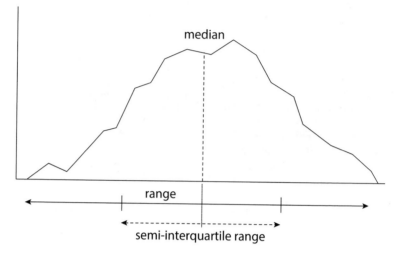

Figure 45 Range and median

may be, and so provides only *ordinal data* which must then be treated by techniques of *non-parametric statistics*. See also *levels of measurement*.

rank correlation coefficient See also *Spearman's rank–order correlation coefficient.*

rapid eye movement (REM) sleep A form of sleep in which the body remains comatose except for the eye muscles, which move rapidly and continuously. When woken from REM sleep, people often report *dreaming*, and if an external stimulus, such as being lightly sprayed with cold water, is applied at this time, the dream content is likely to reflect the stimulus – in this case, the person might dream of being out in the rain. REM sleep occurs in phases throughout the night. Each phase usually lasts about 20 minutes, before the person passes on to one of the deeper, quiescent levels of sleep. The phases become longer and more frequent during the course of sleep. Over the lifespan, the time spent in REM sleep decreases from about eight hours in the newborn

to about 1.5 hours in the elderly. The function of REM sleep is disputed, with theories ranging from those that see it as functional, either in physiological restorative processes or as the phase in which the information acquired during the previous day is processed, to theories that it is left over from a previous stage of evolution. REM sleep is also known as *paradoxical sleep*. See also *sleep cycles*.

rapport A feeling of psychological comfort in interaction with another person, based on feelings of trust and *empathy*. It is used particularly about the relationship that is necessary between a psychotherapist and their client, or between a tester and their subject.

rapport interview An interview that is designed and carried out in such a way as to encourage positive feeling (*rapport*) between the participant and the interviewer.

RAS See *reticular activating system.*

rate coding The idea that the informational content of a neurone may relate to the number of times it will fire in one second. See also *volley principle, summation.*

rating scale A system of measurement, usually of attitudes, in which a person is asked to evaluate some stimulus material or idea on the basis of a predetermined scale that expresses degrees of liking or preference.

ratio scale See *equal-interval scale, levels of measurement.*

rational–emotive behaviour therapy (REBT) A form of *cognitive therapy,* developed by Albert Ellis, based on the idea that people make common logical errors (e.g. believing that it is necessary to be competent in every way, to be loved by everyone, and to have whatever one wants immediately). REBT takes the form of persuading the client, by cognitive, emotional and behavioural means, to see things differently (i.e. correctly) so that their behaviour will be less destructive.

rationalisation

(i) Providing entirely rational and worthy explanations for one's behaviour that are designed to conceal from oneself, or from others, the less acceptable cause of the behaviour (e.g. 'We don't employ older people because the customers would not like it'). The process was identified by Freud as one of the major *defence mechanisms,* but it often takes the form of the basic *attributional error.*

(ii) The process of adjusting information so that it makes rational sense to the receiver, as in Bartlett's 'War of the Ghosts' study of *constructive memory.*

rationalism A philosophical theory most strongly represented by Descartes, that knowledge of the world can only be obtained by the exercise of reason. He claimed as a starting point the famous statement 'I think, therefore I am', as a demonstration both that pure reason could establish the fact, and also that only the exercise of reason, and not observation, could make the claim of demonstrating existence. Try 'I send text messages, therefore I am' or 'I think, therefore I am Descartes'. See also *empiricism.*

Raven's progressive matrices An intelligence test that is designed to be a *culture-fair test.* The test consists of a series of grids or matrices of eight patterns, from which the ninth pattern can be deduced logically, and a set of answers, of which one is the missing ninth pattern and is therefore correct. The special feature of the test is that it is entirely non-verbal, and it is even possible to administer it to someone with whom the tester shares no language at all. Despite the attempt of Raven to make the test independent of culture, it still reflects some cultural assumptions and experience. Three examples of these assumptions are:

(i) solving a puzzle whenever it is presented to you;
(ii) geometric shapes can be manipulated according to rules; and
(iii) familiarity with two-dimensional representation (line drawings).

In some cultures, too, manipulation of and/or interest in abstract forms of this kind are not regarded as particularly desirable human activities.

raw data Data in the form in which it was collected, before being processed ('cooked') by statistical analysis or qualitative methods.

raw primal sketch A basic image extracted from the *optic array*, and formed by linking edges and surfaces. The raw primal sketch forms part of Marr's *computational theory of perception*, which is a *bottom-up approach* showing how the basic elements of the optic array can be combined to form meaningful representations of objects.

reactance The tendency of people to be made uncomfortable by any restriction of their freedom of choice. Once such pressure is perceived, people will often act in opposition to it.

reaction formation A *defence mechanism* by which a person resists and denies an unacceptable motive by acting as if the opposite were true. The classic example of a reaction formation occurs in *homophobia*, in which the individual suppresses their own homosexual inclinations so strongly that they become extremely hostile to anyone expressing overt homosexuality.

reaction time A measure of how quickly a person can produce an accurate response to a stimulus. Reaction time has been used by psychological researchers in a wide range of investigations, including ageing, *decision-making*, drug effects and *vigilance*. It provides a rapid and reliable measure that is highly sensitive to disturbance by additional or extraneous factors. See also *additive factors method*.

reactive aggression Aggression that arises as a direct response to perceived threat. See also *instrumental aggression*.

reactive depression *Depression* that occurs following an event such as a *bereavement*, which is thought to be likely to have caused the disorder.

reactivity Being influenced by or responsive to something. An organism that is responding strongly may be said to be highly reactive.

reading span The largest number of sentences, read for understanding, from which someone can recall all of the words 50 per cent of the time. See also *threshold of response*.

real-world research Research that is conducted in or has very direct application to the lives that people outside of the discipline live. See *action research*, *ecological validity*, *field study*.

realistic conflict theory A model of *intergroup conflict* that emphasises competition for resources or goals as the origin of the conflict.

reality anxiety In Freud's classification of anxiety, he included those situations in which the anxiety is justified by a real external threat. This is reality anxiety. See also *moral anxiety*.

reality principle In Freudian theory, the principle on which the *ego* operates. Whereas the *pleasure principle* is innate, the child has to learn about reality and how to operate in order to satisfy its needs. This developmental process is fundamental to the formation of the ego.

reality testing A fundamental human tendency to check out one's understanding of the real world, particularly one's role in and influence on both physical and social reality. From infancy through early childhood, there is a progressive development of the ability to distinguish between fantasy and reality. A failure to make the distinction in adulthood is taken as an indication of *psychosis*. *Personal construct* theory is largely concerned with the precise forms that reality testing takes.

reappraisal Re-evaluating information, in such a way as to see whether or not it has acquired a new function or can be used in a different way. The term is also used in *emotion regulation*, in which the person identifies and re-evaluates their emotional resposes to an event, as a first step in changing the personal meaning of that event.

reasoning A general term given to those mental activities that are investigated in studies of logical thinking and problem-solving. Although underplayed for much of the twentieth century, the study of reasoning is now a significant aspect of cognitive psychology.

REBT See *rational–emotive behaviour therapy*.

recall The first and strongest of the four forms of remembering identified by Ebbinghaus, recall refers to the retrieval of information on demand from memory storage. The other forms of remembering, in order, are *recognition*, *reconstruction* and *relearning savings*.

recapitulation theory The now outdated idea that individual development retraces the steps of the evolution of the species. See also *ontogeny*.

receiver-operating characteristic (ROC) curve In *signal-detectability theory*, a graph in which the probability of hits and false alarms is plotted against the signal level.

recency effect A learning effect in which the items that were presented most recently in a sequence are more likely to be recalled than those which occurred earlier on. See also *primacy effect*.

receptive field The region of space apparent to the eyes that elicits a neuronal response. The term is also sometimes used to refer to the area of the *retina* that, when stimulated, activates a particular set of *neurones* in the *visual cortex*.

receptor The term is usually used to mean sense receptor – a specialised cell or group of cells that picks up sensory information, either from within (see *proprioception*) or from outside the body, and converts it into electrical impulses for transmission to the *central nervous system*. For example, the light-sensitive *rod cells* and *cone cells* of the eye are receptors, as are the hair cells in the *organ of Corti* in the ear, and the pressure-sensitive cells in the skin.

receptor site A location on the dendrite of a neurone, opposite a *synaptic knob*, which is sensitive to and readily absorbs a specific chemical. The appropriate chemical is released into the *synaptic cleft* from vesicles on the synaptic knob of the opposing neurone, and functions as a *neurotransmitter*, rendering the receiving neurone more or less ready to fire. Receptor sites may also pick up chemicals with a similar structure, and many *psychoactive drugs* exert their effect by being taken up at receptor sites appropriate for other chemicals. The *hallucinogens* LSD and psilocybin are picked up at receptor sites sensitive to the neurotransmitter *serotonin*, while *opiates* such as *heroin* and morphine are picked up at sites appropriate for the *enkephalins* and *endorphins*.

recessive gene A gene which carries a developmental characteristic that only shows in the *phenotype* when the individual inherits a matching gene on the other chromosome. If the paired gene – the *allele* – is of a different type and *dominant*, then the recessive gene will not influence that individual's development, although it could be passed on to children. Many common characteristics, such as red hair or blue eyes, and some genetic disorders, such as sickle-cell anaemia, are carried on recessive genes, and so may skip whole generations and appear in children of later generations.

recidivism Repeated legal offences, such that the person concerned, the recidivist, appears in court on several occasions, not just once. A certain amount of work on *juvenile delinquents* reported by Rutter suggests that recidivism is very strongly linked with a continually stressful home life, at least for teenagers.

reciprocal altruism Helping behaviour that occurs in a social context such that an individual person or animal who receives help, in turn helps the individual who originally helped them. Reciprocal *altruistic behaviour* often occurs over extended periods of time, and may not be recognised by a short-term ethological study.

reciprocal inhibition An approach to *behaviour therapy* which aims to break a learned connection between stimuli by attaching an incompatible response to one of them (e.g. by inducing a relaxation response to a stimulus and so breaking a connection between that stimulus and fear). See also *implosion therapy*, *systematic desensitisation*.

reciprocal liking The name given to a positive relationship between two or more people in which each participant likes the other(s). Positive feelings which are received from someone are reciprocated (i.e. the same degree of positive feeling is directed towards that person).

reciprocity A general term for processes in which action in one direction is responded to by an equivalent action back. It is often used in interpersonal psychology to describe relationships in which both members contribute equally to one another, and is used in *comparative psychology* to describe mutually beneficial relationships between different animals. The term is also used as a component of *moral development*, when the child recognises that it is appropriate to return favours.

recognition

(i)   In memory theory, the second 'level' of remembering identified by Ebbinghaus, in which the person is unable to retrieve an item of information without cueing, but can identify it as correct when they see or hear it.

(ii) In social terms, a level of respect or positive acknowledgement, as in the observation that someone's community service has been recognised by an award.

Ebbinghaus, working with lists of nonsense syllables, demonstrated that material which cannot be *recalled* may nonetheless be recognised as having been in a previously learned set of information. See also *reconstruction*, *relearning savings*, *face*.

recognition heuristic Using information that is recognised as familiar or having been encountered before as the basis for *decision-making*.

recognition memory test A memory test in which people are asked to state whether they have seen a given item before, or not. See also *recognition*.

recollection Remembering specific information, usually from a particular episode. Recollection is generally context-dependent, and can be assisted by using relevant memory *cues*. See also *recognition*, *reconstruction*.

reconsolidation The updating of a *memory trace* which was previously forgotten but has now been reactivated, such that it forms appropriate connections with other memories. See also *consolidation*.

reconstruction Also sometimes known as redintegration, this is the third of the four basic forms by which *memory* may be demonstrated, according to the work of Ebbinghaus. Once people have learned a list of nonsense syllables, in the event of their being unable to recognise or *recall* the items learned, they are often able to reconstruct the list in its original sequence, if provided with the relevant items. Although they will not experience a specific memory of the list, one particular sequence 'feels more right' than any other arrangement. See also *recognition, relearning savings*.

recovered memories Memories from childhood, usually traumatic ones, that have been retrieved in later life. See also *sexual abuse*.

recreational drugs Drugs that are consumed primarily for enjoyment or appreciation of their effects, rather than for medicinal purposes. These include legal drugs such as alcohol, *nicotine* and caffeine, and illegal drugs such as *marijuana, amphetamines* and *heroin*. The use of recreational drugs in some form occurs in all known human societies, and in some cultures it includes the use of very powerful *hallucinogens* such as mescaline. In general, the more powerful drugs are consumed within some kind of *ritual* setting, while less potent ones such as marijuana are taken more casually. Within Western societies, however, the rituals are confined to subcultural habits, and are not often used as a framework for the experience of the drug itself.

red-green colour blindness The most common form of colour blindness, in which the person affected is unable to distinguish between wavelengths of red and the matching wavelengths of green. It has proved difficult to explain this in terms of the conventional *trichromatism* theory of colour vision, and the predominance of red-green colour blindness has been taken as important evidence for the idea of *opponent processing*.

redintegration See *reconstruction*.

reductionism A form of argument which takes the view that an event, behaviour or phenomenon can be understood as being nothing but its component or constituent parts. For instance, the behaviourist insistence that human experience can be seen as nothing but combinations of *stimulus–response learning*, or the view that behaviour may be understood as nothing but the action of 'selfish genes', are both reductionist arguments. Although often superficially appealing, reductionist argument ignores other levels of explanation, such as cognitive explanation or experiential/social factors, in understanding the phenomenon, and as such can only provide a limited understanding of the event under study. Note that even if the most extreme reductionist position is true, and all human functioning is the result of the activities of subatomic particles, it would be nonsense to try to explain a human activity such as a joke in these terms. See also *emergent properties*.

redundancy A term used mostly in information theory for the extent to which a message does not provide new information. Redundant material, like the letters replaced by Xs in this senXencX, can XX put back quite easilX. Because language is highly redundant, we can interpret messages accurately even when they are received in *noisy* conditions. In fact, the lower the *signal-to-noise ratio*, the more redundancy is needed in the message.

reference group A social group that is taken by an individual as providing standards for the modelling of that person's own behaviour. The individual concerned may not actually belong to the reference group itself, but sees the group as directly relevant to their own lifestyle or situation.

referent informational influence A form of influence characterised by referring to a group *norm* – either real or self-inferred.

referential Using words to refer to objects or events, but not with communication as a major objective.

reflex A direct response to stimulation that occurs automatically, without any decision-making input from the *central nervous system* (e.g. the leg jerk which occurs when the knee is tapped). Reflexes are often referred to as involuntary responses, to distinguish them from the *voluntary behaviour* of deliberate action. They are usually mediated directly by the *spinal cord* rather than by the brain itself, although this subgroup is sometimes identified as 'spinal reflexes'. See also *reflex arc*.

reflex arc The term given to the sequence of neurones involved in the simplest unit of behaviour, the reflex. In its most basic form, the reflex arc consists of three types of neurone:

(i) the *sensory neurone*, which carries the information concerning the stimulus to the *spinal cord*;

(ii) the *connector neurone* within the spinal cord, which picks up the information from the sensory neurone and reroutes it; and

(iii) the *motor neurone*, which passes the message from the connector neurone to the muscle fibres, causing them to contract and the reflex action to occur.

Because reflex arcs follow well-defined paths, the failure to display an appropriate reflex can indicate precise forms of damage to the nervous system. Reflexes are therefore used to test newborns, where other responses are less available. See also *Babinski reflex*.

reflexivity The interplay of influence and outcome, such that the outcome becomes the influence, and produces another outcome, which then again becomes the influence.

refractory period The period of a few milliseconds immediately after a neurone has fired and before it is completely restored to full functioning. The refractory period has two parts: (i) the *absolute refractory period*, in which no amount of stimulation will make the neurone fire; and (ii) the *relative refractory period*, in which the neurone will fire only in response to a particularly strong stimulus.

regression In general usage, any return to a previous or simpler state. There are three further contexts that adjust its meaning:

(i) In *psychodynamic* theory, a retreat under stress to an earlier *psychosexual stage*.

(ii) A technique in therapy in which the patient is encouraged to think and feel as they did at a much younger age. The usual objective is to re-experience a traumatic event so that it can be properly dealt with in the supportive context of therapy. *Hypnosis* is often used to help the process.

(iii) In statistics, measures of the extent to which one variable depends on another. It is most commonly encountered in linear regression – the equation of the straight line that provides the best fit (or smallest total discrepancy) when *dependent variable* scores are plotted against the *independent variable*.

regression line The line that, when drawn through the data points of two related variables, has the best fit to them. The regression line indicates the direction and form of the relationship between the two variables.

regulator One of the types of *nonverbal cue* classified by Ekman and Friesen, regulators are those cues that regulate or structure social interaction. Examples of these are the time sequences and turn-taking of conversations, small noises such as 'uh-huh' made to indicate agreement during a conversation and to signify that someone is still listening, and *eye contact*. See also *affect display*.

rehearsal A term used to mean practice, when applied to a memory task. Rehearsal is the repetition of the material to be learned.

reification Treating ideas or concepts as if they were objects or facts (e.g. starting from the fact that people can be seen to behave more or less intelligently, and going on to assume that there is a 'thing' called intelligence). It is easy to slip into reification when talking about cognitive processes. For example, in Broadbent's *filter model*, there is a box labelled 'filter', which is used to indicate a process. The mistake is to represent it as if it must be a mechanism. Another form of this error in psychology is to define a possible phenomenon and then assume it is a fact which then has to be explained. For example, there was a long period in which different theories were proposed to account for some children being obedient and others disobedient, before researchers observed real children and found that none were either consistently obedient or consistently disobedient. The fact that we have a good explanation for something (e.g. male aggressiveness) does not prove that the thing exists as an entity in itself, independently of the context in which it is manifest. See also *labelling*.

reincarnation The belief that after death, people are reborn either as another person or in some other animate form.

reinforcement The process of strengthening learning. See also *reinforcer*.

reinforcement affect model A theory of attraction which says that sharing a positive experience, or at least being with someone else at the time of a positive experience, leads to liking.

reinforcement contingencies The circumstances under which reinforcement will be given. These may vary naturally or be systematically varied, as in the case of behaviour shaping.

reinforcement schedule A particular pattern of applying *partial reinforcement*. There are four main types of reinforcement schedule, each of which produces a distinctive effect on the pattern of responding. Schedules may be either fixed or variable. If they are fixed, then reinforcement is given according to a predetermined pattern; if they are variable, it is given according to a ran-domised sequence that averages out at a particular number. Reinforcement may also depend on the number of responses that have been made since the last rein-forcement, or the time interval which has elapsed since the last reinforce-ment was given. The four schedules are *fixed-ratio reinforcement*, *fixed-interval reinforcement*, *variable-ratio reinforcement* and *variable-interval reinforcement*. Fixed-ratio reinforcement produces a rapid rate of response but a low resistance to extinction. Fixed-interval reinforce-ment produces a low *response rate* and a low *resistance to extinction*. Variable-ratio reinforcement produces a high rate of response with a high resistance to extinc-tion. Variable-interval reinforcement produces a steady, regular rate of response and a high resistance to extinction.

reinforcer Something that strengthens a learned response, and which makes a learned response more likely to occur again. In *classical conditioning*, the rein-forcer is simply the repetition of the pairing of the unconditioned and con-ditioned stimuli. In *operant conditioning*, the reinforcer is the event that occurs as a consequence of the operant behaviour, making it more likely to occur again, and which may be either positive or negative.

related-measures design A design used in experiments in which the same research participants are used in both the experimental and the control con-ditions. Since each person's score is compared with one obtained from the same participant, this technique allows the experimenter to control for indi-vidual differences (e.g. in IQ level or motivation). However, it does mean that *order effects* are likely to become important in the study, and so related-measures designs often involve the use of *counterbalancing* as a control. It is also

known as a repeated-measures design, or a correlated-participants design. The paired *t-test* is used in related-measures designs only.

relational self Our tendency to define ourselves in terms of our relationships with others.

relative refractory period The period after a neurone has fired when it will only respond to a stimulus of unusual strength. This occurs after the *absolute refractory period*, when it will not fire at all, and reflects the cell's renewal of resources after the production of the burst of electrical energy in the form of the *electrical impulse*.

relative threshold The degree by which a stimulus must increase in order for the increase to be perceived. The *threshold* is set at the point where 50 per cent of changes of that magni-tude are perceived. It changes in direct proportion to the intensity of the initial stimulus. The law known as *Fechner's law* expresses this relationship. See also *just noticeable difference*.

relaxation training A range of techniques used to bring about a relaxed state in the individual. It is usually used as a compo-nent in therapy (e.g. in maintaining a relaxed state in a *phobic disorder* patient as they approach the feared object). Many of the techniques used in psychotherapy are based on methods developed for med-itation, such as yoga, or are variations on hypnotic induction procedures. Edmund Jacobson popularised the approach with a procedure in which the subject concen-trates on, and relaxes, different groups of muscles in turn. *Biofeedback* can also be used. See also *mindfulness*.

relay neurone A neurone found within the *spinal cord* and the *brain* that forms multiple connections with several other neurones, and allows information to be routed in several different directions simultaneously. Relay neurones are also known as *connector neurones* or *multipolar neurones*.

relearning savings The fourth (weakest) level of remembering identified by Ebbinghaus in his work on the memorisation processes. He found that there were situations where all traces of memory of a specific set of items appeared to have been lost, in that the set could not be *recalled*, recognised or *reconstructed*, but when the set of items was encountered again, it would take less time to relearn than a comparable set that had not previously been learned.

releaser Something that acts as a signal to trigger off a particular response, usually an inherited one. See also *IRM, sign stimulus*.

reliability The consistency of a measure – how likely it is to produce the same results if used again in the same circumstances. Reliability is a significant concern in the development of *psychometric* tests, and is usually assessed by one of three methods:

(i) *test-retest*, in which the same test is administered to the same participants after a period of time has elapsed;

(ii) *split-half* testing, in which the score that the person achieves on one half of the test items is compared with that obtained on the other half (with both administered at the same time), to see if they give similar outcomes; and

(iii) *alternate-forms* testing, in which two *matched* versions of the test are given to the same people on two different occasions, with their results being compared.

Reliability is an important requirement of any measure that purports to apply to more than just a single individual or case, whether it be a test, a physiological measurement, an observational procedure, or whatever. The other essential requirement is *validity*. A major difficulty in assessing reliability is that scores on successive occasions may differ either because of *practice effects* or because the participants have actually developed or changed in some other way. George Kelly said that reliability is a measure of how insensitive a test is to people changing. More broadly, reliability should be demonstrated over the period for which the function being measured is believed to be stable.

reliability coefficient A measure of the agreement between two sets of data that are attempting to measure the same thing. The data sets may be two presentations of the same test, or a comparison of the two sets of scores obtained by comparing one half of the items with the other half (*split-half reliability*). The reliability coefficient is usually calculated as a correlation and measures the *reliability* of the test.

REM sleep See *rapid eye movement sleep*.

reminiscence bump The way that older people generally remember events that happened in their twenties more clearly than those that happened at other times in their lives. It is thought that this is because there has often been more reminiscence concerning this time of life than about other times.

Remotes Associates Test A test of cognitive functioning that involves finding a word which relates to three other stimulus words.

repair process A speech act in which an attempt is made to correct a misleading utterance or some other source of misunderstanding.

repeated-measures design See *related-measures design*.

repeated-measures t-test See *dependent t-test*.

repertory grid A technique developed by George Kelly for utilising a person's *personal constructs* to examine the significant people in their world, and so identify actual or potential sources of psychological discomfort or stress. The repertory grid is an *idiographic* technique, which enables a therapist to see the patient's world as they see it – a valuable first step in most forms of therapy. The repertory grid is also used more generally in research to indicate how people perceive and understand their worlds.

repetition suppression The observation that repetition of a stimulus tends to produce lower levels of brain activity in response. See also *habituation*.

repetitive transcranial magnetic stimulation A form of *transcranial magnetic stimulation* that involves repeated administration of the stimulation in quick succession. Generally abbreviated to *rTMS*.

replication Repeating an experiment to ensure that the results are reliable, and not due to the particular circumstances or chance at the time of the first experiment. Psychology experiments are particularly open to influence from incidental factors, such as the expectations of participants, and so should always be replicated. However, they are not, for a variety of reasons – it is difficult to get grants for replications, difficult to get them published, and most experimenters would rather run their own new experiment than someone else's old

one. The result is that many of the most famous findings have never been replicated and are not reliable.

representation

(i) In cognitive psychology, this refers to the various ways that knowledge or information is held in the brain, such as *imagery*, *schemata* and *concepts*.

(ii) When one thing stands for, provides an image of, or can be used in place of another. Theories of language are concerned with the extent to which words represent things, while cognitive theories are concerned with how perception represents reality.

representative sample A sample of participants in a study which has all the important characteristics of its parent *population*, so that it can be regarded as typical of that population for research purposes. There are several different techniques for obtaining a representative sample, which include *quota sampling* and *random sampling*.

representativeness heuristic A shortcut used in *decision-making* where the choice falls on the item or information that appears to be most representative, or typical, of the whole set.

repression A *defence mechanism* by which unacceptable thoughts or desires are forced into the *unconscious*. As with all defence mechanisms, the psychological relief is paid for by having to distort one's perception of reality.

reproductive fitness The degree to which an animal is equipped to reproduce. Those that have a higher degree of reproductive fitness will, in general, have more viable offspring, so that their inherited characteristics are likely to become more common in the population. Note that the main interest here is in genetically coded characteristics, so while being a rock star might increase the number of offspring, there may be no relevant genetic characteristics to pass on.

research participant See *participant*.

resilience The ability to 'bounce back' or recover rapidly from setbacks. Setbacks in this context may be physical, psychological or social. Resilience is a powerful sign of psychological health.

resistance In psychotherapy, the attempts by the patient to prevent the therapist from being effective. In analysis particularly, resistance is seen as an inevitable response of the unconscious to the therapeutic process of making it conscious. When a patient rejects one of the therapist's *interpretations*, this will be regarded as resistance and may be taken as an indication that the interpretation was approaching a particularly important *defence mechanism*. However, it must sometimes be the case that patients reject interpretations simply because they are wrong.

resistance to extinction The length of time for which a learned response will carry on without any further *reinforcement*. Resistance to extinction is often used as a measure of *operant strength* – in other words, to indicate how strongly something has been learned.

resource holding power (RHP) An evaluation of the strength or fitness of an animal competitor, expressed in terms of how well it is able to protect or defend its territory or resources against competitors.

respect See *unconditional respect for persons*.

response bias The tendency that people have to produce experimental responses which are socially desirable, or which they think that the experimenter expects. For example, a study involving comparison of reactions to sexually explicit material with reactions to neutral material may show a difference that results from the person's unwillingness to appear overly concerned with sexual matters, or from their embarrassment. If this is not directly the topic under study, it will result in a response bias that could obscure other experimental findings. See also *confounding variable, experimenter effects*.

response conflict Situations in which two or more possible reponses are available, which may be equally desirable, or in which the desired response may not be the easiest or most apppropriate. See also *approach–avoidance conflict*.

response generalisation The tendency to produce a learned response in conditions that are similar, although not identical, to those under which the response was learned. In general, the more similar the conditions are, the stronger the response will be. This is known as the *generalisation gradient*.

response rate The frequency with which a response or unit of behaviour occurs in a set period of time. Response rate is often used as a measure of *operant strength*, or as an indicator of how strongly something has been learned.

resting potential The chemical balance between the external fluid and the chemical components of a neurone when it is not firing. See also *action potential*.

resting state paradigm A way of looking at the brain during scanning sessions, in which the person is not asked to perform any tasks, and the functional connectivity between areas of the brain or networks is measured. This gives an idea of the brain's 'resting state', which can then be compared with how the scan looks when the person is actively engaged in a specific task. See also *fMRI, default mode network*..

restricted code A code of language use identified by Bernstein, which is characterised by a high proportion of personal pronouns, a relatively limited vocabulary, and a considerable reliance on shared assumptions on the part of the speaker and listener. Bernstein saw restricted code speech as mainly being used by working-class individuals, whereas its counterpart, *elaborated code*, was mainly used by middle-class people. Because of the high dependency on context in restricted code speech, Bernstein argued that this made its speakers less likely to deal with abstract concepts and related forms of knowledge – a version of the *verbal deprivation hypothesis* that was highly criticised, notably by Labov, who showed that users of restricted codes demonstrated abstract reasoning just as readily as elaborated code users.

reticular activating system (RAS) A region of the lower portion of the brain that is directly involved in attention, sleep and wakefulness. The RAS appears to operate as a kind of switching mechanism for whole areas of the *cerebral cortex* in the event of wakefulness and alertness, and its surgical removal results in permanent unconsciousness.

reticular formation See *reticular activating system*.

retina The three-cell-deep layer on the back inner surface of the eyeball. The layer furthest away from the lens consists of light-sensitive *rod cells* and *cone cells*, the next layer consists of *bipolar neurones*, and the third layer consists of ganglion cells with elongated *axons* that cross the retina and join together at the blind spot to form the optic nerve. The retina forms a 'screen' on which an image is projected from the pupil of the eye, and the image on the retina is converted into electrical impulses by the rod and cone cells. The point on the retina where the image is focused most sharply is known as the *fovea*, and corresponds to the point where visual attention is concentrated in normal perception. The rest of the retina covers the remainder of the *visual field* (see Figure 46).

retinal disparity The difference in the visual image projected on to each retina caused by the slightly different positions of the two eyes. Closer objects produce more retinal disparity, so the visual system uses the difference to judge distance. See also *depth perception*.

retinal flow The changing patterns of light on the *retina* which are produced by the fact that the observer is moving around in its environment. It is a key process in Gibson's theory of *ecological perception*.

retinal ganglion cells Cells that collect information from the receptive cells in the *retina*, and take it to the brain, bunching together to form the *optic nerve*.

retinal image The inverted image of the external world that is cast on the retina by light rays entering the eye through the pupil, and focused by the lens before falling on the layer of *rod cells* and *cone cells* in the *retina*.

retinal size The term used to refer to the size of the image that an object casts on the *retina*. This will vary in proportion

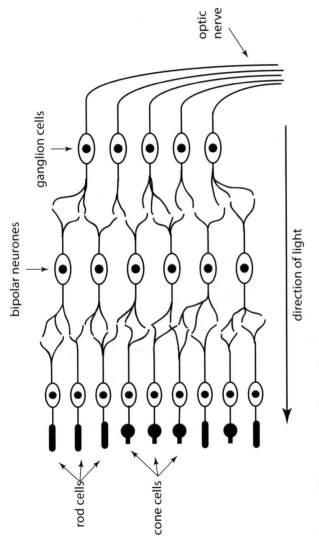

Figure 46 The structure of the retina

to the distance away from the object. For example, a 2-metre pole viewed from 40 metres will cast an image whose retinal size is half that of a 2-metre pole seen from 20 metres. However, due to the process of *size constancy*, the size of the object that is actually perceived by the person does not coincide with its retinal size, and even in young infants some amount of compensation for distance seems to occur.

retinopy See *retinopic organisation*.

retinotopic organisation The way that the *receptive fields* of neurones may be organised in a way which reflects the way that the *retinal image* is organised. The phrase is sometimes abbreviated to retinopy. See also *simple cell, complex cell, ocular dominance columns*.

retrieval A term used to refer to the process of remembering things, in which the information is 'retrieved' or brought back from some kind of storage system. See also *explicit memory*.

retrieval cue An item of information that links with other information stored in *memory*, and so allows that other information to be brought to the surface and recalled. See also *cue*.

retrieval-induced forgetting Forgetting that occurs when the retrieval of a memory causes inhibition of related or competing memories. See also *interference*.

retrieval processes The cognitive operations involved in recalling information stored in *long-term memory*.

retroactive interference The phenomenon that occurs when new information which is being learned interferes with the ability to recall information which was learned previously. For example,

a tennis player who takes up squash may find that their tennis deteriorates for a while. See also *proactive interference, transfer of training*.

retrograde amnesia The form of *amnesia* (memory disorder) in which the person affected is unable to remember things that happened before the event which rendered them amnesiac. Retrograde amnesia usually occurs after some form of brain damage, but can occur in a minor form after concussion. It is not uncommon for people who have been in an accident involving severe concussion to lose all memory of the few minutes leading up to the accident. See also *anterograde amnesia*.

retrograde memory Memory for events that happened before brain damage which led to *amnesia*. See also *retrograde amnesia, anterograde amnesia, anterograde memory*.

retrospective memory Memories of people, events or situations that have been experienced in the past.

retrospective study A study that involves collecting data about events which happened in the past. When information is being provided by people about their past, the possibility of memory distortions is obvious. Many epidemiological studies have been retrospective, using data from the previous records of patients or clients. The weaknesses of this technique are the inadequacy of documented information in the recording of salient or influential events in a person's life, and the tendency for researchers to focus exclusively on the particular feature that they are interested in, and to ignore other information. Where straightforward research on medical conditions is concerned, this may not be a problem, but the technique has been used for far broader research, notably Bowlby's work on *maternal deprivation*, which greatly influenced views of childcare practice from the 1950s to the 1970s.

reversal learning Learning that an act or process which had previously been rewarded is no longer rewarded. See also *extinction*.

reverse inference This is the process of arguing backwards from neural activation to infer that a particular cognitive process is going on.

reversibility The *operation* of returning something to its original state by reversing the process that transformed it in the first case. The concept of reversibility plays an important part in Piaget's theory of cognitive development. Understanding that an operation is reversible allows one to understand important aspects of the world. For example, if a ball of Plasticine can be rolled out into a sausage shape, it can also be rolled back into a ball; if A is larger than B, then B is smaller than A; if 3 squared is 9, then the square root of 9 is 3. Piaget saw an understanding of reversibility as an essential part of the *concrete operational stage*. In particular, it is necessary before *conservation* can be acquired.

reward Something that is provided for an organism, animal or human after a desired piece of behaviour has occurred, and which takes the form of something that the organism wants, needs or likes. The behavioural definition of reward is that it is a stimulus which an animal will work to maintain, and this concept is particularly important in the theory of *operant conditioning*, where reward forms *positive reinforcement* for learned behaviour.

reward pathway Sometimes referred to as the mesolimbic pathway, this is a series of neural connections involving the neurotransmitter *dopamine*, which connects an area of the *midbrain* to the *ventral striatum* of the forebrain, and also receives inputs from the *limbic system* and the *prefrontal cortex*. It is linked with pleasure, positive reinforcement, and the salience of incentives. See also *ESB*, *orbitofrontal cortex*.

rhetoric The study of how language is used to persuade others. Rhetoric was an important part of education from the early Greeks to the mid-nineteenth century, but came to be seen as inferior to the search for scientific certainties. As it explicitly recognises the extent to which thinking is affected by ideology, it is favoured by social constructionists. See also *social constructionism*, *discourse analysis*.

rhodopsin A light-sensitive chemical in the retinal cells of the eye, which responds to changes in light or dark. See also *photopsin*.

Rhine cards See *Zener cards*.

RHP See *resource holding power*.

ribonucleic acid (RNA) A chemical found in the cells of the body, which is involved in genetic protein synthesis, and is capable of duplicating genetic material, DNA, for use elsewhere. It has also been thought to be involved in learning processes.

Ribot's law The observation that people with *amnesia* still seem to retain memories from early in their lives.

right brain A commonly used term indicative of a popular misconception about brain functioning. See also *hemisphere bias*.

right hemisphere The half of the *cerebrum* situated to the right side of the head. It is mainly concerned with the functioning of the left side of the body, and of the right side of the retina in each eye. Following a series of *split-brain studies* by Sperry, it was found that this half of the brain was particularly adept at spatial and artistic tasks, whereas the *left hemisphere* was more readily concerned with language and number. But see also *hemisphere bias*.

rigour A term used to refer to the meticulousness and accuracy of research methods and procedures.

Ringlemann effect The observation that the efforts individuals put into a task is likely to decrease with the number of others involved. See also *social loafing*.

risky shift The finding that when a group of people makes a decision, it tends to be riskier than the decision that they would each have made individually (i.e. riskier than the average of the individual decisions). There are several possible explanations for the risky shift, one being that it is an example of *diffusion of responsibility*, and a second being the 'risk as value hypothesis', that risk-taking is socially valued and so people will want to be seen by the group as more daring. However, some psychologists question whether it really happens. See also *group polarisation*.

rite of passage A *ritual* that marks the progress from one stage of life to the next. All societies have their own rites of passage, with weddings, funerals, and those rituals that mark the transition from childhood or adolescence into adulthood having been most studied by anthropologists.

ritual A strictly defined pattern of behaviour that carries a significant social meaning in a well-defined context. Marriage ceremonies are a clear example of culturally defined rituals, but the term is used more widely to include any meaningful patterns of behaviour carried out according to strict rules, such as the handwashing ritual of an *obsessional* person, Sunday dinner, or a task that a family might be asked to undertake regularly as part of therapy.

ritualisation Types of animal communication that take the form of stereotyped sequences of actions, designed to communicate species-specific messages, such as opposition to intruders or intent to mate. Ritualised actions of this kind are genetically determined, and not easily modified according to the demands of the situation. See also *innate releasing mechanism*.

RNA See *ribonucleic acid*, *messenger RNA*.

robotics The area of research that involves the development of mechanical systems which can perform a set of actions in a manner comparable to that of a human being. Many highly successful robotic systems have been developed and applied, particularly in the manufacturing industries. They have involved considerable research, not just into movement systems, but also into the development of such techniques as optical scanning devices, which can identify and respond to anomalies or changes in the appearance of the material being manufactured. As such, robotics is often considered to form one branch of the research into *artificial intelligence*.

robustness The ability of a *statistical test* to operate in a reasonably appropriate manner, even if it is used inappropriately, with the wrong type of data. The concept of robustness is relatively little understood, but is often used as an excuse to apply *parametric* tests such as the *t-test* to data that would really warrant non-parametric statistics. See also *test power*.

ROC curve See *receiver-operating characteristic curve*.

rod cells Light-sensitive cells in the *retina* of the eye, which respond to very small amounts of light, but are not sensitive to colour. Rod cells are found in all parts of the retina except the *fovea*. Their action is most apparent at the edge of the retina, where their extreme sensitivity provides acute detection of movement in the peripheral vision, and allows very faint objects to be seen. Night vision is due to the sensitivity of rod cells. See also *dark adaptation*.

Rogers, Carl R. (1902–1987)

Carl Rogers was one of the most significant humanistic psychologists of the 1950s and 1960s. He regarded human beings as having two basic needs – for *positive regard* and for *self-actualisation*, which he saw as a process rather than as a goal state. His therapy emphasised providing the client with *unconditional positive regard*, which would free them from approval-seeking so that they could explore their own self-actualisation needs. To this end, Rogers developed *client-centred therapy*, which focuses on helping the client (not the patient) grow in their own way, and so is non-directive. It also emphasises the development of a positive *self-concept*, and helps the client to challenge impractical *conditions of worth* brought about by an unrealistically perfect *ideal self-image*. Part of client-centred therapy involves the therapist honestly reflecting their understandings and feelings back to the client – a practice that aims to reduce incongruence between how clients see themselves and how others see them.

Rogerian A term applied to methods of counselling or psychotherapy that are based on the work of Carl Rogers. See also *non-directive therapy*.

role The part that each individual is expected to play in a social situation. This has been studied particularly in groups in which a role is likely to be allocated to each member – leader, fixer, clown, loyal member, etc. Any individual is likely to play different roles in different groups, and may therefore experience role conflict when two groups come into contact (e.g. when adolescents encounter their family while in the company of their friends). Roles may be held very briefly (e.g. the one who has the next turn), over long periods (e.g. child), or permanently (e.g. gender role). See also *role behaviour, role confusion, role count, role expectation, role play*.

role behaviour Behaviour that is considered to be appropriate for someone who is playing a specific social role. For instance, someone playing the role of a shop assistant is expected to behave in certain ways, to be smart and alert, and to demonstrate specific behaviours such as asking if a customer needs to be served or requires information about prices, etc. Other kinds of behaviour of which the person may be equally capable (e.g. ballroom dancing) are completely inappropriate to the social role of shop assistant. See also *role expectation*.

role confusion In Erikson's developmental theory, a state in which the *identity* is not well defined. It may be regarded as a temporary state (this can occur at any time of life, but is particularly common during adolescence) or as the long-term consequence of having failed to establish a clear identity during adolescence. See also *psychosocial stages*.

role count The sum total of social roles that an individual plays. The concept becomes particularly important in the case of those who have recently retired. The process of retirement results in a drastic reduction in the number of social roles played by the individual, and some researchers consider that it is important for the retired person to replace at least some of those social roles in alternative social activities. See also *disengagement*.

role expectation The implicit but nonetheless very clear ideas that members of a society have concerning the ways in which people ought to behave when they are playing a social role in that society. Behaviour that does not conform to role expectations, at least in general terms, will usually meet with social *sanctions* of some kind (e.g. the exclusion of the person from the group).

role play Taking a particular role temporarily and behaving, as nearly as possible, like a person who actually holds that role. Role play is widely used in training situations and is an effective

way of helping people to understand what it feels like to have the given role. It also allows them to practise the role before being fully committed to it. Acting a role often shifts a person's opinions towards those they have been working with. Preparatory role play may also help to reduce anxiety and improve performance in stressful situations such as interviews.

Rorschach inkblot test A *projective test* based on psychoanalytic theory, in which participants are shown large and elaborate inkblot patterns, and invited to interpret them in terms of images that the blots might represent. The idea is that the responses which they make will indicate the concerns of the *unconscious* mind. The Rorschach test has been found to have poor *reliability*.

Rosenthal effect The finding by Robert Rosenthal and others that one's expectations can have an effect on an outcome that is being observed. The term is used particularly in connection with the finding that when teachers were told that a group of children were very bright, those children subsequently performed better than a similar group that the teachers had been told were all dull. The term is also used for various forms of *experimenter effect* and *self-fulfilling prophecy*. See also *labelling*.

rostral To do with the *anterior* side of a body part, organ or whole animal. See also *caudal*.

rTMS See *repetitive transcranial magnetic stimulation*.

rule-based errors Errors that arise because an established set of rules or procedures have been misapplied – in other words, used in inappropriate circumstances.

Rutter, Michael (1934–)

Sir Michael Rutter was knighted for his services to child psychology and child psychiatry. His re-evaluation of the concept of maternal deprivation in the early 1970s did much to bring attachment theory into a modern context, challenging the oversimplified views of maternal influence and clarifying how disturbed social relationships could produce problems in both childhood and adolescence. His later research into school experiences highlighted a number of social and experiential factors affecting both school performance and delinquency.

S

saccade Rapid, unconscious jerks and tremors that are made continuously by the eye and are thought to be instrumental in preventing *habituation* of the *retinal image*.

SAD See *seasonal affective disorder*.

sadism A psychosexual disorder in which a person obtains sexual arousal by inflicting pain or humiliation on another person. See also *masochism*.

safety needs The second level of Maslow's *hierarchy of human needs*, safety needs refer to needs for security, shelter and freedom from attack. These needs become important once basic *physiological needs* have been satisfied. Once the safety needs in turn have been satisfied, according to Maslow, the next level of needs, namely *social needs*, become important.

salience Something that is particularly noticeable, relevant or likely to be perceived. The salience of an object or event may be due to its physical properties, such as brightness and clarity, or it might arise because the object or event relates to needs, emotional states or meanings on the part of the perceiver.

sample A part of a *population* which is studied so that the researcher can make generalisations about the whole of the original population. Samples can be gathered by means of several different procedures, which include *quota sampling* and *random sampling*. Nearly all psychological research is carried out on samples, because the size of populations, or some other factor, makes studying the whole impossible. Many statistical techniques are concerned with indicating the reliability of a conclusion based on a sample, but cannot identify whether the sample is typical of that population or not. Thus, a considerable amount of experimental methodology is concerned with ensuring, as far as possible, that the samples involved in the study are *representative*.

sampling error The extent to which the results obtained from research may not be truly representative of their population, simply because of the fact that they have been obtained in the real world, and, in psychology, from real human beings, each of which is unique. Most statistical techniques can be seen as ways of addressing or minimising sampling error. See also *null hypothesis*, *statistical analysis*.

sampling procedure The procedure by which a sample is acquired. Sampling procedures need to be carefully defined and reported so that it is possible to judge whether the results obtained for that sample can be generalised to the *population* or to other samples. The ideal form is *random sampling*, in which members of a population are selected at random, with each having had an equal chance of being chosen. In practice, truly random sampling is difficult to achieve because of such influences as volunteer bias. A further disadvantage is that a random sample needs to be quite large to ensure a close fit to the parent population. More sophisticated forms, such as *stratified sampling*, are designed to represent the population in all important aspects, and so allow reliable conclusions to be drawn from a smaller sample. However, in practice, *opportunity sampling* is probably the most common technique.

sanction Some kind of deliberate negative consequence that is applied to a person or group in response to undesired behaviour. Sanctions may include the withdrawal of privilege or opportunity, as well as direct punishment or other unpleasant consequences.

Sapir–Whorf hypothesis The idea that our thinking and understanding are determined by the properties of the language we use for thinking and communicating: the theory of *linguistic determinism*. Benjamin Lee Whorf developed the theory in the 1920s and claimed that people in different societies would have different understandings of the world, and sometimes of their interpersonal interaction, because the words available to them are not the same.

satiation Satiation is defined operationally as the point at which an animal will no longer seek food. It is usually used in investigations of hunger or other motivational states, and it implies that the underlying *need* is temporarily satisfied.

satisficing The *heuristic* strategy in *decision-making* that involves settling on the first solution which satisfies the person's minimal requirements.

saturation This term is usually used with reference to colour, and indicates how 'rich' a particular hue is. However, it may also refer to other forms of stimuli, and in general it is concerned with intensity of content. For instance, 'saturation advertising' occurs when an advertising campaign is so intense that it is considered to have achieved the maximum effective exposure to its target audience.

savant syndrome See *idiot savants*.

savings method A method of measuring memory identified by Ebbinghaus in 1884, in which material that appears to have been entirely forgotten can nonetheless be relearned more quickly than similar material being encountered for the first time. See also *relearning savings*.

scaffolding The setting up of psychological support structures that help someone to build a firmer foundation for their choices, beliefs or learning. The term is used in *personal construct* theory, and is also a significant part of Vygotsky's model of adult influence on the child's *cognitive development*.

scaling The process of organising recorded measures into a scale. By doing this, the measures can be given values with known arithmetical relationships to each other, and statistical analyses can be undertaken. Scaling is particularly important in psychology because many of our phenomena cannot be measured directly, being either subjective or too complex. See also *levels of measurement*.

scanning See *brain scan*.

scapegoat theory The idea that prejudice arises from people seeking to blame others for their own negative circumstances. According to scapegoat theory, poor living conditions, economic depression and frustrating situations lead people to react in hostile ways to others, and this reaction is likely to focus on any individuals who are present but do not belong to the person's own *peer group*. Scapegoat theory has been put forward as an explanation for the growth of *racism* and *sexism* during times when economic circumstances are difficult.

scattergram Also sometimes called a scattergraph, this is a diagram used to illustrate *correlations*, in which the vertical axis (the *ordinate*) represents the values of one set of scores, and the horizontal axis (the *abscissa*) represents the other set. Each pair of scores is plotted as a point on the diagram. This means that the relationship between the two variables can be seen in the way in which the scores are scattered within the area described by the diagram (see Figure 47).

scatterplot See *scattergram*.

schedule of reinforcement See *reinforcement schedule*.

schema A hypothetical model of the way in which information is stored by the brain. It is used to direct action, and in understanding the relationships between events. A schema would include all of the information relating to a particular event or type of event, including representations of previous actions, theoretical and practical

knowledge about the event, ideas and opinions about it, etc. The concept of schemata formed a major part of the theory of *cognitive development* put forward by Piaget, and also Neisser's cognitive theory. The idea of schemata, and their extension and development through experience, provides a useful model for understanding how many different levels of comprehension can be involved in both new and familiar situations. See also *anticipatory schema*.

schizoid Showing tendencies towards *schizophrenia*, but not the extreme form. The term is therefore used for any indication of a mismatch between thought and feeling, and a lack of interest in and ability to form social relationships.

schizophregenic families The idea that some families operate in a way that makes it likely that the children will become *schizophrenic*. One therapist

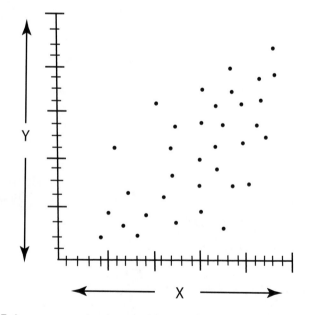

Figure 47 A scattergram showing a positive correlation

claims that it takes three generations to create a schizophrenic. The claim has been largely abandoned, partly because of a lack of evidence, but also because it became used to blame the parents of schizophrenic people.

schizophrenia A broad group of psychoses in which emotion is blunted or is not coordinated with thought and behaviour, and in which thought appears to be disordered. Typical symptoms of schizophrenia are *hallucinations*, incoherent speech and thought, and *delusions*. People suffering from schizophrenia are unlikely to maintain social relationships or to look after themselves adequately. There is considerable controversy over whether schizophrenia is an *organic disorder*, or whether it happens as a result of life experiences, particularly growing up in certain kinds of family. One of the reasons why this dispute has not been resolved is that there is no very clear and widely accepted definition of schizophrenia, and diagnosis of the condition varies widely in different countries. See also *Diagnostic and Statistical Manual of Mental Disorders*, *existentialism*.

school refusal (school phobia) The insistence by a child on staying at home rather than going to school. It used to be thought of as resulting from a fear of the school, hence the term 'school phobia', but is now often seen as being a fear of being away from the home. This is usually associated with the fear either of some disaster happening to the mother or of the parents leaving during the child's absence. Sometimes these fears have a rational basis (e.g. when there is serious discord between the parents or when the child has often been threatened with abandonment). See also *attachment*, *separation anxiety*.

Schwann cell A fatty cell that wraps itself around the *axon* or *dendron* of a neuron, to form the *myelin sheath*.

scotoma A small area of blindness in the visual field, originating in the *primary visual cortex*.

SCR Skin conductance response. See *galvanic skin response*.

script A concept that was particularly articulated by Schank and Abelson (1977), this term refers to the implicit set of social expectations and assumptions which operate in the course of everyday interaction. People act in accordance with these expectations as if their part was 'scripted'. The classic example of this is the restaurant script, in which the roles of customer, waiter, etc. are highly prescribed, with certain actions being expected at certain times. Schank and Abelson demonstrated that the application of a particular script to a given situation can channel and structure what is perceived from that situation – a different script will lead to the individual noticing different features and remembering different facts as salient. Scripts are, for the most part, unconscious and assumed. It is noticeable that people are more likely to remember deviations from a script (e.g. not being asked if coffee is wanted at the end of a restaurant meal) than they are to remember events which conform to the script itself. See also *schema*, *social representations*.

SD See *standard deviation*.

seasonal affective disorder (SAD) A disturbance of affect in the form of depressed mood, which coincides with the reduction of daylight during winter months. People who suffer from SAD experience major depressive episodes each year. Naturally, the condition only operates in populations that live a long way from the equator. It can be treated by prolonged exposure to bright light, called 'phototherapy'.

seasonal territoriality A form of *territoriality* that occurs only for a particular period, such as the mating season or the time of rearing young. Most forms of territoriality among animals are seasonal (i.e. most animals only actively defend their territories against potential competitors at relevant times of the year).

secondary appraisal A term used in stress and coping therapy to describe the person's assessment of the coping resources they have available for use. See also *primary appraisal, transactional model of stress*.

secondary circular reactions *Circular reactions* that have progressed beyond involving the infant's own body, and which now operate through manipulating objects, again in a fixed repeated pattern.

secondary drives Within *drive-reduction theories* of motivation, the attempt to include psychological needs by claiming that they must have acquired drive properties through *association* with *primary drives* such as hunger.

secondary process In psychoanalytic theory, secondary process refers to conscious rational thought. It is so-called in order to distinguish it from *primary processes*, which are the workings of the *unconscious*.

secondary reinforcement Something that has acquired the property of being able to *reinforce* learned behaviour, because it has previously been associated with a *primary reinforcement*. For example, if a 'click' is sounded each time a rat in a *Skinner box* is rewarded with a food pellet, the noise becomes associated with the reward. If the behaviour then undergoes *extinction*, it can return and be maintained simply by making the sound of the 'click', with no food reward being necessary. Moreover, a new behaviour can be increased if it is just followed by the click. The noise has developed reinforcing properties and has become a secondary reinforcer, simply as a result of its *association* with the primary reinforcer. There are many different kinds of secondary reinforcer – in human terms, the most frequently encountered one is almost certainly money.

secondary sexual characteristics Physical characteristics such as beards or breasts that are normally found in mature members of one sex only, but which are not the actual sex organs. See also *primary sexual characteristics*.

second-order conditioning A two-stage *conditioning* process, in which an initial association with a stimulus is learned, and then another condition or stimulus becomes associated with the learned one, and is learned in its turn.

second-order intentionality A degree of *intentional stance* which makes the inference that the individual acting has beliefs and desires, but aso has beliefs about other people's beliefs. So an act may represent an attempt to get others to respond in certain ways. See also *first-order intentionality, third-order intentionality*.

secure attachment A type of *attachment* in which the infant (or older person) is confident in the relationship, and therefore able to cope easily with separation. Securely attached infants will show moderate degrees of upset on being left by their primary *caregiver*, but this soon passes, and they will greet the person positively when reunited. See also *insecure attachment*.

sedative A drug that has a calming effect on the individual, usually producing drowsiness. This is often achieved by dampening the activity of the *autonomic nervous system*. Sedatives are known to produce considerable *tolerance* in the body, with progressively increasing amounts of the drug being required to produce the same effect. The most well-known sedatives are the *barbiturates*, which were traditionally prescribed as sleeping tablets, although this practice is now less common. Although there are known to be large numbers of people who are addicted to barbiturates, the addiction is usually induced through medical prescription – barbiturates are not commonly used as *recreational drugs*.

segementation The process of dividing things into parts. In cognitive psychology, this generally refers to dividing the sounds of speech, which are virtually continuous, into separate words or phonemes.

selective attention Attention that is channelled towards certain stimuli and ignores the presence of others. The most well-known example of this occurs when someone is concentrating on one particular conversation amidst a large amount of background noise, some of which may actually be louder than the conversation being attended to. This was dubbed the *cocktail party effect* in the 1950s, and gave rise to a considerable amount of research, often involving *dichotic listening tasks* and *split-span tests*. The research gave rise to several different *filter models*, which eventually showed that there is a considerable amount of unconscious *semantic* processing even of unattended information. See also *exogenous orienting*.

selective exposure A preference to receive cognitive input that will strengthen our existing views, and a tendency to avoid information which will challenge them. See also *confirmation bias*.

selective serotonin reuptake inhibitors (SSRIs) The collective name for a group of antidepressant drugs that affect the uptake or reuptake of the *neurotransmitter* serotonin (e.g. *Prozac*).

self-actualisation A concept central to the humanistic theories of both Maslow and Rogers, although used in a different way by each. Broadly speaking, self-actualisation refers to the making real (actualising) of human potential, so it involves the individual developing their abilities to the full, exploring options and skills, and experiencing life as fully as possible. For Maslow, self-actualisation takes the form of a 'peak experience', which is only attained once all of the 'lower' levels of the hierarchy of needs have been satisfied (i.e. needs such as *safety needs*, *physiological needs*, etc.). Accordingly, self-actualisation is seen as a relatively uncommon event, which occurs only in a few special individuals.

In Rogers' theory, by contrast, self-actualisation is seen as a continuous process of self-exploration and development that forms an undeniable need for the individual. Most people have ways of developing their potential in day-to-day living, through hobbies, interests and the like, and most recreational pursuits involve some degree of trying to learn or to improve one's abilities. However, in some individuals, the need for self-actualisation comes into conflict with the need for *positive regard* from others. Self-exploration is seen as potentially threatening, in that it might incur disapproval and censure from other people. Accordingly, such people suppress their need for self-actualisation, and Rogers sees this as the foundation of *neurosis*, because the person experiences a discrepancy between the way that they actually act, and their 'inner self'. However, if they have a relationship involving *unconditional positive regard* from someone, the person becomes able to explore their need for self-actualisation, and to balance the two needs in such a way as to achieve personal growth and maturity. Providing such unconditional positive regard forms the basis of Roger's *client-centred therapy*.

self-awareness The conscious feeling of an ongoing, consistent sense of being a person.

self-categorisation A process of deciding that we, personally, fit into certain social, psychological or physical categories. See *social identity theory*.

self-concept The sum total of the ways in which the individual sees themselves. Self-concept is often considered to have two major dimensions – a descriptive component, known as the *self-image*, and an evaluative component, known as *self-esteem*, although in practice the term is more commonly used to refer to the evaluative side of self-perception.

self-consciousness An exaggerated awareness of one's own behaviour, feelings and appearance, combined with a belief that other people are equally aware, interested and critical. Self-consciousness is often particularly extreme during adolescence.

self-efficacy beliefs The belief in one's own power to act effectively, or to influence events. Particularly associated with the work of Albert Bandura

(e.g. Bandura, 1977), self-efficacy theory argues that high self-efficacy beliefs contribute directly to a positive sense of agency in dealing with the world. They are therefore closely linked with an *internal locus of control*. People with high self-efficacy beliefs have been shown to make more efforts to achieve results, and to respond productively to *feedback*, whereas those with low self-efficacy beliefs show a tendency to give up easily, and to fail to use feedback to improve their performance. Although they are closely linked with and perceived as a major contributor to *self-esteem*, self-efficacy beliefs can be highly specific, relating only to particular types of task. However, there is some suggestion that people do show a general tendency towards high or low self-efficacy beliefs in a wide range of contexts. Bandura argues that it is often psychologically healthier for an individual to have slightly higher self-efficacy beliefs than the evidence would warrant, since that will encourage them to take on more difficult tasks, and to persist at those tasks in the face of initial difficulty. This in turn increases their likelihood of success. Some developmental psychologists believe that a strong sense of self-efficacy is built up in infants and small children through *contingencies* provided by caregivers.

self-esteem The personal evaluation that individuals make of themselves, their sense of their own worth, or their capabilities. Excessively low self-esteem is regarded as indicating a likelihood of psychological disturbance, and is particularly characteristic of *depression*. There are several simple questionnaires that have been developed for measuring self-esteem, as well as more sophisticated tests such as the *Q-sort*.

self-fulfilling prophecy A statement that comes true as a result of having been made. The classic example of the self-fulfilling prophecy in action came from work by Rosenthal and Fode, in which undergraduate students were given a set of experimental rats to train in maze-running. Despite the fact that there were no observable behavioural differences between the rats at the start of the experiment, the students were told that they could expect some to be very quick at learning the maze, while others would be very slow. The rats performed according to these predictions, because the predictions had induced expectations on the part of the students that affected how they handled the animals during training. Further studies by Rosenthal and his colleagues demonstrated the power of expectations held by teachers towards their pupils, and the self-fulfilling prophecy is now considered to be a major social influence that needs control in psychological investigation. See also *double-blind control, experimenter effects*.

self-handicapping A tendency to set up situations in such a way that we are bound to fail.

self-image The internal picture that individuals have of themselves; a kind of internal description, which is built up through interaction with the environment and feedback from other people. The self-image may include knowledge about hair colour (although not attitudes towards it), and the *social roles* played by that individual. The person's attitude to self-image plays an important part in their level of *self-esteem*. Most people operate a self-image that gives an exaggerated idea of their own attractiveness, and this seems to be necessary for psychological well-being. See also *body image, identity*.

self-monitoring Being alert to how we come across to other people, so that we can improve, or at least predict more effectively, our effect in social situations. Talking to oneself can also be a form of self-monitoring behaviour.

self-perception theory The idea that we gain knowledge about ourselves by observing our own behaviour (e.g. 'I must have been hungry because I ate an extra sandwich'). Overtly, such an approach may appear naïve, yet there is considerable evidence to suggest that people do make *attributions* about their own behaviour, based on how they have seen themselves acting or reacting.

self-persuasion The modification of a person's beliefs to become consistent with what they observe about their own behaviour.

self-presentation The process of showing a public self to others. Self-presentation commonly involves enhancing those features believed to be regarded by others as positive, while restricting those that might be seen as more negative. See *impression management*.

self-report Data in the form of reports that people make about their own actions or experiences. More broadly, any data provided directly by research participants when they fill in questionnaires or inventories.

self-serving bias A bias in a person's thinking that serves a personal purpose, such as maintaining *self-esteem* or cognitive consistency. The concept is used particularly in *attribution theory* to refer to causal beliefs that are adopted because they are favourable to the individual.

Seligman, Martin E.P. (1942–)

Martin Seligman first achieved fame by reporting a personal experience of *prepared learning* when he became sick after eating his favourite sauce. His interest in one-trial learning led to research into responses to aversive stimuli, which in turn led to his observations of *learned helplessness*, in which dogs gave up attempting to escape from shock as a consequence of previous futile attempts to escape. Seligman drew parallels with depression in humans, but the theory was not fully supported in subsequent research until it was reformulated by bringing in aspects of *attribution theory*. This resulted in the idea of a depressive *attributional style*, which proved useful in various forms of therapy. Seligman continued to study the prediction of behaviour from attributional style, and in recent years has been developing our knowledge of *learned optimism* and *positive psychology*.

Selye, Hans (1907–1962)

Hans Selye was responsible for developing the fundamental model of stress and how it affects the body that is still used today. His early work on endocrinology led to observations about how stressful situations produce hormonal changes; and by examining the effects of both short-term and long-term stress, Selye was able to identify what became known as the *general adaptation syndrome*, later linked to a number of illnesses and maladaptations. Although some of the specifics of his model have been challenged, its overall validity remains widely accepted, and it has proved the jumping off point for much further research, not least into the health benefits of positive thinking.

semantic To do with meaning; the intended communication or meaning that underlies any utterance or signal. The word 'semantic' is usually used in contrast with *syntactic*, referring to the structure of the communication (e.g. sentence structure). Such contrasts are particularly useful in examining the use of *language* in communication.

semantic coding Storing information in memory on the basis of its meaning, rather than using other characteristics, such as *imagery*.

semantic conditioning A conditioning process that uses a *stimulus–response* form of learning such as *operant* or *classical conditioning*, in which the individual is trained to respond to the meaning of a word or phrase. Although the perception of meaning is a cognitive rather than a behavioural event, studies of semantic conditioning are reported to show all the characteristics of behavioural conditioning, such as *generalisation*, *discrimination*, etc. However, there is a certain amount of evidence to indicate that semantic conditioning only 'works' if the research participants catch on to what the study is about, and decide to cooperate.

semantic dementia This is a progressive degenerative neural disorder that involves a gradual loss of *semantic memory*. Most commonly, the patient gradually loses their awareness of the meanings of words, which means it is also sometimes classified as a progressive *aphasia*.

semantic differential A technique developed by Osgood for discovering the underlying features that people associate with individual words. Research participants are provided with *bipolar* lists of features and asked to rate each word. Usually, a small number of rather general features (e.g. weak–strong, active–passive, good–bad) emerge as providing most of the variation.

semantic memory Memory that is concerned with processes (i.e. how to do things). For example, people with amnesia may forget knowledge-based information, but they rarely forget such things as how to walk, boil a kettle or write. These are all examples of semantic memory. See also *episodic memory, procedural knowledge, hub-and-spoke model.*

semantic priming A form of cognitive *priming* that is based on meaning, as opposed to visual appearance or other features.

semantic relations grammar A theoretical approach to understanding the way in which very small children put words together, which emphasises the meaning, or intention, underlying the utterance. The short sentences and limited *utterances* of the child are viewed as *telegraphic speech*, signalling the most important parts of the communication, and only becoming more refined in terms of additional words or word endings later on. The theory was developed by Roger Brown in opposition to the view of language acquisition developed by Chomsky, which largely ignored what the child was intending to communicate and concentrated instead on the structure of the utterance. See also *psycholinguistics.*

semanticisation The cognitive process by which *episodic memories* gradually change into *semantic memories* over time.

semantics The study of meaning.

semicircular canals Structures in the *inner ear* that detect the overall movement of the body, and are particularly concerned with the sense of balance. The canals are filled with a fluid that contains small bony particles known as otoliths, in suspension. As the fluid moves in the canals, the otoliths make contact with hair cells that line the edges, which produce an *electrical impulse*. This is then passed to the brain, particularly those regions of the *cerebellum* that are concerned with balance and equilibrium.

semi-interquartile range Half of the *interquartile range*. This measure can give a rough indication of the *variance* of ordinal data.

semiology The study of symbolism and meanings in everyday life. Semiologists are interested in the metaphors, rituals and symbols that form a large part of our everyday activity, but of which we are almost entirely unconscious.

semiotics The study of patterns in communication of all kinds, including *language, ritual, non-verbal communication,* animal communication, etc. Although primarily concerned with the meanings within such communication, the study of semiotics also sees the form of the communication as providing important clues to that meaning. In other words, a clear distinction between meaning and form is not considered appropriate, as the form will influence the meaning, and the intended meaning will affect the choice of the form. For example, a reminder from the boss to staff in an office about switching off unnecessary lights could be delivered as a spoken communication, a handwritten memo, or a formally typed memo. Although the words might be identical, the form affects the meaning of the communication.

senile dementia A loss of intellectual capacity that apparently occurs through a deterioration of the brain. The deterioration may not be directly attributable to ageing, and is often due to degenerative conditions such as *Alzheimer's syndrome*, which can also affect younger people.

sensation Anything that is experienced through the senses; a general term which is used to refer to sound, visual experiences, smell, taste, tactile or kinaesthetic experiences. It is usually used when it would be inappropriate or misleading to describe the particular form that the experience will take or has taken. See also *perception*.

sensation seeking An approach to everyday choices in which the person deliberately selects options that will maximise emotional or physical challenges. Sometimes considered to be a *personality trait* in its own right.

sensitive period A time period during development in which a given capacity or form of learning can be acquired most easily. Sensitive periods are distinguished from *critical periods* by the fact that the capacity can be acquired outside the set period, although with greater effort.

sensitivity training Training in *interpersonal* skills, such as effective listening and encouragement. Training for counsellors, *psychotherapists* and *clinical psychologists* almost always involves some form of sensitivity training.

sensorimotor stage The first of Piaget's four stages of *cognitive development*, in which the immediate cognitive task that the child faces is the decoding of sensory information and the coordination of motor action. The first step in achieving this, according to Piaget, is the reduction of the infant's *egocentricity* to the point where it can distinguish between 'me' and 'not-me', and has formed its first *schema*, the *body-schema*. Another important milestone during this period is the development of *object constancy*. See also *concrete operational stage*, *formal operational stage*, *preoperational stage*.

sensorimotor transformation The connection between knowledge of the position of the body and the position of objects in space, which allows us to act on objects in our environment.

sensory adaptation The process by which our senses adjust their sensitivity to the surrounding environment. For instance, at night when background sound levels tend to be low, the ear will detect sounds that are far fainter than those which can be detected during the daytime. Similarly, the *rod* and *cone cells* of the *retina* become more sensitive in dim light, and less sensitive in bright light. See also *dark adaptation*.

sensory memory An ephemeral fast-fading memory of very recent stimuli. Includes *echoic memory* and *iconic representation*.

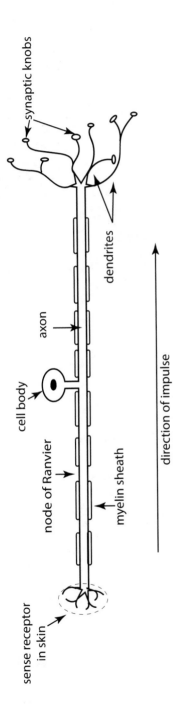

Figure 48 A sensory neurone

sensory-functional distinction The idea that semantic features are grouped together in the brain according to their function and physical properties. However, there are cases where the two types of property have been shown to be distinct (e.g. some people show selective impairments in category-specific cognition, but not for functional tasks). See also *autopagnosia*.

sensory neurone A neurone that carries information from a sense organ or sensory receptor to the *central nervous system*. Sensory neurones are usually bipolar, which means that the cell body occurs in between the two ends, each of which branches into *dendrites*. They are also *myelinated*, which allows them to transmit information extremely quickly (see Figure 48).

sensory projection area Areas of the *cerebral cortex* that receive sensory information, usually via the *thalamus*. There are four major sensory projection areas on each *cerebral hemisphere*, namely the *somatosensory projection area*, the *visual cortex* (also sometimes referred to as the

striate cortex), the *auditory cortex* and the *olfactory cortex*. As there appears to be some kind of correlation between the amount of stimulation and the amount or region of the sensory areas stimulated, it was originally thought that the sensation was 'projected' on to the area as if on to a screen, hence the name (see Figure 49).

sensory threshold The point at which 50 per cent of stimuli will be detected. The nature of the stimuli will depend on the sense being investigated (e.g. faintness of light or speed of exposure for visual thresholds, volume or pitch of sound for auditory thresholds, and so on). See also *threshold*.

separation anxiety The signs of anxiety and distress shown by a young child or other animal when a caregiver to whom they have an *attachment* leaves them alone in a strange situation. Traumatic experiences of separation, or repeated threats of abandonment ('If you're bad, we'll put you in a home') in early childhood are believed to produce 'separation anxiety', in which the child

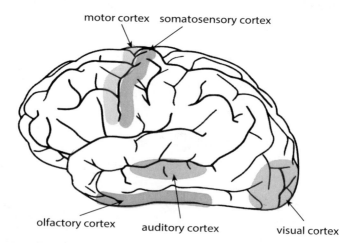

Figure 49 Sensory projection areas

is in a continual state of anxiety about the possibility of losing its primary caregivers. *School refusal* may also reflect separation anxiety. See also *strange situation technique*.

serial Occurring in sequence, one item at a time. For instance, a serial memory search occurs when the memory is searched for items with a definite pattern, one item after another.

serial position curve A graph which shows the probability of recalling an item against the position that item had in the original list of items that was learned. The curve shows higher probabilities for the earliest and latest items in the list, indicating *primacy* and *recency effects*. The curve has also been used to distinguish the operation of *long-term* and *short-term memory*, although this is rather more contentious.

serial processing The processing of information one item at a time. Many early cognitive models assume serial processing in, for example, *problem-solving* or the decoding of *language*, although recent evidence suggests that in fact information is often processed on several levels simultaneously (*parallel processing*).

serial reaction time task A measure of implicit learning in which people are presented with sets of items that involve a repeating sequence, and are asked to respond as quickly as possible to each item.

serial reproduction A research technique, developed by Bartlett, and used for studying the distortions produced by *memory*. In the classic model, one research participant is given information and then reports it to a second subject, and so on. An alternative approach is for the same person to produce successive versions of the material. The progressive distortions in the information provide insight into the types of changes that occur as the material is stored in a person's memory.

serotonin A *neurotransmitter* that is involved in a variety of brain processes, especially those concerned with moods, and including *motivation*, sleeping, relaxation and pain. The *hallucinogens LSD* and psilocybin appear to be picked up at serotonin receptor sites, although the precise mechanisms by which these drugs operate are not fully understood. In some texts, serotonin is referred to as *5-hydroxytryptamine*, or *5-HT*.

set A state of preparedness or readiness for a particular type of experience. Set may be demonstrated with most forms of cognitive process, but the most striking examples of it are *perceptual set* and *learning set*. In each case, information that is relevant to the prepared state is picked up far more quickly and easily than information that is not relevant.

set weight A predetermined body weight, which seems to form the 'natural' weight of the animal concerned. The idea of set weight arose from studies of the *hypothalamus*, in which it was observed that rats with *lesions* in particular areas of the hypothalamus would eat more than usual. At first, it was thought that these areas represented 'feeding centres', but later findings showed that the increased intake only lasted until they had reached a certain body weight. At that point, the rats would adjust their food intake to stay at that level. Experimental lesions in other areas of the hypothalamus produced effects in the opposite direction – rats would cease to eat until their body weight had dropped to a certain point, whereupon they would resume eating, but would eat only enough to maintain the new body weight. It has been suggested that similar mechanisms might be implicated in the case of *obesity* in humans. See also *satiation*.

sex differences Differences between the sexes. Some psychologists reserve this term for biologically based differences, with gender differences being used for socially derived features. However, the distinction is difficult to apply in practice, and it seems likely that few differences between the sexes are either purely biological or purely social in origin.

sex-linked trait An inherited tendency that appears only in members of one sex. The genes for such traits are carried on the pair of chromosomes that determine the biological sex of the individual. Because the structure of this pair of chromosomes differs substantially in males and females, sex-linked traits operate differently for the two sexes. For example, colour blindness, which is *recessive* and carried on the *X-chromosome* alone, will only be apparent in females who have inherited it on both of their X-chromosomes. If it is carried on only one of them, then the gene for normal colour vision on the other X-chromosome will dominate. However, colour blindness will always appear in males who carry it on the only X-chromosome they have. There are therefore more colour-blind men than colour-blind women. It is worth noting, however, that very few biological sex-linked traits of this type appear to have any direct connection with psychological processes. This is partly because genetic psychological processes, if they exist at all, are likely to be *polygenic*.

In human psychology, it is the *phenotype* – the ever-developing outcome of the interaction between genetic and environmental influence – that is the focus of interest. See also *haemophilia*, *Y-chromosome*.

sex-role behaviour Behaviour that is influenced by the person's beliefs about what is appropriate for members of their own sex. The term can also be used to refer to behaviour that conforms to society's definition of appropriate gender behaviour.

sex-role learning The processes by which a child or adolescent acquires an understanding of what is appropriate behaviour for their own sex, as opposed to appropriate behaviour for members of the other sex. Sex-role learning starts very early in life, and 3-year-olds have quite a clear idea of which gender-related behaviours their parents think are appropriate.

sex stereotypes Beliefs that are held in the *culture* about *sex differences* and appropriate *sex-role behaviour*. Like all *stereotypes*, they make a useful starting point for knowing what to expect from a person, but they easily become misleading if used in preference to observing what the person is actually like.

sexism Discrimination against a person on the basis of their sex. It is often more subtle than *racism* because it is likely to be based on assumptions about *sex differences* that are widely held in society. As many of these assumptions have been developed to justify an unfair treatment of women (see *rationalisation*), sexism is often taken to mean discrimination against women.

sexual abuse A form of *child abuse* in which children are involved in inappropriate sexual activities, mostly with adults, and which is known to be psychologically damaging. It is now known that children of all ages, boys as well as girls, can be sexually abused. Typical consequences involve distorting the child's ability to form appropriate relationships, limiting their ability to express affection in non-sexual ways, sometimes producing a high level of sensitivity to sexual cues, and a tendency to misinterpret ordinary interactions as sexual in content. Cases of child sexual abuse are sometimes detected by signs of unhappiness and an inability to concentrate at school. Since most cases of child sexual abuse involve incest, the victims are often afraid of the consequences, and are therefore reluctant to disclose the abuse. Help for individuals who have been the victims of sexual abuse depends on the age at which it is identified, and may include *play therapy, family therapy*, individual *psychotherapy*, or self-help groups.

sexual reproduction Forms of reproduction that depend on combining genetic material from a male and a female. The term is usually used in contrast to 'asexual reproduction' in which the offspring is produced entirely from genetic material provided by a single parent organism. Sexual reproduction has the major advantage of producing new combinations of genetic material and so increasing the diversity of the species. As the process requires cooperation between two members of the same species, it has resulted in the development of a great variety of interesting features, such as courtship rituals, an ability to refrain from eating the sexual partner before their contribution to reproduction is complete, and biological motivations to ensure that the behaviour is undertaken, however unlikely the required activities appear. Sexual reproduction is also widely regarded as being more fun than asexual reproduction.

sexual selection The idea that a particular trait has evolved because it enhances the chances that the individual will be selected for mating by members of the other sex in their species.

shadowing A task extensively used in studies of *selective attention*. Shadowing involves the audible repetition of a spoken message as it is received by the listener. In the classic experiments, participants were presented with two messages simultaneously, one through each side of a pair of headphones (a *dichotic listening task*). They were asked to attend to only one of these messages, and in order to ensure that they were doing so, they would be required to 'shadow' the message. In this way, the effects of information input to both the non-attended and the attended ear could be assessed, as the spoken words would show what the person was consciously noticing.

sham rage An extreme form of uncontrolled rage, produced by direct action on the brain, usually electrical stimulation of the *limbic system*, and which ceases abruptly when the stimulation is switched off. See also *ESB*.

shape constancy The perceptual adjustment which is made by the visual system when viewing objects from different angles, such that the *retinal image* varies. For instance, a cup seen from above casts a retinal image that is very different to that of a cup seen from the side, yet it is perceived as having a constant shape (see Figure 50). See also *colour constancy, size constancy*.

Figure 50 Shape constancy

shaping See *behaviour shaping*.

shock therapy See *electroconvulsive therapy*.

short-term memory (STM) Memory that lasts for only a few seconds (e.g. the kind of memory that is used when retaining a telephone number while dialling). The concept of short-term memory was first introduced by William James (1890), and has been used extensively in psychological theories of memory ever since. One of its notable characteristics is its vulnerability, either through a rapid decay of the memory trace, or through displacement by new material. This means that in order to retain material for any length of time, it is necessary to rehearse it continuously. Another characteristic is its limited capacity, with old information being displaced to make room for new. This limited memory was identified by Miller as consisting of 7 ± 2 items, but the amount of information contained in those seven items could be extended by *chunking* information into meaningful larger units. Some theorists, notably Atkinson and Shiffrin, see short-term memory as an initial stage for material entering *long-term memory*, although they also see it as a completely different

type of memory store. In recent years, the *levels of processing* approach to memory has implied that the existence of two separate memory stores is an unnecessary refinement, and that the characteristics of STM can be seen simply as the effects of the very superficial processing that information receives when it is first perceived. See also *working memory, graphemic buffer*.

sibling A word used to refer to a brother or sister, which has the advantage of not denoting the gender of the person being referred to.

sibling rivalry The commonly observed jealousy between siblings, which may start from a competition for attention and affection from the parents, but then generalises to many or all aspects of their lives.

SIDS See *sudden infant death syndrome*.

sign stimulus A stimulus that triggers a *fixed action pattern* in a particular species.

sign test The simplest of *nonparametric* statistical tests. When the phenomenon being studied can only take one of two values with known probabilities, the difference between the observed frequency and the expected frequency can be checked for *significance*. The simplest case for this simple test is when the two values are equally probable, as in tossing an unbiased coin, or the sex of participants selected randomly from the population.

signal-detectability theory A theory about how weak signals are detected despite the presence of background *noise*. By making simplifying assumptions (in particular, that only the level of noise and the level of signal are to be considered, and that when both are present the levels simply add to the total sensation, rather than interacting or cancelling each other out), it has been possible to produce a mathematical analysis of the process of detecting signals. This approach has been effective in certain restricted cases, and much of the theory is incorporated in the *receiver-operating characteristic (ROC) curve*.

signal-detection task A task used to investigate how long a person can perform effectively when asked to identify one particular type of signal appearing at random intervals amid other distracting stimuli. The task might be auditory (e.g. a tone lasting slightly longer than other tones that are sounded at intervals), or it might be visual (e.g. the detection of one special shape appearing among other shapes). Some signal-detection tasks are replications of the displays that a radar operator would scan, allowing researchers to identify potential sources of error and to investigate possible alleviating measures. See also *sustained attention*.

signal-detection theory (i) A mathematical approach to understanding a person's response to information in terms of their physiological sensitivity to it; or alternatively (ii) their decision *threshold* of responding.

signal-to-noise ratio The ratio obtained by dividing a measure of the strength of the information in a signal by a measure of the *noise* that surrounds it during transmission. It gives a measure of how easy it will be to perceive the signal accurately. For example, a human voice in a loud disco will have a low signal-to-noise ratio and will be difficult to understand.

significance See *statistical significance*.

significance level A level at which it is judged that a statistical finding is unlikely to have occurred by chance. Because chance variation is unlikely, the finding is taken to suggest that a genuine effect may be operating. The significance level should be set before research begins, and should relate to the implications that a finding would have. The lowest significance level conventionally used in psychological research a probability of less than 0.05 (expressed as $p < .05$). But this level of 'significance' would still occur in 1 out of every 20 studies on average if no effect at all was operating. So obtaining this level could just mean that yours was that 1 in 20 chance. If practical use is to be made of a finding, it is more usual to require a probability of less than 0.01, or a 1 in 100 likelihood that it could have occurred by chance. If you were going to use the research to claim that a proven treatment for a serious condition should be abandoned and replaced by a new one, you would demand a much higher significance level. Note that however extreme the significance level, it will never totally exclude the possibility that the finding was due to chance. Therefore, while the possibility that no effect is operating (the *null hypothesis*) may be rejected, it can never be disproved.

significant difference A difference between two sets of scores that has achieved a specified *significance level*.

similarity principle One of the *Gestalt principles of perception* which holds that in the absence of other information, we will tend to group together stimuli that are similar, and regard them as somehow 'linked' or 'belonging'. See also *closure*.

simple cell A type of neurone found in the *lateral geniculate nuclei* of the *thalamus*, and also in the *visual cortex*, which will fire only when a very specific stimulus occurs within the *visual field*. First identified by Hubel and Wiesel, simple cells will respond either to a particular dot or line in a specific part of the visual field, or to a line at a particular orientation in any part of the visual field. There is also some evidence that something like 90 per cent of these cells can adapt their functioning if early visual experience is limited. After a *critical period*, their functioning becomes relatively fixed. It is thought possible that disorders of the arrangements of *simple* or *complex cells* may produce *astigmatism*. See also *hypercomplex cell*.

simulation Any process of modelling or imitating an actual real-life event. The term is often used in psychology to refer to apparatus that mimics a real situation in which training can be more safely carried out (e.g. aeroplane cockpit simulators), to people who act as if they have psychological or physical conditions (e.g. faking epileptic seizures) and in *computer simulation*.

simulation theory The idea that we come to understand other people's emotions or mental states by simulating that state in ourselves. See also *facial feedback hypothesis*, *mirror systems*.

simultanagnosia The inability to perceive more than one thing at a time.

For example, someone with simultanagnosia might have difficulty in using visition to guide their hand movements towards an object, as they are not able to perceive the location of their hand at the same time as the location of the object. See also *optic apraxia*.

simultaneous conditioning A variant of *classical conditioning* in which the *unconditioned stimulus* is presented at exactly the same time as the conditioned stimulus. See also *delayed conditioning*, *trace conditioning*.

single-blind control An experimental control in which the research participants in a study are unaware of the *hypothesis* that is being investigated, but the researcher is aware of it. See also *double-blind control*.

single-case design See *case study*.

single-unit recording See *single-cell recording*.

single-cell recording Also known as single-unit recording or *micro-electrode recording*, this is the measurement of the electrical reaction of a single neurone in response to a stimulus. Because it is an *invasive* method, it is usually only conducted on animals or people already undergoing brain surgery. Research into neuronal activity in the temporal lobe has shown a high degree of specificity – for example, in one case, a person showed activity in a single neurone when looking at a picture of the Eiffel Tower, but not to other famous monuments; or in another, a specific cell was activated when looking at pictures of a famous film star, but not to other film stars, or even to pictures of the same star when she was with her husband. The idea is that these cells have learned to 'tune in' to specific features of the environment. See also *hypercomplex cell*, *grandmother cell*.

SIT See *social identity theory*.

situational attribution In *attribution theory*, this refers to explaining a person's behaviour or experiences as arising from the situation that they are in, rather than from the personality or other internal characteristic of that person (which would be a *dispositional attribution*). See also *fundamental attributional error*.

size constancy The perceptual process by which objects are judged to be consistent in size, regardless of the actual dimensions of the image that they cast on the *retina* of the eye. An object viewed from a distance will produce a *retinal image* that is very different in size to the same object seen at close quarters, but the perceptual system adjusts its recognition of the object, such that in both cases the size is seen as being the same. In extreme conditions, size constancy may break down (e.g. when cars or people are viewed from the top of a skyscraper). See also *colour constancy*, *shape constancy*.

skewed distribution curve A version of the normal distribution curve which is not symmetrical, in that one side is extended further than another. For example, a curve plotted from measurements of simple reaction times will be skewed, because while there is a physiological limit to how quickly someone can react to the stimulus, there is no limit to how long they

can take. So a curve drawn from such measures will tend to 'lean' towards the left, but have a 'tail' that stretches out to the right. This is known as a *positive skew*. A curve that 'leans' in the other direction is referred to as negatively skewed (see Figure 51). See also *measures of central tendency*.

skill The performance of a task at a high level of competence. *Motor skills* (e.g. riding a bicycle) and cognitive skills (e.g. playing chess) have been studied separately, although many common skills (e.g. writing an exam essay) involve components of both. Skills improve through *feedback* and through deliberate use of strategies. Master chess players spend up to four hours each day analysing moves and working out the strategies by which they may have discovered the optimal move. So just doing a lot of handwriting or taking notes in lectures does not necessarily make you better at it.

skill acquisition The processes by which skills are learned or acquired. There have been several models of skill acquisition, but all of them include the idea that informed practice, with feedback, is absolutely necessary.

skill-based errors Errors that have come about because the individuals concerned did not have the expertise or training to deal with the situation.

skin conductance response (SCR) See *galvanic skin response*.

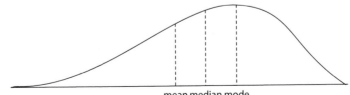

mean median mode

Figure 51 A normal distribution curve with a skewed distribution

Skinner box A device developed by B.F. Skinner for investigating *operant conditioning*. A typical Skinner box will contain a lever, a food delivery chute and a signal light. When a hungry small animal such as a laboratory rat is placed in the box, its exploratory behaviour eventually results in its pressing the lever, at which point a food pellet is delivered. This reinforces the lever-pressing action, rendering the animal more likely to repeat it. The process results in the learning of lever pressing as a means of obtaining food, although the experience of one of the authors suggests that this only happens if the animal feels inclined to cooperate, and is not inevitable. The preliminary phase of getting the animal to push the lever for the first time will be quicker if a *behaviour-shaping* procedure is employed. The signal light can be used as a *discriminatory stimulus*, and the Skinner box may be set to deliver *partial reinforcement* according to a *reinforcement schedule* (see Figure 52).

Skinner, Burrhus Frederick (1904–1990)

Skinner has been described as the most important American psychologist of the twentieth century. His work began with an investigation of the ways in which environments could produce regularities in behaviour, leading him to invent the *Skinner box* and the cumulative recorder. This led him to the principles of *operant conditioning*, which extended the work of *Pavlov* and *Watson* by accounting for the production of novel behaviour. Skinner's work was largely responsible for the widespread influence of *behaviourism* in American psychology throughout the twentieth century, and his later books such as *Verbal Behaviour*, *Walden Two* and *Beyond Freedom and Dignity* reflected his belief that all human experience could be explained in behaviourist terms. He worked at Harvard for most of his career, and received a tremendous number of awards in recognition of his contribution to psychology, including no less than 25 honorary doctorates.

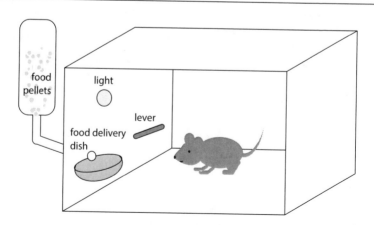

Figure 52 A Skinner box

sleep cycles Patterns of sleeping that involve changes in *EEG* recordings produced by a sleeper, and corresponding differences in how easy the person finds it to wake up. During a typical night, sleepers pass through the different levels of sleep in a cyclic fashion between five and seven times. Levels 1 and 2 are light sleep characterised by irregular EEG patterns; the deeper levels 3 and 4 show regular wave patterns in EEG recordings. Typically, the sleeper will cycle through the levels every 40 to 80 minutes, and then enter REM sleep for a period before starting a new cycle. During a period of normal sleep, deeper stages become shorter and then cease completely, while the REM stage becomes longer. See also *orthodox sleep, rapid eye movement sleep* (see Figure 53).

sleep spindles Distinctive patterns on EEG sleep records, which show short bursts of very rapid, high-amplitude activity contrasting with the less intensive and lower-amplitude pattern that is dominant most of the time. See also *sleep cycles*.

sleeper effect An experimental effect that is not apparent immediately but which may appear later. For example, an item might be stored in memory but not be accessible on testing soon after the acquisition. However, it may be recalled the next day.

slippery slope argument The argument, often made, that an innocent or innocuous first step will eventually lead to a much larger and undesirable outcome. See also *fallacy*.

SMA See *supplementary motor area*.

smoothing A process used in brain mapping studies in which the random acitvity of neurones is smoothed out by applying a normal distribution curve to probability of activity generated by each *voxel*.

SNARC effect This stands for 'spatial-numerical association of response codes', and has to do with the connection between motor and brain activity. Typically, people who are asked to make judgements about numbers such as whether they are odd or even tend to react faster with their left hand for small numbers, but faster with their right hand for larger ones. The effect is

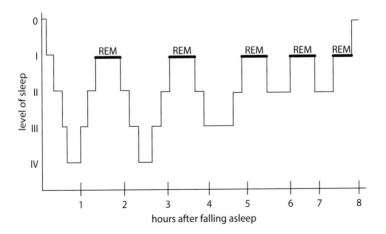

Figure 53 Sleep cycles

reduced if *transcranial magnetic stimulation* is applied to both lobes of the brain.

snowball sampling A method of obtaining research participants whereby a small group is selected, who in turn find other participants, who in their turn find others. In other words, a sampling technique that taps into pre-existing social networks in order to obtain a reasonable sample size. See also *random sampling, representative sample, sampling procedure*.

sociability The ability to engage in an appropriate range of social relationships and activities. The different forms that sociability takes at different ages and the means by which it develops is one of the major topics of *developmental psychology*.

social attribution A branch of *attribution theory* that attempts to integrate the social orientations of *European social psychology* with analysis of the nature of individual everyday explanation. Where more traditional versions of attribution theory, such as the *covariance* approach, have treated attribution as the product of individual cognitive processes, social attribution emphasises the social nature of many of the explanations adopted by people, and tends to focus more on intergroup similarities and differences than on individual problem-solving. See also *lay epistemology, social identity theory, social representations*.

social bonds These are social connections between individuals or between an individual and the group, which involve a sense of loyalty towards the individual or group, and often a sense of well-being or positive affect in its presence. See also *relationship, social identification*.

social class The classification of people according to their occupations and economic circumstances. Naturally, such a classification generates all kinds of problems, but the finding of widespread differences between different classes is consistent enough to motivate researchers to continue to categorise people in this way. It is important to recognise that social class in itself cannot be an explanation of anything, although it is often used as one. A problem in interpreting social class differences is that, since the different classes differ in almost every way possible (education, income, health, smoking, religious attitudes, etc.), it is not usually possible to say what is the cause of any particular difference. The most commonly used criterion for allocating social class in the UK is called the Registrar General's Classification, which consists of a list of occupations allocated into classes from 1 to 5. The term *socio-economic status* is sometimes used in an attempt to avoid the undesirable implications of 'class'.

social cognition

(i) The branch of social psychology concerned with people's understanding of what is going on in social interaction. This tends to be mainly concerned with identifying the different forms of social assumptions and social explanation. Social cognition therefore includes the study of *social schemata* and *scripts*, as well as *social representations* and *social attribution*.

(ii) In *developmental psychology*, an approach to cognitive development which states that social interaction is the most important factor in the development of the young child's cognition. Work in this field has produced some re-evaluation of the classic Piagetian findings concerning *conservation* and *egocentricity*, as it appears that the traditional responses obtained from children were more a product of the child's interpretation of the social demands of the experimental situation (saying what the experimenter wanted to hear, etc.) than with any inability to conserve or decentre on the part of the child. Work by Judy Dunn and others indicates that children show cognitive abilities within social interactions at much earlier ages than they can show them in the context of physical science, which was the basis of Piaget's investigations. Other studies have examined the influence of social expectation and *modelling* in cognitive development.

social comparison Social comparison is concerned with the way in which we automatically draw comparisons between different groups and individuals. It leads to a number of outcomes, including *social identification*, as people assess the relative status, power, etc. of their own group relative to others. Festinger also proposed that social comparison leads to a tendency towards shared beliefs, particularly with respect to social judgements. In the case of beliefs about the physical world, beliefs can be directly tested – we can observe directly that glass is fragile by breaking some. However, in the case of social beliefs (e.g. whether a socialist form of government leads to greater prosperity), we have no such access to direct factual information, and consequently will come to depend more on the views of others. Here, social comparison comes into play, as we will be more likely to accept the views of those we consider to be similar to ourselves than of those we see as different. See also *social representations*.

social constructionism The position taken by some social psychologists that social reality is constructed between people, rather than being an objective phenomenon of which there can only be one true description. More broadly, it is a position in the social sciences that meaning is socially constructed through interaction, especially through discourse. Therefore, it is more useful to study the social construction of meaning than to attempt to study the 'reality' that our meanings are about. See also *account analysis, constructivism, positivism, transaction, discourse analysis*.

social desirability scale A set of items hidden in *psychometric* tests or self-report questionnaires that detects whether the person taking the test is exaggerating their positive qualities in order to appear more socially acceptable.

social determinism The view that human behaviour and experience are caused by social and cultural forces. Therefore, culture and society should be studied as existing in their own right, and not just explained as the outcome of the actions of large numbers of individual people.

social exchange theory The idea that social functioning operates according to a basic rule that people should benefit from a social exchange to about the same extent as they have contributed to it. See also *equity theory*.

social exclusion A term, becoming popular with politicians, that refers to the effect of conditions that prevent people from benefiting from full participation in society. Poverty and disability are what people usually have in mind, and referring to social exclusion suggests that problems arise more from the ways in which society excludes these people than from lack of money, learning or mobility. See also *labelling*.

social facilitation The finding that performance is usually improved by the presence of others. Simple and well-rehearsed tasks are most likely to be facilitated, so if the presence of others is a source of arousal, the phenomenon follows the *Yerkes–Dodson law*. See also *coaction*.

social identification The process by which individuals identify themselves with the groups to which they belong, especially by searching for differences between their group and other groups.

social identity theory (SIT) The theory, developed particularly by Tajfel, which proposes that membership of social groups actually forms a highly significant part of the *self-concept*, rather than being some kind of external act or role. Social identity theory draws on two fundamental psychological mechanisms. The first of these is the cognitive mechanism of *categorisation*, whereby objects, events and people are classified into categories. The second is the tendency for people to seek sources of positive *self-esteem*. The outcome of these two processes is social identification, as the tendency to categorise also leads people to compare their social groups with others. If their group membership provides a source of positive self-esteem, the individual will come to identify with the group, and to incorporate group membership as part of their self-image. If such comparisons do not reflect positively on the self-concept, the individual will seek to leave the group (social mobility), to distance themselves from it, or to alter the perceived status of the group to which they belong (social change). Social identification may also lead to the emergence of shared beliefs, or *social representations*, within a given group.

Social identity theory is a core theory in the school of thought known as *European social psychology*. This school is particularly distinguished from the majority of social psychological theories by its emphasis on the realities of social life in terms of differences in social status, relative power and access to economic resources. Other theories of this school include social representation theory and some versions of *attribution theory*. See also *social comparison, minimal group paradigm*.

social impact theory An American social psychological theory proposed by Latané, in which the strength of social impact in phenomena such as conformity is perceived as increasing with the number, immediacy and strength of the sources. In other words, social impact or social pressure is higher if there are more people exerting it, if those people are closer to the individual rather than distant, and if they are important people rather than simply random strangers. The second aspect of the theory concerns diffusion of impact, proposing that the strength or influence of a source decreases with the number, immediacy and importance of the targets towards which it is directed.

Social impact theory has been hailed by some social psychologists as providing a higher-order model that can account for a number of diverse findings in social psychology. However, it has also been sharply criticised for its *reductionist* approach, in that it sees social influences simply as the product of the actions of individuals, and fails to take account of either the *emergent properties* of social groups, or the importance of social contexts. It therefore represents a direct contrast to the school of thought in social psychology known as *European social psychology*.

social influence The influence exerted on an individual by other people, social groups, social institutions, or internalised *social norms* or beliefs. See also *conformity*.

social intelligence The ability to understand complex social interactions and to respond appropriately in complex social situations.

social intelligence hypothesis The idea that the need for high levels of *social intelligence* produced the evolutionary pressure that resulted in the *evolution* of higher cognitive processes and other aspects of *intelligence* such as increased brain size.

social interaction A process in which two people or animals directly influence each other's behaviour. Social interaction is the core phenomenon of *social psychology*, and the complex regulation of forms of social interaction is an important part of the young child's *socialisation*.

social learning theory An approach to child development which states that children develop cognitively through learning from the other people around them. Social learning theory emphasises the processes by which children come to adopt the rules, norms and assumptions of their society (e.g. *operant conditioning*, *imitation* and *identification*). In general, social development is seen as a continuous learning process, rather than as happening in stages, and many theorists consider that it continues throughout adult life. See also *stage theories*, *modelling*.

social loafing The situation that occurs when a person in a group becomes less active, allowing the rest of the group to do the task. Social loafing is considered to be one of the factors involved in crowd behaviour, but contrasts with *deindividuation*.

social needs The third level in Maslow's *hierarchy of human needs* is concerned with group identity and membership, love, and positive interaction with others. According to Maslow, social needs become important once the basic *physiological needs* and *safety needs* have been satisfied. Once the social needs have been adequately met, *aesthetic* needs become important. At the top of the hierarchy is *self-actualisation*, which Maslow considers to be possible only once all the other levels of need are satisfied. Many psychologists criticise this model of human needs on the grounds that it does not account for many instances of human behaviour in which 'higher' needs are apparently put before basic ones, the classic example being the case of the 'starving poet'. There are also many examples of *prosocial behaviour* in the face of physical deprivation.

social neuroscience A growing field that links social behaviour to neurological processes within the brain. See also, for example, *mirror systems*.

social norms Forms of behaviour that are widespread within a society and/or are widely accepted as appropriate. Often it is the second condition that is more important. For example, there are probably more people in our society who abuse children than who work professionally for their welfare and protection. Yet concern for children, rather than abuse of them, is accepted as the norm. Acceptance of a person in a society is usually based on the extent to which that person follows, or at least expresses agreement with, social norms. See also *conventional norms*.

social psychology The branch of psychology that is particularly concerned with the nature and form of social interaction and how people come to influence each others' behaviour. As such, it includes the study of social phenomena, such as *conformity*, *obedience* and *non-verbal communication*, as well as aspects of social cognition such as social *perception*, *attitudes* and *attribution*. In recent years, a distinction has been developing between the problem-centred and individualistic (some say *reductionist*) approaches to the understanding of social phenomena seen as particularly typical of American social psychology, and the group-based, highly contextual form of social psychology that has become known as *European social psychology*.

social referencing In neuroscience, this is a term which refers to the way that a previously neutral stimulus may become associated with someone else's positive or negative emotional response, and as a result be either regarded positvely or avoided by another person.

social representations A concept developed and articulated by Moscovici (e.g. Moscovici, 1984), social representations are the shared beliefs adopted by groups of people and used to explain social experience. Social representations vary in scope from the large-scale ideological beliefs shared by a society in general, to smaller-scale beliefs adopted by members of a specific social group or subculture. However, despite their shared nature, social representations are dynamic, negotiated through social interaction and conversation, and modified or adapted as they become incorporated into the world knowledge of the individual. One of the major contributions to the group of theories known as *European social psychology*, social representations act as the cognitive interface between individual action and ideology, and have been studied in terms of several social movements, including changes in health and dietary beliefs over time. See also *lay epistemology*, *social attribution*.

social responsibility of science The principle that scientific research occurs within a social context and affects real people, and therefore should reflect ethical and responsible values and practices.

social role See *role*.

social schema A form of *schema* that is particularly concerned with social cognition and social interaction. As with other forms of schema, the social schema serves not just to assimilate and interpret experience, but also to direct action. A number of different types of social schema have been identified, among them *scripts*, role-schemata, which are particularly concerned with the social roles to be played in society, and person-schemata, which are concerned with structuring and applying knowledge about people. In view of the overwhelming evidence for the importance of social factors in the development of the self-concept, the self-schema has also been identified as a type of social schema.

social sciences A collective term for those academic disciplines that involve the study of human beings interacting with one another. As such, it includes *psychology*, *sociology*, *anthropology*, *linguistics*, economics, geography, etc.

social self The aspect of one's self that is shown to other people.

social skill learning The approach to social interaction that treats it as a learned skill. With this basis, socialisation is understood using *learning theories* and studies of *skill acquisition*. Social skills training has been used to help people with psychological problems (e.g. loneliness).

socialisation The process by which a child becomes integrated into society by adopting its *norms* and values, acquiring the necessary skills of *social interaction*, and learning to adopt acceptable *roles*.

sociobiology A *reductionist* approach to the study of social behaviour, in which the identification of a 'unit of natural selection' that could possibly form the basis for a social phenomenon is taken as an 'explanation' for the phenomenon. The 'unit of natural selection' is referred to as a 'gene', although it is not biologically equivalent to the *gene* as studied by geneticists. All behaviour is seen as being directed towards the perpetuation and replication of genes. Even *altruistic behaviour* is interpreted in terms of the perpetuation of the 'selfish gene', through the mechanism known as *kin selection*.

There are many weaknesses in the sociobiological approach, one of which is its retrospective approach to methodology, in which explanation involves three stages:

(i) the identification of some kind of 'universal' in behaviour;

(ii) the identification of a possible 'unit of natural selection' that could produce such behaviour; and

(iii) the development of a plausible account of how that behaviour could (or, more often, 'must') have evolved.

Other objections stem from the highly selective approach both to the 'universals' of behaviour – which usually emphasise only the more negative human traits – and those examples of animal behaviour taken as evidence, in which behavioural variations are largely ignored, and only cases that support the argument are acknowledged.

sociocognitive conflict A form of discontinuity or contradiction between the individual's personal awareness or cognitions, and their knowledge of what is accepted or acceptable in their society. The avoidance of sociocognitive conflict can be a significant *motivator* for people, acting in a similar way to *cognitive dissonance*.

socio-economic status An elaborate way of referring to *social class* while attempting to avoid the unwanted implications and problems of definition and distinctions involved in the concept of class.

sociolinguistics The study of social forms of language, and the ways in which language is used in society. Sociolinguistics inevitably shows considerable overlap with, and can make contributions to, *social psychology* (e.g. in the study of the social influence of accents and dialect and in the study of *elaborated* and *restricted codes* of language).

sociology The systematic study of societies and other social institutions, their effects on people, and how people operate within them. There is some overlap between sociology and *social psychology*.

sociometry An approach to attitude measurement that involves charting the links and affiliations in a particular group of people. Sociometric diagrams usually consist of circles representing the individuals, with arrows representing the direction of influence or affiliation between those people.

sociopathy A *personality disorder* marked by an inability to form lasting commitments or relationships, *egocentric* and impulsive thinking, and a disregard for social consequences. It has been noted that relatively high numbers of successful business people and politicians score strongly on *psychometric* measures of sociopathy, without it being regarded as a clinical problem. In clinical terms, it is now generally referred to as *antisocial personality disorder*.

solipsism The belief that only oneself and one's experience exists. It refers to a philosophical position taken in order to explore the question of what we can know, rather than to a psychological disturbance.

soma The cell body.

somatic To do with bodily structure or functioning.

somatic marker hypothesis The idea that states of the body (such as emotional states or moods) which have been associated with previous behaviours can be a significant factor in *decision-making*. Somatic markers are thought to form a link between the *cortical* memories of events or behaviour, and the emotional feelings registered in the *amygdala* and associated areas. It has been proposed that these somatic markers are stored in the *ventromedial frontal cortex*.

somatic nervous system The network of nerve fibres that carries messages from around the body to and from the *central nervous system*. 'Somatic' means 'of the body', and this nervous system consists mainly of *sensory* and *motor neurones* throughout the body, linked by the *spinal cord* and the *brain*. This allows

bodily sensations, movement and experience to be recognised in the central processing areas of the nervous system. See also *autonomic nervous system*.

somatic theory of emotion The idea that emotion arises as a result of bodily changes. See also *James–Lange theory*.

somatic therapies The treatment of psychological disturbance by using physical techniques that have a direct effect on the body (e.g. *chemotherapy*, ECT or *psychosurgery*).

somatosensation Sensory information about the state of the body. There are many different forms of somatosensation, which includes internal senses such as kinaesthesia and information about internal discomfort, as well as information about balance, proprioception, etc.

somatosensory projection area A strip running alongside the *central fissure*, in the *parietal lobe* of the *cerebral cortex*. A.k.a. the *sensory projection area*, this is particularly concerned with the sensation of touch. Different parts of the somatosensory area correspond to different areas of the body; those parts of the body that are more sensitive have a correspondingly greater amount of surface area on this strip of cortex.

somatotype An overall body shape, which has been thought by some researchers to provide an indication of personality. One of the most famous researchers in this area was Sheldon, who classified human bodies into three main groups: (i) ectomorphs, with a tall, slender physique; (ii) endomorphs, who were plump and rounded in shape; and (iii) mesomorphs, who were sturdy and muscular. Sheldon saw this as indicative of *personality*, considering that ectomorphs tended to be introverted and were often nervous and intellectual types, endomorphs tended to be friendly and relaxed people, and mesomorphs tended to be noisy, hearty and often callous in their interpersonal interactions. Although Sheldon's studies involved an impressive sample size, they were methodologically flawed, and took little account of experimenter bias (see *experimenter effects*) or *self-fulfilling prophecies* (see Figure 54).

spaced practice See *distributed practice*.

spastic Affected by muscular spasms. The term used to refer to people suffering from *cerebral palsy*, but as it then entered the common language as a derogatory label for clumsiness, it is now rarely used within psychology.

spatial intelligence The ability to recognise and manipulate shapes, patterns, areas or locations. See also *multiple intelligences*.

spatial resolution How accurately it is possible to measure the exact location of something, or how close it is to something else. See also *temporal resolution*.

Spearman's rank–order correlation coefficient A measure of *correlation* that can be applied to *ordinal data* and which is usually used for small *samples*. In the event of it being used for a large sample (e.g. over 60 pairs of scores), the final coefficient obtained from the test is considered to be equivalent to a *Pearson's product–moment correlation coefficient*. See also *scattergram*.

special child A term adopted to refer to all children whose qualities or abilities are well outside the normal range. It represents an attempt to avoid the automatically negative implications of terms such as 'mentally handicapped' and 'retarded', and to make an association between children who need special resources because of some disadvantage

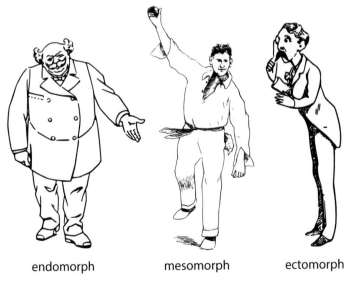

endomorph   mesomorph   ectomorph

Figure 54 Somatotypes

and those who need special attention because they are exceptionally gifted in some way. More recently, the expression 'children with special needs' has been adopted to reduce the possibility of *labelling*.

special learning difficulties See *mental handicap*.

species-specific behaviour Behaviour that occurs in all members of a given species and which does not appear to take place in animals of other, even closely related species. One obvious example is language in humans. Whether or not one believes that other primates can be taught a language, the fact remains that only humans develop this complex means of communication spontaneously, and it occurs in all human societies, so making it a species-specific behaviour. There are many other examples of species-specific behaviour. Courtship rituals in different species have been extensively studied, and it is thought that the development of elaborate mating patterns serves to prevent inappropriate cross-mating between members of similar species. It is usually assumed that if a behaviour is species-specific, it is likely to have an *innate* component.

specific hunger Hunger that is directed towards a specific food or kind of food (e.g. a hunger for sweet foods or for salt). Specific hungers are often experienced during pregnancy, and may serve the function of supplying specific nutritional needs.

spectrogram A graph that plots the frequency of sound against time, so an intense sound will make a taller, dark image, while a faint one will make a small, low image (see Figure 55).

Figure 55 A sound spectrogram

speech acts Segments of speech that are intended to bring about some effect. The focusing of attention on to speech acts is one attempt to narrow down the study of *language* to more specific areas so that it becomes more manageable, and also to draw attention to the way that people use language to achieve particular ends.

speech register A mode of language use that is tailored to the social context in which it is used, and which involves different styles of grammar and often a different vocabulary. Speech registers range from the formal, used in highly structured social situations such as an official address or a lecture, to the intimate, used only between those with very close relationships and comprising a number of shared assumptions and a high level of implicit meaning. Conversations with friends, using an affiliative speech register, will involve different kinds of language use from the consultative register involved in, for example, asking a stranger for directions. See also *accent*, *dialect*, *psycholinguistics*.

speech therapy The profession that helps people who have some kind of problem with *verbal communication*. Speech therapists use many techniques from psychology, particularly behavioural methods, and are increasingly paying attention to social factors in the disruption of communication.

speed-accuracy trade-off The relationship between the time taken to perform a given task, and the accuracy with which it is completed. The speed-accuracy trade-off is a *negative correlation*, since accuracy tends to decrease as speed increases. It is therefore also sometimes formulated as a deliberate option in strategic *decision-making*.

spillover effect In reading, rare words are looked at for longer than common words. An increased length of visual fixation appplies to the word immediately following it as well, which is the spillover effect.

spinal cord The bundle of nerve fibres that runs up the channel within the spinal cord. The spinal cord forms a pathway between the *somatic nervous system* and the brain, mediates some basic functions such as pain reflexes and, in the higher segments, some of the functioning of the *autonomic nervous system*. In cross-section, the spinal cord can be shown to consist of an outer layer of *white matter*, with an inner part of *grey matter*, and a small central canal at the core, which contains *cerebrospinal fluid*. As the spinal cord is the medium through which the brain transmits information to the body, lesions of the spinal cord can result in paralysis, the extent of the paralysis depending on how far up the spinal cord the lesion occurs: lesions closer to the brain producing a more total paralysis (see Figure 56).

spinoreticular pathway A pathway of nerve fibres passing from the spinal cord through the *reticular formation* and into the *thalamus*. It is particularly involved in *nociception*.

split-brain studies Studies of people in whom the corpus callosum and the optic chiasma are severed. Originally resulting from an operation on humans as an attempt to control severe epilepsy, the condition was found to permit the study of the independent functioning of the two *cerebral hemispheres*. This work extended knowledge of localisation of function in the brain (e.g. the finding that logical/mathematical functioning is mainly localised in the left hemisphere, while artistic abilities and spatial awareness are more highly developed in the right hemisphere). It also led to the discovery that the two halves of the brain could operate virtually

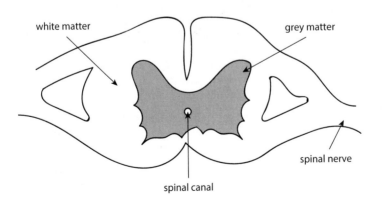

Figure 56 Cross-section of the spinal cord

independently as decision-making and intelligent structures.

split-half reliability A technique for assessing the *reliability* of a *psychometric* test by calculating a score from first one half of the items and then the other half, in order to see whether the two scores agree.

split-personality See *multiple personality*. Do **not** see *schizophrenia*!

split-span tests Tests first developed by Broadbent to study *selective attention*, in which a succession of digits is presented to an individual through headphones with two different digits presented simultaneously, one to each ear. Broadbent observed that, when asked to repeat the digits they had heard, research participants did not mix digits from different ears, but instead reported a succession from one ear only or from each ear in turn, thus implying a 'filtering' approach to attention. See also *sustained attention, filer models*.

spontaneous recovery The sudden reappearance of a *habituated* or a learned response after it has undergone *extinction* due to lack of reinforcement. Spontaneous recovery occurs during a period in which the eliciting stimulus is not presented, and has been demonstrated in both *operant* and *classical conditioning*. If the spontaneous response is reinforced, it can lead to the reappearance of the learned behaviour at full strength, very quickly.

spontaneous remission When an illness or disorder disappears and appears to have been 'cured' without any particular medical treatment or therapy.

spoonerism An error of speech that involves swapping the initial consonants of words – as in the classic phrase 'fighting a liar' as opposed to 'lighting a fire'.

spreading activation theory The idea that activating a set of neurones which correspond to a particular concept or word in the brain will cause neural activation to spread to other, related words or concepts. While a popular idea in *cognitive psychology*, it depends on a one-to-one correlation between neurones and concepts that has yet to be demonstrated.

SPSS A computer calcuation package comonly used in *quantitative research*, capable of undertaking complex statistical analysis with very large samples.

SQUID A device used to detect changes in the tiny magnetic fields generated by electrical activity from *neurones* in the brain. The acronym stands for 'superconducting quantum interference device'.

SSRIs See *selective serotonin reuptake inhibitors*.

stabilised retinal image The finding that *rod* and *cone cells* in the *retina* habituate quickly if they are exposed to a stable image. This does not normally occur because of *saccades*, but has been achieved experimentally by the use of small projectors and screens attached to contact lenses. The effect of maintaining the image of an object at a fixed position on the retina is that the person ceases to be able to see it (see Figure 57).

stable attributions *Attributions* in which the cause that has been identified is of a kind that will apply again in similar situations in the future. For example, believing that you have failed a summer exam because of your hayfever is a stable attribution, in that you are likely also to have hayfever for future summer exams.

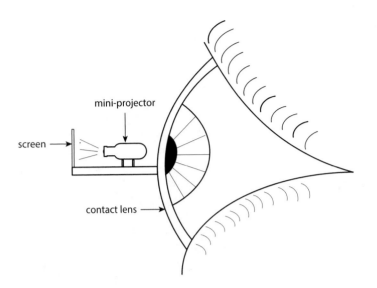

Figure 57 Creating stabilised retinal images

stage theories Many theories in developmental psychology are based on the concept of development from stage to stage. Major examples are Freud's *psychosexual stages*, Gesell's *maturational* stages, Piaget's cognitive stages, Erikson's psychosocial stages and Kohlberg's stages of *moral development*. In all cases, it is assumed that each stage must be completed more or less successfully before the next stage can be adequately tackled. This means that stages will occur in a fixed order, since later stages depend on earlier ones. The theories differ in whether they see the transition from one stage to the next as gradual or abrupt, and in what happens to the earlier stages. Some, such as Kohlberg's, assume the earlier stage becomes irrelevant and is abandoned once a new stage is reached. Freud sees the earlier stage as something to be relinquished if possible, but likely to continue to exert an influence. Piaget, Erikson and Gesell see earlier stages as built on and incorporated into later functioning, but no longer used in their original form. Another developmental stage theorist, Heinz Werner, saw earlier stages as more primitive modes of functioning that may still have their uses in certain circumstances, and which can still be used when the occasion arises – a rather more positive view of the process that Freud identified as *regression*. Broadly speaking, stage theories imply *qualitative differences* in functioning at different ages, and can be contrasted with behavioural approaches such as *social learning theory*, which assume that the same processes apply throughout the lifespan.

standard deviation (sd) A statistical *measure of dispersion* in a normally distributed population. Calculation of the standard deviation is a basic step in *parametric statistics*. Simply knowing that two scores are 5 points apart tells you nothing unless you know how widely the scores in the population are dispersed. If the sd is 1, then a difference of 5 points indicates a wide divergence on what is being measured. If the sd is 100, 5 points represents no real difference at all. The sd is the square root of the *variance* (see Figure 58). See also *z-score*.

standard error A measure of *variance*, which expresses the *standard deviation* of a particular sample or set of samples.

standard scores Scores that have been converted to a standard form in relation to the *standard deviation*. The conversion used most often is to *z-scores*, and these are sometimes referred to as standard scores.

standardisation Establishing a set of *standardised procedures* for a test, with the aim of ensuring that results are comparable when obtained in different settings. The term can refer either to procedures for administering the test, or to data that indicate the expected range of scores in specified populations (*norms*).

standardised instructions A predetermined set of instructions that is given in the same manner and using the same words to each subject taking part in a given experimental procedure. The use of standardised instructions is intended to provide a control against *experimenter*

effects in research or testing, but is of dubious value when dealing with human beings.

standardised procedures A set of experimental procedures, or a sequence of events, which has been established in advance such that it will be carried out in the same way for each subject. This is one way of controlling unconscious *experimenter effects* that could influence the results of a study.

standardised responses Preestablished and regularly patterned ways of responding to questions or situations. Often used in questionnaires, they present problems in that they often present an unrealistic picture of what people actually do. See also *questionnaire fallacy*.

Stanford–Binet test The most extensively used *intelligence test*, developed at Stanford University in 1916, using Binet's test as a starting point. The test has been revised several times, but has a major limitation in only giving a single *IQ* score. Later tests such as the *Wechsler Adult Intelligence Scale* and the *British Abilities Scale* provide independent measures of various aspects of intelligence.

startle response A pattern of rapid reactions to a sudden and unexpected

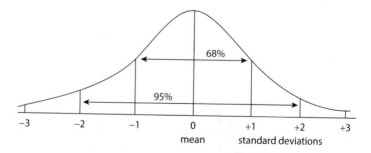

Figure 58 Standard deviations from the mean

stimulus. It can vary from whole body flexion, particularly in infants, to a brief reflex action of the eye muscles. In infants, it is similar to the *Moro reflex*, but not quite identical.

startle-eyeblink measure A measure obtained by placing electrodes under the eye, which can detect the tightening of the eye muscles of an eyeblink, as a *startle response*. The eyeblink becomes more frequent in response to threat or fear, and can also be elicited by sudden stimuli that startle the individual.

startle probe A stimulus designed to elicit a *startle response*, so that the researcher can observe consequent changes in behaviour or neural activity.

state A term with many meanings, but in psychological contexts usually used to describe a temporary condition influenced by the immediate environment, and contrasted with an ongoing *personality trait*. For example, state *anxiety* might reflect anxiety brought about by, say, a testing situation, while trait anxiety would reflect a more general and ongoing tendency towards anxious behaviour. Other states might include hunger, sexual desire or expectation. See also *emotion*.

state-dependent learning Learning that is recalled most effectively when the individual is in the same physiological state as when the information was originally learned. For instance, information learned when someone is under the influence of alcohol is often most readily recalled at times when the person is again under the influence. State-dependent learning has been similarly demonstrated with a range of drugs, including *amphetamines* and *tranquillisers*.

statistic A measure of some aspect of a sample. Measures of a population are called *parameters*.

statistical significance A statement of how likely it is that the outcome of a study or comparison has simply occurred through chance factors. Statistical significance is usually expressed in terms of a ratio of '*p*' (e.g. '*p* is less than [or equal to] .05' or '*p* is less than [or equal to] .01'). In such expressions, '*p*' stands for the probability that the *null hypothesis* is correct (i.e. the probability that the results have simply occurred through sampling error). Before a study is conducted, the level of significance considered to be acceptable to the researcher will have been decided; $p < .05$ means that there is only a 5 per cent chance (or less) of the null hypothesis being correct, and this may be acceptable to the researcher. Alternatively, in a study with important social or ethical implications, such as the testing of a new drug, a far more stringent level of significance might be required, such as $p < .0001$, and this too will have been decided in advance. Given the highly variable nature of the subject matter in psychology, the concept of statistical significance is at the core of most psychological research. See also *Type I error*.

statistical test A mathematical procedure designed to identify whether it is likely that a particular set of results has occurred purely by chance. There are many different statistical tests, each of which is appropriate for different conditions and types of data. Selecting the appropriate test for the research is rather important because using the wrong test can give completely invalid results. See also *statistical significance*, *t-test*, *Type I error*, *Type II error*.

statistics Mathematical techniques designed to summarise raw data and indicate the conclusions that can be drawn. Statistical techniques are largely concerned with either summarising information (*descriptive statistics*) or determining whether a given result could easily have been obtained by chance (*inferential statistics*). See also *hypothetico-deductive method*, *non-parametric statistics*, *parametric statistics*.

status The perceived measure of social worth or measure of an individual's standing in a social group. See also *face*, *power*.

status quo bias Not a preference for heavy rock bands, but a general preference for keeping things the way they are rather than acting to change them. It is a common heuristic in *decision-making*, but frequently encountered in other walks of life as well.

stem cell A non-differentiated cell that has the capacity to develop into a variety of specialised cells depending on its chemical and neurological environment. Stem cells are plentiful in embryos and *neonates*, producing physical development, and in adults can be found in blood marrow and some other areas of the body. One of the most exciting developments in modern physiology, stem cell therapy offers the potential for self-repair of damaged organs and regeneration of nerve tissue. See also *neuroblast*.

stereopsis Another term for binocular disparity: the small differences between the *retinal images* received by the two eyes, which is a significant cue in *depth perception*.

stereoscope A device much used by early investigators of perception, which allows a researcher to present two different pictures to a research participant simultaneously, one to each eye.

stereoscopic vision Vision that provides a direct perception of depth or of a three-dimensional image. It is achieved by integrating information received through two eyes simultaneously. The cortex integrates the information from equivalent parts of the *retina*, which will be receiving slightly different patterns from the same source because of the distance between the eyes, and uses those differences to construct stereoscopic vision. This can only occur in animals with frontally mounted eyes, such as humans and other primates, cats, owls, etc., and cannot take place in animals such as rabbits or blackbirds, which have eyes at the side of the head. Stereoscopic vision is particularly useful for the accurate judging of distance, through the process of *binocular disparity*, and it is thought that this may provide an evolutionary explanation for its development in the largely arboreal (tree-living) primate group.

stereotactic normalisation The first step in the process of dealing with individual differences in brain functioning by averaging them out to produce a common map of functioning. This first step involves mapping each individual brain (which will vary in size and proportions) on to a standard reference brain. This is followed by a smoothing process, in which the individual differences in results from all of the different brains are averaged out, by redistributing brain activity from neighbouring *voxels* so they emphasise the main activity and minimise other, irrelevant neural activation. See also *stereotaxis*, *Talairach coordinates*.

stereotaxis A techique for identifying precise locations within the brain. It uses an external 3D frame of reference based on three orthogonal coordinates, generally labelled x, y and z.

stereotype A belief about a class of people that is then applied to individual members of the class to express expectations about the person. Stereotypes enable us to begin interaction with strangers with an expectation of better than chance success in choosing an appropriate style and topic of conversation. Stereotypes can therefore be seen as highly functional in a setting that involves frequent interactions with people of whom one has limited knowledge. The view of stereotypes as undesirable arises from assuming either that they will be inaccurate or that they will persist despite contrary information. Neither assumption is necessarily true. If a stereotype is inaccurate, negative and adhered to despite contrary information, it qualifies to be called a *prejudice*.

Sternberg, Robert (1949–)

Robert Sternberg presented a major critique of *IQ tests* and measures of intelligence, arguing that the practical and creative aspects of intelligence were just as important as the relatively limited number of abilities tested by conventional IQ tests, and proposing a *triarchic theory of intelligence* as an alternative. Sternberg also conducted research into loving and cognitive styles, and had a productive career as an American educational psychologist, academic and consultant.

---

steroid hormones Hormones that are able to get inside a cell and bind to DNA structures. In this way, they influence the creation of new proteins inside the body.

stigma A mark or identifier that singles out a person for social shame, and is therefore likely to be a source of embarrassment.

stimulants Drugs that produce heightened activity of the *central nervous system*, often used to combat fatigue or tedium. The most commonly used stimulant is probably caffeine, which is consumed daily in the form of tea, coffee or cola by many people worldwide. In medical use, *amphetamines* are one of the most common groups of stimulants, and are also used as *recreational drugs* for the same purpose, as is *cocaine*. One of the more common uses of amphetamines is as an appetite suppressant, and many other stimulants appear to have similar properties, although to a lesser degree.

stimulus Any event to which an organism – human, animal or plant – responds. 'Stimulus' is a general term that avoids specifying the form in which stimulation is presented. Essentially, it refers to anything that is detected by the sensory equipment possessed by the organism.

stimulus deprivation An experimental condition in which sensory input is reduced to a minimum. Early studies found that the condition produced extreme cognitive disturbances, but later replications found much weaker consequences.

stimulus discrimination The form of discrimination shown in *stimulus–response* *learning*, in which a response will occur to one specific stimulus, but will not occur in the presence of similar ones. Unlike *stimulus generalisation*, which occurs without prior training, stimulus discrimination is learned by the organism through *reinforcement*. Responses made in the presence of one stimulus are reinforced, while those made to the other are not. In this way, the organism comes to discriminate between the two.

stimulus generalisation The phenomenon that occurs when a learned response is produced to a stimulus different from the one to which it was originally learned. Stimulus generalisation often shows a *generalisation gradient* whereby the response is strongest to those stimuli that are most similar to the original.

stimulus–response learning Learning that occurs as a result of the association between a stimulus and some kind of behavioural response. In general, there are thought to be two basic forms of stimulus–response learning – *classical conditioning* and *operant conditioning*. Some psychologists classify *one-trial learning*, in which such an association is formed as a result of only one learning trial or experience, as a third form, while others regard it as a special form of classical conditioning.

STM See *short-term memory*.

storm and stress A model of adolescence which holds that hormonal disturbances coupled with a battle for increasing independence make it almost inevitable that the adolescent's relationship with its parents at this time will be characterised by temper tantrums and rebellion. However, this is only one model of adolescence, and in many cases adolescents experience a much more peaceful passage into adulthood.

strange situation technique A standardised method developed by Mary Ainsworth to study attachments in 1-year-old children. The child is brought into an unfamiliar environment by its mother, then a stranger enters and the mother leaves. Finally, the mother returns. The reactions of the child are recorded in a standard way, and the quality of the attachment is judged. Ainsworth classified attachments as either secure (Type B), anxious (Type A) or ambivalent (Type C). This technique has made it possible to study the consequences of these different forms of attachment.

stratified sampling A technique of collecting a *sample* that is designed to make the sample represent, as accurately as possible, the *population* from which it was recruited. The major groupings (e.g. social class) in the population are identified, and the sample is recruited from each of these groupings, so that each can be analysed separately if necessary. See also *opportunity sampling*, *quota sampling*, *random sampling*.

straw man fallacy Appearing to challenge or discredit an idea by misrepresenting it, and then refuting the misrepresentation.

stress Usually, the effect on a person of being subjected to noxious stimulation, or the threat of such stimulation, particularly when they are unable to avoid or terminate the condition. Major changes in one's life (*life events*) have been found to be a common source of stress that leave people vulnerable to *depression*. Hans Selye found similar physiological and psychological reactions to prolonged stress, regardless of the nature of the source (see *general adaptation syndrome*). While stress is unpleasant and often damaging, it is also recognised that it may be actively sought (as when apparently sane people jump out of aeroplanes for fun), and is an important source of motivation. The term is also sometimes used for the source of the stress (noise, poor housing, etc.), but it would be better if such conditions were always called 'stressors'.

stressor Something that causes *stress*.

striate cortex See *visual cortex*.

striatum The part where the *brainstem* joins the bottom of the *cerebral hemispheres*, forming part of the *basal ganglia*.

stroboscopic motion The phenomenon that forms the basis of film projection, whereby a series of separate pictures shown in rapid succession will seem to produce a continuous movement. Stroboscopic motion can also be demonstrated using lights that flicker on and off, as in the *phi phenomenon*, and takes its name from the brief appearance of each image, in the same way that a stroboscope (a light which flashes rapidly on and off) produces a succession of 'flash pictures'.

stroke A disabling problem arising from the disruption to the blood supply of the brain, caused by bleeding or the blocking of a blood vessel. A common mnemonic to inform people about what to do (and to do it quickly) if they think someone is having a stroke is the word FAST, which stands for:

- Face weakness. Is one side of the person's face drooping? Can they smile properly?

- Arm weakness. Can the person raise both of their arms, and keep them raised for 10 seconds or more?
- Speech problems. Can they speak clearly, or has their speech become slurred?
- Time. If the person has any of these three symptoms, you should call medical help immediately, so normal blood supply can be restored as quickly as possible.

See also *aneurism*.

Stroop effect A reliable experimental effect that demonstrates how powerful routine cognitive processing can be. The Stroop effect is normally demonstrated using colour names. Two sets of different colour names (orange, red, blue, etc.) are written on cards. One set is written in the appropriate colour for the word, while the other set is written in a different colour (e.g. 'orange' written in green ink). On being asked to identify the colours in each list, research participants take longer to process the information on the cards that contain the discrepant information. Reading the colour name occurs as an automatic cognitive subroutine, which interferes with the recognition of the colour itself. See also *problem-solving, go/no-go test*.

structuralism An approach to theory in which psychological phenomena are explained as the natural outcome of the way in which the organism is structured. The proposed structures may be physical and open to direct examination (e.g. accounts of aggression based on interpreting brain structure) or hypothetical. Examples of the latter are Freud's personality structure and Piaget's cognitive structures. Structuralist approaches in anthropology and sociology are concerned with the social structures within which people function, although these are often taken to be outward manifestations of mental structures. The term is also applied to attempts to understand how language works by examining its structure. Structural theories are contrasted with *functional* approaches.

structured observation A form of observing in which the behaviour that is to be observed has been carefully precoded, and the observation takes the form of recording when and how often these precoded behaviours occur.

STS See *superior temporal sulcus*.

study skills The set of techniques, strategies and behaviour patterns that form a structured approach to learning, often based on psychological theory, but also on experiences acquired and transmitted less formally. Study skills can be related to the theoretical area of *metacognition*, but are usually treated as a separate topic in their own right. They include such features of effective study as reading skills, effective revision techniques, organising study time, and examination strategies. See also *mnemonic*.

subconscious Material of which the person is not consciously aware but which could be made conscious if required. The term has the same meaning as *preconscious*, but is not so strictly tied to Freudian theory.

subcortical structures Those parts of the brain that are found below the *cerebrum* – in other words, all the parts of the brain except for the *cerebral hemispheres* (see Figure 59).

subgoals Goals that allow the person to progress some way towards an ultimate goal, but are easier to reach. See also *superordinate goals*.

subjective Personal and liable to be open to bias because of personal ideas or experience.

sublimation In Freudian theory, the redirection of instinctual energies towards more socially acceptable goals. During development, direct expression of psychosexual drives is prohibited and the energies are diverted into substitute activities that are more acceptable. In this way, society's restrictions on the direct gratification of instinctual needs result in energy being made available for

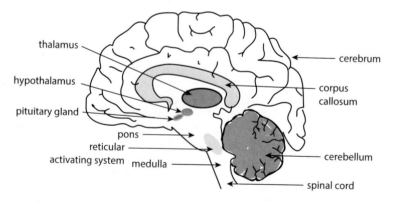

thalamus
hypothalamus
pituitary gland
pons
reticular
activating system   medulla
cerebrum
corpus callosum
cerebellum
spinal cord

Figure 59 Subcortical structures

purposes that are valued by society. A more general term is *displacement*.

subliminal perception Perception which occurs in such a way that the person is unconscious of it. Several studies have demonstrated that information may be absorbed by the perceptual system extremely rapidly, and in such a way that it does not penetrate to consciousness, but may nonetheless influence people at an unconscious level. Studies that involved presenting threatening or offensive stimuli subliminally have demonstrated marked alteration in the person's *arousal* level as a consequence. Subliminal advertising is prohibited in the UK by the Broadcasting Act, but is permitted in private locations such as supermarkets, provided that a notice is displayed informing the public that this is occurring. In such cases, it normally takes the form of faint auditory messages embedded in music.

subscales Measuring scales that form smaller parts of more general measuring scales. For example, a general measure of verbal *intelligence* might actually consist of a number of subscales, each testing a different aspect of people's abilities to use words (e.g. a comprehension test, a vocabulary test, a sentence completion test, etc.).

subset A group or set, usually of data, which forms a distinctive or identifiable part of a larger set.

subtising The capacity to identify immediately, and without counting, an exact quantity of objects.

subvocal speech Using features of speech without producing speech sounds. The term is often used about movements of the vocal apparatus while reading or talking to oneself. It was of interest to early behaviourists who wanted to study thinking but believed it was only possible to study observable behaviours. They therefore suggested that thinking is really invisible subvocal speech. However, studies involving *curare* showed that this idea, although convenient, was not in fact true.

successive approximation See *behaviour shaping*.

sudden infant death syndrome (SIDS) Also called *cot death* or *crib death*. Babies appear to go through a vulnerable period at around 2 to 4 months of age, and during this time a significant number are found dead in their cots, having shown little or no sign of illness or any other warning signal. Some research suggests that it may be associated with a failure to learn how to restart breathing early in life following *apnoea*, but most research has concentrated on possible medical causes. Cot deaths are of major concern to psychologists because they are relatively common and an extremely distressing form of *bereavement*.

sulci The plural of *sulcus*.

sulcus A groove or fissure in the *cerebral cortex*.

sum of squares A calculation used in *analysis of variance*. It is obtained by calculating how much each score differs from the mean, squaring each difference, and adding them up.

summation The cumulative effect of several neurones transmitting information to one neurone at the same time. If a single *synaptic transmission* is received, from one other neurone only, it is unlikely to be enough to produce a response in the next cell. However, the total effect brought about by several *receptor sites* receiving the *neurotransmitter* at the same time will produce the effect. See also *synapse*.

sunk-cost effect A common *decision-making* trap in which people continue to invest additional resources to justify a previous commitment that has so far not been achieved ('We've put too much in to give up now'). See also *entrapment*.

superego In Freudian theory, the third component of personality, which forms after the *id* and *ego* have become established. The superego is formed in early childhood by internalising the parents' system of rewards and punishments, so that the child comes to operate according to these rules even when the parents are not present. It is not quite the same thing as the conscience, as it retains an infantile version of the parents' rules, which is likely to be severe and intolerant. The adult conscience is more realistic and sophisticated, and so may come into conflict with the superego. See also *psychoanalysis*.

superior Towards the top, or above. See also *inferior, posterior, anterior*.

superior colliculi A group of cells in the *midbrain* that form part of the *visual system* by playing a significant role in processing incoming visual information.

superior olivary nuclei Nuclei in the *medulla* that are involved in auditory perception.

superior temporal sulcus (STS) An area of the *temporal lobes* that responds to the changeable aspects of a face – important for identifying cues in social interaction, but less so for *face recognition*. See also *fusiform face area*.

superordinate goals Overarching goals that shape and give general structure to more immediate goals. For example, someone might have a general goal of becoming a professional athlete. This would involve several *subgoals* such as winning competitions. But they might also have a superordinate goal of ultimately becoming an Olympic champion, which would influence how they approached competing and training.

superposition One of the *monocular depth cues* in which an object that obscures another is perceived to be nearer to the viewer. Sometimes incorrectly written as superimposition, which is a tautology.

superstitious learning An *operant conditioning* process in which the occurrence of a cue at the same time as a reinforcer gives that cue control of the operant behaviour. If you notice that a particular person is nearby every time you win on a slot machine, the presence of that person may make it more likely that you will play. It is a form of *autoshaping*, but is so named because it usually refers to situations where the *association* is accidental, so the conditioning produces an arbitrary or superstitious connection. See also *one-trial learning*.

supplementary motor area (SMA) Another name for the *medial premotor cortex*.

surface dysgraphia A condition that results from brain damage, and results in poor spelling of irregular words, but with reasonable spelling of regular words and often the ability to spell non-words 'correctly'.

surface dyslexia *Dyslexia* in which the problems are only with the forms of the words themselves, and the person has no difficulties with their meaning. See also *deep dyslexia*.

surface structure The term coined by Chomsky to refer to the pattern of grammar and sentence structure that is found in a particular language, and which distinguishes it from other languages. The term is used in contrast with *deep structure*, which, Chomsky argues, is common to all languages and which forms the fundamental set of principles inherited by the young child, which it uses to decode the surface structure of the language that it hears around it from birth. The process of *transformational grammar* was developed as a method of identifying the deep structure components of specific phrases or sentences in a particular language.

survey A technique of investigation that involves collecting information, attitudes or opinions from large numbers of people, usually by the use of careful *sampling* procedures. Although a survey rarely allows for in-depth investigation of a topic, it can be extremely valuable for investigating general patterns of human behaviour, such as surveys of sleeping habits or attitudes.

sustained attention Also referred to as vigilance in many accounts, this refers to an extended period of concentration on a relatively simple task. Studies of sustained attention became important during the Second World War, with the development of complex defence technology, since errors brought on by fatigue or distraction could have serious effects, especially in the case of radar surveillance. Overall, studies of sustained attention have tended to take the form of *signal-detection tasks*. Performance on these has been shown to be positively affected by such variables as the presence of others, a limited

amount of extraneous noise, a high degree of *introversion* in the individual concerned, etc. One theoretical explanation which has been suggested is that all of these factors relate to the degree of *arousal* experienced by people as they are carrying out the task. See also *selective attention*.

switch cost The additional time taken for a cognitive task which involves rejecting a previous schema and adoping a new one.

syllogism A type of problem that involves two statements or premises, and a conclusion. This type of problem is often used in studies of deductive reasoning, where the conclusion may or may not follow logically from the premises.

symbol grounding problem The problem of defining exactly what a concept is (i.e. what a symbol represents) without actually referring to that concept.

symbolic interactionism A way of understanding social behaviour by describing it in terms of social *roles* and *role behaviour*. The use of symbolic interactionism allows researchers to distance themselves from the individual people concerned, and to look at what is happening in terms of social expectations and assumptions.

symbolic representation The third of the *modes of representation* described by Bruner, in which information is stored as symbols, such as numbers, words or signs. Bruner argued that this mode of representation enables the child to organise and categorise information, and to perceive relationships which might not otherwise have been readily identifiable. As such, he regards

the development of symbolic representation, especially through the use
of language, as being of paramount
importance in cognitive development.
See also *enactive representation, iconic
representation*.

sympathetic division One of the two
divisions of the *autonomic nervous system*, the sympathetic division is the set
of nerve fibres that, when stimulated,
increase *arousal* and may trigger off the
fight or flight response, producing a rapid
burst of energy and preparing the body
for action. The operation of the sympathetic division is accompanied by
the release of *adrenaline* into the bloodstream, which serves to maintain the
activated state of the body over a longer
period of time. See also *stress, anxiety*.

sympathy A feeling of compassion
for another person, brought about by
awareness of their negative circumstance or situation.

synaesthesia A condition in which
information from different sensory

modes becomes confused, so sounds
may be perceived as tastes, or touch as
sound. While pure synaesthesia is relatively rare, synaesthetic *imagery* appears
to be a reasonably frequent form of
memory *coding*.

synapse The term given to a junction
point between two *neurones*, by means
of which information is transmitted
from one neurone to the next. Synapses
may be *inhibitory* or *excitatory* (i.e. they
may render the next neurone more or
less likely to fire). Normally, stimulation
from several synapses (summation) will
be required for the full effect on the next
neurone to be achieved (see Figure 60).

synaptic button See *synaptic knob*.

synaptic cleft The small gap between a
synaptic knob and the *receptor site* on the
adjacent neurone.

synaptic knob A swelling at the end
of the *dendrite*, which contains small
pockets known as *synaptic vesicles*.
Each vesicle contains a small amount

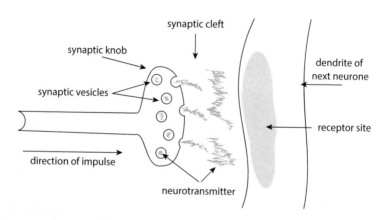

Figure 60 The synapse

of a particular *neurotransmitter*, which is released into the *synaptic cleft* when stimulated by an electrical impulse passing along the dendrite.

synaptic transmission The transmission of information from one *neurone* to another by means of electrochemical processes. When the neural impulse reaches the *dendrites* of a given neurone, vesicles in the synaptic knob release a *neurotransmitter* into the gap between it and the dendrite of the opposing neurone. Part of the dendrite is specialised to form a *receptor site*, which will pick up only that neurotransmitter or chemicals with a similar structure. The absorption of the neurotransmitter produces chemical changes in the cell, rendering it either more likely or less likely to fire. Should enough *synapses* be stimulated in this way, the next neurone will either fire, or have a raised *threshold of response* such that it will not fire easily.

synaptic vesicle The small reservoirs found on the synaptic button, which contain the neurotransmitter chemical. See also *synapse*.

synaptogenesis The process by which the *axons* and *dendrites* of nerve cells grow and form new *synapses*. It is aided by a protein known as NGF, or *nerve growth factor*.

synchronicity A concept developed by Jung, in which he argued that certain events and ideas possess a resonance with deeper, more meaningful layers of experience than most, and so have far greater psychological or even psychic implications than ordinary events or ideas.

syndrome A set of symptoms or physiological events that tend to occur together, forming a functional group.

syntactic To do with grammatical structure and organisation, rather than with meaning. See also *semantic, syntax*.

syntax The set of rules and principles concerning the structure of a language; how the words should be combined to form what is accepted by users of the language as a grammatical sentence or phrase.

systematic desensitisation One of the ways in which *classical conditioning* has been applied to the treatment of *phobias*. The process of systematic desensitisation involves the learning (conditioning) of new responses to the feared stimulus. The new response is deliberately incompatible with the old response of fear, so that once it has been learned, the phobia is extinguished. Usually, *relaxation training* is used to provide the new response, and the person gradually learns to relax in the presence of the stimulus. A hierarchical list of feared stimuli is drawn up, and the training process begins with the least frightening situation. Once the new response to this has been learned, the person moves on to the next situation. Since the learning takes place gradually, with each stage building on the gains of the previous one, the new response gradually comes to supplant the old one and the phobia dies. See also *implosion therapy*.

systems analysis The analysis of a complex process. In social sciences, the term is taken to mean analysing interconnected groups of people and the social systems that influence them. Systems analysis also includes the use of computers to analyse complex systems and develop ways of improving their functioning.

systems theory A set of theories based around the idea that all complex systems will share certain properties. Thus, it should be possible to transfer ideas obtained from studying one kind of system to one that is very different. Often this has meant taking principles from engineering systems (including guided missiles) and applying them to the behaviour of individuals or to groups such as families. See also *family therapy, negative feedback*.

T

T group A form of *encounter group* intended to produce a close, therapeutic relationship between the group members. T groups are traditionally free-floating and unstructured, involving a high degree of self-revelation on the part of members, and with the aim of breaking down established *defence mechanisms* and barriers to open communication with other people. However, an alternative view is that defence mechanisms should not be broken down unless the person also receives constructive help in dealing with whatever it is that they were defending against. For this and other reasons, T groups have been accused of being more destructive than helpful.

T maze A device used to assess learning in laboratory rats or other animals, consisting of a straight passage from a starting box leading to a junction at which the animal is obliged to make either a right or left turn to reach a goal box, which may or may not contain a reward (see Figure 61).

t-test Probably the most widely used statistical test within psychology, t is a *parametric statistic* that is obtained by comparing the *means* of two data samples in order to determine whether any differences which occur between them are *statistically significant*. The *null hypothesis* of any given study will predict that any differences which have occurred between two sets of data have occurred simply by chance. In other words, all of the scores have come from the same population, and differences between the means are simply due to random variation. On the other hand, if the means of the two sets of data are very different, it is unlikely that they have come from the same population; they are more likely to have resulted from two different populations. In that case, the null hypothesis would be refuted. The t-test looks at the mean of each set of data, bearing in mind the *standard deviation* of each one. By giving a final statistic that expresses the strength of the differences between the two samples, it allows the user to judge just how likely it is that these differences have arisen by chance. The t-test is one of the more powerful tests in that it is able to detect significance when present, and it is also very *robust* (i.e. it can cope if the conditions of its use do not conform strictly to those for parametric tests). See also *F ratio*.

TA See *transactional analysis*.

tabula rasa A *blank slate*. It is used as a summary term for Locke's theory that humans are born with no knowledge or mental structures, so that their mental processes are entirely formed by experience. Since slates have not been used in education for some time, the *metaphor* of an unformatted computer drive might convey the idea more effectively.

tachistoscope (t-scope) A device used to present visual stimuli for precise amounts of time and/or at precise levels of intensity. Tachistoscope studies are frequently used to demonstrate the power of *set* in perception, and were used extensively by cognitive and social psychologists during the 1950s and 1960s.

tactile stimulation Information that is received through the sense of touch.

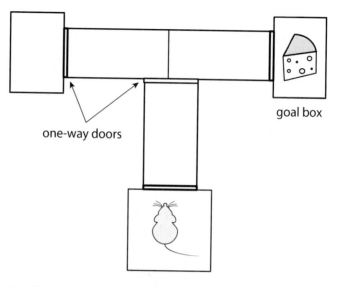

Figure 61 A T maze

Tajfel, Henri (1919–1982)

Following his experiences as a Polish Jew in the Holocaust, Tajfel developed a major analysis of *prejudice* and *intergroup conflict*. His work began with explorations of the cognitive dimensions of prejudice, but soon led him to recognise the importance of motivational factors, and in particular the sense of belonging involved in group membership. Tajfel conducted experiments in which 'minimal groups' were artificially put together on some unimportant basis, and showed that the members still developed loyalty to their own group, and *intergroup rivalry* if put in conflict for resources. Tajfel saw group membership as fundamental to an individual's *identity*, and his *social identity theory*, in which the identity and functioning of the individual is seen as a product of their social and cultural setting, was a major factor in the development of *European social psychology*.

Talairach coordinates These are ways of describing precise locations in the brain. They relate to an atlas of the brain created by Talairach and Tournoux in 1988, which used the anatomical data from a single post-mortem brain to define x as locations on the left/right axis, y as locations on the front-back axis, and z as locations on the top-down axis.

task switching The cognitive act of changing from one schema to another. See also *Wisconsin card-sorting test*, *multitasking*.

task-resource artefact The finding that performance on a task will suffer if another task or activity is taking up the relevant cognitive resources.

TAT See *thematic apperception test.*

taxonomy A system of classification that groups members of a data set into successive levels. The classic taxonomy is the biological classification of organisms that includes 'orders', each of which contains many kinds of 'genus', which in turn contain many 'species'.

tDCS See *transcranial direct current stimulation.*

telegraphic speech Concise speech that leaves out *redundant* words, as in a telegram, but still conveys the essential meaning. Telegraphic speech is used by children of around 2 years of age, who typically combine only two or three words at a time in each utterance. Identified as such by Roger Brown, it formed the basis of his approach to *language acquisition,* which rejected the prevailing structural approaches to infant speech and instead focused on the child's communicative intentions. The overall approach was known as *semantic relations grammar.*

telemetry Sending measurements over a distance, using radio frequencies, or more recently, WiFi or Bluetooth. Telemetry is used to monitor the physiological responses of freely moving individuals such as athletes, children at play and migrating birds.

telencephalon Part of the forebrain, which consists of the two *cerebral hemispheres,* the *basal ganglia* and the *limbic system.*

teleology A form of logical reasoning in which the outcome is regarded as responsible for the cause (e.g. 'It rains to make the flowers grow'). This type of thinking is regarded by logicians as a mistake, by developmentalists as immature thinking, and in systems theory as valid in some circumstances. In philosophy, teleology refers to the study of ultimate purpose – a teleological approach to scientific investigation is one in which describing the function that something has is considered to be an adequate form of explanation, as in many biological explanations, or in *sociobiology.*

telepathy The communication of *cognitions* (thoughts, etc.) by means other than those understood in conventional science. There is considerable dispute as to whether the phenomenon occurs, and its definition precludes rational explanation – if a communication can be explained, it is not telepathy. See also *extrasensory perception, parapsychology.*

temperament The stable aspects of the character of an individual, which are often regarded as biologically rooted and as providing the fundamental dispositions that, through interaction with the environment, produce the *personality.*

template An abstract model or schema that indicates what something is usually like, or how it generally fits together.

template matching theory A theory of pattern recognition which holds that we identify objects by comparing their images to general templates that we have stored in memory, and assessing the degree of 'fit' between them.

temporal Concerning time, or the experience of time.

temporal coding Conveying information through the timing of events. In neuroscience, this generally refers to the way that populations of *neurones* synchronise their firing in response to different strengths of signal. See also *volley principle.*

temporal contiguity Two events occurring next to each other in time. Temporal contiguity is an important factor in conditioning, since it is usually necessary for the *unconditioned stimulus* to be temporally close to the response or reinforcement.

temporal lobe The area of the *cerebrum* found below the lateral fissure at the side of each *cerebral hemisphere*. It was once thought to be the seat of the soul, and of *time perception*, although there is little formal evidence for this. The temporal lobe does, however, contain the *olfactory cortex* and the *auditory cortex*. See also *temporoparietal junction*.

temporal resolution How accurately it is possible to measure just when something is happening, or how long it takes. See also *spatial resolution*.

temporal summation A situation where the accumulation of stimuli arriving close together in time produces an effect that would not happen if the stimuli arrived at longer intervals. Some nerve impulses are passed from one *neurone* to another through summation.

temporoparietal junction An area of the brain where the *temporal* and *parietal lobes* meet. It incorporates information from the *visual*, *auditory* and *somatosensory* systems, and also from the *thalamus* and the *limbic system*. It is known to play a significant role in *theory of mind*, and damage to this region can produce impairment of moral decision-making and sometimes *out-of-body experiences* (OOBs). It is connected to the *frontal lobes* by the *arcuate fasciculus*.

tender-mindedness A personality characteristic put forward by William James, and later elaborated by H.J. Eysenck, characterised by a gentle, optimistic and idealistic approach to the world. Its opposite, *tough-mindedness*, is characterised by a harsher, more pessimistic approach.

teratogens Substances or agents that can affect *foetus* development, such as alcohol or pollution.

terminal button See *synaptic knob*.

territoriality The defence and protection of one area to the exclusion of other members of the species. It has been studied mainly by *ethologists*, with particular reference to those aggressive acts that deter potential sexual competitors. The concept has been extended speculatively, and with varying degrees of sense, to account for all manner of human behaviour, ranging from international warfare to crowd violence and stress in high-density housing. See also *personal space*.

tertiary circular reactions The final stage of *circular reactions* in Piaget's theory of cognitive development, in which the infant introduces variations in the repeated behaviour. These variations change successively, eventually becoming very different from the behaviour with which the infant started out.

tertium quid The possibility that what looks like a relationship between two variables may actually have been caused by a third variable, acting independently on each of the others.

test A standardised means of assessing the abilities or characteristics of individuals. See also *intelligence*, *personality*, *projective test*, *psychometrics*, *reliability*, *validity*.

test administration A standard way of presenting a *psychometric* test to ensure that results obtained from respondents by different testers are comparable. See also *standardised instructions*.

test battery A combination of psychometric tests that provides a comprehensive account of an individual's functioning, such as a set of tests used for the assessment of memory disorders or reading skills.

test items The individual items in a psychometric test.

test power The potential that a particular statistical test has to detect significance, if it is there in the data. Some tests are better at this than others, and these tests are often more popular with users than the data would strictly warrant. See also *levels of measurement*, *robustness*.

test profile The (usually graphic) portrayal of the characteristics of an individual as assessed by a test or test battery. A test profile involves the presentation of a range of scores from the subtests, rather than a single score.

test-retest A method of assessing the *reliability* of a measure by applying the same measure, or test, on two separate occasions and *correlating* the results.

test standardisation The administration of a test to a large *sample* of the *population*, ideally a *representative sample*, which serves to provide *norms* against which the results of particular individuals or groups can be compared.

test statistic The final number obtained when a *statistical test* has been carried out. The test statistic is then compared with the appropriate *critical value* for that test, in order to identify whether the results have achieved *statistical significance*.

testee An ugly word for a person to whom a test is administered.

testes Male gonads – glands that form part of the *endocrine system* of the body, and which are particularly responsible for the manufacture of *androgens*.

testing effect The way that *learning* is enhanced by spending some of the learning time retrieving information, rather than concentrating on committing it to *memory*. An important thing to know when revising for exams.

testosterone A male sex hormone (*androgen*) that is responsible for the development of the *primary sexual characteristics* of males, and plays a major role in sexual and related activities throughout life.

tetrachromatism A theory of colour vision which assumes that there are four primary colours – red, blue, green and yellow. See also *trichromatism*.

texture gradient The loss of visual definition of objects with increasing distance, such that the details are seen less clearly and general textures appear to be smoother. Gibson's *ecological perception theory* argues that textural changes in the visual field are the source of most *depth perception*, and that top-down models of perception which assume that it relies on *hypothesis testing* are largely unnecessary in the explanation of usual experience in everyday life.

thalamus The area of the brain found just below the *cerebrum*, where information is relayed from the sensory receptors of the body to the *cerebral cortex*. It is involved in some basic information processing. Hubel and Wiesel found the basics of *pattern perception* to be related to the arrangement of *simple*, *complex* and *hypercomplex cells* in the *lateral geniculate nuclei* of the thalamus.

Thanatos The name of the Greek god of death, which was used by Freud to refer to the death instinct – a concept he developed in order to account for the interpersonal and intrapersonal aggression of the First World War.

thematic apperception test (TAT) A *projective test* in which research participants are asked to interpret and explain ambiguous scenes. The nature of their response (e.g. whether they perceive a recumbent figure as dead, drunk or sleeping) is taken as an indicator of hidden anxieties or defences of the *unconscious* mind. Typically, research participants will be shown about 8 or 10 different pictures, and asked to explain what is happening in each one.

thematic qualitative analysis A form of *qualitative analysis* in which the salient material is organised into distinct themes. The themes may be data-driven, in which case they are identified during the analysis itself by grouping together recurrent ideas or concepts that seem to represent significant concerns which are being expressed by the interviewees. Alternatively, themes may be identified before the data are collected, in which case they have generally been derived from theory, and will usually relate to explicit hypotheses.

theory An overall explanation given for a set of observations, which links them all into a coherent pattern or *model*. Scientific theories are usually considered to be of no value unless they give rise to *hypotheses* that can be tested against reality and can be shown to be false. However, exceptions to this are often made in the case of theories that are particularly appropriate to the mood of their times, such as *sociobiology* or *psychoanalysis*. See also *hypothetico-deductive method*, *positivism*.

theory-driven analysis An approach to data analysis, particularly common with *thematic qualitative analysis*, in which the essential issues or themes that are being used to structure the data have been derived beforehand, from theory. This contrasts with *data-driven techniques*, which tend to be more reflexive, and in which the themes of the analysis emerge from the data themselves.

theory-led investigation An approach to research in which the topic of study, and/or the way in which it is undertaken, has been derived entirely from theoretical perspectives rather than from empirical research or social need.

theory-theory Particularly used in *neuroscience*, this is the idea that human social understanding is based on formulating theories about mental states and how they govern behaviour, and storing them as explicit knowledge. See also *personal constructs*.

theory of mind (TOM) A recent development of child psychology in which the child's understanding of other people's cognitions and emotions is the focus of study. An aspect of *cognitive development*, the child is said to develop a theory of mind between 4 and 6 years of age. The area has generated many interesting ideas and issues that are being vigorously investigated. Many characteristics shown by *autistic* children can be summarised by the idea that they have not developed a theory of mind.

theory of reasoned action The idea that intention determines behaviour, and that intention itself is determined by perceived *norms*, *attitudes* and behavioural control.

theory of the humours A *type theory* of personality originating from the second century BC, and popular throughout the Middle Ages. It identified four main types of personality, each of which was supposed to come about through the action of particular body fluids. The four types are:

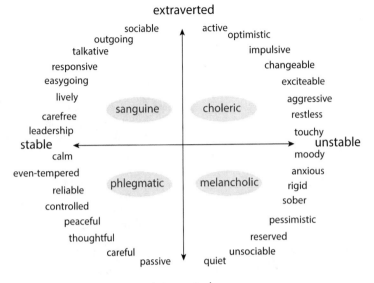

Figure 62 Humours and the EPI dimensions

(i)   choleric, thought to result from an excess of yellow bile;

(ii) sanguine, from blood;

(iii) melancholic, from black bile; and

(iv) phlegmatic, from phlegm.

That this was a popular theory can be seen in the way in which many words have retained meanings that derive directly from the theory. It was this view of the origins of human personality that led to the word 'humour', which had previously only meant bodily fluid, coming to mean 'mood' or 'temper' (see Figure 62).

therapeutic A term used to refer to something that is useful as an agent or tool in *therapy*.

therapy The treatment of an individual by physical or psychological means. When applied to psychological treatments, the term implies that the client is ill and should be cured. See also *behaviour therapy, client-centred therapy,* *cognitive therapy, family therapy, Gestalt therapy, medical model, psychoanalysis, psychotherapy, rational–emotive behaviour therapy, transactional analysis.*

thinking A general term which that be defined in several different ways:

(i)   The use of symbolic processes by the brain.

(ii) Any chain or series of ideas.

(iii) Ideation, the sequence of producing ideas concerned with the solving of specific problems or incongruities in models of reality.

Thinking is usually taken to mean conscious cognitions. Unconscious processes such as those referred to in psychoanalytic literature are seen more as responses of *affect* or motivations. Most psychological investigations of thinking have concentrated on *problem-solving* or *concept formation*. See also *creativity*.

third-order intentionality A degree of *intentional stance* which makes the inference that the individual who is acting holds beliefs about what other people may believe about things or people, and that these are directing the person's actions. An example might be acting in the belief that another person is aware that a third person knows how to achieve a result. It may sound complicated, but it happens remakably often in day-to-day living. See also *second-order intentionality*, *first-order intentionality*.

third turn repair A process identified in *conversation analysis*, in which the individual tries to repair a misunderstanding or failure to communicate the next time they have a turn in the conversation.

thought disorder A tendency to produce sequences of ideas that appear unconnected or illogical to the observer. It is a symptom of *schizophrenia*.

threat display A form of inherited behaviour in which an animal acts in a manner that serves to emphasise its size and strength, and so discourages competitors, or attempts to do so. Threat displays often involve exhibitions of natural weaponry (horns, tusks, teeth, etc.), of power and strength (beating the chest, roaring) and also of size (standing tall, engaging the *pilomotor response*). All of these behaviours are designed to intimidate the other animal as much as possible.

threshold The lowest level of stimulation at which an event can be detected. Although the term 'absolute threshold' may also be used, there is nothing absolute about it. There is no fixed point at which a stimulus changes from invisible to visible, just an increasing probability that it will be detected. A threshold is therefore usually set at the point where 50 per cent of the signals are detected by the person.

This point itself is easily influenced by factors such as *sensory adaptation*, set and fatigue, so the threshold obtained will depend very much on the conditions of the experiment. See also *relative threshold*, *word recognition threshold*.

threshold of response The point at which a stimulus, or a change in a stimulus, becomes detectable. Since these can fluctuate from moment to moment, the threshold itself is taken as the point where 50 per cent of trials indicate that the stimulus has been detected. An absolute threshold is the point where the presence of a stimulus has been detected 50 per cent of the time, while a relative threshold is the point at which a change in the intensity of a stimulus has been detected. Differences between relative thresholds are sometimes referred to as *just noticeable differences* (jnds).

timbre The tonal quality of a sound, especially used of voices. Combinations of different tones and harmonics give sound its distinct timbres.

time and motion A method of analysing working patterns developed by F.W. Taylor in 1903, involving a systematic breakdown of movements and skills. By breaking down work sequences into sequences of actions with maximum economy and minimum effort, Taylor showed how productivity in industry could be dramatically increased, and his work is often considered to be the foundation of *ergonomics*. Although it is still used from time to time, it has proved to be of only limited value on the factory floor, as people have an understandable aversion to being treated as if they were robots.

time-based prospective memory A form of *prospective memory* that involves remembering to do things at the appropriate time.

Tinbergen, Niko (1907–1988)

Nikolaas Tinbergen was a Dutch ethologist who conducted extensive research into the role of inherited recognition signals and other aspects of animal behaviour. In 1973, he shared the Nobel Prize with Karl Frisch and Konrad Lorenz for their contributions to ethology. Among other things, Tinbergen identified the importance of sign stimuli in setting off innate releasing mechanisms, and is best known for delineating the 'four questions' that need to be addressed in order to understand animal behaviour. These are: causation, ontogeny, evolution and function.

time perception The subjective awareness of the passage of time, which does not correspond precisely with objective time. Time perception has been studied experimentally to determine the effect of various forms of cognitive tasks, and of *psychoactive drugs*.

time sampling An observational technique in which the occurrence of specified events is noted during successive time intervals. The observer may use a grid with each column representing, say, 60-second units. Each row is a defined event, the observer moves to a new column each 60 seconds, and a tick is placed against every event that occurs during the next 60 seconds. The technique is used for *observational studies* of relatively frequent events. See also *event sampling*.

tip-of-the-tongue (TOT) phenomenon A phenomenon of memory in which the individual experiences the feeling of knowing the desired information but is temporarily unable to bring it to consciousness.

tit-for-tat A strategy in which participants adopt matching approaches, such that cooperation leads to cooperation, while non-cooperation leads to non-cooperation. See also *game theory*.

TMS See *transcranial magnetic stimulation*.

token economy The application of B.F. Skinner's techniques of *operant conditioning* to establish an environment in which desired behaviour is *reinforced* with tokens that can then be exchanged for goods or privileges. Token economy is proposed as an efficient way of modifying behaviour, especially of long-stay *institutionalised* patients. However, there is some evidence that any improvements found in patients using token economy systems may be a by-product of raising morale through providing them with apparently meaningful tasks, rather than through the direct operation of conditioning. See also *Hawthorne effect*.

tolerance Adaptation to the effects of a drug so that increasing doses are needed to achieve the same effect.

TOM See *theory of mind*.

tomography A method of investigation of brain functioning, mostly used for medical purposes, which involves building up a three-dimensional picture of the brain through a succession of X-ray photographs or ultrasound images, in order to identify abnormal structures or growths.

tone The quality of sound expressed in terms of the number of different frequencies which make up that sound.

A pure tone consists of sounds of one frequency only, but most sounds are combinations of several different frequencies at differing strengths, often with one frequency being dominant over the others, which becomes identified as the pitch of the sound.

tonotopic organisation The principle that sounds which are close to one another in frequency stimulate neurones which are also close to one another. This is the way that neurones in the *organ of Corti* in the *cochlea* are organised.

top-down approach An approach to research that emphasises the general or social functions of the processes being studied, and explores the nature of the processing using that as its starting point. A good example is Gregory's theory of *perception*, which works on the principle that the brain is actively hypothesising about meanings for the information it is receiving. See also *bottom-up approach*, *raw primal sketch*.

TOT See *tip-of-the-tongue phenomenon*.

TOTE Abbreviation of 'Test Operate Test Exit', proposed as the basic component of planned actions by Miller, Galanter and Pribram in *Plans and the Structure of Human Behaviour*. They proposed that the organism 'tests' the environment, 'operates' on it to bring about change, 'tests' again to see whether the outcome is satisfactory, and, if so, 'exits' from the sequence. See also *negative feedback*.

tough-mindedness See *tender-mindedness*.

Tourette's syndrome This is a psychiatric disorder considered to have neurological origins, which is characterised by repetitive actions such as motor tics or repeated vocalisations. Although sometimes those repetitions are of obscene or offensive language, this is not typical of all Tourette's sufferers. It is thought to begin in early childhood, and has similar characteristics to *obsessive–compulsive disorder*.

trace conditioning A form of classical conditioning in which the *conditioned stimulus* is presented immediately before the *unconditioned stimulus*, rather than simultaneously. See also *delayed conditioning*, *simultaneous conditioning*.

trace decay The vanishing of a *memory trace* with time. See also *echoic memory*.

tradition A distinctive pattern of behaviour or customary approach to doing things that is shared by members of a social group, and transmitted to new members over time.

trait An aspect of *personality*, such as sociability, impulsiveness, conventionality, etc. See also *trait theory*.

trait anxiety A source of personal anxiety, or tendency towards anxiety, which is believed to come from a *personality trait* rather than an immediate reaction to situations.

trait theory A theory of *personality* in which personality is considered to consist of a collection of differing, usually measurable traits. One of the best-known examples is that of R.B. Cattell, whose *personality inventory* measures 16 different personality factors (and so is called the 16PF). See also *Minnesota Multiphasic Personality Inventory*.

trance An *altered state of awareness* in which *decision-making* and executive functions are partially suspended, and attention is highly focused. Trance can be achieved by *hypnosis*, meditation, some drugs and some clinical conditions.

tranquilliser A drug used to reduce stress or anxiety temporarily.

transaction A chain or sequence of interactions between two or more individuals which is based on the idea that *interactions* can only be understood if it is recognised that each person influences the other. Each person acts on the basis of the meaning they give to how the other treats them, and that treatment is itself the product of an *attribution* made by the other person. For example, a baby becomes upset while feeding, the mother responds by being anxious during feeds, and this makes her treat the baby differently, causing further upset to the baby, and so on. In general, transactions mean that two people negotiate the environment in which they will both have to function in the future, rather than one person defining the environment for the other. The concept of transactions is particularly useful in the analysis of interactions between parent and infant, but can also be applied to most areas of social behaviour. See also *coevolution*, *social constructionism*.

transactional analysis (TA) A scheme developed by Eric Berne for interpreting the way in which *ego-states* lead people to relate during interpersonal interaction. Each person in a given pair or dyad may operate as a Child, an Adult or a Parent. Acting in a submissive, dependent manner (Child) may provoke the partner of the dyad to adopt a Parental role. Acting in a dominating manner (Parent) may produce submissive behaviour from the other, etc. This model has been usefully applied in individual and group *psychotherapy*, particularly by uncovering the recurrent patterns of social interactions described in Berne's *Games People Play*.

transactional model of stress A model of *stress* and *coping* in which the person

first appraises the stressor, and then assesses the resources they have available to deal with it. See also *primary appraisal*, *secondary appraisal*.

transactional theory A theory of perception, developed by Ames, which states that perception develops as a result of constant interaction with the environment.

transcendental meditation A technique, derived from Hindu practice, of sustained concentration on a brief phrase (*mantra*) in order to induce relaxation. See also *altered states of awareness*, *hypnosis*, *trance*.

transcoding The conversion of symbols from one type to another (e.g. from written symbols to spoken words).

transcortical sensory aphasia A condition in which the person is able to repeat spoken words, but has very little comprehension of both spoken and written language.

transcranial direct current stimulation (tDCS) This is a procedure that involves stimulating the brain externally, using a coil held over the scalp. By interrupting the brain's functions in that region, it is considered to produce a 'virtual lesion' in that particular area. See also *transcranial magnetic stimulation*, *cathodal tDCS*, *anodal tDCS*.

transcranial magnetic stimulation (TMS) A method of investigating brain function by disrupting brain function in a particular area by short bursts of magnetic stimulation, and exploring how this interferes with task processing.

transcription The process of converting audio or videotape recordings into written text. Preparing transcripts is an essential early step in many forms of *qualitative research*. A reasonably competent typist will take about six hours to transcribe one hour of tape, so even a basic transcript is quite an investment of effort. Some research methods such as *conversation analysis* require much more detailed transcripts in which intonations, stresses, the exact length of pauses, grunts, etc. are precisely indicated.

transcription factor A chemical product of a particular *gene* that affects how other genes function.

transducer

(i)   A device used to convert a biological signal such as heartbeat or skin resistance into an electrical signal suitable for recording.
(ii) More generally, any sort of device that converts energy into a different form.

transduction A term that is usually used of sensory receptors (e.g. in referring to the conversion of photons [light] into electrical energy by rod and cone cells in the retina). See also *transducer*.

transfer of training A phenomenon in which the learning of one particular task either helps or hinders the learning of a subsequent task. Positive transfer involves the facilitation of subsequent learning, while negative transfer impedes it. See also *proactive interference*.

transfer RNA (tRNA) This is a form of nucleic acid that can move from one cell or part of the body to another. It is closely related to and works alongside the genetic information contained in DNA. See also *messenger RNA*.

transference The way in which feelings derived from a previous relationship may be transferred to someone new. This is particularly used in psychoanalysis, in which the analyst deliberately maintains a neutral, colourless personality so that such transfer becomes easy for the patient (e.g. when the therapist is responded to as the patient's father). Transference is similar to *projection*, and was first regarded by Freud as a nuisance, but is now regarded as an essential source of information about the patient's early relationships. Interpretation of transference has been claimed as the major or only source of therapeutic change. See also *counter-transference*.

transformational grammar A set of rules that specify how one sentence can be transformed into another in a language, particularly converting *deep structure* into *surface structure*. The concept was originally proposed by Chomsky as part of his explanation of how children acquire language. A complete set of transformational rules amounts to a grammatical description of a language.

transgenerational transmission The passing on of environmentally acquired characteristics to subsequent generations (e.g. the underfeeding of one generation of rats at a *critical period* may result in reduced size of the adult rats two generations later). Similarly, extreme malnutrition for a pregnant woman may have subsequent effects on the child.

transmitter substance See *neurotransmitter*.

transparency assumption This is the assumption that *lesions* in the brain will not produce entirely new cognitive systems. Instead, they are thought simply to influence pre-existing cognitive systems. The transparency assumption is a major assumption of much *cognitive neuropsychology*, justifying the use of data from damaged or abnormal brains to infer functioning in the normal brain. However, it has been challenged by discoveries of neural plasticity (e.g. in accident victims where the recovery from damage to specific pathways has sometimes been shown to generate entirely new pathways within the brain).

transsexual A person who changes sex, either from male to female or from female to male, usually through a course of hormone therapy and surgery. Although typically transsexuals have always experienced themselves as being 'really' the other sex, the main part of transsexualism involves the learning of a new sex role. Many transsexuals have to spend an extensive period of time, at least a couple of years, passing as a member of their desired sex before being allowed treatment.

transvestite A person who enjoys dressing as a member of the opposite sex, and may do so quite elaborately. Most transvestites are *heterosexual*, although transvestism can sometimes be associated with *homosexuality*. Transvestites in general tend to be contented with their own sex and sex role, and do not usually experience problems of sexual identity.

trauma

(i) An experience that, because of its intensity and unexpectedness, is damaging. The initial reaction is shock, which may or may not be followed by recovery (see *post-traumatic stress disorder*). Freud came to believe that all *neuroses* were caused by childhood traumas that remained unresolved in the adult.

(ii) In medicine, bodily injury caused by an external object.

triadic interactions In *social psychology*, this generally tends to mean interactions between three people,

but it may also be used to refer to interactions between two people and an object.

trial-and-error learning Learning that takes place as a result of trying out a variety of responses to a given *stimulus*, until one response achieves the desired effect, whereupon it becomes more likely to be repeated. Thorndike proposed that trial and error was the basis of all learning, but work on *latent learning* by Tolman brought this into question.

triangular theory of love A theory of love developed by Sternberg in 1988 that identifies three significant components: passion, intimacy and commitment. In Sternberg's model, different forms of loving involve different proportions of the three components.

triangulation A method of research that involves adopting several different approaches or methods of study, enabling comparison of their different outcomes. This makes it possible to 'home in' on an idea, if all the studies give similar results or have similar implications. For example, it is not possible to undertake research that provides definitive proof of a connection between social violence and the content of the mass media, yet many different research methods have shown strong correlations between the two. While no one method provides definitive evidence, the very similar findings and implications of many different approaches indicate that there may be something valid in the argument.

In *family therapy*, triangulation refers to a communication system in which one person is caught in the communications between two others. It is often seen in families where a child may be being used so that the two parents can send contradictory messages without coming into direct conflict with each other.

triarchic intelligence A theory of *intelligence*, outlined by Robert Sternberg, which consists of three separate sub-theories. Each sub-theory concerns a different aspect of manifest intelligence:

(i) *Contextual intelligence*, which is concerned with intelligence in its sociocultural setting.

(ii) *Experiential intelligence*, which is concerned with how the individual's own past experience influences the way in which they approach a given task or situation.

(iii) *Componential intelligence*, which is concerned with the cognitive mechanisms by which intelligent behaviour is achieved. The componential sub-theory incorporates an earlier theory of intelligence (Sternberg, 1977), in which components of intelligence are classified in terms of function and level of generality.

The triarchic theory is therefore distinctive in that it treats intelligence as mental activity that is directed towards purposive activity in the real world, rather than as a reified, context-free cognitive exercise. By integrating sociocultural and experiential intelligence with the specific tasks generally involved in intelligence testing, it also provides a theoretical framework for the selection of appropriate content for *intelligence tests*. See also *reification*.

trichromatism A theory of *colour vision* which proposes that it results from perceiving combinations of just three colours – red, blue and green (not the same as the primary colours of red, blue and yellow for pigments).

tricyclic antidepressants Antidepressant drugs that work by increasing the amount of serotonin and noradrenaline available to the *synapse*.

trigram A standard item in studying memory for meaningless material. It consists of three letters in the order of a consonant, a vowel and a consonant (e.g. GIK).

Triesman, Anne (1935–)

The career of Anne Triesman as a psychologist spanned the areas of attention, object perception and memory. However, she is best known for her *attenuation* model of *selective attention*, and later for her development of feature integration theory: an approach to the study of attention which emphasises the way that different kinds of attention may contribute to the experience of attention as a whole.

tRNA See *transfer RNA*.

Turner's syndrome A genetic disorder in which the individual has one less *chromosome* than normal, resulting in sexual abnormalities.

two-factor theory A model of intelligence proposed by Spearman, who argued that any particular intelligent act originates from two different intelligence factors – a 'g' (general) factor, common to all behaviour, which is characteristic of the individual's general functioning, and an 's' factor, specific to the problem in hand, which is the relevant skill for that particular behaviour (e.g. mathematical, verbal, spatial, manipulative, etc.).

two-factor theory of emotion The idea that *emotion* results from both our physiological state and our cognitive assessments of what is going on. The cognitive appraisal determines the emotion we experience, while the physiological state determines its intensity. Contrast with *somatic theory of emotion*.

two-point threshold A test of tactile sensitivity that involves touching the skin with two points close together and measuring how far apart they have to be before the subject feels two points, not one.

two-process theory of memory First proposed by William James, and developed further particularly by Miller and by Atkinson and Shiffrin, this theory holds that two distinct forms of memory exist, each with its own characteristics – immediate or *short-term memory* (STM) and *long-term memory* (LTM). There is dispute as to how far these forms of memory are in fact distinct. See also *levels of processing, dual memory theory*.

two-tailed hypothesis A hypothesis that predicts a result from either end of a frequency distribution of the *null hypothesis*. For example, a prediction that scores will vary on a task from one day to the next would be two-tailed, whereas a prediction that scores would improve from one day to the next would be one-tailed, as only one of the two kinds of outcomes (improving or getting worse) is predicted.

two-tailed test The use of a statistical test to investigate a *two-tailed hypothesis*.

Suppose the research hypothesis is that distraction by loud noise will affect the amount remembered. When you examine the memory scores of the distraction group, you need to test whether they are significantly higher *or* lower than the mean for the control group. This may amount to a significance level of $p < .05$, meaning that their mean falls either within the lower 2.5 per cent or the upper 2.5 per cent of the normal distribution. Compare this judgement with that for a *one-tailed test*.

two-way ANOVA An *analysis of variance* applied to two sets of data. When two or more data sets are analysed in this way, it becomes possible to test for the significance not just of differences between groups, but also of the *interactions* between the variables.

two-way mirror A sheet of glass inserted in a wall that looks like a mirror from the brightly lit side but acts as a window from the dark side. Two-way mirrors are used to observe without being seen, so that people do not know they are being watched (which is no longer ethically acceptable without prior consent in psychological research). They are used in *focus group* research and *family therapy* so that researchers or therapists can take notes, discuss and undergo training without too much interference in the group process.

Type I error A statistical term for the mistake of rejecting the *null hypothesis* when it should have been retained. In *experimental* as opposed to *correlational* studies, this would mean concluding that a difference in the *dependent variable* is attributable to the *independent variable* when in fact it was due to other factors (e.g. deciding that a difference in the performance of two classes was due to different teaching methods when in fact it derived from *individual differences* in the students concerned). *Statistical significance* levels are usually set so as to make Type I errors unlikely, but in some circumstances one would tolerate a high risk of Type I error (e.g. a cheap, safe and easy way to prevent cancer). See also *alpha level*.

Type II error A statistical term for the mistake of retaining the *null hypothesis* when it should have been rejected. In experimental studies, this would mean concluding that the *independent variable* had no effect on the *dependent variable*, when in fact it did have some influence. This is usually regarded as the less costly kind of error (see *Type I error*). Note that this is not a statistical error, as statistics merely assess the probability of relationships. The error arises in the conclusions that are drawn from the statistics.

Type A and Type B behaviour As outlined by Friedman and Rosenman, these refer to styles of working shown by company executives. Type A individuals are typically anxious, driven people, who find it difficult to delegate tasks to other people, and who tend to worry about their work when at home. Type B individuals may work just as hard, but have a more relaxed style, and an easy-going approach to problems, dealing with each difficulty as it arises rather than worrying about them all. Friedman and Rosenman found these styles to correlate strongly with susceptibility to heart disease, Type A individuals being far more likely to suffer heart attacks than Type B individuals.

type theory A theory of *personality* in which people are classified according to common characteristics. Sheldon grouped people according to types of physique – their *somatotype* – with personality characteristics supposedly associated with particular kinds of bodily build. Jung also grouped people according to personality type, most famously *introversion* and *extraversion*. The *theory of the humours* provides another example of an early type theory of personality. A more restricted approach in the study of personality is the 'narrow-band' approach, involving the identification of a single type, such as the *authoritarian personality*.

typicality effect The way that categorisation happens more quickly with a 'typical' example of the category than it does with an example which differs more strongly.

U

ultimate attribution error The way that people make *attributions* that will enhance or defend their own *in-group*, while making more negative attributions for *out-groups*. See also *fundamental attributional error*.

ultrasound Sound that is too high-pitched to be detected by human beings. Ultrasound can be detected by many animals, including dogs (it is the basis for 'silent' dog whistles) and cats. It has also been shown, by dedicated researchers, that rats emit an ultrasonic screech after mating. See also *infrasound*.

unconditional positive regard A prerequisite for mental health and personal growth, according to Carl Rogers. Rogers identifies two basic human needs – the need for *positive regard* from other people, and the need for *self-actualisation*. The person must satisfy both of these needs, but if their only experience of positive regard is conditional upon 'good' or appropriate behaviour, then much of their behaviour will be directed towards obtaining that approval. This means that they will not feel free to explore their own potential and their need for self-actualisation because of the fear of engendering social disapproval. However, most individuals have at least one person at some time in their life who gives them unconditional positive regard. In that relationship, they can be sure of the other person's affection and warmth, and this means that they can feel free to develop and explore new aspects of themselves. Unconditional positive regard is usually provided by parents during childhood, although Rogers believes that it is not tied to the early years of life. The formation of such a basis of unconditional positive regard is at the heart of Rogers' *client-centred therapy*.

unconditional respect for persons The recognition that each person is an autonomous individual entitled to respect as a human being and the acknowledgement of their personal integrity. Although this is the basis of most human rights manifestos and political constitutions, it has been under-represented in psychology, but the increased emphasis on *ethical issues* and *qualitative research* means that it is now becoming a significant concept.

unconditioned response (UR) A response that occurs automatically to a particular stimulus, and does not have to be learned. For example, pulling the hand away from a burningly hot surface is an unconditioned response – it happens as a *reflex*, without the need for conscious recognition of what is happening. See also *classical conditioning*, *conditioned response*, *conditioned stimulus*, *unconditioned stimulus*.

unconditioned stimulus (US) A *stimulus* that automatically produces a response in an organism (animal or human being). The term 'unconditioned' means 'not learned' – a stimulus of this kind will produce an effect automatically, with no learning being necessary. It forms the basis for *classical conditioning* as the new, *conditioned stimulus* becomes linked with the unconditioned one.

unconscious Lacking in conscious awareness. The most important use of the term is in *psychoanalytic theory* as a reference to mental activity that is not available to consciousness because it concerns material which is too threatening to the *ego* to be recognised directly. Freud believed that the unconscious has its own way of working (see *primary process*) which is different to that of the conscious mind. For example, there is no awareness of time in the unconscious, so all threats are felt as if they were still present, even if the source of the threat disappeared years ago. See also *preconscious*.

unconscious motive A motive of which the person is unaware but which continues to have an effect on behaviour. For example, a student may underachieve during exams owing to an unconscious rebellion against parental pressure to succeed. Although consciously they will be trying to do as well as possible, the chosen revision strategies are ineffectual, relying on rote learning or simply reading through notes, and this ensures that the student does not do as well as they could. Unconsciously, they have shied away from being too successful. Human behaviour is often influenced by such unconscious motives, and disentangling them such that the individual becomes aware of what is going on can be one of the main tasks of a *psychotherapist*.

unconscious transference In *eyewitness testimony*, this is the observation that a familiar but innocent face is sometimes misidentified as the perpetrator of a crime.

underadditivity The observations that there is less brain activity when two tasks are performed together, than if each is performed separately.

underspecification The use of simplified expressions to reduce the cognitive demands of speech processing.

uniform connectedness The observation in *visual perception* that objects which are next to one another and have uniform or very similar properties (e.g. colour) will be seen as linked. See also *Gestalt principles of perception*, *Law of Prägnanz*.

unilateral neglect A problem encountered in *clinical neuropsychology* in which the person ignores information coming from one side of the visual field. Although the *retina* and *optic nerve* appear to be working normally, there is no cognitive recognition of input from that side, and as a consequence images, judgements and other types of output become unbalanced.

unipolar depression A depression that is similar in form to a *bipolar depression*, but in which the manic phase is absent. The person simply has the depressive periods without the swings to *mania*.

universal grammar The theory that there is some kind of basic, elementary grammar underlying all human languages. It is not known whether such a thing exists, but it is a significant article of faith among most structural linguists, and considered to be the source of the young child's ability to acquire language easily and fluently.

universalistic meanings Meanings of words or phrases that are abstract or general and not tied to a specific context or social meaning. See also *particularistic meanings*.

unresponsive wakefulness syndrome See *vegetative state*.

unusualness heuristic The use of unusual events or findings to stimulate or introduce new areas of enquiry or lines of research.

Urbach Wiethe disease A brain disease that results in the destruction of the *amygdala* and areas near to it.

utterance Something that is said; a simple unit of speech or language. The term is often used when describing spoken language, as it avoids making assumptions about the grammatical form of what was said. Describing something as a 'sentence' or a 'phrase' might not be accurate, but calling it an 'utterance' merely makes the assumption that it was actually uttered.

V1 See *primary visual cortex*.

V4 A region just outside the *striate cortex* that has been shown to respond distinctively to colour. See also *achromatopsia*.

V5 A region just outside the *striate cortex* that has been shown to respond distinctively to movement. It is also sometimes known as MT, which stands for the middle temporal *visual cortex*. See also *akinetopsia*.

valence A positive or negative weighting (e.g. of emotional experience).

validity Validity refers to how far a given measure assesses what it was intended to measure. There are generally considered to be three main types of validity – surface or *face validity*, *criterion validity* and *construct validity*. Surface validity is judged simply in terms of how far the measure seems appropriate – it is an assessment of how plausible the chosen measure is. A questionnaire item asking how people feel about sex discrimination has surface validity in that it appears, on the surface, as though it will allow us to find out about sex discrimination.

Criterion validity occurs when the measure being used is compared with some other measure or standard which assesses the same thing. Criterion validity may be of two basic forms. *Predictive validity* involves the measure being compared with some future event, such as assessing the validity of IQ tests by looking at how well they correlate with later examination success. *Concurrent validity* involves the measure being compared with a measure obtained at the same time, such as comparing stated attitudes towards sex discrimination with behavioural measures of participation in housework. More usually, a new test may be compared with the results from an existing and widely accepted test.

Construct validity refers to how far the measure being examined truly represents the theoretical construct that it is supposed to measure. The most well-known example of this is the question of how far intelligence tests truly measure intelligence. In this case, 'intelligence' would be the theoretical construct, and the IQ score the measure being assessed for construct validity. The assessment would be made by examining whether people with higher IQ scores in fact behave in ways that would be judged as more intelligent. See also *ecological validity*.

values Ideas or principles that are of central importance to the individual, and which are used to form an evaluative standard against which actions or ideas are judged.

variable Anything that varies; something that can have different values. Any measure of performance or behaviour taken in a study is referred to as a variable, because it can have different values depending on circumstance. If its value depends on the particular experimental situation that was set up, then it is known as the *dependent variable*. The conditions set up by an experimenter in a formal experiment also vary. Typically, there is an experimental and a control condition, and often there may be several variations of the experimental condition. For this reason, that, too, is known as a variable – the *independent variable*. Other features of a study can also vary (e.g. background noise or time of day). If these variables are randomly distributed, so that they can affect any of the conditions of the independent variable equally, then they are referred to as random variables. However, if they are likely to affect certain conditions of the independent variable more than others, they are known as *confounding variables*.

variable-interval reinforcement A *reinforcement schedule* in which the delivery of a reinforcement depends on the amount of time that has passed since the last one was given. The amount of time between each rewarded response varies, but works out to a set average within a given time period. For instance, a VI 10 schedule would mean that an average of 10 seconds would have to elapse after each reinforcement before another reward could be obtained, but the actual time might be less or more than that on any given trial. Variable-interval reinforcement schedules tend to produce a steady *response rate* that is highly resistant to *extinction*. See also *partial reinforcement*.

variable-ratio reinforcement *Reinforcement* given during *operant conditioning* in such a way that not every response made is reinforced, only a certain proportion of them. The ratio of reinforced to non-reinforced responses varies randomly, but will average out to a preset proportion. For instance, a *reinforcement schedule* of VR 10 would mean that, on average, one in every 10 responses would be rewarded, but the number of responses which had to be made before each reward given would be randomly varied. Variable-ratio reinforcement produces a very rapid *response rate* that is highly resistant to *extinction*. Many naturally occurring reinforcement schedules are in the form of a variable ratio. For example, a child who demands attention may only receive it unpredictably, and this would result in a high level of demanding, which is very resistant to extinction. See also *partial reinforcement*.

variance A parametric *measure of dispersion*, obtained by subtracting each score from the *mean* of the sample, squaring these differences, and averaging them. Mathematically, it has the advantage so that scores which are only slightly different from the mean have very little effect, while more extreme scores (because the differences are squared) have more influence. The square root of the variance is the *standard deviation*. See *F ratio*.

variance ratio A statistical measure that describes precisely the way that scores are spread out around the mean.

variation

(i)   In statistics, it is the degree to which scores in a set differ from the measure of central tendency of that set. Variation is assessed in different ways depending on the data, and can be measured using the *standard deviation* or the *semi-interquartile range*, among others.

(ii)   In evolutionary or biological theory, it is the extent to which the individuals in a particular species differ from one another. Individual variation is the ultimate basis for evolutionary change: if all members of a species were identical, natural selection would be impossible.

variation ratio A *descriptive statistic* that expresses the proportion of scores in a data set which are not *modal*, as opposed to those which are.

vasoconstriction Constriction of blood vessels. It occurs in the skin in response to cold, and also in conditions of threat (when it would have the effect of reducing bleeding from a wound). It can therefore be used as an indicator of anxiety.

vasopressin A peptide hormone released by the *pituitary gland*, which is involved in *attachment* formation and may also have a wider role in reducing anxiety. See also *oxytocin*.

VBM See *voxel-based morphometry*.

vegetative state A condition in which people appear totally inert, although measures of brain activity indicate that they are in a state of partial *arousal*. It is classified as a disorder of consciousness, and after four weeks becomes described as persistent vegetative state. Legal definitions vary in different countries, but after three to six months it may be classified as permanent, raising debates about euthanasia, although the fact that a few people have recovered from this condition makes such decisions tricky. The existence of brain activity means that some prefer to call it *unresponsive wakefulness syndrome* rather than vegetative state.

ventral Towards the bottom, sometimes referring to the front or forward part of the body or body part. 'Ventral' comes from the Latin word for 'belly'. See also *dorsal, lateral, medial*.

ventral stream A term used to describe the visual pathway that extends from the *occipital lobes* to the *temporal lobes*, and is involved in memory, semantics and object recognition. See also *dorsal stream*.

ventral striatum This is the part of the *basal ganglia* that is particularly associated with the *limbic circuit*, and has been particularly associated with learning the emotional value of an action, and the *reward* value of a decision.

ventral tegmental area A part of the *midbrain* that is believed to be the origin of the *dopaminergic* system associated with rewards. See also *reward pathway*.

ventral visual stream See *ventral stream*.

ventricle Hollow areas in the brain that contain *cerebrospinal fluid*.

ventromedial frontal cortex The area on the *frontal lobe* of the brain towards the bottom and also towards the midline of the two hemispheres. It is thought to be associated with *decision-making*. See also *Iowa gambling task, somatic marker hypothesis*.

ventromedial nucleus (VMH) A region of the *hypothalamus* that seems to be particularly concerned with *satiation*. Stimulation of this region in rats will cause them to cease eating even when previously they have shown strong signs of hunger, and lesions in the region result in rats becoming obese through overeating. It is thought that some cases of human obesity may arise from some kind of disorder within this region of the hypothalamus.

verbal behaviour Speech or speech-related actions, such as sign language. The term was made popular by B.F. Skinner, who used it as a way of denying the relevance of cognitive processes in speech or language.

verbal communication Communication that uses words to convey the important messages.

verbal deprivation hypothesis The idea, put forward by Bernstein and others, that the form of language learned by a child could be a disadvantage when it came to learning or handling abstract forms of information. Bernstein argued that *restricted codes* of language, with their relatively limited vocabularies and reliance on shared assumptions on the part of the listener, meant that children would find the kind of conceptual and abstract learning which they encountered in school inherently more difficult than children who use *elaborated codes*. This idea was hotly disputed by many researchers, notably Labov, who demonstrated that children who used highly restricted codes of language, such as Black American English, were perfectly capable of handling abstract and theoretical concepts, so long as those concepts were introduced in a setting in which the children felt confident.

verbal memory

(i) The storing of mental images by using words as a form of coding for information. In this case, verbal memory is simply a variation of *symbolic representation*, with all the associated features and advantages.

(ii) Memory for words. Much laboratory research on memory, especially in the early years, concentrated initially on asking people to memorise lists of words, partly because they were able to state clearly exactly what they remembered, which was not always easy with visual or auditory images. However, there is considerable recent evidence to suggest that this form of learning is qualitatively different from the way in which people remember connected prose or speech, and even more different to everyday memory.

(iii) In its most general sense, the term verbal memory includes memory for speech and prose.

vesicle A small reservoir found at the *synaptic knob* that contains a *neurotransmitter*, and which breaks open and spills that neurotransmitter into the *synaptic cleft* if it is stimulated by the arrival of an appropriate electrical impulse.

vestibular system The sense receptors that inform the body of orientation and balance, brought about by the arrangement of *semicircular canals* in the *inner ear*. It is important in the two senses of *proprioception* and *kinaesthesia*.

vicarious learning Learning through observing what happens to others. Vicarious learning was particularly investigated by Bandura in studies of imitation in children. He found that children who saw others being rewarded for aggressive acts were more likely to imitate them. Behaviour patterns may be acquired or abandoned as a consequence of seeing other people being rewarded or punished for them. See also *identification*.

vigilance See *sustained attention*.

vignette A brief verbal story or account used in research and clinical studies in order to create impressions, attitudes or assumptions that can then be examined.

visual To do with vision.

visual buffer A brief *short-term memory* store, proposed as a kind of *echoic memory* but for visual rather than auditory information.

visual cache The part of the *visuospatial scratch pad* that stores information about shape and colour. See also *working memory*.

visual cliff Apparatus designed by Gibson and Walk to investigate whether animals have an *innate* perception of depth. A newborn animal (e.g. a chick or goat kid) is placed on a centre board over a sheet of strong glass that covers a steep drop. If the animal shows fear or refuses to cross over the drop, it is assumed that the ability to perceive depth is present. Since the animal is newly born, this cannot have been learned, and therefore must be regarded as innate. The results are more difficult to interpret when human babies are used, since they are not mobile at birth (see Figure 63).

visual cortex That part of the *cerebral cortex* which is responsible for the decoding of visual information. The visual cortex is found at the back of the brain, in the *occipital lobe*. Also known as the striate cortex, this area

forms the main *sensory projection area* for vision. Electrical stimulation of this area produces vivid visual sensations.

visual field The 'scene' or expanse of visual information that is encompassed by the *retina* at any moment. When we are looking at something, the object of our attention is at the centre of the visual field, and we see it most clearly. However, we also receive a visual impression of our surroundings, and this stretches for quite a long way around the focus of vision. A slight movement at the side of the visual field will usually cause us to turn slightly and focus on a new centre of visual attention. The visual field then covers a different, but overlapping, range of visual stimuli.

visual form agnosia The inability to recognise or identify specific forms, or shapes, visually, even though the same forms or shapes may be recognised by that person using touch.

visual illusions Figures that appear to be other than they really are, as a result of the ways in which the brain interprets information. Visual illusions have been extensively studied by psychologists, as it is thought that investigation of the errors of perception can throw light on

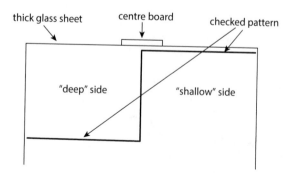

Figure 63 A visual cliff

how normal perceptual processes work (e.g. they formed a significant aspect of Gregory's inferential theory of perception). The visual illusions most commonly studied by psychologists fall into three main categories:

(i) *geometric illusions*, usually in the form of simple line drawings (see Figure 64);

(ii) illusions of movement, such as the *phi phenomenon* or the *waterfall effect*; and

(iii) colour illusions.

visual perception The analysis and interpretation of information received and processed through the *visual system*. See also *perception*.

visual search The process of scanning, or looking for particular types or items of information in the visual field.

visual stimulation Any form of light that reaches the *retina* and causes the *rod* or *cone cells* to react. The term is usually used to refer to a visual image that is received by the eye. See also *stimulus*.

visual system The general name given to the set of *neurones* and brain structures involved in the processing of visual information. The visual system includes the eye, in particular the *retina*, the *optic nerve*, the *optic chiasma*, the *lateral geniculate nuclei* of the *thalamus* and the *visual cortex* (see Figure 65). See also *lateral interparietal area*, *ocular dominance columns*.

visuo-spatial scratch pad A component of *working memory* that is considered to be a temporary memory store used particularly to contain visual or graphical images for very brief periods of time. See also *inner scribe*.

visual word form area (VWFA) An area in the ventral *visual stream* that responds preferentially to the visual presentation of strings of letters.

VMH See *ventromedial nucleus*.

vocalisation The production or articulation of audible speech sounds. The term is particularly used when referring to the *babbling* or crying noises made by babies before they have recognisable speech.

vocational guidance tests *Psychometric* tests that are designed to help people to find out what kinds of jobs they are best suited for.

voice recognition systems Computer systems that can analyse the distinctive features of the human voice, and

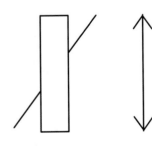

the Poggendorf   the Müller-Lyer   the Ponzo

Figure 64 Some visual illusions

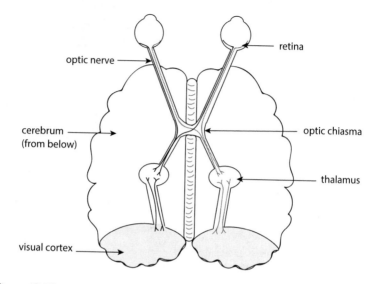

Figure 65 The visual system

respond to key words which have been spoken. The development of voice recognition systems forms a major area of research in the field of *artificial intelligence*, but represents no easy task, owing to the wide differences in articulation shown by different people. Systems have now been developed that can interpret continuous speech (i.e. they do not depend on the speaker saying each word separately, but they still need to learn the pronunciation of the speaker). This is usually achieved by the individual concerned reading out a set of key words and phrases, which the computer system uses as a baseline for identifying their characteristic speech patterns, and retains for when information is next received from that person. See also *artificial intelligence, expert systems*.

voice stress analyser A device for analysing the acoustic properties of the voice, which examines in particular the minute variations of tone and pitch that occur as vowel sounds are produced. In a relaxed voice, there are many of these variations, but they occur rapidly, and the overall impression is that the sound is smooth and regular. The variations can be seen clearly on a spectrograph, which gives a visual image of the sound. If someone is under stress, even though they may try to keep their voice sounding normal, and although it may sound the same to a listener, the effort of keeping their vocal cords steady will mean that, when analysed by a spectrograph, the sound appears to be 'flattened out', without the normal small variations. Accordingly, the analysis of speech by a spectrograph provides a sensitive and reliable measure of stress. Voice stress analysers are sometimes used in an attempt to detect when a speaker such as a politician or someone doing business on the telephone is lying. See also *galvanic skin response, polygraph*.

voice timbre See *timbre*.

Völkerpsychologie One of the earliest forms of *social psychology*, which was the study of the collective mind developed by Wilhelm Wundt in the 1860s.

volley principle In *audition*, and in several other sensory systems, the intensity of a *stimulus* is signalled by means of the rate at which *electrical impulses* are fired to the brain. This signal can be achieved by each *neurone* firing very rapidly, but owing to the *absolute* and *relative refractory periods*, there is a limit to how fast each neurone can fire. In the case of very intense stimuli, the neurones fire in relays or volleys – a set of neurones will fire, closely followed by another set, and then another. In this way, the brain receives a series of impulses at a rate that would not be possible for the neurones if each was firing singly.

voluntary behaviour Behaviour that forms a deliberate action on the part of the individual. Such behaviour is usually contrasted with involuntary, or reflexive, behaviour. *Operant conditioning* and the higher forms of learning are usually concerned with the training of voluntary behaviour, except in the case of *biofeedback*.

Classical conditioning is typically concerned with involuntary behaviour.

volunteer effects Research outcomes that result from participants trying to be helpful, or to behave in ways that they believe are appropriate for the study, because they have volunteered and want to be cooperative.

volunteer sample A method of *sampling* that consists of using people who have volunteered to take part in the research project. See also *volunteer effects*.

voxel The 3D equivalent of a *pixel* (i.e. a minimal volume-based unit).

voxel-based morphometry (VBM) A technique used to separate and measure differences in the concentration of *white* and *grey matter*.

vulnerability model The idea that certain people have a predisposition to conditions such as *schizophrenia*, but that these dispositions are not deterministic and the condition will only develop under certain conditions of stress or damage. See also *diathesis-stress model*.

VWFA See *visual word form area*.

Vygotsky, Lev Seminovich (1896–1934)

Vygotsky was one of the new Soviet psychologists, working closely with the neuropsychologist Luria in an attempt to develop a psychology in keeping with the ideals of Marxist ideology. However, he was well informed about European psychology, including the work of Piaget in Switzerland. Although he managed to continue to operate effectively while alive, after he died (of tuberculosis) his work was suppressed by Stalin's regime, and it only re-emerged in the early 1960s. Vygotsky's approach was distinctive in that he was concerned with the interaction of cultural and educational influence with the child's cognitive development. This led to the concept of the *zone of proximal development*, as a result of which his theory has now become a major influence in modern developmental psychology. His model of thought and language showed how language was used for both cognitive structuring and communication by the young child.

W

Wada technique A method for detecting which *cerebral hemisphere* is dominant for speech, which consists of anaesthetising one half of the brain and seeing whether the person's speech is immediately affected or not.

WAIS See *Wechsler Adult Intelligence Scale*.

warrior gene A term given to a *polymorphism* of the monoamine oxidase A *gene* that is associated with increased aggression, particularly in males.

waterfall effect A special case of a *negative aftereffect* involving the perception of steady movement. If someone looks steadily at movement that occurs consistently in one direction (e.g. if they gaze at a waterfall, then when they look away at a stable background), they experience an illusion of movement in the opposite direction. In the case of the waterfall, this involves the impression that the bank or surroundings are moving steadily upwards. If the effect is as a result of the movement of a train, then the train may appear to be moving backwards when it stops at a station.

Watson, John B. (1878–1958)

J.B. Watson is best known as the father of *behaviourism*. His main work was conducted at Johns Hopkins University in America, where he rose to lead the psychology department at the age of 31 years, following a scandal that caused the resignation of the previous professor. (Another scandal forced his own resignation in 1920, whereupon he left academic psychology and pursued a successful career in advertising.) His work on learning in laboratory rats led him to develop a model of *stimulus–response learning*, based on Pavlov's research into conditioned reflexes, which he cited in his APA presidential address in 1915. In this address, he first introduced the concept of behaviourism. He continued to develop the idea, and his book, *Psychology from the Standpoint of a Behaviourist* (1919), could be argued to be the most influential in the history of psychology. Another book, written with his ex-secretary and now wife Rosalie Watson (née Rayner), entitled *The Psychological Care of Infant and Child* (1928), attracted tremendous public debate, as a result of which behaviourism became even more widely known and influential. Much of the history of Western psychology in the second half of the twentieth century can be viewed as attempts by psychology to break free of the influence of behaviourism.

weapon focus Studies of eyewitness testimony have shown that some aspects of a scene (e.g. a weapon) attract so much attention that it impairs memory of other details. See also *eyewitness testimony*.

Weber's law A law discovered by Ernst Weber in the early years of psychology, during which *psychophysics* was being developed. The law states that the amount by which a stimulus needs to be changed in order for the change to be noticeable (the *just noticeable difference*) is a constant proportion of the strength of the stimulus. The value of this constant proportion is known as Weber's constant. In practical terms, the implication of Weber's law is that stronger stimuli will need to increase or decrease by greater amounts than do smaller stimuli before they are perceived as being different. See also *Fechner's law*, *power law*.

Wechsler Adult Intelligence Scale (WAIS) One of the major *intelligence tests*, produced by David Wechsler. Although it produces an overall *IQ* score, this can be subdivided under two general headings of verbal IQ and performance IQ, each of which is composed of different sets of items (six sets for verbal and five sets for performance IQ). In principle, it is possible to identify specific kinds of disability or deficit using such tests, but in practice, for differences between subset scores to be large enough to be significant, the deficit in the person's performance would be obvious anyway.

Wechsler Intelligence Scale for Children (WISC) A version of the *WAIS* designed for use with children. It will measure *IQ* from 6 to 16 years.

WEG Acronym for warmth, empathy and genuineness – the three therapist attributes that have been proposed as the most important factors in the effectiveness of *psychotherapy*. WEG is thought to be more important than any specific therapeutic technique.

well-being A positive condition of mental and physical health, often identified as a goal in *positive psychology*.

Wernicke's area The area of the *cerebral cortex* that is particularly concerned with the interpretation and understanding of language. Damage to this area produces *aphasia* or difficulties in the comprehension of speech. See also *angular gyrus*, *Broca's area*.

Westermarck effect The tendency not to feel sexually attracted as an adult towards someone who was familiar in the earliest years of life (e.g. a close sibling).

white matter The term used to refer to the densely packed masses of *myelinated* nerve fibres that are found in the *central nervous system*. In the *brain*, this is found on the inside, with *grey matter* (consisting of unmyelinated fibres and cell bodies) covering the outer surface. In the *spinal cord*, this is reversed, the white matter being on the outside and the grey matter being on the inside, surrounding the central canal.

Whorfian hypothesis See *Sapir–Whorf hypothesis*.

Wilcoxon signed-ranks test A statistical test used for *repeated-measures designs* and *ordinal data* to identify *significant differences* between two samples.

WISC See *Wechsler Intelligence Scale for Children*.

withdrawal symptoms Temporary physical disorders that occur as a result of the person failing to receive their normal dose of a drug on which they have become *dependent*. Withdrawal symptoms can be quite severe, depending both on the drug concerned and on the extent to which the subject has become *habituated* to the drug. Many ordinary drugs, such as caffeine, can produce quite strong withdrawal symptoms if the individual has previously had a high regular intake and suddenly ceases to take the drug altogether. The existence or otherwise of withdrawal symptoms is one of the main indicators of physiological *addiction*.

within-group variance A statistical measure of the variation within a group. It may be used to indicate something about a *population*, or as a measure of variability in the scores within an experimental condition, especially when using an *analysis of variance*.

within-subjects design A form of research design that takes two or more sets of measures from the same individuals, thereby controlling for individual differences such as age or personality. See also *related-measures design*.

Wisconsin card-sorting test This is a test of executive functioning, in which people are asked to match up cards containing numbers, shapes and colours, according to one of those three criteria. After a few goes, they are asked to change criteria. Typically, people with prefrontal cortex damage show *perseveration* (i.e. they fail to shift from the previous criterion to the new one).

wolf children Children found living in the wild, whose behaviour led people to believe that they had been brought up by wolves. Also known as feral children, such children were of great interest to psychologists in order to identify critical periods for abilities such as language acquisition. However, it is suspected that in most cases, the children had

been abandoned relatively recently because of severe mental disturbance, and that it is that disturbance which is responsible for the unusual behaviour and restricted abilities.

word blindness See *alexia*.

word length effect The finding that verbal *memory span* is decreased if longer words are presented.

word meaning deafness A specific condition in which the person has impaired understanding of spoken language, although they have no difficulty understanding the written word.

word recognition threshold A measure of the minimum degree of exposure to a word necessary for someone to identify it. The normal procedure is to vary the time during which the word is exposed. Other conditions could involve presenting the word more or less faintly, or at different distances. The *threshold* is usually taken to be the point at which the word is recognised 50 per cent of the time, as the exposure necessary will vary according to the conditions under which the word is presented. Recognition thresholds are usually measured using a *tachistoscope*.

word superiority effect The way that letters can be detected more rapidly if they are presented in the context of a word than if they are presented in a nonsense or random letter string. See also *word recognition threshold*.

working memory An alternative to *short-term memory*, proposed by Baddeley and Hitch, who put forward the idea that immediate memory may be like a computer's working memory. The basic working memory system comprises a central executive, a *visuo-spatial scratch pad*, an *articulatory loop* and an input register. See also *dorsolateral prefrontal cortex*.

working memory capacity The amount of information that can be held in *working memory*.

worrying Cognitive activity characterised by repetitive *anxiety*-provoking thoughts. It is one of the main symptoms of *anxiety disorders*.

Wundt, Wilhelm M. (1832–1920)

Wundt is widely regarded as the 'father of experimental psychology'. He became Professor of Psychology at Leipzig University in 1875, and established the first experimental psychology laboratory, where he investigated a number of different topics, the most well known of which were investigations of the role of *sensations*, *association* and *attention* on *consciousness*, which led to the publication of his textbook *Grundzüge der physiologische Psychologie* (*Fundamentals of Psychology*) in 1873. Less well known in Britain and America, however, were a series of investigations in *social psychology*, which led to his 10-volume *Völkerpsychologie*, published between 1900 and 1920. His wide interests, his development of systematic research methods, and his central influence in academic circles meant that many others were attracted to his laboratory, and took his approach as the model for the new discipline.

x A term normally used to represent a raw score in a set of data, usually plotted as the *abscissa* (or horizontal axis) of a graph. The term is also used for any unknown score or the value of an *independent variable*.

X An abbreviation often used to refer to the *mean* of a set of scores.

x-axis The horizontal *axis* of a graph or chart.

X-chromosome A distinctive chromosome, named for its appearance under the microscope, which carries information that directs the development of sexual characteristics. In women, the X-chromosome is paired with another, similarly structured X-chromosome, but in men it is paired with a small, truncated chromosome known as a *Y-chromosome* (Fig. 66).

X-ray tomography See *tomography*.

xenophobia An irrational and excessive fear of strangers or strange (foreign) cultures, which can become converted into intense, jingoistic patriotism and/or racial or cultural *prejudice*.

XX An abbreviated reference to the combination of chromosomes shown by women. Men are referred to as XY. See also *X-chromosome*, *Y-chromosome*.

XXY syndrome See *Klinefelter's syndrome*.

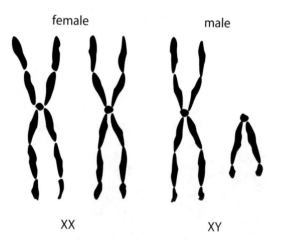

Figure 66 X and Y chromosomes

Y

y A term used for scores from a second set of data, usually plotted as the *ordinate* (or vertical axis) of a graph; *x* is the term used to refer to those from the first set.

y-axis The vertical *axis* of a graph or chart. See also *ordinate*, *abscissa*.

Y-chromosome A distinctively shaped chromosome whose presence as one of a pair indicates that an individual is male. The other one of the pair will be an *X-chromosome*. See also *sex-linked trait*.

YAVIS A term used to describe the typical patient considered suitable for *psychoanalysis*. The term stands for 'young, attractive, verbal, intelligent and successful'. Patients who do not fit these criteria are frequently allocated to other less expensive forms of treatment (e.g. *behaviour therapy*). Although this idea is only semi-serious, it contains more than a grain of truth in terms of the types of patients with whom many psychoanalysts feel they can be most effective.

Yerkes–Dodson law An expression of the relationship between a person's state of physiological *arousal*, and his or her performance of a task or job. When plotted on a graph, it takes the form of an inverted U-curve. Up to a point, increased arousal improves performance, but beyond that point further increases in arousal will cause performance to deteriorate. Furthermore, the shape of the curve will vary with the complexity of the task, simple tasks being less affected by high levels of arousal, and showing a wider, flatter curve, and complex tasks reaching their optimal level at a relatively lower state of arousal, increasing and falling off more sharply (Fig. 67).

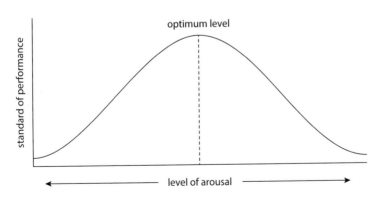

Figure 67 The Yerkes–Dodson law

Yerkish An artificial 'language' developed during experiments in chimpanzee language training at the Yerkes primate laboratory in Georgia, USA. Initially developed for use with a chimpanzee named Lana, it consists of a series of symbols used in a fairly arbitrary fashion to stand for concepts and conjunctions. There is considerable debate as to just how far Yerkish can be regarded as a language rather than just an arbitrary set of symbols.

yoked control An experimental set-up in which the experimental group and the control group are paired, such that any member of the experimental group has one of the control group receiving exactly the same experiences. The pairs are linked ('yoked') in such a way that what happens to one also happens to the other (e.g. if one receives a reward or punishment, the other does, too). This makes it easier for the experimenter to ensure that any differences which arise between the two are produced by the *independent variable*, rather than by variations in experience.

Young–Helmholtz theory A theory of colour vision which argues that colour is perceived through the stimulation of receptors which are sensitive to red, green and blue light. Other colours can be perceived by combinations of these three, in the same way as the coloured dots on the screen of a colour television produce a complete spectrum by combination. See also *opponent processing*.

z-axis The axis of a three-dimensional graph that is at right angles to both the *x-axis* and the *y-axis*.

z-score A measure of how far a specific score is from the mean of its group. The raw scores are converted to a standard form so that the z-score is the number of *standard deviations* by which the score differs from the mean. In a *normal distribution*, knowing the z-score gives a direct measure of the *significance level*. For example, a z-score of 1.96 identifies the point in a normal distribution beyond which only 5 per cent of the scores will fall.

Zeigarnik effect A feature of memory, that a task or activity is more likely to be remembered if it is interrupted before completion.

zeitgeber A German word meaning 'time-giver'. The term occurs in studies of *circadian rhythms*, referring to environmental events that provide the organism with a precise timing to which their innate rhythms can be attached. For example, the daily alternation of light and dark is a zeitgeber that enables the circadian rhythm to adjust to precisely 24 hours.

zeitgeist The 'spirit of the times' – in other words, the social and cultural climate within which an event occurs or a theory is developed. Scientific theories are very rarely, if ever, independent of their cultural climate, and the form that a theory takes and the information

which counts as acceptable evidence for a theory can vary dramatically from one period to the next. By and large, those scientific theories that become popular tend to be the theories which 'fit' the zeitgeist best.

Zener cards A standard set of cards used in experimental studies of *extrasensory perception*. There are usually 25 cards, each bearing one of five simple symbols (cross, wave, circle, star or square). In a typical experiment, research participants are asked to guess which pattern is on a card that another participant (out of sight) is looking at. These cards are also sometimes called *Rhine cards* (see Figure 68). See also *parapsychology*.

zero-order intentionality A level of *intentional stance* in which it is assumed that the actor is acting directly (e.g. instinctively) without having any particular beliefs or desires.

zero-sum game In games theory, the class of games in which a fixed quantity of resources is distributed between the players, so that for anyone to do better, someone else must do worse. Zero-sum games are of particular interest to social psychologists because it has been found that people may operate according to the same principles even when they are not in a zero-sum situation. That is, people will sometimes work hard to ensure that others fare worse than them even if this has no effect on their own gains, and in some cases may even mean sacrificing them.

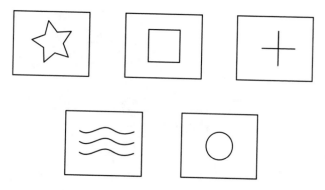

Figure 68 Zener cards

Zimbardo, Philip (1933–)

Philip Zimbardo is a social psychologist best known for the Stanford Prison experiment, a prison simulation in which he showed that interpersonal brutality is not particularly dependent on manifest personality, but under certain conditions could be manifest by people who would normally not act in such ways. Zimbardo went on to study shyness and other features of social interaction, and also conducted an extensive research programme investigating how ordinary people become capable of torture. More recently, his research has focused on the more positive area of how ordinary people can become heroes. See also *deindividuation*.

Zöllner illusion A particularly powerful visual illusion in which parallel lines appear to converge as a result of being crossed by short diagonal lines set at angles to the main ones (see Figure 69).

zone of proximal development (ZPD) The term proposed by *Vygotsky* for the area of competence that a child is ready to develop into, if provided with the appropriate environmental and social stimulation. It is identified as the things that children cannot learn on their own, but would be able to do with appropriate help. It is important that parents and educators work within the

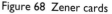

Figure 69 The Zöllner illusion

ZPD, because this is where the development of competence can occur.

zoology The study of animals. Zoology includes the study of animal physiology and animal behaviour. In the latter area, it frequently overlaps with *comparative psychology*.

zoom lens model The idea that our visual attention can be either narrowed and tightly focused or broadened out – much like the zoom lens on a camera.

ZPD See *zone of proximal development*.

Zurich school The group of psychoanalysts who joined Carl Gustav Jung as he developed an alternative school of analysis after his break with Freud. Jung's method is referred to as *analytical psychology*.

zygote An *ovum*, or egg, which has been fertilised and so is capable of developing into a young member of the species.

Appendix 1

Key references

Adler, A. (1930) *What Life Could Mean to You*. Center City, MN: Hazelden.

Adorno, T.W., Frenkel-Brunswik, E., Levinson, D.J. and Sanford, R.N. (1950) *The Authoritarian Personality*. New York: Harper & Row.

Ainsworth, M.D.S. (1979) Attachment as related to mother–infant interaction. *Advances in the Study of Behaviour*, **9**, 2–52.

Allport, G. (1937) *Personality: A Psychological Interpretation*. New York: Holt, Rinehart, & Winston.

Ames, A. (1951) Visual perception and the rotating trapezoidal window. *Psychological Monographs*, **65**(7), 324.

Argyle, M. (1987) *The Psychology of Happiness*. London: Methuen.

Asch, S.E. (1956) Studies of independence and conformity: a minority of one against a unanimous majority. *Psychological Monographs*, **70**(9).

Atkinson, R.C. and Shiffrin, R.M. (1971) The control of short-term memory. *Scientific American*, **224**, 81–90.

Baddeley, A.D. and Hitch, G. (1974) Working memory. In: G.H. Bower (ed.), *The Psychology of Learning and Motivation* (vol. 8), pp. 47–90. New York: Academic Press.

Bandura, A. (1977) *Social Learning Theory*. Englewood Cliffs, NJ: Prentice Hall.

Bandura, A. (1997) *Self-Efficacy: The Exercise of Control*. New York: W.H. Freeman & Co.

Bartlett, F.C. (1932) *Remembering: A Study in Experimental and Social Psychology*. Cambridge: Cambridge University Press.

Bateson, G., Jackson, D., Haley, J. and Weakland, J. (1956) Towards a theory of schizophrenia. *Behavioural Science*, **1**(4), 251–64.

Baumrind, D. (1964) Some thoughts on the ethics of research: after reading Milgram's 'Behavioural study of obedience'. *American Psychologist*, **19**, 421–3.

Beck, A.T. (1976) *Cognitive Therapy and the Emotional Disorders*. New York: International Universities Press.

Berkowitz, L. (1965) The concept of aggressive drive. In: L. Berkowitz (ed.), *Advances in Experimental Social Psychology 2*. New York: Academic Press.

Berlyne, D. (1960) *Conflict, Arousal and Curiosity*. New York: McGraw Hill.

Berne, E. (1973) *Games People Play*. Harmondsworth: Penguin.

Bernstein, B. (1965) Social class and linguistic development: a theory of social learning. In: A.H. Halsey, J. Floud and A. Anderson (eds), *Education, Economy and Society*. New York: The Free Press of Glencoe.

Binet, A. and Simon, T. (1905) Méthodes nouvelles pour le diagnostic du niveau intellectuel des anormaux. *L'Année Psychologique*, **11**, 245–336.

Bowlby, J. (1951) *Child Care and the Growth of Love*. Harmondsworth: Penguin.

Bowlby, J. (1969) *Attachment and Loss 1: Attachment*. London: Hogarth.

Broadbent, D.E. (1958) *Perception and Communication*. Oxford: Pergamon.

Brown, R. (1973) *A First Language*. Cambridge, MA: Harvard University Press.

Bruce, V. and Young, A. (1986) Understanding face recognition. *British Journal of Psychology*, **77**, 305–27.

Bruce, V. and Young, A. (2012) *Face Perception*. London: Psychology Press.

Bruner, J.S. (1973) *Beyond the Information Given: Studies in the Psychology of Knowing*. New York: W.W. Norton.

Burt, C. (1958) The inheritance of mental abilities. *American Psychologist*, **13**, 1–15.

Campbell, H.J. (1973) *The Pleasure Areas*. London: Eyre Methuen.

Cannon, W. B. (1929) *Bodily Changes in Pain, Hunger, Fear and Rage*. New York: Appleton.

Cattell, R.B. (1946) *Description and Measurement of Personality*. New York: World Book Company.

Chomsky, N. (1957) *Syntactic Structures*. The Hague, the Netherlands: Moulton.

Craik, I.F.M. and Lockhart, R.S. (1972) Levels of processing: a framework for memory research. *Journal of Verbal Learning and Verbal Behaviour*, **11**, 671–84.

Cumming, E. and Henry, W.H. (1961) *Growing Old: The Process of Disengagement*. New York: Basic Books.

de Bono, E. (1966) *Lateral Thinking*. Harmondsworth: Penguin.

Deutsch, J.A. and Deutsch, D. (1963) Attention: some theoretical considerations. *Psychological Review*, **70**, 80–90.

Donaldson, M. (1978) *Children's Minds*. London: Fontana/Collins.

Dunn, J. (1988) *The Beginnings of Social Understanding*. Oxford: Blackwell.

Ebbinghaus, H. (1885) *Memory: A Contribution to Experimental Psychology*. Republished 1964. New York: Dover.

Ekman, P. and Friesen, W.V. (1969) The repertoire of non-verbal behaviour: categories, origins, usage and coding. *Semiotica*, **1**, 49–98.

Ellis, A. (1977) The basic clinical theory of rational-emotive therapy. In: A. Ellis and R. Grieger (eds), *Handbook of Rational–Emotive Therapy*. New York: Springer.

Erikson, E.H. (1963) *Childhood and Society* (2nd edn). New York: Norton.

Eysenck, H.J. (1953) *The Structure of Human Personality*. London: Methuen.

Eysenck, H.J. (1985) *The Decline and Fall of the Freudian Empire*. Harmondsworth: Penguin.

Fairbairn, W.R.D. (1952) *An Object-Relations Theory of the Personality*. New York: Basic Books.

Festinger, L. (1954) A theory of social comparison processes. *Human Relations*, **7**, 117–40.

Festinger, L. (1957) *A Theory of Cognitive Dissonance*. Evanston, IL: Row, Peterson.

Festinger, L., Riecken, H.W. and Schachter, S. (1956) *When Prophecy Fails*. Minneapolis, MN: University of Minneapolis Press.

Freud, S. (1900) *The Interpretation of Dreams* (trans. J. Strachey, 1953). London: Allen & Unwin.

Freud, S. (1901) *The Psychopathology of Everyday Life*. Republished 1953. In: J. Strachey (ed.), *The Standard Edition of the Complete Psychological Works of Sigmund Freud Vol 6*. London: Hogarth.

Friedman, M. and Rosenman, R.H. (1974) *Type A Behaviour*. New York: Knopf.

Galton, F. (1883) *Enquiries into Human Faculty and Its Development*. London: J.M.Dent & Co.

Galton, F. (1884) *Hereditary Genius*. New York: Appleton.

Garcia, J. and Koelling, R.A. (1966) The relation of cue to consequence in avoidance learning. *Psychonomic Science*, **4**, 123–4.

Gardner, H. (1985) *Frames of Mind: The Theory of Multiple Intelligences*. London: Paladin.

Gesell, A. (1929) Maturation and infant behaviour patterns. *Psychological Review*, **36**, 307–19.

Gesell, A. and Ilg, F.L. (1949) *Child Development*. New York: Harper.

Gibson, E.J. (1969) *Principles of Perceptual Learning and Development*. New York: Appleton-Century-Crofts.

Gibson, E.J. and Walk, R.D. (1960) The visual cliff. *Scientific American*, **202**, 64–71.

Gibson, J.J. (1950) *The Perception of the Visual World*. Boston, MA: Houghton Mifflin.

Gould, S.J. (1981) *The Mismeasure of Man*. New York: Norton.

Gregory, R.L. (1966) *Eye and Brain: The Psychology of Seeing*. New York: McGraw Hill.

Harré, R. (1979) *Social Being*. Oxford: Basil Blackwell.

Haxby, J.V., Hoffman, E.A. and Gobbini, M.I. (2000) The distributed human neural system for face perception. *Trends in Cognitive Science*, 4(6), 223–33.

Hayes, N.J. (1995) The magic of sociobiology. In: N.J. Hayes (ed.), *Psychology in Perspective*. Basingstoke: Macmillan.

Hayes, N.J. (1998) Psychological processes in organisational cultures I: social representations and organisational semiotics. *Human Systems*, 9(1), 59–65.

Hebb, D.O. (1949) *The Organisation of Behaviour*. New York: Wiley.

Heider, F. (1944) Social perception and phenomenal causality. *Psychological Review*, 51, 358–74.

Hering, E. (1878) *Outlines of a Theory of the Light Sense*. Cambridge, MA: Harvard University Press.

Herzberg, F. (1959) *The Motivation to Work*. New York: John Wiley & Sons.

Hewstone, M. (1989) *Causal Attribution: From Cognitive Processes to Collective Beliefs*. Oxford: Blackwell.

Holmes, T.H. and Rahe, R.H. (1967) The social readjustment rating scale. *Journal of Psychosomatic Research*, 11, 213–18.

Hubel, D.H. and Wiesel, T.N. (1979) Brain mechanisms of vision. *Scientific American*, 241(3), 150–62.

James, W. (1890) *Principles of Psychology*. New York: Holt.

Jung, C.G. (1933) *Psychological Types*. New York: Kegan Paul.

Jung, C.G. (1964) *Man and His Symbols*. New York: Doubleday.

Kelley, H.H. (1973) The processes of causal attribution. *American Psychologist*, 28, 107–28.

Kelly, D. (1955) *The Psychology of Personal Constructs*. New York: Norton.

Kempe, C.H., Silverman, F.N., Steele, B.F., Droegemueller, W. and Silver H.K. (1962) The battered child syndrome. *Journal of the American Medical Association*, 181, 71.

Klein, M. (1932) *The Psycho-Analysis of Children*. London: Hogarth.

Kohlberg, L. (1969) *Stages in the Development of Moral Thought and Action*. New York: Holt, Rinehart, & Winston.

Köhler, W. (1925) *The Mentality of Apes*. New York: Harcourt Brace.

Kruglanski, A.W. (1980) Lay epistemo-logic, process and contents: another look at attribution theory. *Psychological Review*, 87, 70–87.

Labov, W. (1972) *Language in the Inner City: Studies in the Black English Vernacular*. Philadelphia, PA: University of Pennsylvania Press.

Laing, R.D. (1965) *The Divided Self*. Harmondsworth: Penguin.

Lamarck, J.B. (1914) *Zoological Philosophy*. London: Macmillan.

Lashley, K.S. (1929) *Brain Mechanisms and Intelligence*. Chicago, IL: University of Chicago Press.

Latané, B. (1981) The psychology of social impact. *American Psychologist*, 36, 343–56.

Lewin, K. (1936) *Principles of Topological Psychology*. New York: McGraw Hill.

Lewin, K. (1946) Action research and minority problems. *Journal of Social Issues*, 2(4), 34–46.

Locke, J. (1700) *An Essay Concerning Human Understanding* (4th edn). Republished in 1959. New York: Dover.

Loftus, G.R. and Loftus, E.F. (1975) *Human Memory: The Processing of Information*. New York: Halsted Press.

Lorenz, K. (1958) The evolution of behaviour. *Scientific American*, 199(6), 67–78.

Lorenz, K. (1966) *On Aggression*. New York: Harcourt, Brace & World.

Marler, P.R. (1982) Avian and primate communication: the problem of natural categories. *Neuroscience and Biobehavioural Reviews*, 6, 87–94.

Marler, P. (2005) Ethology and the origins of behavioral endocrinology. *Hormones and Behavior*, **47**, 493–50.

Marr, D. (1982) *Vision: A Computational Investigation into the Human Representation and Processing of Visual Information*. San Francisco, CA: W.H. Freeman & Co.

Maslow, A.H. (1970) *Motivation and Personality* (2nd edn). New York: Harper & Row.

McGarrigle, J. and Donaldson, M. (1974) Conservation accidents. *Cognition*, **3**, 341–50.

Milgram, S. (1973) *Obedience to Authority*. London: Tavistock.

Miller, G.A. (1956) The magical number seven, plus or minus two: some limits on our capacity for processing information. *Psychological Review*, **63**, 81–97.

Mischel, W. (1968) *Personality and Assessment*. New York: Wiley.

Monitz, E. (1936) *Tentatives opératoires dans le traitement de certaines psychoses*. Paris: Masson.

Moreno, J.L. (1946) *Psychodrama Volume 1*. Beacon, NY: Beacon House.

Moscovici, S. (1980) Towards a theory of conversion behaviour. In: L. Berkowitz (ed.), *Advances in Experimental Social Psychology*, **13**, 209–39.

Moscovici, S. (1984) The phenomenon of social representations. In: R.M. Farr and S. Moscovici (eds), *Social Representations*. Cambridge: Cambridge University Press.

Neisser, U. (1976) *Cognition and Reality: Principles and Implications of Cognitive Psychology*. San Francisco, CA: W.H. Freeman.

Osgood, C.E. (1966) Dimensionality of the semantic space for communication via facial expression. *Scandinavian Journal of Psychology*, **7**, 1–30.

Pavlov, I.P. (1927) *Conditioned Reflexes: An Investigation of the Physiological Activity of the Cerebral Cortex*. New York: Dover.

Perls, F., Hefferline, R.F. and Goodman, P. (1951) *Gestalt Therapy*. Harmondsworth: Penguin.

Piaget, J. (1952) *The Origins of Intelligence in Children*. New York: International Universities Press.

Piaget, J. (1959) *The Language and Thought of the Child*. London: Routledge and Kegan Paul.

Popper, K. (1959) *The Logic of Scientific Discoveries*. London: Hutchinson.

Reich, W. (1933) *The Mass Psychology of Fascism*. London: Condor Books.

Rogers, C.R. (1951) *Client-Centred Therapy*. London: Constable.

Rogers, C.R. (1961) *On Becoming a Person: A Therapist's View of Psychotherapy*. London: Constable.

Rosch, E.H. (1973) Natural categories. *Cognitive Psychology*, **4**, 328–50.

Rosenthal, R. and Fode, K.L. (1963) The effect of experimenter bias on the performance of the albino rat. *Behavioural Science*, **8**, 183–9.

Rotter, J.B. (1966) Generalised expectancies for internal vs external control of reinforcement. *Psychological Monographs*, **80**(1).

Rutter, M. (1981) *Maternal Deprivation Reassessed* (2nd edn). Harmondsworth: Penguin.

Schank, R. and Abelson, R. (1977) *Scripts, Plans, Goals and Understanding: An Enquiry into Human Knowledge*. Hillsdale, NJ: Erlbaum.

Schjelderuppe-Ebbe, T. (1922) Beiträge zur Sozialpsychologie des Haushuhns. *Zeitschrift für Psychologie*, **88**, 225–52.

Seligman, M.E.P. (1975) *Helplessness: On Depression, Development and Death*. San Francisco, CA: Freeman.

Seligman, M.E.P. (1991) *Learned Optimism*. New York: Knopf.

Selye, H. (1956) *The Stress of Life*. New York: McGraw Hill.

Sheldon, W.H. (1954) *Atlas of Men: A Guide for Somatotyping the Human Male at All Ages*. New York: Harper & Row.

Skinner, B.F. (1938) *The Behaviour of Organisms*. New York: Appleton-Century Crofts.

Skinner, B.F. (1948) *Walden Two*. New York: Macmillan.

Skinner, B.F. (1957) *Verbal Behaviour*. New York: Appleton–Century–Crofts.

Skinner, B.F. (1972) *Beyond Freedom and Dignity*. Harmondsworth: Penguin.

Spearman, C. (1923) *The Nature of 'Intelligence' and the Principles of Cognition*. London: Macmillan.

Sperry, R.W. (1964) The great cerebral commissure. *Scientific American*, **210**, 42–52.

Spitz, R.A. (1945) Hospitalism: an inquiry into the genesis of psychiatric conditions in early childhood. *Psychoanalytic Studies of Childhood*, **1**, 53–74.

Sternberg, R.J. (1977) *Intelligence, Information-Processing and Analogical Reasoning: The Componential Analysis of Human Abilities*. Hillsdale, NJ: Erlbaum.

Sternberg, R.J. (1985) *Beyond IQ: A Triarchic Theory of Human Intelligence*. Cambridge: Cambridge University Press.

Stevens, S.S. (1957) On the psychophysical law. *Psychological Review*, **64**(3), 153–81.

Stratton, P.M., Heard, D., Hanks, H., Munton, A., Brewin, C.R. and Davidson, C.R. (1986) Coding causal beliefs in natural discourse. *British Journal of Social Psychology*, **25**, 299–313.

Tajfel, H. (1981) *Human Groups and Social Categories: Studies in Social Psychology*. Cambridge: Cambridge University Press.

Talairach, J. and Tournoux, P. (1988) *A Co-Planar Stereotactic Atlas of the Human Brain*. Stuttgart, Germany: Thieme Verlag.

Taylor, F.W. (1911) *The Principles of Scientific Management*. New York: Harper & Row.

Tennov, D. (1979) *Love and Limerence: The Experience of Being in Love*. New York: Stein & Day.

Thorndike, E.L. (1911) *Animal Intelligence: Experimental Studies*. New York: Macmillan.

Thurstone, L.L. (1938) *Primary Mental Abilities*. Chicago, IL: University of Chicago Press.

Tinbergen, N. (1953) *Social Behaviour in Animals*. London: Methuen.

Toffler, A. (1970) *Future Shock*. New York: Random House.

Tolman, E.C. (1932) *Purposive Behaviour in Animals and Man*. New York: Century.

Torrance, E.P. (1972) Characteristics of creatively gifted children and youth. In: E.P. Trapp and P. Himmelstein (eds), *Readings on the Exceptional Child: Research and Theory*. New York: Appleton–Century–Crofts.

Triesman, A. (1964) Verbal cues, language and meaning in attention. *American Journal of Psychology*, **77**, 206–14.

Vernon, P.E. (1971) *The Structure of Human Abilities*. London: Methuen.

Vygotsky, L.S. (1962) *Thought and Language*. Cambridge, MA: MIT Press.

Ward, J. (2015) *The Student's Guide to Cognitive Neuroscience* (3rd edn). London: Psychology Press.

Watson, J.B. (1924) *Behaviorism*. New York: J.B. Lippencott.

Watson, J.B. and Rayner, R. (1920) Conditioned emotional reactions. *Journal of Experimental Psychology*, **3**, 1–14.

Werner, H. (1957) The concept of development from a comparative and organismic point of view. In D. Harris (ed.), *The Concept of Development*. Minneapolis, MN: University of Minnesota Press.

Whorf, B.L. (1956) *Language, Thought and Reality*. New York: MIT Press.

Woollett, K. and Maguire, E.A. (2011) Acquiring 'the knowledge' of London's layout drives structural brain changes. *Current Biology*, **21**(24), 2109–14.

Wundt, W. (1900–1920) *Völkerpsychologie: Eine Untersuchung der Entwicklungsgesetze von Sprache, Mythus und Sitte*, 10 vols. Leipzig, Germany: Engelmann.

Wynne-Edwards, V.C. (1962) *Animal Dispersion in Relation to Social Behaviour*. New York: Hafner.

Zimbardo, P. (2007) *The Lucifer Effect: Understanding How Good People Turn Evil*. New York: Random House.

Appendix 2

Study notes – how to write an essay

An essay has two purposes. One is that it is an attempt to answer a question (in French, *essayer* means to try). The other is to show off to the person marking the essay just how much you know about the subject and how good you are at organising that knowledge.

Work out your answer

So the first thing you need to consider when choosing an essay topic is what your answer should be. Not the details of your answer – its essence. Ask yourself what you would say if a friend asked you that question in the cafeteria (it may be unlikely, but that's what your imagination is for!). If your answer would be 'I dunno', then that probably isn't the right essay question for you – either that, or you haven't really thought about it enough.

To write a good essay, you need to be able to adopt a position – to give an answer to the question – and then describe arguments or evidence which show that your position or answer is the best one to adopt, or at least a really good one. The idea is to convince other people that you really know what you are talking about. That means giving your essay a good, clear structure, and making sure that what you have said all leads to the conclusion you draw – in other words, your answer.

Essays work best if you plan them out. If you don't, you can end up just rambling, with no clear direction. But once you know the short answer to your essay question, you know where your arguments are going, and what your conclusion will be. So that will help you to stay on track, and at that point you can start planning your essay.

Select your evidence

Your essay needs to be organised, and for that you need to use paragraphs. So the best way to plan your essay is as a list of paragraphs. Each paragraph should make just one point, and back it up with some kind of argument or evidence – whatever counts as important in the particular subject you are taking.

For example, in English literature, the evidence you would use would be reference to things in the text or direct quotations. In creative writing, it would be examples drawn from your ideas, imagery or experience. In history, it would be reference to source material of some kind. In psychology, it would be reference to research studies, or critiques that have challenged research evidence. Learning any subject involves learning what counts as evidence and what doesn't, and by the time you are writing an essay, you should have a pretty fair idea of what kind of evidence matters for that particular subject.

Plan your paragraphs

A paragraph states an idea and then amplifies it. Usually, it will be between 50 and 100 words long. (How long paragraphs are depends on how much you need to say to amplify the point that it is making.) Knowing this means that you can work out how many paragraphs you will need, according to how long your essay is supposed to be. A 500-word essay will usually need about eight paragraphs, while a 1,500-word essay will need about 12–18 or so. If it's an exam essay, begin by working out how much time you are supposed to give to the essay. In some exams, you can calculate this by how many marks are given to the question, by comparison with the other questions you have to answer. In all-essay exams, just divide the time of the exam by the number of essays you need to write. Then deduct five minutes per essay for planning (believe us, it's worth it!) and allow five minutes for writing each paragraph. So 45 minutes of exam time means eight paragraphs plus five minutes' planning time.

Bearing that in mind, you can make up your essay plan as a list of paragraphs. Two of them are done for you: the first, where you introduce the subject and outline the main argument you are making – if you like, where you give the short answer to the question – and the last, where you sum up how all that evidence shows that your short answer was the best answer for this question. In between comes the detail of your essay, so on the plan, number your paragraphs and list briefly what each point is going to be. Don't go into any details – a one-word reminder is plenty.

Remember, though, that in many essays, you don't just want to give your own arguments – you also need to show that you are aware of any opposing ideas or other arguments which might lead to different conclusions. A paragraph describing one of those would begin by stating what it was (to prove that you know it) and then give evidence or arguments for why it is wrong, or irrelevant to this particular question. So some paragraphs will be criticising other ideas, and some will be backing up your own.

In a well-balanced essay, that would normally be about half and half, but it can vary depending on your subject. In a science essay, for example, the ideas you are criticising might just be very old-fashioned ones, which would only need a couple of paragraphs to describe, or in an English essay you might concentrate more on producing the evidence to support your own idea and not bother as much with what other people have said. But if you are writing about a controversial topic, or one where people have very strong views, then you definitely need to show that you are familiar with the arguments on both sides of the case – and then challenge the arguments of the side that you disagree with, saying why you don't think they should really count.

The essay task

How you go about organising your paragraphs and deciding what to put into them depends on the task that your essay is trying to do. Often, the essay title itself will give you an idea of how you are meant to go about writing the essay. Here is a list of some of the more common essay tasks, and what they expect you to do.

Compare and contrast

Write about the similarities (compare) and the differences (contrast) between two things. That means writing some paragraphs describing things they have in common, and roughly an equal number of paragraphs describing ways that they are different.

Criticise

Write about the weak points of the topic or idea that you are writing about, or say what you think is wrong with it. Describe criticisms that other people have made, as well as giving some of your own if you can. But remember to begin with at least one paragraph showing that you do understand the idea or thing that you are criticising.

Discuss

Write about both the good points and the bad points of your topic, and try to look at whether there are any implications or conclusions that would follow naturally from it. Try to look at it from more than one point of view.

Describe

Write about the topic plainly and simply. Give as much detail as you can in the time or number of words, but stick to the plain facts – don't give your own opinions, or if you do keep them for a very limited contribution right at the end.

Explain

Give a set of reasons for why something happens or has come about. That often means writing about the stages or steps which have led up to it.

Illustrate

Give specific examples that highlight or amplify the particular topic which you are writing about (but don't forget to describe the topic first). Do not draw pictures as your answer, unless you are sure that this is appropriate. It usually isn't.

Outline

Simply describe the main facts of the topic, but leave out all of the unimportant details. Give as much information as someone would need in order to be able to understand the most important features of the topic you are describing.

Write clearly

If you follow this advice, your essay plan will end up as a list of paragraphs, each of which is making a different point. Once you've got your plan, you can expand all the points into paragraphs, and while you're writing you'll know pretty well what you are going to say next. That means that you can keep your arguments clear and incisive, and avoid unnecessary repetition.

Make sure, too, that you really have said what you mean to say. Even a small difference in spelling can change the meaning of a sentence so it looks as though you mean something completely different. To affect something, for example, means to influence it. But to effect something means to bring it about or make it happen. Confusing the two won't be picked up by a spellchecker because they are both real words. You don't want a little spelling mistake to make it look as though you're talking nonsense, do you?

Getting it right

Not only that, but carelessness with grammar or spelling makes a really bad impression. So here are 16 of the most common spelling and grammatical problems – errors which you need to avoid and rules which you need to follow:

1   Be consistent in singular and plural. Not 'there is 23 of them'.
2   Latin words that end in 'a' tend to be plural (e.g. data and media). Therefore, 'data are reported'.
3   Apostrophes give endless trouble. They indicate either a possessive (something which belongs to the noun concerned) or an abbreviation (a word or part of a word which has been shortened). But APOSTROPHES NEVER INDICATE A PLURAL! 'The department's student's ...' implies they only have one student and you are about to be told about something that person possesses. If the possession refers to several people, then the apostrophe comes after the s (e.g. if it belongs to several students, it is the students' opinion). If the word is already plural, such as people, the apostrophe comes after the plural word: people's party. Sometimes the spelling changes: the plural of family is families, but the possessive relating to one family is family's. The possessive of many families is families'.
4   The usual use of an apostrophe as in 's is as an abbreviation for his, hers or its (e.g. 'A student's opinion' = one student – her opinion).
5   The other main use of an apostrophe is when it is used to indicate an abbreviation, or something missing, as in don't for 'do not'.
6   'Its' is already possessive. It only gets an apostrophe if it is functioning as an abbreviation of 'it is', as in 'it's a lovely day'.
7   'There' is a place, 'their' refers to possessions. So do not write 'we solved there problems'.
8   Sentences in the form of a question should have a question mark at the end.
9   Try to split up sentences that have become too long and complicated. It's generally a good idea to do the same for paragraphs when they become too long, too.

10   When a sentence or, worse, a paragraph starts with 'this', it is often unclear what, in the preceding material, it refers to. Think of it as a vague hand-wave backwards to what you have recently written. Make a rule to avoid using 'this' unless you say what 'this' is, or unless it is so clear that there couldn't possibly be any other subject. This (referring to the first sentence of this paragraph) also reminds me that it is important to minimise the use of commas, but even more important to use them correctly.

11   While we're on the subject, A COMMA IS NOT THE SAME AS A FULL STOP! A comma indicates that you are developing, or amplifying, the idea behind your sentence. A full stop tells you that that particular statement or idea has been completed. If you want to say more, you should introduce the next idea – another point on the same topic, like this one – in the next sentence. Using commas when you should be using full stops makes you appear illiterate. That's not an impression you want to give to anyone, really.

12   'Effect' and 'affect' often cause problems for psychology students. They have different meanings when they are used as nouns or verbs. For example, something can have an effect (noun). But if something 'effects a change' it means to bring about a change. Similarly, an affect (noun) means a feeling or emotion, while to affect things (verb) means to influence it. If in doubt, look up these words in the main text of this dictionary.

13   A similar confusion between noun and verb occurs with practice (noun) as in 'the practice of psychotherapy' and practise (verb) as when you 'practise your guitar solos'. People do not usually get confused between 'advice' and 'advise', which follow the same rule, so you may find you can use that to remember whether you want to say practice or practise.

14   For some reason, when writing about activating a response, instead of writing 'elicit' people often write 'illicit', which is an adjective meaning that it is underhand or illegal. Try not to confuse the two.

15   'This finding highlights that value for money is an important issue for customers'. Do not use 'highlights' – it is a cop-out to save you thinking of the word you should really use. It makes the sentence ungrammatical, when it would have been simpler and more informative to have used 'shows' or 'suggests'. Or should it have been 'proves' or 'emphasises'?

16   Don't begin a sentence with 'So, …' unless it is genuinely a logical conclusion from the sentence or paragraph you have just written. It should not be used as a general beginning for a topic, no matter how often you might hear people using it that way in everyday life.

Pay attention to presentation

Finally, make sure you present your essay neatly. In an exam, there's not all that much you can do, but do remember that you are trying to impress your examiner, and you won't do that if your handwriting is so bad that they can't decipher what you have written. If you are writing an essay for an assignment, make sure that you print it out, or if you really don't have access to a printer, write it out very neatly.

Separate the paragraphs clearly, choose a clear font and a readable line spacing, and leave proper margins. It might not get you extra marks, but it all contributes to the impression that you really know what it is that you are supposed to be doing, and have made an effort to do it well. And that can only be a good thing!

Happy writing!

Nicky Hayes and Peter Stratton

Appendix 3

List of abbreviations

5-HT	5-hydroxytryptamine
AA	ambulatory assessment
ACTH	adrenocorticotrophic hormone
ADD	attention deficit disorder
ADHD	attention deficit hyperactivity disorder
AI	artificial intelligence
AIDS	acquired immune deficiency syndrome
AIP	anterior intraparietal area
ANN	artificial neural network
ANOVA	analysis of variance
ANS	autonomic nervous system
BAS	British Ability Scale
BOLD	blood oxygen level dependency
CA	conversation analysis
CAL	computer-assisted learning
CAT scan	computed axial tomography
CDS	child-directed speech
CNS	central nervous system
CR	conditioned (or conditional) response
CS	conditioned (or conditional) stimulus
db	decibel
df	degrees of freedom
DLPFC	dorsolateral prefrontal cortex
DNA	desoxyribonucleic acid
DSM-V	*Diagnostic and Statistical Manual of Mental Disorders*, 5th edition
ECT	electroconvulsive therapy
EEG	electroencephalogram
efMRI	event-related functional magnetic resonance imaging
EMA	Ecological Momentary Assessment
EPI	Eysenck Personality Inventory
EPQ	Eysenck Personality Questionnaire
ERP	event-related potential
ESB	electrical stimulation of the brain
ESM	Experience Sampling Method

ESN	educationally subnormal
ESP	extrasensory perception
EST	electroshock therapy
FDR	False Discovery Rate
FEF	frontal eye field
FI	fixed-interval reinforcement scale
fMRI	functional magnetic resonance imaging
FR	fixed-ratio reinforcement scale
FRU	face recognition unit
FTT	failure to thrive
FWE	Family Wise Error
g	general intelligence factor
GAF	Global Assessment of Functioning scale
GAS	general adaptation syndrome
GIGO	garbage in garbage out
GPS	general problem-solver
GSR	galvanic skin response (or resistance)
HCI	human–computer interaction
HRTF	head-related transfer function
Hz	hertz
ICD	International Statistical Classification of Diseases and Related Health Problems
ICSS	intercranial self-stimulation
IQ	intelligence quotient
IRM	innate releasing mechanism
jnd	just noticeable difference
LAD	language acquisition device
LAS	language acquisition system
LH	lateral hypothalamus
LIP	lateral inter-parietal area
LOC	locus of control
LSD	lysergic acid diethylamide
LTM	long-term memory
LTP	long-term potentiation
MA	mental age
MBD	minimal brain dysfunction
MEG	magneto-encephalography
MMN	mismatch negativity
MMPI	Minnesota Multiphasic Personality Inventory
MRI	magnetic resonance imaging
MS	multiple sclerosis
MVPA	multi-voxel pattern analysis
N-Ach	need for achievement
NAI	non-accidental injury
NEO	neuroticism, extraversion and openness to experience
NGF	nerve growth factor

NIRS	near-infrared spectroscopy
nm	nanometer
NREM	non-rapid eye movement (sleep)
ns	nanosecond
NVC	non-verbal communication
ODD	oppositional defiant disorder
OOB	out-of-body experience
PALS	Psychological Applied Learning Scenarios
PDD-NOS	pervasive developmental disorders not otherwise specified
PDP	parallel distributed processing
PET	positron emission tomography
PIN	person identity node
PK	psychokinesis
PRP	psychological refractory period
PSE	point of subjective equality
PSP	post-synaptic potential
PTSD	post-traumatic stress disorder
RAS	reticular activating system
REBT	rational emotive behaviour therapy
REM	rapid eye movement (sleep)
RET	rational emotive therapy
RHP	resource holding power
RNA	ribonucleic acid
ROC	receiver operating characteristic
rTMS	repetitive transcranial magnetic stimulation
SAD	seasonal affective disorder
SCR	skin conductance response
sd	standard deviation
SIDS	sudden infant death syndrome
SIT	social identity theory
S–O–R	stimulus–organism–response
SQUID	superconducting quantum interference device
S–R	stimulus–response
SRT	social representations theory
SSRIs	selective serotonin reuptake inhibitors
STM	short-term memory
t-scope	tachistoscope
TA	transactional analysis
TAT	thematic apperception test
tDCS	transcranial direct current stimulation
TMS	transcranial magnetic stimulation
TOM	theory of mind
TOT	tip-of-the-tongue phenomenon
TOTE	Test, Operate, Test, Exit
tRNA	transfer RNA
UCS	unconditioned (or unconditional) stimulus

UR	unconditioned (or unconditional) response
VI	variable interval reinforcement schedule
VMH	ventro-medial nucleus
VR	variable ratio reinforcement schedule
WAIS	Wechsler Adult Intelligence Scale
WEG	warmth, empathy and genuineness
WISC	Wechsler Intelligence Scale for Children
YAVIS	young, attractive, verbal, intelligent and successful
ZPD	zone of proximal development